D0957114

Endorsements

You hold in your hands the product of one woman's decade of exploration, experimentation, and success. Kathy Jackson came to the study of self defense eager to master skills that would give her the best options for protection of herself and what were then her five small children. That quest has grown into a devotion to helping people who seek answers to the same problems she faced, who need the self assurance she has developed. The solutions she outlines are many, so set aside some time and absorb with an open mind the facts, concepts and attitudes she offers, because you are sure to find much useful information between these covers.

– Gila Hayes
Operations Manager, The Firearms Academy of Seattle
Author of "Effective Defense" and "Personal Defense for Women" –

Kathy Jackson's wise and insightful research and experience have long made the Cornered Cat website one of my standard referral points for students and readers. I'm delighted to see it become available in book form. A great resource for anyone of any gender who keeps or carries defensive firearms, and particularly valuable for armed women!

– Massad Ayoob
Founder, Massad Ayoob Group
Author, "In the Gravest Extreme" –

Cornered Cat is all about women that have chosen or are considering choosing firearms for self defense, sport, or just wanting to understand more about what their menfolk find so fascinating. This book contains a wealth of information presented in Kathy's warm and often humorous style. She tackles the serious considerations of using deadly force in defense of oneself and loved ones in a thought-provoking, non-judgmental, "between girlfriends" prose that is neither threatening nor sugar-coated, just very real.

– Diane Walls
Instructor, The Firearms Academy of Seattle
Popular National Gun Writer–

"The Cornered Cat may be subtitled A Woman's Guide to Concealed Carry, but I would recommend this to anybody that does, or is even thinking about, carrying a gun. Kathy Jackson touches on every gun-toting topic possible with a lot of class, humor, and wisdom."

– Larry Correia,
New York Times Bestselling Author–

Kathy is as skillful with a handgun as she is with a computer! Watching her shoot, it becomes obvious that she has put in the time and effort it takes to be truly proficient with a handgun. As importantly, she has the drive and vision to be a first rate trainer, as well. I highly recommend her new book, whether you are a woman learning to take care of yourself, a man involved in training female students, or just a gun owner looking for solid, no b.s. advice on a truly life and death topic. Pay heed to Kathy's words, she knows what she is talking about.

– Tom Givens
Owner, Rangemaster, Memphis, TN–

Although there are many fine books available on the topic, The Cornered Cat is THE must read for the woman who has made the decision to carry a firearm for personal defense or is even considering it. As her co-author in 'Lessons from Armed America', I could not be more proud of Kathy and her efforts in furthering firearm knowledge, safety and training. Kathy Jackson has penned the definitive work on the subject of women and guns in The Cornered Cat.

– Mark Walters
Co-author of 'Lessons from Armed America'
Concealed Carry Magazine columnist
Nationally syndicated host of Armed American Radio–

the Cornered Cat

A Woman's Guide to
Concealed Carry

by Kathy Jackson

"If you have to fight... fight like a cornered cat."

 www.CorneredCat.com

Published by White Feather Press, LLC in 2010

ISBN 978-0-9822487-9-9

Printed in the United States of America

Cover Design by Betty Shonts

White Feather Press

Reaffirming Faith in God, Family, and Country!

Disclaimer: The author of this book believes you are an adult human being capable of making your own choices and taking responsibility for same. If you are not an adult, or are not capable of taking responsibility for your own choices, STOP. Do not read anything else in this book. The author has made a reasonable, good-faith effort to assure that every chapter in this book is accurate and contains good advice, but hereby advises the reader that the author is a normal human being who makes the normal number of human mistakes. Deal with it. If something in here sounds stupid to you, don't do it. The author accepts absolutely no responsibility whatsoever for anything you might say or do as a result of reading anything in this book. Live your own life!

Contents

Dedication

To every woman who has ever wondered what she can do to protect herself...

To every man who has ever wondered what he can do to help the women in his life understand the elements of self defense...

And to the wonderful, intelligent, brave, and savvy people whose stories are told in these pages:

This book is for you.

Laying the Foundations

Dear Gunhilda,

Why do you carry a gun?

~ Critical in Carson City

Dear Critical,

Because I can't carry a policeman.

~ Gunhilda

The Cornered Cat

Some folks say the most dangerous place in the world is between a Mama Bear and her cubs. It may be so. I've never met a Mama Bear, myself. The most dangerous place I ever stood was between a cornered cat and an open door.

When a cat feels threatened, she gets away from the danger as quickly as she can. She doesn't care what damage she inflicts on her way to safety, but she's not interested in fighting for fighting's sake. She does only as much as she needs to do in order to escape. She doesn't deal in revenge. If she feels threatened, she simply leaves. Efficiently.

Until she needs to use them, her claws stay sheathed. She doesn't go around threatening to maul people. She's cuddly, she's cozy, she likes to curl up next to a crackling fire on a warm winter's day. She's great company.

But don't try to trap her in a bad situation.

This book is about women and guns, not about cats. But in a way, it's about the cornered cat in all of us. It's about the determination to get away from an attacker if you need to. It's about making the decision to say, "Not me. Not mine. Not today." And it's about the tools to make that decision stick.

Fight Like a Cat

The cornered cat is a parable, of course. It's just a word-picture, intended to help us understand one way to think about self defense. But it's a handy word picture, because nearly everyone is familiar with a domestic cat. Nearly everyone who has shared a home with a cat has seen how their cat responds when frightened. Nobody in their right mind tries to hold on to a frightened cat. Even though cats are very small in comparison to humans, most cat owners soon develop a healthy dose of respect for feline teeth and claws.

There are other ways to think about self defense. Some people like to think of themselves as *sheepdogs*, charged with the duty to protect other people. That's a valid and noble picture, isn't it? But to sheepdogs, other people are like weak and foolish sheep that cannot protect themselves. That's not very flattering to our friends and neighbors who have decided not to travel the same road. If we want others to respect our choices about self defense, the least we can do is to respect the choices others make.

Some people think of women who are armed as *Mama Bears*. Don't get between a Mama Bear and her cubs, they say. That's another great word picture... right up until the children grow up and leave home. Is Mama Bear's life still worth defending, once her children grow up and she is all on her own? Of course it is! Her life would be valuable and precious even if she'd never had children. She doesn't get her worth or her dignity from the act of procreation. She gets it from being a unique individual, precious in the sight of the God who made her.[1]

So I've chosen to use the imperfect word-picture of a cornered cat to describe my perspective on self defense, a word-picture that describes a friendly and capable person who can protect herself if she needs to, and whose only goal, if she must fight, is escaping to safety. This picture isn't about something you have or think or plan. It's about something you *are*. What you *are*, is worth defending. Here are some other things I have learned about self defense from my own friendly domestic cat.

Avoid Danger: She generally avoids dangerous situations in the first place, and somehow vanishes when there's trouble brewing. She pays attention to what is going on around her, and slips away at the first sign of any unpleasantness that might threaten her.

Get Away: Once danger is spotted, she gets away from it as quickly as she can. Her ears go up, her eyes get wide, her tail fluffs up, and she's outta there quicker than you can say, "Scat!" She doesn't stick around for the social niceties and she doesn't worry about her dignity. She simply *leaves*.

Don't Bluff: She doesn't threaten. You never see her pull out her claws unless she is ready to use them. Her claws only come out when she needs them.

Use Your Voice: She has a wonderful and unmistakable command voice, that low growl that means, "Stay away. Don't touch me. Keep your distance." Everything about her body language says that grabbing her at that moment

---

1   *Of course, whether you choose to believe in God or not does not alter your worth, value, or dignity as a human being.*

would be a *very* bad idea.

Do Whatever It Takes: If she feels trapped, she does whatever she needs to do to escape and get to safety. She'll run right over you on her way out of the room. If you grab her, every part of her body turns sharp and dangerous. You quickly learn that she has teeth and claws underneath that fluffy exterior, and she goes all out to defend herself. Did you ever notice that there's no "sorta" setting on a cat? Whatever she does, she does with her whole heart. If she's curled up on your lap, purring, that's all she's doing right then. If she's trying to get you to feed her, she dedicates her whole self to doing that. And when she needs to get away from danger, that's *all* she's doing. She's not indecisive about it. She doesn't hold back for fear of hurting someone. She doesn't worry a bit about being embarrassed. She simply does whatever she needs to do to get away.

Don't Stick Around: As soon as she escapes, she's gone. She doesn't stick around to see what happens next. She's *gone*—and she doesn't come back to seek revenge against whatever scared her.

Move Toward Safety: When she leaves, she doesn't scamper every which way looking for a place to hide. She heads straight for someplace she *knows* is safe.

Of course, like any other analogy, the cornered cat is not a perfect picture of human self defense. One place it falls down is that cats don't call for help when they're in over their heads. As a human, as soon as you've gotten away from an attacker and reached a place of safety, you need to call the police and report what happened.

A Word to Survivors

If we lived in the best of all possible worlds, a book like this would never be necessary. In that world, women's lives would never be threatened by violence. Criminal attacks against women would be vigorously prosecuted in every single case, and every person would rightly understand that the criminal's guilt does not depend upon the survivor's lifestyle choices. There would be no shame in surviving a violent crime—*any* type of violent crime, under *any* circumstances—because blaming the survivor for any part of the criminal's activity would rightly be considered an insane thing to do.

Back here in the real world, life gets a bit more complicated. This isn't a defense of the way things are, but simply an acknowledgement that things are that way. Lest there be any doubt: if you have survived a violent crime, **YOU ARE NOT TO BLAME FOR ANY ASPECT OF THAT CRIME.** Period, full stop. The criminal—and only the criminal—is to blame. Not you. Not in any way. Not ever.

To some people, any discussion of ways to avoid or limit the damage from a criminal assault just smacks of blaming the victim. There's a very fine line indeed between saying, "Avoiding this thing may reduce your risk of being attacked" and saying, "Doing this thing causes criminals to attack." Complicating matters even more, crime victims often say something like, "There wasn't anything I could do." They're saying they were without blame in the situation, it wasn't their fault it happened, and the criminal was entirely in control of the crime. And all of those things are perfectly true.

On the other hand, every happening has variables that, if changed, would create an entirely different event or perhaps a similar event with a different outcome. Playing with those variables is one way we learn from other people's experiences—and from our own. But because "there wasn't anything I could do" is so important to a survivor's healing, when others discuss those variables as they relate to violent crime, survivors often feel others are removing their blamelessness and denying the thought that has allowed them to heal.

That's one reason some survivors become angry at the suggestion that women should arm themselves. If being armed might prevent other crimes similar to the ones they survived, then maybe they could have prevented their own criminal encounters. That's an unbearable thought, because it means they might have avoided being as helpless as they were under the circumstances—which in turn leads almost inescapably to, "If I could have been in control, but wasn't, I was in part to blame for what happened." (But of course they weren't!) Seeing how the entire train of thought so readily runs down the rails to land in Blame-the-Victim Station churns the stomach and creates tremendous, visceral anger. This isn't an unreasonable reaction to such a painful outcome, but it's also not helpful for the survivor once she begins looking for ways to increase her own power in the world.

Predators prey. It's what they do. They find opportunities to attack other people. To help innocent people avoid becoming victims necessarily means discussing the opportunities predators take: how those opportunities happen, when and where they happen, ways to avoid allowing them to happen. Does that mean we're giving the predator a free pass, or blaming the innocent victim for the crime? Nope. Not at all. All the opportunities in the world won't cause a good person to turn into a predator. No matter how abundant the opportunities, it is the presence of the predator *alone* that makes the difference between a crime that happens and a crime that never happens. No matter what the victim did or didn't do, it is the predator—and only the predator—who chooses whether an opportunity actually becomes a criminal attack.

Put another way, every criminal attack involves a combination of predator plus opportunity. In this imperfect world, we can't tell who the predators are until they have used one of those opportunities to attack an innocent person. Even worse, we have no control over what choices others (including predators) might make. We can only control our own choices. The predator might attack or walk away without attacking, a choice utterly beyond our control. But that does not mean we have no power at all. We do have power: the power to limit the number of opportunities we offer to the predators among us, and the related choice of how we respond if we are violently attacked.

And that is the topic of this book.

Three Good Questions

For the most part, this book is intended for people who have already decided that firearms are something they are interested in, or for people who are in relationships with gun owners and want to understand a bit more about gun ownership and self defense. Although I am very enthusiastic about educating newcomers, I'm not really interested in trying to convince people to do anything they are uncomfortable with or unwilling to do. I believe my readers are adult, responsible human beings who are perfectly capable of making their own decisions about what they are—and are not—willing to do to protect themselves.

Nevertheless, people sometimes ask, "Why a gun? Why don't you use some other, less violent, less lethal way to defend yourself?" Or they jovially tease, "Are you compensating for something?" Or they want to know, "Why do you carry it with you?" These are good questions, and they deserve an answer.

Why a Firearm?

It's surprising to me, the number of people who think the purpose of carrying a gun is to "kill someone." Most emphatically, it is not. Firearms are indeed useful for defense, and they can indeed kill people, but their usefulness does not happen simply because they can be lethal. Rather, they are useful because they are the most effective (and perhaps the only reliable) means of stopping a determined criminal attack before an innocent person is gravely injured, crippled for life, or killed.

For those who would rather use a less-lethal means of defense, I absolutely support your right to choose whatever tools or techniques you feel you need, and we will talk about some of those tools later in this book. Kudos to you for your determination to stay safe! Like you, I see that awareness, avoidance, de-escalation, and deterrence are the absolute best first line of defense. Whenever possible, the smart choice is to avoid situations which may make physical self defense necessary. Stay away from dangerous people and places. Pay attention to what is happening around you. Listen to the little voice that tells you something might be wrong, and get away before trouble starts. Do not escalate unpleasant encounters, but rather use your calm, confident demeanor to remove yourself from the situation as quickly as possible. Use whatever means you can contrive to convince the potential attacker that it is not worth the effort it will take to assault you. Learn the body language of empowerment and use it. If you do get attacked and believe you cannot defend yourself physically, remember that negotiation, misdirection, and outright lying in order to escape are all perfectly acceptable and just as praiseworthy as more direct methods. If the criminal just wants stuff, give him stuff; stuff is less valuable than human lives. These simple, intelligent precautions can save you from a world of grief.

But when all that fails, what's left? Do we ignore the danger from a brutal, determined, vicious assailant simply because we are afraid of using a more effective defense? Do we choose *not* to defend ourselves to the uttermost because our best means of defense may result in the criminal's death?

Here is what it boils down to. If the attacker pushes the incident clear to the desperate place where someone—either the intended victim, or arriving officers armed with deadly weapons—must make a choice between either sparing the attacker's life or saving the victim's life, I firmly believe the intended victim's innocent life should be saved, without question and without hesitation.

If a criminal attacks me without provocation, why should he—the aggressor, the malefactor, the bad actor—get to choose which one of us survives his violent act? In initiating extreme violence, the criminal has chosen that at least one person will die or be seriously injured. The law allows for lethal self defense because wise people through the ages have recognized that in some circumstances, literally the only choice left for another person to make is whether the intended victim or the violent attacker will be the one to survive.

At this point, those who are skeptical about the necessity of using lethal defensive force may be thinking, "Yes, but isn't there some other way?" And the answer is, not really. Not when the attacker is both aggressive and determined, and the defender's life is in immediate danger.

If it were *always* possible to protect oneself and others using lesser weapons, law enforcement officers would not carry firearms at all. They certainly have other tools available to them. Nearly all officers these days are armed with bare-hands skills, batons, pepper spray, Tasers, and less-lethal ammunition such as pepperballs and beanbags for their shotguns. Police officers have radios and backup officers ready to rush to their aid on a moment's notice.

9

And they use all of these tools regularly... but they still carry firearms. And the firearms they routinely carry are always loaded with lethal ammunition, not the exotic less-lethal type. Why is that?

Contrary to what some anti-police propaganda might suggest, it isn't bloodthirstiness or bloody-mindedness. Every law enforcement agency in America has a detailed use-of-force policy telling its employees that lethal force is the absolute last resort, to be used only in desperate situations where all other means of protection have failed or are clearly not viable. In most law enforcement departments, management isn't exactly happy when ordinary cops use deadly force.

So why do police carry firearms when so many other tools exist and using lethal force is so often a public-relations nightmare? Here's why: because experienced law enforcement personnel recognize that in the most dire and desperate of circumstances, *only* a firearm can reliably stop a determined and aggressive criminal. The firearm is the least-used tool on any law enforcement officer's belt, but it is utterly indispensable because no other tool can do what it does. It enables an officer to save his or her own life, or the life of an innocent other, in circumstances where no other tool will reliably do the job.

> *Police carry firearms in order to save innocent life when all other means of protecting life have failed. Shouldn't ordinary people have the same choice?*

So even though less-lethal options do exist, and are used by preference nearly all of the time, nearly all law enforcement departments require officers wait for backup (at least one other officer) before engaging a known, dangerous felon with less-lethal tools. And what is the backup officer supposed to be doing? He or she is supposed to be posted in a defensible position (ideally behind cover) with the firearm in hand and the muzzle oriented toward the threat. The backup officer is prepared to use the firearm to save the other officer's life, just in case the preferred, less-lethal method of dealing with the dangerous criminal does not work.

To save an innocent life in case the less-lethal method of dealing with the criminal does not work. Ponder that thought for a long moment, please.

Even with all the advantages they have, even with at least one other officer already present on the scene, even with immediate radio contact with the 911 operator and police dispatcher, law enforcement officers still do not trust their own lives to less-lethal methods when they are dealing with a dangerous, belligerent criminal. The individual officer is expected to delay contact with a truly dangerous criminal until at least one backup officer is on the scene and prepared to shoot if necessary, in case the less-lethal methods fail.

Of course, what the police need to do in order to fulfill their jobs, I do not need to do as a private citizen. I do not need to seek out wrongdoers and bring them to justice. That's not my job. As a private person, if I am interacting with a criminal, it's because the criminal attacked me without provocation. The criminal gets the element of surprise, and he chooses when, where, and whether to attack me. I may get to choose my response, but I don't get to choose the time or the place. And I do not get to choose whether or not the conflict is "worth" a human life; *the attacker does.*

Whatever form my response to the attack might take, it has to happen immediately. It simply will not wait for someone else to arrive on scene. Unlike the police officer planning an arrest, the ordinary citizen does not have the luxury of waiting to initiate contact with a criminal until the time is right. The criminal attacks with little or no warning. The odds are already stacked against the intended victim, or the criminal would not have chosen that time and that place to attack her.

Because ordinary people do not seek out criminals, our chances of being assaulted are much lower than those faced by a law enforcement officer. But by the same token, if we are physically assaulted, it is relatively more likely that the criminal intends to maim or kill (rather than to simply escape), and very much less likely that we will have anyone else standing by prepared to protect us if our first response fails. As an ordinary citizen, whatever defense I ordinarily carry is very likely the only defense I will have available when the conflict begins, and perhaps for some time thereafter. I have to get it right the first time.

The most reliable means of stopping a determined criminal attack, a firearm, may likely result in the criminal's death. That thought is horrible. But far more horrible than that is the thought of an innocent person losing her life simply because some violent predator decided to amuse himself by killing her. More horrible still is the knowledge that the criminal, unstopped, could go on to attack the innocent again, and again, and again, with multiple fresh victims abused and killed for the murderer's pleasure. A serial killer survives and thrives in part because the only people who ever learn he is dangerous are the people who meet him at the very moment he is most deadly, at the time and place of his own choosing when he violently and unexpectedly attacks. Think of Ted Bundy, the Green River killer, Coral Eugene Watts, the Nightstalker, Dennis Rader, the Bike Path Rapist, the Central Park Rapist, and the Hillside Strangler. These serial offenders could each have been stopped by *just one* intended victim who carried an effective tool to defend herself and had the mindset to use it if necessary. Although each was eventually caught and brought to justice, at what cost to the innocent did these predators continue so long undetected and undeterred?

That is the lure of the firearm for self defense. For the armed citizen as well as for the law enforcement officer, the firearm fills a role that no other defensive weapon can fill. In the worst of all possible circumstances, an available firearm can save innocent life.

Some people, presented with such a discussion, immediately start shaking their heads in denial. "Using a firearm doesn't work in *every* situation," they rightly point out. "There are armed officers killed every year in this country, and having a firearm did not save them." This is true. And it is a tragedy.

Related to this, some point out that in many situations where people later say that the victims may have been able to protect themselves if only they'd been armed, the reality is that we don't know what might have happened if a gun had been brought into play. For example, a friend and I were talking about the Nikki Goeser story. Nikki Goeser was a newlywed, married just over a year, when her husband was murdered in cold blood right in front of her. She had a permit to carry a concealed weapon, but in obedience to the laws of her home state, she was unarmed at the time of the murder. She has since become a vocal proponent of improved laws which would allow legally-armed citizens to carry in more locations.

As my friend and I discussed this situation, my friend shook her head. "You can't know that her having a gun would have saved her husband's life," my friend said passionately. "Maybe it would have made the situation worse." Indeed, it might have.[2] They say hindsight is 20/20, but that is not really true. Hindsight only tells you what *did* happen. It never tells you what *would have happened if.*

When it comes down to it, I would rather have choices than *not* have choices. I fully recognize that using a firearm will not always be an appropriate choice. I realize that shooting the assailant may not be enough to save me. I understand that not every criminal attack will be survivable, no matter how I respond. If God intends me to die that day, I will die that day regardless of what tools I carry with me. But just because I might one day encounter a non-survivable situation does not mean I must therefore remain helpless in every other situation![3]

This kind of argument makes as much sense to me as the patient who,

2 Though it is difficult to picture what "worse" would have looked like in this particular case. There are few things worse than watching helplessly as a loved one dies.
3 "If fate means you to lose, give him a good fight anyhow." – William McFee

upon being told that he should take medication to lower his risk of heart attack, immediately retorted, "I won't take that heart medicine unless you can guarantee that it will also protect me against cancer, dandruff, broken bones, and herpes." How ridiculous! There is no medicine in the world that treats or prevents *every* medical condition. Similarly, carrying a firearm won't solve *every* criminal encounter, nor even every life-threatening criminal encounter. What it will do is give you the choice to live in certain specific situations that would otherwise almost certainly end in your death.

A few years back, media outlets hummed with the story of Meredith Emerson, a vibrant young woman who went missing one afternoon. I never met Meredith. She didn't even live in my part of the country. The news pictures show her to be a beautiful young woman—strong, vibrant, *alive,* posing with her dog, smiling for the camera. She looked like a joyful sort of person. Although I never met her, the horror that struck me after reading the account of her death followed me for days. When I read the news, I was so angry I literally shook from the emotion.

Shall I retell the entire gruesome tale? I'd rather not. Let us repeat only the important facts, mercifully blurring over details. Meredith Emerson went for a hike one beautiful day. She was young, in her early 20s. She was in good health. She'd had training in the martial arts, and knew how to take care of herself. And she took her big dog with her on her hike. She should have been safe.

But on that hike, she met Gary Michael Hilton, then 61 years old. He briefly befriended Meredith, spoke to her. For a short spell, they hiked together. But, he told police later, Meredith soon outdistanced him. Hours later, she returned along the same trail. While she hiked, Hilton had armed himself with a baton and a knife. And when she returned, he attacked her.

She fought. She fought like a wildcat. He reported later that she nearly got the best of him. She did disarm him successfully, just as she'd been taught to do. She knocked the knife out of his hand. She knocked the baton away. This petite, martial-arts trained young woman fought with everything she had. And she disarmed him. They rolled away from the baton and away from the knife. Barehanded, she fought him. And she almost won.

Almost.

Four days later, she was dead. Months later, her attacker returned to the crime scene, to tell the story to the officers who had arrested him for her kidnapping and eventual murder. She almost won, he said. She almost got away.

This is just another sad news story of a pathological creep overpowering a young woman, raping her, and finally killing her. It happens every day in America, in towns and cities, in state and national parks, and on private property. It has happened in your neighborhood—if not this year, then last year or the year before.

Just another serial killer, without pity and without remorse.

Just another innocent victim whose mangled body was found in the woods.

Just another beautiful, vibrant soul snuffed out to give a few minutes' sick pleasure to a man who had no soul of his own.

The day after I heard the news, I was talking to a friend who asked why I was upset. I told him I'd been listening to the news, and couldn't get over the story of Meredith Emerson. He asked me what had happened to her, so I told him. "The thing is," I told him, "she was young, strong, healthy. She had martial arts skills. Her big dog was with her. She fought with grit, determination, bravery. She fought with everything she had. She did all the right things ..."

My friend said slowly, "... but the attacker had a gun?""

No, I replied. The attacker did NOT have a gun. *He* didn't need one.

So what's the lesson? "Give the attacker what he wants"? Oh no. What the attacker *wanted* was to kill, to deliberately and gruesomely slay, this vibrant young woman. What he *wanted* was to watch her suffer and struggle, to watch as her life slowly ebbed away, to take his sick pleasure from her pain and her death. Should this sociopath have simply been given what he wanted? Gah! That's not the lesson.[4]

The lesson certainly is not that martial arts are useless. For every Meredith, I can point to dozens of women in slightly less-desperate circumstances who survived and prevailed because they had the physical skills they needed in order to escape their attackers. Only a short-sighted person would tell a woman that she is so helpless there's no sense in even trying to defend herself if she is caught unarmed. If someone you love is ever caught in a horrific situation as Meredith was, I hope that person uses as much determination and intelligence as Meredith did in her efforts to survive and escape.

So what is the lesson? Here's one part of it: women should know that they

---

4   From John Lott: *Having a gun is consistently the safest course of action when someone is confronted by a criminal. Research by academics such as Gary Kleck and Larry Southwick have used the National Crime Victimization Survey, which surveys about 100,000 to 150,000 people each year, to directly measure how different types of victim reactions impact the probability that they will be injured by the attack. The data from the 1990s indicated that the probability of an injury after self protection with a gun is 3.6 percent; for running or driving away, 5.4 percent; screaming, 12.6 percent; threaten without weapon, 13.6 percent; and passive behavior, 55.2 percent. Quote from "An Interview with John Lott"* published on Free Market Mojo by Ariel Goldring at www. freemarketmojo.com/?p=9988. Accessed 6/23/2010.

are not, by nature, incapable of defending themselves, no matter what the "women can't..." brigade might tell us. Most women can benefit from martial arts training, sometimes to an amazing degree. In part this is because training boosts self-confidence, and confidence often provides its own protection during the prey selection process.

This is the heart of the lesson: our lives are worth defending! From an early age, girls should be taught that their bodies are precious, that their spirits are their own, and that they have a *right* to protect and defend themselves with a clear conscience. Knowing their own worth and valuing their own place in the world, young women should learn to use every ounce of strength, savvy, and grit that they can summon to avoid danger and to get away if they are attacked. Our daughters should learn how to escape from a grab, where to strike, how to use misdirection, why sometimes it is necessary to fight back. They should be determined to defend themselves with every ounce of force, every smidgeon of guile and every trickery they can concoct. Above all, they should know to never, ever, ever give up.

And there is one more thing, the final lesson. For Meredith's sake, we should teach our daughters that they may someday come to a place where a larger and stronger attacker can overpower them, where their physical skills are not enough and where their natural intuition has catastrophically failed. In the gravest extreme, they may need a gun.

And in that final and desperate place, only a gun will do.

Are You Compensating for Something?

I suppose we've all heard the accusation: "Gun owners are compensating for something." Usually said with an evil grin and a you-know-what-I-mean kind of chuckle.

Well, guess what? It's absolutely true! By and large, people who own guns for self-protection are indeed compensating for something. At the time I first began carrying a concealed firearm, I was compensating for having children who were too small to beat off a kidnapper with their bare hands. The day my first baby was born, I looked into his eyes and swore I would never let any harm come to him that I could prevent. I took that vow seriously. I suppose you could say that I began carrying a firearm to compensate for that.

These days, I'm not as young as I once was. I'm in pretty good shape for a sedentary middle-aged woman, but I'm no martial artist. You won't see me on the silver screen doing one of those spectacular spinning back-kicks that miraculously knock deadly weapons out of the hands of people standing clear across the room. I've had just enough martial arts training to know that, in a physical fight between two people, the smaller of the two is generally at a tremendous disadvantage. Unless that gap is narrowed by significant training, the smaller person is going to be in a world of hurt—and this goes doubly if the smaller person is a woman fighting an aggressive man. I'd give it my best rather than simply giving up or giving in, but I'm a realist. Realistically, an undersized middle-aged woman defending herself against an enraged young man is going to get her rear end stomped. By carrying a gun, I'm compensating for that.

> **What are *you* compensating for?**

Somehow I've never been able to wrap my brain around the idea of throwing myself on the mercy of the merciless. I cannot imagine betting my very life or the lives of my children on my ability to reason with the unreasonable. Nor am I alone in that skepticism, because you know what? SWAT teams often negotiate—in fact, most such teams have members who are trained extensively in negotiation skills—but every member of most SWAT teams, including the trained negotiator, also carries a gun. I guess those guys are compensating for having the same skepticism about the sweet reasonableness of dangerous criminals that I do.

It seems unlikely that the intended victim could simply *talk* a Son of Sam or a BTK or a Hillside Strangler out of a killing spree. In some circumstances, it's worth trying, since you never know if you're up against the next Green River Killer or whether you're simply dealing with a criminally confused youngster who fell under bad influences. You're a lot more likely to succeed at talking someone out of doing something he really didn't want to do in the first place. But it's sure not worth putting all your survival eggs in that basket, because not every criminal is actually a non-violent kid with a good heart. Most are just what they seem: hardened, vicious, nasty people who don't give a damn about you or anyone else. So I'm compensating for wanting a decent back-up plan in case kissing the Blarney stone doesn't work.

Come to think of it, I'm also compensating for not having a policeman in my back pocket. The average police response time to an emergency call inside city limits in America is around ten minutes. That time can stretch literally to hours if you live outside city limits or if the dispatcher does not understand that it is an emergency call. A violent self defense situation typically explodes in just seconds, and an awful lot of very bad and very permanent things can happen in ten long minutes. It's enough time for a shooting, a stabbing, a strangulation, a successful kidnapping, a rape. There's never a police officer around when you need one, is there? This is no slur on officers, by the way. These are good people doing a thankless task. Being there when a crime begins is simply not in their job description. Their job is to catch evildoers who have *already* committed a crime. So I guess you could say I'm compensating for not wanting to be the dead victim of the next murder my local police will be investigating after it happens.

Why Carry It With You?

Many people understand keeping a gun in the home just in case of a criminal intruder, but cannot wrap their brains around the notion of carrying a firearm regularly when outside the home. Sad to say, this puzzlement is sometimes more extreme when the gun carrier is a woman, and it sometimes leads to odd conclusions about that woman's state of mind. People wonder, "What in the world would prompt a woman to do something like that?" Because it sounds a little odd, many people conclude that an armed woman must live in a constant state of worried fear.

For me, I've found that the confident reality of living an armed lifestyle is far different from the paranoid fear conjured up by puzzled fantasy. Knowing that I am prepared and equipped to cope with the worst life might throw at me allows me to be calmly confident as I go about my day. It isn't something I have to constantly fret over. Rather, it is similar to having a spare tire and a good tire jack in the trunk of the car, and knowing you have the skills to swiftly change the tire if needed. You don't have to obsess over that spare tire, or even think about it at all, in order to be reassured by its presence.

As anyone who's ever tried it already knows, carrying a gun can be uncomfortable.[5] The gun literally and figuratively gets in the way of some activities. When I first began carrying, I coped with a constant, uneasy awareness that many of the folks I cared about would be unhappy with me if they knew I carried a gun. Nevertheless, I worked through those feelings and continued to carry, because I discovered that having my firearm with me is generally more comfortable than *not* having it.

A story from a few years back illustrates why this is true. At the time, my five children ranged through late elementary to early middle school ages. One day in mid-summer, I went to pick up two of my children from their session of summer camp, and drop off the other three for the next session at the same camp. The camp is about three hours from my house, in a rural area. The road we travel to get there is a two-lane highway, scenic and beautiful. And we were traveling in broad daylight.

Before I left the house, I put my gun on. Did I expect any trouble? Nope. I just wear it as a matter of course. It's what I ordinarily do and so that's what I

---

5   *We'll talk about ways to make it less so a bit later. There are options!*

did on this ordinary day.

After dropping off the older set of kids and picking up the younger set, the younger kids and I wandered down to the beach. We walked along a nearly empty boardwalk and enjoyed the sunshine and the crisp breeze. Yes, I still had my gun on. I didn't leave it in the car simply because I expected no trouble. I carried it, because that's what I always do.

Because we were enjoying ourselves, we stayed at the beach a bit longer than I had originally intended, and so it was nearly sunset before we got back in the car for the ride home. We got back in the car and I noticed the car needed fuel, so we stopped at the gas station. After I filled the tank, I got back in the car... and the car didn't want to start.

Hmph.

My sons and I push-started the cruddy little car and I mumbled a few choice comments under my breath. After the push-start, the car was running smoothly enough, and the engine sounded all right, but the ride home was going to take about three hours. We'd piddled around at the beach so long that I knew it would be full dark before we arrived home. This particular stretch of road is notorious for its lack of cell service. Was the car reliable enough to drive down the deserted rural highway? Should I risk it? If I didn't risk it, what would I do instead? There were no repair shops open in this tiny town on a Saturday night, nor were there likely to be the next day. I know almost nothing about engines (hey, that's what God made mechanics for!) and had no idea what was wrong. Maybe I'd left the headlights on while we were walking the boardwalk? If so, driving for awhile would take care of the problem. The car really did sound okay once it started up, and I couldn't think of any really great alternative plans.

So we started back on that empty stretch of road. And of course, as soon as we got a few miles out of town, the car died. Fiddlesticks and other comments. So there I was, a woman alone with two young boys, with no cell phone, on a deserted two lane highway just before dark.

Was I worried? About the car, yes. But I wasn't worried about our physical safety. We had warm blankets in the trunk along with bottled water and even some energy bars, so we'd be comfortable enough. Furthermore, I knew I had both the training and the tools to protect myself and my children even in the very unlikely event that a human predator came along before help did.

Shortly after the car died, another car pulled over and the man driving it asked if we needed help. Was I worried about his intentions? Nope, I was relieved to see him. I didn't have to worry about him or what he might do, because I knew I could protect myself if he turned out not to be the Good

Samaritan he appeared to be. Having the means to defend myself allowed me to be friendly and confident in talking to a stranger in what could have been dangerous circumstances. I gave him the phone number for AAA and asked him to call for me. He said, "All right, I'll do that—and I'll come back and let you know what they said so you'll know I got ahold of them okay." Nice guy.

Fifteen minutes later, the man returned, handed us three cold Cokes, and told me AAA was on the way. The kids and I thanked him profusely.

An hour after that, I was still sitting on the side of the road, waiting for my tow truck. The boys and I had run out of things to talk about. I was bored, a little worried that AAA had forgotten us, and we were all getting hungry and sleepy. Finally, the tow truck showed up—a greasy driver who talked a mile a minute. Of course he was greasy, that's his job. But a woman stranded on a lonesome country road knows in her bones that any kind-seeming man might be a rapist of opportunity. Did I worry about that? Truthfully, I didn't even think of it, because I knew I had the means to take care of myself and my kids if I needed to. Because I had that confidence, I could be friendly and forthright, without fear or even worry.

Eventually, the whole situation worked itself out, as these things do. Nobody offered me the slightest violence and because I was calmly confident of my ability to take care of it if they did, I was able to be outgoing and friendly rather than churlishly suspicious in dealing with other people, even in what I considered to be risky circumstances.

Although the stereotype is that gun owners, and especially people who carry their firearms with them, are after some sort of a "power rush," I never have felt super-powerful or invincible when carrying a gun, nor anything remotely like that. Instead, in a low-key sort of way, I simply feel confident that I am equipped to handle an unpleasant or even deadly situation if I really need to do so. Because I know I could cope with the worst that could happen, I am free to go about my regular business without a lot of that low-level, back-of-the-mind feeling of vulnerability that so many women experience on some level in their daily lives. When I first began carrying, I really liked having that feeling of calm confidence which came from being prepared to cope with danger if I needed to. I loved knowing that I could protect myself, but more than that, I *really* loved knowing that I had done what I could to prepare and therefore need not waste any more emotional energy on the problem.

If, after reading this book, you decide to purchase a firearm to defend yourself, or if you have already made the decision to do so, your reasons for making that choice will probably be somewhat different than my own. For instance, you might have lived through a specific danger in the past, and be seeking a way to avoid it again in the future. You might be striving to please a loved one, or worried about protecting yourself from a known problem such as a stalker or a jealous ex-boyfriend. You might simply be curious what the fuss is all about. That's okay. However you got here, I hope the pages of this book will help you understand the choices others have made—and more important, I hope that reading it helps you think about and understand *your own* choices well enough to explain them to others. Most of all, I hope that by reading this book you are able to find your own balance point, the place where you can truly say that you are prepared but not fearful, equipped but not obsessed.

With a clear understanding that your own life is worth defending and with calm confidence that you are able to defend yourself if you need to, your mind and your energy become free to concentrate on much more pleasant things!

Saving the Life of a Stranger

The concealed-carry firearm exists to save innocent life when there are no other alternatives. A bit later, we will discuss the elements of Ability, Opportunity, and Jeopardy, factors that must be present in order to justify the use of deadly force. But you already know that using a firearm is a serious thing, and that its use is reserved for when human life is threatened. But what if the life at risk is not your own? Should you intervene to save the life of a stranger?

Generally speaking,[6] you may legally use force in defense of others if the person at risk would legally be able to defend himself using that same level of force if he were physically able to do so, or if you reasonably believe that he would be justified in doing so. Using a very old legal concept, in many jurisdictions, a bystander could legally "stand in the shoes" of the person at risk, using the same level of force that that person would be justified in using. If that person would be legally justified in using deadly force to protect himself or herself, then you also would be legally justified in using deadly force on that person's behalf.

> **The Basic Standard**
>
> *Use deadly force only when there is an immediate and otherwise unavoidable danger of death or grave bodily harm to the innocent.*

There's a mighty big IF hidden in the previous paragraph: in places where the "stand in the shoes" standard applies, you would only be justified in using lethal force IF the person you were defending was actually justified in using it. If it later turns out that the person you defended knew something you didn't—if, for instance, they'd actually been the aggressor; or if they knew that their life wasn't really in danger because they were just play-acting; or if they

---

6 *Laws about use of force do vary from one place to another, and laws also change from time to time. The laws where you live may be more restrictive or less restrictive than the ones mentioned here. Don't just take my word for it! Look up the laws in your own jurisdiction for yourself.*

were fighting with an off-duty cop or a legitimate bail bondsman—then your intervention would not be legal even though you acted in good faith and with the best of intentions. That's a fairly significant issue!

It doesn't work like this in every jurisdiction, by the way. Many places recognize a less-strict "reasonable belief" standard rather than the stricter "stand in the shoes" standard. In those places, if you reasonably believe the person would be justified in using deadly force, you may use deadly force on their behalf even if it later turns out you were wrong about crucial facts. But many places do use the stricter standard. Be sure of your own local laws before you act.

Completely apart from legal concerns, in order to avoid the truly awful danger of taking an innocent life, it's a good idea to follow the stricter "stand in the shoes" standard even in less strict jurisdictions. If you intervene only when you are overwhelmingly sure of the circumstances, you will never be placed in the horrible position of knowing your mistake killed a good guy.

When you use a defense gun, you are gambling everything you have on getting it right. You are gambling your physical life. You are betting your job, your home, and every penny you have in the bank. At risk is your marriage, your ability to share a bed with the person you love, and your ability to watch your children grow up in person instead of from jail. You place on the table every friendship you've ever made, every dollar you've ever earned or will earn, and your family's future happiness. You are risking sleep disruptions, flashbacks, nightmares, sexual disturbances, anorexia and other eating disorders, alcoholism, drug reliance, and a long and bitter lifetime of regret if you get it wrong. That is the gamble you take when you use a firearm against another human being.

To take a gamble that big, it's a good idea to be overwhelmingly certain there's no other way out. Is the life of a stranger worth a gamble that size? Depending on your personal morals, maybe it is. But never in an ambiguous situation, especially when you didn't see the prelude and don't know the players.

Occasionally, you will encounter a person who reacts angrily when told it's a gamble to physically intervene during an apparent criminal attack, or that taking that gamble might be a bad idea. Some people scoff at the idea of being overly concerned about legalities. Sometimes they imply that if you are not willing to rush in without full knowledge, you must believe that your bank account matters more than an innocent life. This visceral reaction is understandable and even laudable, because we all know that the only thing it takes for evil to triumph is for good people to do nothing.[7] When Kitty Genovese died in New York City in 1964, at least a dozen and possibly as many as forty people heard her pleas for help and did nothing. Do we want to live in that type of society? No, we do not. Heaven save us from people who "do nothing" when others are in danger! These honorable people are absolutely correct when they assert that as civilized, competent, compassionate humans, we must be prepared to act to save the life of another. We must not do nothing.

In their rush to condemn those who "do nothing," however, sometimes these honorable folks lose sight of this: there is a lot of territory between using a firearm to shoot a presumed criminal, and "doing nothing" to save an innocent life. Calling the police isn't "doing nothing." Writing down license plate numbers isn't "doing nothing." Shepherding others to a safe haven is not "doing nothing." Watchfully being prepared to act if the situation escalates is not "doing nothing." Testifying in court and identifying the criminal to the authorities is not "doing nothing." There are many actions a good and honorable person might take that do not require the use of a firearm, and those actions are not "doing nothing." Only doing nothing is doing nothing.

Please don't get me wrong. Although I hope I have been clear about the potential monetary costs of intervening, the true dilemma is not about getting sued. It's not about *things*. Things can always be replaced. The question is a challenge because of the awful risk of killing an innocent person if you get it wrong. That is far more serious than losing a few dollars, or even everything you own, in court.

In the case of jumping into a raging river to save someone from drowning or rushing into a burning building to pull someone from the flames, there's no chance at all of killing an innocent person if you get it wrong (unless, of course, you count yourself and the risk to your own life). By jumping into such situations, you will not put the innocent person into any more danger than they are already experiencing. But wielding a firearm creates a substantial risk of killing an innocent person if you do not completely grasp the situation—or if you are unable to hit a fast-moving, distant target without hitting innocent others.

One of the things I have learned through training and study: the greatest physical danger to an out-of-uniform law enforcement officer who intervenes in dangerous criminal events actually comes from other cops when they first arrive on scene. "Friendly fire" is a horrendous oxymoron for the kind of devastating tragedy which can happen when someone goofs during a rapidly-de-

---

7   *Edmund Burke reportedly said that.*

veloping, chaos-filled, confusion-driven event. Trained professionals some-times kill the wrong person when they arrive at the scene of a life-or-death struggle. Why? Because the responding officers did not see the entire prelude. They don't have all the facts when they get there. The danger of a mistaken identity shooting is every bit as acute for an armed citizen who intervenes in a stranger's situation as it is for law enforcement officers arriving at the scene of a reported attack. Heartbreaking mistakes happen on both sides of the blue line. And they happen most often when the person who shoots intervenes not see the beginning of the event and does not know the people involved.

If you see an unambiguous situation develop from scratch; or if you know the people involved so that you know that the apparent intruder is in fact an intruder, and that the apparent aggressor is in fact the aggressor; and if you are overwhelmingly certain of the circumstances, you are probably standing on very firm ground when you act in defense of the innocent. But if there's any ambiguity, you're better off getting away and calling the authorities.

On the other hand, if you did not see how it started but you do see that blood is actively being shed—that is, you didn't just see "someone with a gun" in the middle of chaos,[8] but you see a murderer in the very act of killing peo-ple—then there's no doubt about what's happening and that's the time to act decisively. If your own life is not immediately endangered, stopping the mur-derer will likely require a shot from a distance, under great stress, at a small and rapidly-moving target. Because there are innocents around that target you *must not miss*. Is your training up to that? Are you absolutely sure?

If it bothers your conscience to think of running away from a mass shoot-ing rather than intervening to save lives, I strongly suggest you seek out pro-fessional firearms training. Good training may make it physically possible for you to do the job that needs to be done, when it needs to be done. And what a tragedy it would be if an armed citizen were on the scene yet lacked the skill to defend innocent life.

Because we are human, we want simple answers. Unfortunately, real life is sometimes a bit messier than our plans, and this entire question of when to use the firearm to defend another or when to stand down and be a good witness is nowhere near as simple as people want it to be. The more you learn about how these things often work out in real life, the better you will be able to make solidly sensible, reality-based decisions when you need to—and the more likely it becomes that your actions will be successful when you do act.

---

8   *Which is a good description of yourself at that moment, too.*

Christians and Self Defense

Christians often have unique ethical and moral concerns about using deadly force—or sometimes, about using any force at all—in self defense. For this reason, and because I am a Christian myself, I've chosen to address these concerns here. If this doesn't apply to you and your worldview, please feel free to move along to the next chapter without offense.

Is It a Sin to Kill in Self Defense?

> *"Is it moral to take the life of another? No. Is it moral to allow my family to be assaulted to the threat of death? No. Do I trust God enough to protect them at the moment of threat-to-life while I'm there with the means to protect them instead? To my discredit, no, but I believe God will work out every severe consequence (Romans 8:28) for His glory and testimony for those that are saved..."*

When I first came across the above paragraph where it was posted on a now-defunct online discussion board, I was still fairly new to the concept of self defense. The post bothered me, with its flat assertion that taking the life of another was always immoral. It disturbed me with its implication that self defense was evidence of a lack of personal faith. And so I thought about it for a long while. Much of the material in this chapter was first hammered out on the anvil of my personal faith during several interconnected discussions on that old board.

As I thought about the ethics of self defense, I looked through the Bible to see what I could learn. And what I found then—and am still finding, every day—is that God is more concerned with the heart than with outward behavior, and that He fully and freely blesses people who act in faith. But what faith actually *is*, and how it expresses itself, is an intensely personal thing. It varies from person to person. So I want to be very clear here that my attempts to articulate this aspect of my own faith is in no way intended to judge others for *their* faith or what they believe in these areas. It is simply an attempt to grapple with these issues for myself, and then to turn around and share with others the journey God has led me through.

One of the first things many children learn in Sunday school is the Ten Commandments. If you're familiar with Christianity at all, you've heard of those: those are the laws that Moses brought down from Mt. Sinai, etched on two stone tablets, rules that were supposed to bind all of humanity for all time. And one of those commandments was, "Thou shalt not kill." This is the basis for much religious and Judeo-Christian thinking about self defense. If an act of self defense kills another human being, it is thought, the person who defended himself or herself actually broke this commandment. According to this line of argument, breaking one of the Ten Commandments is immoral, and therefore, killing another person—even in self defense—is always immoral.

There are two problems with this reasoning. First, many scholars tell us that the Hebrew word commonly translated as "kill" in English Bibles would more accurately be translated as "murder" or as "unlawful killing." It did not refer to killing in wartime or to self defense.

Second, if the commandment meant that every act which led to the death of another was an immoral act, then God commanded His people to act in immoral ways when He told them to take the Promised Land, laying siege to its cities and conquering its farms. When God called King David a man after His own heart, He was talking to and about a man who was responsible for more deaths in battle than any other ruler in Jewish history. Would God really call King David someone who pleased Him, if every one of King David's most famous and public actions had been immoral from start to finish? So we are left with a contradiction: if it is *always* immoral to take a human life, then God Himself is immoral, because He commanded His people to do immoral things, and rewarded them for doing those things! Since as Christians we believe that God is *not* immoral, then there must be at least some circumstances where it is *not* immoral to kill a human being.

The question then becomes, "Under which circumstances *is* it moral to kill another human being?" If there are any circumstances at all in which it is moral to kill someone, I would say that doing so with the specific intent to protect the innocent, without malice, and while defending the people you love would certainly be one of them. What kind of a man would simply *allow* a rapist to abuse his wife or daughter? What kind of a mother would simply *allow* her child to be kidnapped and murdered, without trying to prevent it? If defending one's family in such circumstances is immoral, then I submit that the word "moral" has no meaning at all. Nor am I alone in this assessment.

Here's a quote from well-known Christian theologians, Dr. Norman Geisler and JP Moreland:

"...to permit murder when one could have prevented it is morally wrong. To allow a rape when one could have hindered it is an evil. To watch an act of cruelty to children without trying to intervene is morally inexcusable. In brief, not resisting evil is an evil of omission, and an evil of omission can be just as evil as an evil of commission. Any man who refuses to protect his wife and children against a violent intruder fails them morally." [9]

But is it right to defend *your own life* with the same tenacity you would use to defend someone you love? I think it is. While a Christian may voluntarily decide to lay down her life for the sake of another, God gave you a body and He wants you to take care of it.[10] God designed you to protect your body, so it is not a sin, but a virtue, to protect it.

This is my reasoning and my belief. It need not be yours. This is one of those areas where good people often disagree. Each person's conscience belongs to that person alone. If, after considering the material in this book, you decide it is wrong to kill in self defense, then owning a defensive firearm is not for you. Indeed, I would never want to be a Christian who thought it was a sin to defend myself—and yet planned to do it anyway. The Bible tells us that for anyone who believes something is a sin, for *that* person, it is a sin.[11] If you believe that it's morally wrong to defend yourself with deadly force, then for you, it really *is* wrong. And that can be true for you even if others are able to do the same thing without guilt.

If the questions in this chapter trouble you, and especially if you are convinced that self defense is a sin, I suggest, gently but emphatically, that you put your defense firearm away and work out these issues in your own mind before you pick it up again (if indeed you ever do). You do not want to do what is wrong to you and then have to live with yourself afterward. You really, *really* do not want to be standing there with your brain frozen solid, wondering about the ethics of shooting someone when you have *no time, no time at all*, to think or to consider or to pray or to change your mind before the decision has to be made. The time to consider such ethical dilemmas is *before* you are faced with life or death peril.

---

9   *The Life and Death Debate: Moral Issues for Our Time*, by Dr. Norman Geisler and JP Moreland, Greenwood Publishing, 1990.
10   1 Corinthians 3:16-17
11   Romans 14:14, 23

Must Christians be Pacifists?

"You have heard that it was said, 'Eye for eye, and tooth for tooth.'
But I tell you, Do not resist an evil person. If someone strikes you on
the right cheek, turn to him the other also. And if someone wants to
sue you and take your tunic, let him have your cloak as well. If some-
one forces you to go one mile, go with him two miles. Give to the one
who asks you, and do not turn away from the one who wants to bor-
row from you. You have heard that it was said, 'Love your neighbor
and hate your enemy.' But I tell you: Love your enemies and pray
for those who persecute you, that you may be sons of your Father in
heaven.... Be perfect, therefore, as your heavenly Father is perfect."[12]

Any Christian understanding of the warrior ethic certainly has to include an honest handling of Jesus' words in the Sermon on the Mount, recorded in Matthew chapter five. Years ago, I thought this passage was pretty clear: if someone wants to insult you, attack you, or murder you, your job as a Christian was simply to take it. All straightforward and tidy and completely impossible, which was why Jesus tossed in the bit about being perfect (that's impossible, too).

But now when I look at this passage, I see a lot of things that I didn't see back then. First, I see that it is part of a larger context. The passage comes from the Sermon on the Mount. In that sermon, Jesus sets forth some common mis-understandings of the old law. The Jews in Jesus' day had the books we call the "Old Testament," but they also had rabbis whose comments supplemented the Mosaic Law. Over the years, these extra teachings became nearly as important to them as the Bible itself. There were errors in the rabbis' teachings as well as simple misunderstandings of what the law really said. In the Sermon on the Mount, Jesus addressed these errors. Each is prefaced by, "You have heard that it was said ..." and then corrected with the formula, "But I say to you ..."

When Jesus said, "You have heard that it was said, 'An eye for an eye and a tooth for a tooth,'" He was referring not to the Mosaic Law,[13] but to the hu-man tradition surrounding the law. Jesus addressed the fact that people often treated "eye for an eye" as if it were a personal command, when in fact it was a requirement for how their courts were supposed to function. The courts were supposed to be strictly just and without favoritism. Under the Mosaic Law, the punishment given to a criminal was required to always remain in proportion with the damage done to the victim. That is what it meant when the old law commanded "an eye for an eye." And yet many of the rabbis had

12 *Matthew 5:38-48 (NIV)*
13 *Exodus 21:24*

begun to teach, and many people erroneously believed, that this point in the law meant that individual people were entitled—or even required—to seek personal revenge for wrongs that were done to them. So Jesus pointed out that the individual was not commanded to seek strict parity. The individual could choose to forgive rather than to seek vengeance, and that is what God's people should also do if they are able.

In verses 38-42 of Matthew 5, Jesus mentions three situations in which the His followers should not fight back:

☑ **For an insult:** "If someone strikes you on the cheek." A slap on the cheek isn't a deadly force assault. Especially in Jewish culture at that time, a slap on the face was simply an insult. An insult isn't worth fighting, killing or getting killed over.

☑ **For a matter that can be settled by the courts:** "If someone wants to sue you and take your tunic, let him have your cloak as well." Settle your disagreements out of court if you can, even if such a settlement costs more than was originally asked of you. (Besides, the lawyers will take more than just your coat and shirt once they get involved!)

☑ **For a hated legal requirement:** "If someone forces you to go one mile, go with him two miles." This was the Roman right. Under Roman law, any government official, at any time, could force any ordinary person to carry a load one mile. You can imagine how deeply hated such a law would be. But Jesus said for His followers to stay so far on the right side of this hated law that there would be no question at all whether they had obeyed it. Do twice what the law demands, if you need to, rather than risk fighting, killing, or dying over it.

Look at the list again: none of those situations involves a threat to your life. This is all just good tactical advice in situations that do not call for deadly force.

Jesus then went on to correct another misunderstanding of the old law: "You have heard that it was said, 'Love your neighbor and hate your enemy.' But I tell you: Love your enemies and pray for those who persecute you...." At this point in the Sermon, Jesus is still talking about seeking vengeance. If you are praying for your enemy, it is because you are still alive. Whatever form your enemy's attack against you took, you have survived it. That is when faith kicks in. You don't need to hunt your enemy down after you have survived his attack and you don't have to shoot him in the back as he flees. If you and your enemy are both still alive after your encounter, you can choose to let him live and allow the law to deal with him. You can choose to let go of anger and bitterness, to embrace mercy and pray for justice.[14]

Oh, and that bit about being perfect? The other meaning for the word "perfect" is "mature or complete." It means, don't deal with these issues incompletely. Don't leave out the uncomfortable bits. Don't engage in sloppy or wishful thinking. Instead, think the issues all the way through and act accordingly. Strive for your understanding of these things to be as complete, as finished, as perfect as God Himself.

Here's another difficult passage often used to promote Christian pacifism.

With that, one of Jesus' companions reached for his sword, drew it out and struck the servant of the high priest, cutting off his ear. "Put your sword back in its place," Jesus said to him, "for all who draw the sword will die by the sword. Do you think I cannot call on my Father, and he will at once put at my disposal more than twelve legions of angels?"[15]

Another account tells us the disciple who drew his sword was Peter.[16] People usually remember this whole passage as, "Those who live by the sword will die by the sword"... and that's often true. People who live by fighting generally die violently. But take a look at the sentence after the famous one. Jesus goes to some pains to point out that He *wasn't* defenseless. Jesus could easily have protected Himself if that was His plan, and He didn't need His followers to do foolish things on His behalf. He had the situation under control. He carefully told His disciples that they didn't need to worry about Him, since He had the ultimate in concealed carry—a dozen legions of avenging angels!

Jesus didn't want Peter getting himself killed foolishly (one guy with a sword against a large crowd is just plain foolish). So He said, "Peter, put that away, you'll get yourself killed! Look, you know who I am, I've got a dozen legions of angels in My back pocket, but you'll have to trust Me for the plan..."

Jesus' plan was to die. But notice that even when His plan was to get Himself killed, He still had the means to protect Himself. That was the whole point of His death: it was His free choice to sacrifice Himself for us. If He really was without the power to choose, His sacrifice would have been no sacrifice at all, and wouldn't have had any meaning. It would have just been a

---

14 *Look at the imprecatory Psalms for an example of how to pray for an enemy. It doesn't have to be sweetness-and-light. There is nothing unbiblical about praying for justice!*

15 *Matthew 26:51-53 (NIV)*

16 *John 18:10*

gruesome story of some guy killed by a mob. But instead, He freely chose to lay down His life for us.

So I think we can see several interesting things in this passage. First, Christ's disciples were normally armed: Peter had a sword. Jesus wasn't surprised when Peter drew his sword (there are also other passages where Jesus refers to His followers' swords).

Second, it's okay to carry weapons. Jesus didn't tell Peter to throw his sword away. He just told him to put the sword back where it belonged, on his belt.

Third, it's not always in God's plan for His followers to use weapons. Sometimes there's a better plan than taking on a whole mob by yourself. (But Jesus didn't tell Peter not to *ever* use his sword; He simply told him not to use it right then.)

Finally, being able to protect yourself isn't a sin, since Jesus Himself was definitely able to protect Himself and He did not sin. The simple ability to defend yourself is morally neutral, neither good nor bad.

There are lots of other passages in Scripture about using force, and it would be the work of a lifetime to find them all and try to understand what they mean. At first glance, it isn't hard to understand why so many Christians embrace pacifism. But in my own studies, I have found the strongest Scriptural support for living an armed lifestyle often comes from the very passages that seem toughest at first. If there is a Bible passage that troubles you as you grapple with these issues, I urge you dig into that passage and really study it. Compare it with other verses. Check out a few commentaries. Ask your pastor for help understanding it. Pray over it and read it regularly until you come to a place of peace.

Can You Defend Yourself and Still Have Faith in God?

Even after accepting that self defense is moral in some circumstances, and that pacifism is not required of every Christian, there's still one more hurdle many Christians need to cross on the road to determined self defense. That hurdle is the apparent contradiction between trusting God to protect us and carrying a gun to protect ourselves. If we *really* trust God to protect and provide for us, the reasoning goes, we will not need to provide for our own protection—and indeed, if we do so, this must be evidence of a lack of faith.

After a lot of soul-searching on this issue, I've come to realize that trusting Him to protect me isn't at odds with having the tools to defend myself—not any more than having a fridge full of food is at odds with trusting Him to provide my daily bread. God created human beings as tool-users with creative minds. Built right into the human body is a very deep-seated desire to defend your own life. Try holding your breath until you pass out, for example. It is *very* hard to do, and even if you succeed, your body takes over and starts breathing again as soon as you lose consciousness. Self-protection is a design feature the Creator gave us.

The Creator also set human beings into a universe governed by cause and effect, in a world where our actions have consequences. Although He undoubtedly could have made the world some other way, He designed it so that human actions would affect what happened next. It could hardly be a sign of faith in the Creator who did all those things to relinquish our creative minds, ignore cause and effect, and think that He must take care of us without any action on our own part! But sometimes that almost seems like what people mean when they talk about trusting God... they mean, sitting back and letting whatever happens, happen.

I don't think that's what trusting Him means. I think trust means believing that God is still good even when the world doesn't go the way we want it to. I think trust means accepting that God is in control of the results, after we tried our best to make it happen a different way. I absolutely believe God is in charge of results, no matter what I do or don't do. At the same time, I think of myself as a farmer: God makes the crop grow, if it grows, by sending rain and sunshine in the right proportions and at the right season. I can't force those things to happen. I can't guarantee success. But what kind of a farmer would I be if I sat on my porch and said, "I don't need to plant or plow. God will provide"?

So if I work hard to provide for my family, it doesn't mean I don't trust God to provide what we need. It means I am doing the work God set in front of me. Same thing with protecting the people I love. I may not be able to protect them in the end (that's up to God), but carrying a weapon and knowing how to use it is simply doing my part of the work He's given me to do.

God doesn't usually say, "Let this happen" or "Make that happen." *He uses people to do things.* God doesn't just add zeroes at the end of your bank account so you won't starve to death—He gives you hands and a brain, so that you can earn a living for yourself and your family. He does miracles, but He works through people to do those miracles. Someone prays, someone acts. Moses raised his staff and parted the Red Sea; the widow poured out her last oil for Elijah; the servants brought the jugs of water to Jesus and gave the wine to the wedding guests. God uses human actions to do His will. Some prayers for healing are answered by a doctor's handiwork, some are simply answered. Is it a sin for the doctor to perform surgery, to give medicines, to use his knowledge and skill to help heal? Is it a lack of faith to use a doctor's expertise?

I don't think so. I think God wants us to act. He gave us brains for a reason, after all. If God had wanted mindless automatons, if He wanted brainless and will-less toadies, He could have created us that way. But that wasn't His plan. His plan was to use human beings and human wills and human actions.

If God has allowed you to be put in a place where you have both the means and the ability to defend yourself or your loved ones, and you don't do it, you can't blame your choice or its consequences on Him. It would be your choice to act or to not act. You can't say, "Well, I thought God was going to step in and fix it for me." Maybe His ideal and best plan was for you to grow by taking care of it, and that's why He let you be put in that spot.

Dying of Embarrassment

I'm going to tell you a little secret. Ready? Here it is: It is okay to break the rules in order to defend yourself. A lot of times, when I say something like that to firearms people, they respond instantly, "Oh! You mean like, it's against the rules to shoot someone, but if you need to defend yourself, then you can break that rule?" That's a good thought, and it's not inaccurate. That is one of the things I mean. However, I think it needs to start a lot farther back than that, and deal with the question of how to stay out of trouble in the first place.

One of the things that criminals are good at—must be good at, in order to do their jobs—is using the social rules to their own advantage. Here are some examples of the social rules we in America obey every day:

- Don't draw attention to yourself.
- Don't make people uncomfortable.
- Don't order a meal and then leave.
- Don't lie.
- Don't go out of the house naked.
- Don't lock the keys in the car.
- Don't be late for your appointment.
- Don't be rude.
- Don't tackle the waitress.
- Don't ignore people talking to you.
- Don't leave your purse behind.
- Don't talk too loud.
- Don't steal an old man's cane.
- Don't use the "employees only" door.
- Don't trip your husband.
- Don't leave your card in the ATM.
- Don't stand too close.
- Don't run a red light.
- Don't knock over a little old lady.
- Don't leave home without your keys.
- Don't break a window.
- Don't talk in the movie theater.
- Don't knock over your cubicle walls.
- Don't take things that aren't yours.
- Don't drive on the lawn.
- Don't run in church.
- Don't leave without saying goodbye.
- Don't barge in.
- Don't yell in the library.
- Don't abandon a full shopping cart.
- Don't throw food.
- Don't let baby ride without car seat.
- Don't jump over line dividers.
- Don't shove through a crowd.
- Don't run over a pedestrian.
- Don't act racist.

- Don't leave your laundry.
- Don't drag children by their arms.

That's quite a list, isn't it? Did some of those items make you laugh out loud for their sheer *obviousness*? We live with a million rules, a billion rules, every day. Most of them are so ingrained in us by the time we're adults that they become like a force of nature. Just as a fish is probably never aware that it is wet, humans are rarely conscious of the social rules that constrain us. And the more obvious the rule may seem, the less likely we are to notice it in daily life—or to deliberately break it in order to get out of trouble before it starts.

Here's a challenge for you: read the list again. This time, as you read each one, picture a situation where violating the rule would be one way to get out of trouble. For example:

- "Don't drive on someone's lawn"... unless the lawn is next to the road, and there's a young child on the road, and you cannot possibly stop in time to avoid that child. In that case, steering toward the lawn might be just the thing.
- "Don't tackle the waitress." Can you picture a situation where it might be good or even necessary to do just that? What if you see that your waitress is about to be shot by another customer? Would she thank you, later, for pulling her to the ground and out of danger?
- "Don't make a fuss in public." Are you willing to be the *first* person who responds to a fire alarm in a crowded restaurant, even though the other patrons choose to play it cool and keep eating? Would you stand up and loudly announce that everyone needs to evacuate until the fire department has arrived to take control?

Not long ago, I was out of town when my cell phone rang. At the other end of the phone, one of my friends sounded worried as she described her situation. She was inside a large convention center waiting for an event to start. The event was nearly sold out, yet twenty minutes after the planned start time, the auditorium remained only about three-quarters filled. More ominously, my friend could see significant law enforcement activity taking place just a few sections over from where she was seated. Rumors were flying through the crowd and my friend really believed there was a bomb in the building, although no official announcement had been made.

As we discussed my friend's options, I asked how far she was seated from an exit. "I don't know," she replied. "I haven't looked yet." She was worried enough to call me, but because she was rattled, she hadn't yet thought to look for a way out. I encouraged her to do so, and she noted that there was an exit door just one section over. After a moment, she said, "No, wait, I can't go out that way. I would have to climb over some seats to get there, or else go down to the area that's all blocked off and then come back up." I asked if the seats between her and the exit were occupied. They were not. Were the seats particularly tall, or was there anything else blocking her way to the exit? There was not. At this point, I realized that the only thing holding my friend in the building where she clearly felt extremely threatened was the fear of others seeing her break the social rules by climbing over a few seats.

Another friend of mine tells a similar story. He was eating in a restaurant one day when the building's smoke alarm began to sound—an earsplitting, unmistakable klaxon blare. The room was crowded, with many tables sharing a large area, and he was seated just a few feet from the door. And yet he did not get up and walk out that door when the alarm sounded. Rather, he looked around the room and saw that other people remained seated, some looking around and some simply continuing to eat. So my friend, playing it cool, stayed in his seat and resumed his meal as the wail of the alarm filled the air around him. A few minutes later, he smelled a whiff of smoke. Just a whiff. A minor, easily-ignored scent. Of course, it was a scent that didn't belong and that signaled extreme danger in a crowded building. But no one else had moved from their seats. And he hadn't yet paid for his meal. So he continued to eat, a bit more uneasily but still determined not to make a fool of himself. He continued to play it cool, in fact, right up until the fire department arrived and the fire marshal, in no uncertain terms, yelled at every patron in the restaurant to GET OUT NOW, because the building was, in fact, on fire. Standing in the street a few minutes later, the marshal then proceeded to dress down the manager in front of everybody present, pointing out that it was the manager's job "to see that the damned fools in your establishment don't ignore the fire alarms and get themselves killed."

Both of my friends' reactions were perfectly normal. This is the way people normally think. It isn't until the building has actually collapsed that the earthquake victim realizes she should have dived for cover when the first, mild tremor began. It isn't until the fire rages out of control that the person cooking dinner gets excited about the little grease flare on the stove. It isn't until the stolen car actually speeds away that the owners realize their car alarm wasn't chirping simply to annoy them. And it isn't until it is literally too late to escape that most people begin looking for a way out of a developing danger.

Because social rules are so rarely spoken aloud, they have a power to compel us far out of proportion to their purpose. When we see another person violating those social rules, we are often alarmed or dismayed—and often with good reason!—but the taboo against talking about the rules often *also* prevents us from being able to articulate exactly what we find so threatening about their behavior. Even worse, when another person violates the social rules, many of us are still respectfully bound to obey those same rules. That prevents us from being able to respond immediately, appropriately, and effectively to the developing threat.

As an example, when I was around thirteen years old, I was at an amusement park with some friends when lunchtime rolled around. The park was very crowded and the line for refreshments was terribly long, so I agreed to stand in line for all of us while my friends found us a place to sit. So I was standing in line by myself when an older teen came up and stood alongside me. I didn't know him. He was just there: long-haired, scraggy beard, smelled like stale cigarette smoke and something I couldn't identify. Since I didn't know him and didn't know what to do about him standing right next to me like that, I decided to pretend he wasn't there, looking away from him as if I hadn't even noticed his presence. A moment later, he crowded extremely close to me, standing right next to my side, literally touching shoulders with me. I moved away from the unwanted touch, but still didn't say anything. It was too weird. He wasn't acting right. He should have gone to the back of the line if he wanted to buy something, I thought. I edged away from him and he took a step toward me. He didn't say anything. I didn't say anything. The line moved forward and as it moved, he put his foot right up against mine, bumping his hip against mine in intimate offensiveness. I again moved to one side—and now *he* was standing in the line and *I* was standing to one side of the line. And just at that point was where the line narrowed down into those little metal bar people-separators, and he got my place in line and I was left standing stupidly to one side. I didn't know what to do. So I turned to walk away, and as I turned, he finally spoke. "Nice try," he said.

At any point during the humiliating process of "giving" a stranger my place in line, I could have spoken up. We were surrounded by people. I could have stood my ground and looked him in the eye and said, "NO. This is MY spot." I could have talked to the people behind me—people who had just as much interest as I did in not allowing others to cut in front of them—and told them what was going on. I could have yelled for the security guard standing just across the way. But I did nothing. And for years it bothered me, in a vague sort of way. Why did I just *let* him take my spot? Why did I do nothing?

Looking back as an adult, I finally realized exactly why I felt uncomfortable and alarmed from the very beginning of our encounter. It was because he began by breaking the unspoken rules of social behavior: Don't stand too close to people you don't know. I was worried and I was angry, but at the time I could not have told anyone what it was, exactly, that bothered me the most. Far more than his specific behavior, far more than the lost spot in a lunch line, and even more than the unwanted touch, what bothered me the most—then and now—was that his actions, in a form much louder than words, told me he did not consider himself bound by the rules that bind other people. A man who isn't bound by the rules of the civilized society around him is a dangerous man, and some part of me understood that even then.

At the same time, even though he had just told me in the most convincing possible way that social rules had no power over him, I said and did nothing *because I was still bound by those same social rules.* I was a good person, a nice kid, not given to drawing attention to myself. So even though he didn't consider himself bound by any social constraints, he still used the social rules to control *my* behavior. He gambled that I would follow the rules while he broke them. And he was right.

Does this matter? In one sense, not at all. The meal I stood in line for twice was eaten long ago, and its delay cost me not a whit. But in another sense, it matters deeply, because it illustrates so clearly how a good person can get trapped in a situation where she really does have other choices, when those choices lay outside the standard social contract: making a scene in a crowd simply isn't allowed under the rules most people live by. It serves to illustrate another point too, one that's fairly critical. Although all I lost was a few more minutes standing in line, the reason I lost my spot was because the scraggly guy got the reaction he was hoping for when I did not speak up. In a sense, he "interviewed" me for the job of victim that day, and I passed his interview with flying colors. But this is one interview a woman never wants to pass.

Self defense instructor Marc MacYoung details what he calls the five stages of violent crime on his very worthwhile DVD, *Street Safe.*[17] MacYoung notes that crime and violence are processes that take time to develop. The attack itself is not the first step. Rather, there are certain necessary building blocks that must be in place first. Likewise, the initial attack is not the conclusion of the criminal's activity. Here are the five stages of crime, as MacYoung identifies them:

1) Intent
2) Interview
3) Positioning

---

17 *Street Safe: How to Avoid Becoming a Victim of Violent Crime (Marc MacYoung, Paladin Press, 1993/LOTI, 2007).*

4)   Attack

5)   Reaction

MacYoung notes, "During the first three stages, you can prevent an attack without the use of violence. These are where the criminal decides whether or not he can get away with it. He may want to (Intent), but if he doesn't have the opportunity (Positioning) he cannot succeed. The Interview is his way to double check if you are safe for him to attack. If these conditions are not met, he will not attack!"[18]

Criminals, especially predatory criminals, make a living by reading people. In order to stay alive and stay out of jail, they learn to watch the signals other people send. They literally gamble their lives and their freedom on choosing the "right" people to attack—people who will be good victims and follow the script the criminal has prepared. One important part of that script includes you, the good person, following little social rules even when those rules narrow your choices and finally trap you in a dangerous situation you could easily have escaped otherwise. Don't fall for it!

Cst. Sandra Glendinning, a member of the Vancouver (Canada) Police Department, tells the story of a reported disturbance at a local bank. Working nearby, she responded to the call, which initially provided few details. In her own words, here's what happened next:

The main doors led into the ATM machine area, which was separated from the rest of the bank by a set of glass doors and a glass wall.

I had time to take in a woman and a young child at the ATM when a flash of yellow drew my attention to the inside of the bank. The flash of yellow was the jacket on a security guard. He was darting around on the other side of the glass and pointing frantically to another area of the bank. Several staff members were running around behind him, and one woman ducked beneath the counter. "Oh shit," I said under my breath, and my hand dropped to my sidearm.

"Radio to the units at the bank," our dispatcher broke in, her voice full of concern, "The manager's on the line—there's a man with a gun inside the bank."

The officer with me went to contain the other exit as I drew my pistol and started to take cover. Then I remembered the woman and child at the ATM—they would be in clear view of anyone inside the bank and would make ideal hostages. I could not go to them as I did not

---

18   From MacYoung's website at *www.nononsenseselfdefense.com/five_stages.html.*

want the gunman to know the police were there, so I stayed rooted in the doorway and called out to them.

The woman turned and gasped, drawing her daughter tight to her side when she saw my uniform and gun. I told her to come to me NOW but she balked. "What's wrong?" she asked in a whisper.

"There's a man with a gun inside the bank and I need you and your daughter to come here now," I said, beckoning her with my free hand. I hoped she could tell by the tone of my voice that I was not messing around.

The woman instinctively placed her body between her child and the doors of the bank and started towards me. Just when I thought she was going to be out of harm's way the woman stopped and pointed backwards.

"My bank card!"

And with that she stepped back to the machine with her child, pressed a button, and waited for the machine to spit her card out.[19]

Do you suppose this woman really intended to put herself and her child in mortal danger? I doubt it. I think she was just stuck in the "social rules" loop. The social rules tell you not to leave valuable belongings lying around in public. They tell you not to block the use of a public facility for the next patron. They tell you not to leave your card in the ATM.

This dynamic doesn't just come into play with *criminal* danger, by the way. It happens with other types of danger too. For example, at International Training, Inc. (ITI) in Texas, professional drivers teach students how to safely avoid collisions even when operating at high speed.[20]

One training drill at ITI places a student behind the wheel with an instructor in the passenger seat on a closed driving track. Laid out on Texas flatland, with hard-packed caliche clay on both sides of the road and no trees for miles, the track at ITI provides the perfect environment for this type of training. Before the drill begins, the instructor tells the student that the exercise has only one rule: do *whatever it takes* to avoid hitting the cones. The cones represent kindergarteners. Or your own loved ones. Or a pack of peace-

19 "Today's Would-Be Hostage," blog post dated 9 October 2009, Policing in Vancouver blog at www.behindtheblueline.ca.
20 ITI Texas, 10700 South Interstate Highway 35, Dilley, TX 78017. (830) 334 2990. www.itiwsi.com

ful nuns crossing the road in front of you. Whatever happens, the instructor says, the student must not hit the cones. That's the only rule. The instructor then blocks the student's view of the road ahead, and steers for the student as the student brings the vehicle to full speed. The instructor yanks the vision blocker away when the vehicle is nearly on top of a crowd of traffic cones, and the student must deal immediately with the sudden view—braking, steering, and otherwise doing whatever is necessary to avoid driving over any of the orange cones.

The trick—and it *is* a trick and a nasty one!—is that the cones completely block the roadway. There is no way to avoid those suicidal little cones unless the student immediately opts to steer off the pavement and onto the packed clay alongside the road. Most don't. Most freeze, panic, and drive *thump thump thump* over the cones. All because they cannot break the "rule" (never given by instructors!) that says good drivers never let their wheels leave the roadway.

Is a traffic law more important than human life? No, it is not. But just like minor social rules, traffic laws usually help people navigate safely and reasonably around other people. Even though obeying the traffic codes and following minor social rules helps society run smoothly most of the time, those same rules occasionally put human life at risk. For this reason, a truly safe driver must be prepared to do *whatever it takes* to keep the people around her safe—even if it means ignoring a rule that she normally obeys. And someone interested in protecting herself and her loved ones must make the same decision to do *whatever it takes* to stay safe.

Whatever it takes. A lot of times, concealed carry people jump on that phrase with great abandon. "OH YEAH, I'll do whatever it takes! I'll shoot the—." But what if *whatever it takes* means apologizing to the scuzzy little punk and backing away from the situation? What if it means leaving early from a concert you'd paid to attend? What if it means being thought of as a wimp or a girly-girl or a silly little fool because you chose to avoid potential danger? What if it means giving in, backing down, backing away? Are you really, truly willing to do *whatever* it takes to stay safe and keep your family safe?

A while back, I had an interesting conversation with Caleb Giddings of the Gun Nuts Radio podcast.[21] At the time we spoke, Caleb had recently been involved in an attempted mugging and had defended himself. On a bright Saturday morning, he exited his downtown office and was confronted by a

---

21 *www.GunNutsRadio.com.*

man wielding a large knife. Caleb's little pocket gun snagged on the draw, so as he worked to get his firearm out, he also hurled a cup of hot coffee at his assailant. The criminal ducked and fled, and Caleb never even had to fire a shot. Definitely a victory! During our conversation, Caleb told me that his wife had asked what he would have done if he didn't have the coffee with him. "I probably would have thrown my new iPhone at him," Caleb told her. He quite reasonably believed that buying himself enough time to save his own life was certainly worth the cost and hassle of replacing a cell phone.

Unfortunately, this type of quick thinking under stress does not come naturally to many—perhaps most—people. Especially when it involves a violation of the social norms. By thinking through these types of potentially-embarrassing ways to avoid danger or to escape once trouble starts, we can begin to set both the optional social rules and our own physical safety in the proper perspective. Swallowing the bitter pill of a little social embarrassment beats dying, every time.

Turning Fear into Safety

"The difference between fear and panic is knowing what to do. If you have a reliable, effective solution then fear is an asset. You know what to do and fear just makes you do it faster. On the other hand, if you don't know what to do—or don't trust what you know—then you will freeze in terror, because you have no clear goal or way to get there. Fear helps, panic hinders. Fear is your savior, panic your nemesis."—Marc MacYoung

One of the odd things about fear is that ignoring it can make it grow stronger. It can become this giant, amorphous thing that haunts the back of your mind, growing ever larger as you ignore the shadows in which it hides.

You start by being afraid of some specific thing—being attacked and raped by a stranger, for example. You don't want to think in detail about that, because it certainly isn't a pleasant thought. Because you don't want to think about it, you never study the Uniform Crime Reports to learn that stranger rapes are the rarest type of rape there is, so you never learn that most involve women who make high-risk lifestyle choices. Because you avoid this unpleasant subject, you tune out information about ways you could reduce your already-small risk of experiencing this unlikely type of attack. So that quiet little spot in the back of your mind, unexamined, grows into this huge black hole in which all strangers—or maybe even all men—become dangerous aliens to avoid.

So how does one set about reducing this oversized black hole of fear back to its proper proportions?

Listen to Your Fear

The first step is to face your fear and acknowledge it for what it is. This may not be as easy as it sounds, because while the emotion is easy to identify, figuring out exactly what prompted it might not be so simple.

If you have trouble sleeping in an empty house, for example, you might lie awake listening to unfamiliar noises, jumping every time the branches outside your bedroom window creak in the wind and tensing up with every miniscule settling sound the house makes as it cools down in the night. You're an adult and you know that noises don't hurt people. But the noises frighten you all the same. How could this be?

A little analysis might help you realize that the *noises* aren't the thing you fear. Instead, the noises just get your imagination going. You actually fear a danger that the noises suggest. So it is time for a little introspection: might you fear that someone is in the house with you? Or that someone is trying to break in? That is one possible explanation. It isn't enough to look for the thing that triggered your fear, because often the trigger isn't really threatening after all. You need to take it a step further, and figure out how the thing that triggers your fear implies a real threat that could harm you.

Educate Yourself

The next step is to educate yourself about the possible threat, and find ways to reduce your risk. For example, if you are worried about being carjacked, research ways to reduce the likelihood of it happening to you. Ask how you can lessen your risk of being harmed if it does happen. This could be as simple as learning that many carjackings begin when an intruder opens the unlocked door on the passenger side and climbs in. Just locking your car door will reduce this risk significantly. It doesn't cost anything and it doesn't take any real time. It's a no-brainer! But it's the sort of no-brainer that someone avoiding fear will never discover, because denial is less frightening than reaching over to lock a door.

But if you've already locked the door, and are still concerned about criminal activity while you drive, perhaps your subconscious mind is telling you that you haven't done enough. You may need to dig deeper, and do a little more research into how these events take place, how often they occur in your neighborhood, and who is most at risk from them.

If you fear violent crime, you may want to study Marc MacYoung's five stages of violent crime, which you can find on his excellent website (www. NoNonsenseSelfDefense.com) and in greater depth on the DVD, *Street Safe.*[22] MacYoung teaches that it takes time to build up to violence, even though it often seems to the victim as if the crime "came out of nowhere." Criminals have goals they are reaching for, and certain steps they must take before they can reach those goals. Once you know what those steps are, you will be in a much better place to counter the steps and thus avoid violence. When you know

---

[22] *Street Safe: How to Avoid Becoming a Victim of Violent Crime* (Marc MacYoung, Paladin Press, 1993/LOTI, 2007).

what a criminal needs to accomplish in order to attack you, you have a better idea of when and where to be alert, and more important, what you are looking for when you are alert. You also know when you may breathe a sigh of relief because you are temporarily able to relax your vigilance. In this, knowledge is your friend. And knowledge begins by facing your original fear nose-on.

Nightmares and Dreams

A new shooter often found herself fighting off recurring nightmares and vivid dreams about guns and self defense. Night after night, she battled shadowy bad guys, reaching for her gun only to find it missing. Or she drew the gun, and it would not fire no matter how hard she pulled the trigger. A masked intruder entered her dreams, and she stood frozen, unable to lift the gun to fire at him even as he reached for one of her children. The dreams made her feel puzzled, powerless and angry. She was frustrated about her interrupted sleep, and worried that the dreams meant something was really wrong with her.

This isn't an uncommon tale. A fairly high percentage of those who venture into the self defense world as adults will experience some level of sleep disruption as the subconscious mind struggles to integrate new thought patterns and organize the new information. Our brains are wired to process new information all the time, not merely when we are awake. The more fundamental the new information, the more the brain struggles to integrate it with what is already there.

Learning to cope with these active dreams can be an ongoing challenge, but it is possible to tap into such dreams and make them work for you. Here's how.

- **Find a comfortable place.** This can be your own bed, immediately after you awaken from the dream, or it can be an easy chair or a comfortable couch the next morning.
- **Relax**. Consciously slow your breathing as you deliberately let go of muscle tension.
- **Visualize**. Once you have relaxed, allow the dream to replay itself as a movie in your mind. Visualize each small detail, every bit of it, and don't shy away from anything. Accept the dream and the fear contained within it.
- **Take control**. As your reverie reaches the climax of your dream, the part that woke you up, take control, changing key details. Rather than visualizing being frozen in fear, visualize yourself reacting with calm confidence. Picture yourself calmly reaching for your

firearm and drawing it smoothly, doing what is necessary to stop the imminent attack. Consciously feel capable and strong; hear your steady voice command the attacker to stop. If necessary, visualize pulling the trigger smoothly with the front sight centered on the attacker's chest, and visualize the gun responding as it should.

- **Fix what you need to.** As you allow the changed storyline to play out in your mind, you may discover that you do not know what to do in the event that an attacker does some specific thing (enters from the dining-room window, perhaps). This is your opportunity to spot holes in your defensive plans that your conscious mind may not yet be aware of. If necessary, figure out what you will do to patch these holes and then visualize yourself doing that thing.

Visualization works to erase the immediate sting of the nightmare and begins reprogramming your mind to fight and win if you must. Together with sensible safety precautions to allay conscious fears, careful visualization can help put your nightmares to sleep for good.

Let It Go

The final step to conquering fear, as incongruous as it sounds, is to get on with your life. Once you have set your safety measures in place—whether they are passive measures like better locks or active measures such as a lifestyle of being alert—it is time to let go of your fear and focus on more positive thoughts.

A lifestyle of awareness is not about fear. It's about living life to the full. It's about paying attention to the world around you, walking through life with your eyes wide open and your senses fully extended, seeing the details other people miss. It's about smelling the roses, cherishing the daffodils, and never stepping on the bee that's hiding in the clover.

As Tim Schmidt, president of the United States Concealed Carry Association (USCCA),[23] says, "The whole idea of proper preparedness and a healthy, second-nature sense of awareness is to allow your mind to think about the important things in life." Fear doesn't have to run your life and it should not run your life. It can be instead a welcome ally in the quest to live safely, secure in the knowledge that you are able to protect yourself.

---

23   *United States Concealed Carry Association. (877) 677-1919. www.usconcealed-carry.com.*

Making the Decision

Those who carry a gun also carry a heavy responsibility. With the power to take a human life comes the responsibility to use that power wisely. Later, we'll discuss the laws governing deadly force. But weighing the moral and ethical issues you might face won't wait. It should be done immediately. Jumping past these basics might be tempting, but it drastically increases the risk of making the wrong decision under stress, perhaps even killing an innocent person. Neglecting to consider these moral dilemmas also increases the risk that you'll end up in jail, in the morgue, in the hospital, or in the suicide-watch wing of the local loony bin— again as a result of making the wrong decision under stress. In

Four Basic Questions
☑ Is it ever morally permissible to kill another human being?
☑ Am I myself able to pull the trigger if that is what it takes to survive?
☑ Under what circumstances am I willing to fight? Under what circumstances am I willing to take a human life?
☑ What are my state and local laws about using lethal force?

short, carrying a gun but failing to think about this stuff in advance is both poor citizenship *and* poor tactics.

Is it ever okay? Could I do it myself?

When wondering about carrying a firearm, one of the first questions you might ask yourself is, "Is it ever morally permissible to kill another human being?" Within your moral view, are there any circumstances—any at all—in which you believe it is not wrong to kill another person? Is it acceptable for the police to use deadly force? For the military? For adults protecting their children? This need not, in fact should not, be a personal question. It is philosophical in nature: is it *ever* okay for *anyone* to kill another person?

If you answer this first, most basic, question with a "Yes," it's time to get personal. The logical follow-up is, "Am *I myself* willing to pull the trigger if that is what I must do in order to survive?" Choosing to carry a gun means you are willing to risk killing an attacker in order to save your own life. Can you reconcile your religious, ethical, and moral paradigms with that?

If your deliberate action kills another human being, will you be able to live with yourself afterward? If you cannot, you have no business carrying a gun. That is nothing more than a tragedy waiting to happen. Instead of carrying a handgun, you may want to look into less-lethal defense options, such as pepper spray or martial arts classes. Although these intermediate steps will never level the playing field the way a gun does, they are an acceptable choice for those who are unprepared to use lethal force. Be aware, though: pepper spray is no magic potion. And many martial arts can be just as deadly as using a firearm, only more messy and less certain. The firearm fills a unique niche in defensive tools.

Under what circumstances?

The next question to ask is, "Under what circumstances am I willing to take the life of another human being?" Of course you will not be able to list every conceivable circumstance! And you certainly won't want to dwell on all the nasty possibilities. Nevertheless, you need to consider some potential decision points in advance. Some of mine are:

- **I will not go anywhere at gunpoint.** If the bad guy wants me to go somewhere else, it's because he will be able to do something to me there that he is unwilling or unable to do to me *right here, right now.*[24] Therefore I will not be moved. No matter how bad the tactical situation seems, *right here, right now* represents my best chance to fight back and I intend to use it.
- **I will not be tied up.** If the bad guy wants to tie me up, it is because he wants to do things to me that I would be able to resist if I were not tied up. Therefore, I will not allow him to tie me up.
- **I will not kneel.** No one is going to execute me. If I die, I'll die fighting.
- **If someone tries to take one of my children, I will fight** even at the risk of my child being killed during the struggle. I plan this not because I have positive assurance that I would be successful, but because I would not be able to live with myself if I simply "allowed" my child to be taken, brutalized, and his body perhaps never found. I'd rather watch him die in front of me.[25]

---

24 *Muggers and thieves don't need extreme seclusion. Rapists and murderers do.*
25 *No denial allowed. These are the basic worst-case possible outcomes of the choice*

I made this list for myself because I understand that the natural thing to do, when something bad happens, is to deny that it is happening: "This can't be happening to me!" Even if you get past that thought (a lot of victims never do), it's tempting to tell yourself that if you wait, if you do what the other person says, things will get better. The situation will work itself out. All you have to do is cooperate. The attacker will take your wallet, your car keys, whatever, and leave you alone. Just do what he says and everything will be okay. That's what most people who are attacked tell themselves—and in most cases, that's a good plan. Good people carry firearms to defend innocent life, not to fight over personal property or to protect their own egos.

But while cooperating with the attacker might sometimes be a good survival strategy, there are a few very specific situations where waiting and cooperating are the worst things the victim can possibly do. A woman forced into a car by an attacker, for instance, has an incredibly high chance of getting killed if she complies. Wherever the criminal plans to take her, he will have more control there. Even if it seems likely the attacker will kill her if she *doesn't* get in the car, her odds of escaping right then are the very best they will ever be. They might be lousy odds, but they aren't going to get any better. Similarly, a woman forced into a back room on her knees, with her back to the attacker, has just been put into the execution position. When someone is forced into this position, a bullet in the back of the skull often comes next. Once on your knees, you don't have any choices left, even if you realize what is about to happen. If you're going to save your own life, you have to make the choice to fight back *before* you're on your knees. If you comply by kneeling, you are choosing to place yourself entirely at the dubious mercy of a violent criminal.

So the purpose of analyzing this stuff beforehand is to make sure that even my frozen brain and my in-denial guts cannot lull me into cooperating if I am ever in one of the extreme places where a victim really needs to fight immediately if she is going to survive. Because I've thought about this stuff in advance, if something like it ever happens, even my frozen brain will have a definite decision point.

Your decision points need not be the same as mine, of course. And even though you should make your ultimate choice on the spot, based on the exact circumstance, you should also set some crucial decision points into your mind beforehand. If you don't, you may end up frozen in place while your attacker takes all your choices away.

---

whether to fight or not to fight. In a clear cut case where the criminal plainly intends to kidnap your child, would you fight? Would you fight even if—?

What are the laws?

The final, critical part of this advance decision-making process is to understand the lethal-force laws in your state. If someone breaks into your home, can you shoot them as they enter even if they are not visibly armed? Do you have a duty to retreat in your own home? If someone attacks you in public, do you have a duty to retreat? Under what circumstances may you legally display your weapon?

Find out the answers to these and other legal questions if you can. Chances are that your state's laws are online, and you can look them up. If you have taken or will take a concealed-carry class, ask your instructor about the laws governing lethal force. Read Massad Ayoob's book *In the Gravest Extreme,* or better yet, enroll in a MAG-40 class from the Massad Ayoob Group.[26] Join the Armed Citizens' Legal Defense Network (ACLDN) and participate in their members-only online discussion forum.[27] If all else fails, hire a lawyer and spend an hour of the lawyer's time going over the lethal-force laws where you live. The better your understanding of the laws, the more free you will be to act in a moment of crisis. When you *know* what the law is, your mind will be free to consider tactics instead of freezing on the legal question. You should be able to simply do what needs to be done.

When you think you have a basic academic understanding of your local laws, get in the habit of mentally applying those laws to situations you hear or read about. When you watch the evening news, or read the newspaper, and come across a news story about violent crime, see if you can determine whether the victim could legally have fought back using lethal force. Were the important lethal-force elements present? At what point *could* the victim have fought back? If the victim could *not* have used a firearm legally, what element(s) in the story would need to be different so that she could have done so? What information was missing from the news reports, and how could the missing information have affected the legal question?

Train yourself to recognize the basic elements of a legally good or legally bad shoot. Learn to do this when you are not under stress. If you cannot do this while you are not even subject to the accompanying emotions, sounds, smells, and sights of a deadly attack, making the right decision under extreme stress might be only a matter of dumb luck.

On the other hand, if you carefully consider all such questions in advance,

---

26 *Massad Ayoob Group, PO Box 1477, Live Oak FL 32064. www.massadayoobgroup. com.*

27 *Armed Citizens' Legal Defense Network, PO Box 400, Onalaska WA 98570. www. armedcitizensnetwork.org.*

and nail them into your consciousness with purposeful role play and considered imagination, then when the moment of truth arrives you may be able to simply do what needs to be done, without getting hung up in a deadly cycle of doubt and denial.

What Will I Tell My Mother?

When I first thought about getting a concealed carry permit, I talked to everyone about it. I told my mom and my husband and my kids' teacher and the lady at the grocery store. I babbled to friends and friends of friends and friends of friends' friends. It wasn't long before I discovered that not everyone wants to know or needs to know about your private life. And don't get me wrong: the decision to protect yourself is an intensely *private* one, with all sorts of personal ramifications. You may not be quite the extrovert I was, but if you're new to concealed carry at all, you've probably already told at least one person that you now wish you hadn't.

Here's the secret I wish someone had told me early on: You don't have to talk about concealed carry with anyone you don't want to. If you have friends with whom it isn't pleasant to talk about guns, you don't need to talk about guns with those friends. If it makes your gut clench to think about telling a particular person about your carry permit, you don't have to tell that person about it. You can instead continue on in your normal way, talking about all the other things you've always talked about with them. That goes for friends, extended family, acquaintances, and strangers. You have the right to protect your private life from public view.

Unfortunately, keeping your own counsel doesn't always work. Maybe the cat's already out of the bag—you started talking before you realized that some of your friends were against guns. Or perhaps it's an extended family thing, where you told your mom and she told Aunt Jane and now your cousins keep asking about it. Even worse, perhaps you're married to someone who doesn't like firearms and doesn't understand your fascination with being able to defend yourself. Now what?

Close family members

Starting with the most difficult case, the anti-gun spouse, expect to walk an emotional tightrope for awhile. But since you love each other and are committed to working things out, there's reason for optimism. You'll get through this conflict just as you've gotten through others.

Let's discuss the concept of boundaries. In short, boundaries mean that you get to decide what *you* do, while he gets to decide what *he* does. You can choose to be armed or unarmed. He can choose to go with you or not go with you. He doesn't get to "make" you disarm, and you don't get to "make" him go with you. Your actions are yours and his actions are his. He cannot later blame you for going somewhere without him if you chose to go armed and he refused to accompany you, because staying home would be *his* choice. You cannot blame him later if you choose to make him happy by leaving the firearm at home and then something untoward happens, because *you* chose to go unarmed. You entirely own every choice within your boundary—and that includes any fallout that happens as a result of those choices.

Put differently, you don't need anyone else's permission to carry, not even your husband's. You don't need his permission to own personal property, whether it's a firearm or anything else. However, because you love him, you might find that some part of you needs him to approve of the choices you make. That's where things get tricky, but try to keep the distinction between permission and approval very clear in both your mind and his. You can bargain for his *approval* (and you often will), but he has no moral right to either grant or deny *permission*.

A lot of folks have found that just quietly doing what they do, without fuss and without making a big deal out of it, gradually lays their partner's fears to rest. As time goes on, the other person eventually realizes that you're not doing anything except going through life just as you were before. However, if you choose to make a visible power struggle out of it, talking endlessly, badgering him to "agree" to "let" you do stuff rather than simply doing what you do and letting him choose how to react, the conflict can last for years and become quite nasty.

Your husband needs to see that you are committed to safety and that you intend to keep your firearms out of the hands of people who should not have them. If you don't already own a safe, get one. If you can't afford a safe, purchase some cable locks and find a secure place to hide the locked firearms when they are not in use.[28] Make security a visibly high priority and don't ever skimp on it. Whenever possible, enlist his help. Have him help you choose a location for the safe, or research safe types. Ask him whether he believes the not-in-use firearms are better stored in Place A or Place B with their cable

---

28 *For example: the firearm on the nightstand behind your locked bedroom door while you are sleeping is "in use" as a self defense tool. But the firearm on the nightstand during the day while you are out is not in use and should be locked up for safety's sake.*

locks in place. Discuss how you intend to manage your children's safety education as it relates to firearms. Ask for his feedback on such matters, listening to his worries and non-defensively accepting his concerns as the valuable data points they are.

Without asking permission to do things related to firearms, enlist his help doing those things safely and with the least amount of impact on your family life. If he hates that you take time away from the family on the weekends to go to the range, for example, discuss family time management with him rather than getting entangled in an argument about firearms use. Remember: your choices are yours, his choices are his. He has no veto power over your right to go to the range and practice. But it's best to choose range times that will least affect your family time. Rather than risk getting into an argument about whether you will go to the range, sit down and discuss how to protect family time while also allowing each of you to have time for yourselves. How can you schedule your "me" time without negatively affecting your shared time? How you spend your alone time isn't up for negotiation. But scheduling your calendar is a shared concern, so respect that by bringing it up with him before he has time to resent that you haven't.

Cutting into family time isn't the only reason your husband might object to your trips to the range. Be alert for other concerns—such as worried fears that you are spending time alone in a place traditionally populated only by men. If that's the problem, try inviting him to the range with you. That could be a win for all involved, because he will see that you're not flirting with anyone there, while you have an opportunity to let him shoot and find out it's not so scary after all. But if that doesn't work, consider taking a female friend or two to the range with you whenever you go, so that he realizes he doesn't need to be worried or jealous about what you do while you're there. Again, remember you're not bargaining for permission, but for approval, and always keep your discussion on those grounds. What can you do that will help him feel better about the choices you make?

Your beloved might not be able to express his deepest fears about your decision to protect yourself. Sometimes it just hits too close to home. If he loves the romantic notion that he will always be your rescuer, your hero, your knight in shining armor, he might feel betrayed when you begin learning the skills to be your own hero. He might even feel that you are competing with him when you learn how to protect yourself! But he might not be able to say this to you. Because this one hits so hard at such a gut level, he might not even consciously realize that's what he's feeling. If you suspect something like this might be at the root of his objections, take time to reassure him that he will always be your hero and that you will always need him in your life.

Anti-gun friends and extended family

If the cat's already out of the bag with friends and extended family members who don't like firearms, you have some hard choices to make. Don't get discouraged—that's just the way life goes sometimes. I wish I had some great advice that worked for everybody, everywhere. But I don't. Please take the words below as food for thought and nothing more. Run it through your common sense filters and chart your course based on your own good ideas about how to deal with your friends' concerns.

Even when dealing with people who appear very hostile to the subject of gun ownership, do your best to avoid being defensive. You don't need to justify how you live your life, and you don't need to insist that others see things your way. Have enough confidence in yourself and your good choices to address your friends' concerns without getting entangled in troublesome emotions.

Most of the time, questions from friends and family spring from curiosity rather than hostility. If you answer such questions freely, openly, and without defensiveness, you may find an unexpected ally. But sometimes, the questions might seem outright hostile, more like accusations than genuine questions. Again, remember that *you* choose whether to continue the conversation or gently end it. You are not obligated to put up with rude behavior even from people you love, and you do not have to expose your private life to the world. This goes back to confidence again: when you are confident in your own choices, you don't need to prove anything when the subject comes up. You can answer questions to whatever level of detail you wish, or you can gently direct the conversation elsewhere if you feel unwilling to cope with hostility. Both choices are equally acceptable, and neither makes you a bad person.

For some people, their first concern is what you will do on their property. Provide reassurance by discussing the nuts and bolts of concealed carry with them. Try to center the discussion on the ways you avoid accidents while carrying. Explain how you prevent other people from being able to get your gun while you're wearing it. Discuss how well your holster covers the trigger and holds your firearm firmly in place so that it cannot come out of the holster unintentionally. Explain that modern firearms are drop-safe and that they will not—can not!—fire without someone pulling the trigger. Note that you worry about leaving your firearm locked in your car, where a prowler could break in and steal it. Try not to get bogged down in lengthy philosophical arguments about why you need or don't need a gun inside the home of good friends who are themselves no threat to you. Instead, talk about how much safer you feel when you run errands while armed, or about your default setting of having the firearm with you, and how important it is to you that your carry method is a safe one so that no one else can possibly be unintentionally harmed by your decision to carry.

Some anti-gun friends will firmly tell you that you aren't welcome in their home when armed. Expect this and be prepared for it. It's up to you where to go from that point, but you might decide to move your friendship off their property. Tell them—once, politely—that you will respect their wishes on their property. Then drop the subject. When you want to visit, invite them over to your house. Or offer to meet at a local restaurant. If you intend to remain armed, politely decline invitations to their home without stating your reasons, countering with an invitation of your own. In this way you can keep the friendship alive while avoiding unnecessary confrontations and power struggles.

If such friends ask about your carry status when you get together off their property, politely and gently change the subject without answering the question. Just because someone asks a nosy question does not mean you need to answer it! If they ask you if you left the gun in your parked car, change the subject without answering and without making a big deal of it. The status of your firearm and its location are nobody's business but yours... unless you choose to make it so. If your anti-gun friends aren't willing to accept a cease-fire on the subject—which is what your decision to avoid butting heads over your carry status really is—then they aren't really willing to remain friends. That's their choice, not yours. But chances are you will be able to reach a truce and carry on.

Be realistic

While the initial reactions might range from cheerful interest to horrified fascination, eventually family and friends will adjust. That's the good news.

The bad news is that if you ever need to shoot someone in self defense, you can expect to lose some or all of your anti-gun friends—even your closest ones. All their early fears about you and your firearms will come roaring back to life. They might call you a murderer and worse. They may shun you, talk to the media about you, keep their children away from you. That's the sort of things anti-gun people do when people they know and care about are involved in self-defense shootings. This loss of social support can be absolutely devastating.

For that reason, when you decide to carry a firearm for self defense, you also need to reach out to other like-minded folks who will provide emotional and social support when you most need it. You certainly don't need to shun anti-gun friends. Keep them and love them! But for your own mental health, make sure your social circle includes people who will be there to support you afterwards if you need to defend yourself.

Could You, Really?

A few years back, a female relative approached me and said, with elaborate casualness, "Kathy, your husband tells me you've been taking a lot of shooting classes...?" I admitted I had, and told her about some of the classes I'd recently taken. She continued, "Well, as long as you enjoy it. You know, guns really scare me. I like shooting at paper a little bit, but... I'd never be able to shoot it, like at another person I mean. My husband kept telling me I should carry one, back when I was doing all that driving every weekend by myself. But I thought, you know, I'm not going to use it, I really wouldn't."

I told her, "I understand what you're saying. I think you're safer without a gun than with one, if you aren't sure you could use it."

She nodded, looking thoughtful. "Anyway," she said hesitantly, "I was wondering about—well, I wanted to ask you—do you think you could use a gun, like that? Really?"

She obviously expected me to say no. Instead I took a deep breath and jumped in with both feet. "Yes, I could." She blinked. I added, "I wasn't sure at first, but I got thinking about the kids. If someone tried to hurt or kill one of my babies—"

She finished the thought for me by saying, "You'd tear his head off!"

I laughed. "Yeah, I would, too. Wouldn't have to think about it at all. Don't touch the kid."

"But, what if it was just you?" she asked.

"Just me? Well, growing up without a mom would hurt the kids, wouldn't it?"

She was quiet for a long minute, then said slowly, "Yeah, I can see how you could get there that way." Then she changed the subject so abruptly that I had to wonder if she'd just decided that I was the moral equivalent of an axe murderer.

Obviously all such conversations are not nearly so peaceful and non-confrontational. Answering concerns like this can be a difficult task. Although "protect the kids no matter what" is hard-wired into most parents, not everyone has children. Further (I'll probably get kicked out of the Women's Club for saying this so baldly), I believe *my* life would be worth defending even if I had never had children. You don't need to have kids in order to justify your right to protect your life! So even though I pulled the for-the-kids card in this conversation, it's not really the line of thought that resonates most strongly for me.

Another way to answer the question could be to point out that every animal from the lowliest worm up to the largest carnivore has a built-in reflex to protect its life. Human beings have this reflex, too. When you were a kid, did you ever try to hold your own breath until you passed out? Most people can't do it. Even if you are one of the very rare people who can, your body takes over for you and starts breathing again as soon as your conscious mind is out of the way. When you are calmly sitting in your living room, it's easy to claim, "I'd let him kill me before I would ever fight back." But your body, threatened with death, will have different ideas. It has a built-in reflex to fight back and defend itself. When you *know* death is the alternative, you will fight to protect yourself. If you have an effective defense tool within your reach, you will use it.[29]

The drawback to using this approach is that while the defensive-instinct argument is absolutely true, it isn't convincing to people who have never been near death. And most people have some level of denial about what they are capable of doing under stress. But it may be worth mentioning, if you think you can get away with it, because people will think about it later if they are honest with themselves.

When someone asks, "Could you really…?" sometimes they mean that the worst that could possibly happen, if they didn't defend themselves, is that they would die. For a religious person that's not such a threat. But is death really the worst thing that could possibly happen? Not to my way of thinking! I don't want to sicken you with grisly and unnecessary tales of disgusting events. You watch the news as often as I do. Having your loved ones slowly killed in front of you, while you watched helplessly—that would be one thing far worse than dying outright. Living with yourself after something like that might not even be worthwhile. I'm sure you can think of other horrible possibilities too, and if you can't, I want your imagination. My own is too vivid.

Sometimes the question means the person believes no human being, no matter what he has done, really deserves to be killed for his actions. Such an argument usually shows that the person making it does not understand the nature and purpose of self defense. Contrary to what Hollywood might have

---

29 *This is one reason it's a very bad idea to carry a gun unless you have squarely considered and accepted the consequences. If you carry it but intend to use it only to bluff, and your bluff doesn't work, you may find yourself in the position of having killed someone despite your original intention never to fire the gun. That's a bad place to be.*

us all think, self defense is not about revenge, and it's not about punishing the attacker. It isn't even about justice. Someone who defends herself is not passing judgment on her attacker. She is simply trying to survive until society's watchdogs arrive to stop him and then (eventually) to pass judgment on him.

Occasionally, "Could you really...?" comes from a man who has quaint notions about women's physical capabilities and odd beliefs about women's emotional resolve. Were it not for the fact that women ask this question of other women nearly as often as men do, I might be tempted to slap an ugly label on the question itself. It isn't, but there's no denying that sometimes it comes from people who are motivated by some very offensive ideas. I've never found a good way to deal with such people except to ignore them and move on. You can't please everyone!

After the Shooting Stops

Let me start this chapter with a disclaimer: I have never killed anyone. I do not personally know what it is like and I hope to God I never do. I am not a psychologist, psychiatrist, counselor, trauma therapist, or any other brand of professional listener. My only qualifications to talk about this stuff are that I am a dedicated firearms student and an autodidact with a wickedly obsessive reading habit. The information below came from a wide variety of sources, but I'm particularly indebted to Massad Ayoob of the Massad Ayoob Group (MAG). Through his ongoing studies of self defense cases, and through his expert witness experiences, Ayoob regularly contacts people who used lethal force in self defense. He has had a ringside seat at far too many trials for those who courageously defended themselves and others. And he generously shares what he learns with his students.

Most researchers agree that women generally do better than men dealing with the emotional and social aftermath of a defense shooting. In part this is because society gives us a lot more leeway. Few people expect a woman to defend herself with her bare hands, or to take a beating "like a man" before a reasonable person would allow her to use lethal force.

It's also because our society gives women permission to express feelings. Therapists say that unexpressed or denied feelings lead to many of the worst aftereffects of using lethal force. Similarly, religious folks tend to do better than non-religious folks. After all, even if you can't talk to your buddies, at least you can pour out your feelings to God in prayer, or to the universe via meditation.

I also suspect women often do okay after defense shootings in part because of the social stigma against women who are prepared to defend themselves with lethal force. Before picking up a firearm for defense, we first have to question and reject a lot of feminine stereotypes. That's a difficult thing to do, requiring some introspection.

In this culture, self defense with lethal force is very rarely (if ever) a default setting for women the way it can be for some men; it has to be a deliberately embraced *choice*. As a result, women who carry guns have usually thought through the ethical, social, and emotional issues a lot more thoroughly than our male counterparts have needed to do.

Carrying a gun is not part of the culture of being female. When they find out a woman carries a gun, very often one of the first questions friends ask is, "Could you really shoot someone?" The answer our friends expect to hear is, "No, not really, I'd just scare him." And the way the question is asked often implies we should be unable to face the idea of killing. But women get asked that question often enough that it makes it really hard to sidestep the reality of what the gun is, or why you carry it. You're pushed to think about it, think about it hard and in detail, simply because you are asked that question so often and need to think about your answer every time you give it.

Contrast that with the typical gun-carrying guy. Although many men consider these issues in great detail, social pressure rarely forces them to do so. There's also a lot of chest-beating and emotional denial that takes place. A guy's buddies probably won't ask him if he's emotionally able to handle taking a human life, and if they do, they expect the guy to make some flip comment like, "Kill 'em all and let God sort 'em out!" After a shooting, a guy's buddies might expect him to feel proud of himself, his enemies probably expect him to feel smug and self-satisfied, his wife could expect him to be the rock she can lean on—and if he has any feelings to the contrary, he's probably going to stuff them down inside rather than admitting them to others. This is not a recipe for mental health.

This doesn't mean women get a free ride. After any kind of violent encounter, there are predictable aftereffects. I'm told it's kind of like the grieving process, and that some emotional and physiological reactions are only to be expected. But you needn't fear that living through a lethal force encounter will be more difficult for you, "just because you're a woman." Nothing could be further from the truth.

Social Issues

Dear Gunhilda
,

> At my husband's cousin's wedding last week, my
> big-mouthed spouse told everyone that I carry a gun.
> The women all bolted for the other room to gossip
> about me, and before I knew it I was surrounded
> by a crowd of garrulous old men who wanted to tell
> me intimate details about their guns, their medical
> problems, and their politics. What should I do?
>
> ~ Beleaguered in Birmingham

Dear Beleaguered
,

> Well, depending on how intimate
> those details were, you might consider
> blackmail.
>
> ~ Gun+

Would You Carry a Gun to _____?

Sooner or later, every person new to concealed carry asks this question, sheepishly, of other people they know who carry. "Would you carry a gun to _____?" they ask. The blank can be filled by any number of things. Would you carry a gun when you go camping? Would you carry to your mom's house? to work? to church? to the movies? to your kids' Little League games?

The question, earnest as it is, always bemuses me somewhat. You see, I don't usually carry a gun *to* anywhere in particular, but I do go places and do things. And I carry.

Years ago I made a decision that my default setting would be to carry my gun wherever I went and whatever I was doing. As a result, if I'm ever not carrying, it is because I made a deliberate decision to leave the gun at home. I take my gun with me unless I have a good reason not to. In every situation where I haven't carried in the past couple of years, it's been either specifically illegal, or literally impossible to conceal.

When I carry, it is never because I think I'm going somewhere really dangerous or doing something risky. If I think it's dangerous, I either don't do it at all, or I find a way to do it more safely—such as going wherever it is during the day instead of at night, or traveling with a friend instead of alone. A lot of people do the exact opposite. Their default setting is to leave the gun locked up at home. If they carry, it's because they made a conscious decision to carry, generally because they thought they were doing something dangerous. The only time they carry a gun is when they think they have a specific reason to do so.

I don't do it that way simply because my crystal ball has never been very good and I've noticed that bad things generally happen to me when I'm not expecting it. Nobody has ever left the house expecting a car accident, but we wear our seat belts anyway. Similarly, I don't leave the house expecting trouble, but I bring my firearm anyway. It's my default setting.

People whose default setting is to leave the gun at home often believe that someone who would carry to _____ (fill in your own blank) must be paranoid. After all, there's no specific danger at _____. So why would anyone carry a gun there?

The only answer I have for that is to ask another question: is there really a good reason not to?

Carrying in Your Own Home

Consistent with my default carry idea, I carry a handgun on my body even when I am at home.

Why?

Well, oddly enough, the entire reason I got a handgun in the first place was so that I could wear it at home. It wasn't until I'd purchased the gun and looked into the laws that I realized I wanted to carry outside the home. It happened like this: When we moved into our rural home, my husband and I realized that our home security needs would be different than they had been when we were city dwellers. For one thing, our nearest neighbors were well over a quarter mile away, and rarely home. We couldn't count on country neighborliness to bail us out if anything bad happened. Furthermore, because our county is large but lightly populated, a fast police response would take over a half an hour on a good night. Finally, my husband had gotten a job which forced him to work irregular hours, and he often was gone late into the night, leaving me home alone with our young children.

For all these reasons, I decided that I really wanted to have a firearm available to protect myself and our children when my husband wasn't around to do the job. But my very active children had taught me that they could get into more trouble more quickly than anyone else would ever believe, and I was worried about keeping them safe. How was I going to keep them from getting the gun?

At first I thought I would use a long gun, probably a shotgun, to defend our home and family. Since I had very little experience with handguns, but had handled shotguns as a youngster, a shotgun seemed more familiar and easier to work with. Furthermore, nearly anyone you ask will tell you that a shotgun is an ideal home defense weapon, because it is very powerful, very threatening, and because (this one cracks me up), "You don't have to aim it."[30]

So I thought about it. And I asked myself, if a kidnapper or murderer came slamming through my front door, would I have time to fetch a shotgun from

---

[30] *Just for the record, that's not true at all. You do have to aim a shotgun, even inside the house at room distances.*

the next room in time to save my children's lives? Possibly not, especially if the gun were securely locked up apart from its ammunition, with its ammunition secured behind a second lock, as many safety experts recommend.

Worse still, if someone did come slamming in the front door, or slithering in through a window, would I have to make the awful choice to leave my children alone in the room with him in order to grab the gun? What if he grabbed one of my kids and just... left? I shuddered at the thought! Then I considered leaving the shotgun accessible to me in the living room instead of in a back room. But what if we were all in the back of the house and an intruder entered? The location changed, but the dilemma remained the same.

I also wondered, if I could easily get the gun, what would stop the children from getting it? They'd already taught me that they could get into nearly everything in the house when I wasn't looking. I'd long considered childproof locks a sick joke. So what could I do?

There had to be a better way.

Around this time, a friend of ours revived his own interest in handgunning, and invited me to shoot with him and some mutual friends. Why not? As I fired a handgun for the first time in my adult life, it suddenly occurred to me that I was holding the answer to our home-defense needs in my hands. At that moment, I decided that I would get a handgun, learn how to use it, and keep it with me at home.

Just Paranoia?

- Of the 207,240 rapes and sexual assaults in America in 2004, 30% happened inside the woman's own home.

- Of the 83,920 rapes and sexual assaults committed by a stranger, 42% happened inside the woman's own home.

- Of the 99,130 incidents of completed robbery in which the victim was injured, 31% happened inside the victim's own home.

- Of the 895,340 cases of aggravated assault, 18% happened within the victim's own home.

After all, I reasoned, I never have any idea what the little darlings might be up to in the next room. They might have figured out the combination to the safe, and they might have snuck away with my keys to try them all out on the ammunition cabinet. But no matter what my pestilential children might do out of my sight, I knew that I could keep a gun underneath my personal clothing without them getting their grubby little paws on it. At least, not without me noticing.

So I set out to do just that. I decided I would carry a gun at home. Not long after that watershed moment, and with the help of that same family friend, I purchased my first firearm, belt, and holster. It took me about 24 hours to realize that a woman with curves cannot comfortably carry on the hip, and I moved the holster around to in front of my hip instead. It took another day to realize that it was just silly to lock the gun away when I left the house. After all, bad stuff happens in public too. Furthermore, with multiple toddlers, I was already fed up with taking what seemed like sixteen dozen trips in and out of the house every time we went anywhere.[31] I surely didn't need to add yet one more thing to our leaving routine.

At this point, you are probably wondering about practical little questions—stuff like, "What do you do with the gun at night?" and "But what about kids sitting on your lap?" and "Isn't that uncomfortable?"[32] Those questions each deserve a long answer of their own, but for now it should be enough to say that we worked things out. Because the gun is concealed, and because I defused the kids' curiosity early on, I've never had that much trouble hugging them or cuddling them or playing with them while wearing the gun. I learned to keep them from bumping the gun when we were playing, and otherwise it simply doesn't come up.

At night, I lock my bedroom door. I leave the gun inside a fanny pack lying in an open lockbox near the bed. If the kids need me in the middle of the night, I either lock the lockbox before I open the door, or pick the fanny pack up and put it on with my robe. Undoubtedly others could find other solutions to this problem, but this solution has worked pretty well for our family.

Is carrying a gun at home for everyone? No, most decidedly not. It takes a certain commitment to carry it off. But I'm here to tell you it's not impossible. For me, carrying the gun at home seemed the easiest and simplest answer to the question, "How do I keep the gun away from the children but accessible to myself?"

Carrying to Friends' Houses

This may be the most difficult subject in this series, dancing as it must between the sharpened horns of multiple dilemmas. So let me say this right

---

31 You know the routine. Trip one is the diaper bag and playpen. Trip two is kid one. Trip three is the kid's favorite toy that he dropped on the way out. Trip four is the other baby. Trip five is the pacifier which he dropped. Trip six is the purse I set down by the door. Trip seven is bringing kid one back in to change the stinky diaper. Trip eight is the other baby because he can't stay in the car by himself while I change the diaper ...
32 At least, I hope that's what you're wondering. I'd feel bad if you were actually wondering which mental hospital you should contact on my behalf.

at the outset: I am not the keeper of your conscience. You are. My intention in writing this piece is to give you some ideas to consider as you make your own choices. And that is my entire goal. If you disagree with some of the ideas below, that's only to be expected. It's a contentious topic.

The Legal Dilemma

Depending on your jurisdiction, it may be outright illegal to carry into someone else's home without their informed permission. In other places, the law for private dwellings may be similar to the law for private businesses, and it is legal to carry there unless the owner specifically announces you may not. Nearly everywhere, if the owner asks you to leave for any reason, you must leave immediately or you will be guilty of trespass.

You must find out what the law is in your own state. You, and you alone, are responsible for your own choices about when and where to carry, and only you are responsible if you ignorantly or deliberately break the law. While I would never advise anyone to do that, it is worth pointing out here that breaking the law on purpose, while being fully aware of the consequences and prepared to cope with the risk, is much less personally risky than it is to stupidly run afoul of a law you didn't even know existed. If you intend to be a law-abiding citizen, it is well worth your while to go look those laws up and figure out how they apply to you. Especially in the internet age, ignorance of the law really is no excuse.

The Ethical and Social Dilemmas

So you've passed the legal hurdle, and you've found out that in your state, you may legally carry concealed nearly anywhere you go with very few exceptions. Your friend's home is legally clear. But should you carry there? If you don't, where will you leave your firearm while you are visiting her? If you do, should you tell your friend that you are armed? If your friend is married, do you need to tell her husband, too? Or is it enough to tell just one of them? If you do inform someone of your carry status, how and when should you do so? Do the answers change if you are staying overnight instead of just visiting for the evening? Or if they have children? Or if you know they don't like firearms? Or if they are relatives, not really friends? Or if one half of a married couple hates firearms but you know the other one won't mind? Or if... or if... or if...?

These are questions it is not easy to answer, especially because the answers may vary greatly depending upon the circumstances and upon your relationship with your friend. Here are some things that I've thought about over the years. These aren't answers that will work for everyone—it's only my take on things.

Over the years I have become very close-lipped about carrying. My immediate family knows, of course. My readers know it. And a jillion people in the mythical world called the internet know about it. In person? Not so much. I used to indiscriminately tell everyone I met. But these days, if we met in person, you'd never even know I own firearms. Even among my closest friends who know I carry regularly, I don't often discuss my carry status unless someone has a specific need to know. It's kind of like my underwear: of course I wear them everywhere, but there's no need to talk about them in polite company.

Remember that concealed carry is my default status. I don't look for specific reasons to carry somewhere. I look for specific reasons not to. And those reasons, for me, are very few and far between: if it's illegal to carry, or literally impossible to conceal in the situation, I'll take my gun off. Otherwise, I'm wearing it.

All of the above means that I do carry into friends' homes, and most of them never know it.[33]

There's are practical reasons for this. For one thing, because I am nearly always literally surrounded by my children, it's very hard for me to discreetly remove the firearm in the car. Picture me pulling up in front of someone's house and then doing the watusi in the front seat, trying to get the gun off my waist and into a lockbox without anyone seeing it, while the kids ask helpful questions like, "Mom, why does your face turn funny colors when you scrunch over to reach under the seat?"

Ethical Meets Practical

If you are not ethically or emotionally comfortable carrying in a friend's home, it's a bad idea to do it anyway. Your own nervousness, shown in your body language, will very likely cue your friend that something is wrong.

Then there's the question of security. I cannot bring myself to leave a gun in the car, even a locked car, without adding a little extra security with a lockbox. But secure as the lockbox is, a thief could always just drive away with the whole car, lockbox and all. On my waist, the gun is safe. Out of my sight, who knows? So I prefer to keep it on my waist if I can.

I've never had anyone catch me carrying in their home without permission. Perhaps I'd feel differently about this if anything like that had ever hap-

---

33 *Actually, um. I guess they do now. Hi, friends!*

pened. Instead, the single most uncomfortable moment I've ever had while carrying came before I adopted the tight-lips policy, when I tried to be a good (relative) and inform my (relative) that I was carrying in her home. She didn't quite kick me out of the house, but it was a near thing. I think the only thing that saved me was her knowledge that if she'd tried, her husband and mine would probably both have pitched a fit on my behalf. I felt guilty about that for years, and still do, because there really was no need to make her so uncomfortable. She didn't need to know I was carrying in the first place! My gun was going to stay out of sight and under my control at all times. There was nothing she needed to do differently simply because I had a gun with me. It was only my own selfish need for approval that made me tell her.

After that, I gradually got more and more close-mouthed. But I kept carrying. And it works that way for me. But things might be different for you. Maybe your conscience wouldn't allow you to smuggle a gun onto your friend's property. Or maybe you simply doubt your ability to get away with it, and would rather have permission in advance. Or maybe... well, there are as many possible "or maybes" as there are people in the world. In any case, I would not urge you to do anything that makes you uncomfortable or uneasy. You are the one who has to live with yourself, after all.[34]

If you decide to come clean, I think it's best to do so well in advance, not after you have already unpacked your bags for a long visit. You'll want to give your hostess enough time to think about it, and perhaps discuss it with her family before you arrive. Probably the biggest practical benefit of telling your friend right up-front is that if she consents at all, you will have an ally to help you figure out how to keep the gun secure. That's excellent—but remember, keeping the gun away from children, the criminal and the clueless is still your responsibility.

The Practical Dilemmas

Carrying into other people's homes presents several practical dilemmas. Starting with the obvious safety issue: If you carry off-body in a purse, or if you temporarily put the gun into a suitcase or pack, you must keep the purse or pack within your personal control at all times unless the gun is securely locked up. This is non-negotiable. There is no "just this once." If you cannot commit to keeping positive control over your firearm every single second of every single minute no matter where you are, you should not take the

---

34 *And back on the practical level, if you are uncomfortable or nervous or worried, other people are likely to pick up on your feelings and wonder what's going on. For best concealment, unless you're a really, really good actress, you have to be emotionally and ethically comfortable with the choices you make.*

firearm with you.

This is especially important if your friend has children. But even if your friend does not have children, security and unauthorized access remain important issues. Remember, children are only one of the Three C's from which firearms must be kept: the Criminal and the Clueless are still out there. Unless your friend and every other person who might enter her home while you are there are all competent with firearms safety, without a single exception, you don't get a free pass to set your gun purse down and forget it.

This isn't such a big deal if you are only visiting for an afternoon, especially if you carry on-body. Whatever carry method you've chosen, you've probably worked security out for yourself during daylight hours. But what about overnight visits? Assuming your friend is a gun owner and has a gun safe, you may want to simply tell her you're carrying, and ask her to lock it up for you at bedtime. Ohhhh, if it were always that easy!

Some Bedtime Options

With no lock on the bedroom door...

- ☑ You could unload the firearm, put a cable lock on it, and shove it to the bottom of your suitcase.

- ☑ You could partially disable your semi-automatic, drop the pieces into the the bottom of your bag, putting the ammunition in a separate pocket.

- ☑ You could unload the firearm and put it into a bag or case that you've equipped with a travel lock.

- ☑ You could purchase a small, hard-sided lockbox to keep in one corner of your suitcase. The gun is out of sight and secure wehn it is in the box, and when it is locked securely it is safe to leave the gun loaded inside.

If the guest-room door has a lock on it, you could lock the door when you go to bed, then put your firearm somewhere analogous to where you would leave it in your own home at bedtime. When you wake up in a strange place, you're likely to be slightly disoriented, so you may prefer to leave the gun across the room rather than near the bed where you might grab it before you are fully awake. If you go with this plan, you will probably want to get dressed, including putting on the firearm, before you open the bedroom door in the morning. In no case will you leave the firearm in the room with the door unlocked when you are not in the room.

If there's no lock on the door, or if the sleeping arrangements have you sharing the living room couch with the family's St. Bernard, you are going to have to be a little more creative about bedtime. Leaving the gun lying around someone else's home, accessible to anyone who walks in while you are sleeping, is simply not an option.

Of course, if you lock your gun up at bedtime, it won't be accessible in the middle of the night. Maybe that doesn't appeal to you much. It doesn't appeal much to me, either. But if the bedroom door doesn't lock, there really aren't a lot of other really safe choices. You're going to be sound asleep, after all. When you do awake, you'll probably wake up slightly disoriented because it's not your own bed. Since the door doesn't lock, people might wander in, and anyone who wanders in may easily spot your firearm and pick it up.

Sleeping on the living-room couch has one more drawback besides all the obvious ones: if you intend to put the firearm into your suitcase when the family goes to bed, you might find it pretty hard to get it off your belt, unloaded and locked, and then get it into your suitcase without being spotted. A really nonchalant attitude helps with this. If you look sneaky and nervous, your body language may give you away. But if you are casual and easygoing about it, you're more likely to carry it off if someone does walk back into the room.

If your suitcase is small, maybe you can take the whole suitcase into the bathroom with you when you make your bedtime ablutions. More likely, though, you're going to have to figure out some subterfuge: carry an opaque shower bag or makeup bag with you into the bathroom, and temporarily place the cable-locked (or unloaded and reholstered) gun into the bag after you remove it from your belt. Or hide the gun within a pile of clothing about which you're understandably embarrassed because your dainties are in it. Or fold or roll it into a towel to carry casually out of the bathroom with you. The goal is to get the gun off your body in privacy, unload and secure it, then move the gun to your suitcase without arousing suspicion. That means that whatever you choose to transport it has to be something you would normally carry with you into and back out of the bathroom near bedtime.

Be aware that unloading a semi-automatic makes an easily-identified noise, unless you work very hard at keeping it quiet. Although this should go without saying, be very aware of the gun's muzzle direction whenever you absolutely must load or unload it—it would not do to accidentally shoot the family dog while you were trying to secure the gun where the toddler couldn't get it.

Practical Issues and Group Dynamics

It's important you try to anticipate times when you will need to secure the gun, and plan accordingly. For instance, if everyone begins talking about going swimming in your hostess' swimming pool, you'll know that it will soon be necessary to get the gun off your body and locked up securely before someone throws you in. How are you going to do that? If the group is making plans to visit some facility into which it is illegal to carry, you can anticipate in advance that you'll need privacy to lock your gun away when you get there, so figure out how you're going to get that privacy before you climb into the car. Or figure out how to get the gun off your belt and locked into your suitcase before you leave the house. Try to stay a step ahead of the crowd. Before you arrive at your friend's house, visualize everything that is planned, and any possible variations that might happen, and figure out how you'll cope with each one. It is best to think these things out carefully beforehand, rather than being caught by surprise when they happen.

Once you've got a good basic plan, take a moment to think of ways the plan could change if needed. For instance, you plan some specific excuse which will allow you to slip back to the car to lock your gun up before the group enters some forbidden location. What will you say if someone wants to accompany you back to the car? Anticipate it, visualize it, then forget it unless it's needed. It probably won't come up, but if it does, you'll be ready.

Carrying to the Doctor's Office

An email exchange with a friend reminded me of something that happened a couple of years back, when I went to the doctor to get some better allergy drugs. Of course I carried my gun into the doctor's office, since I carry all the time and it is legal in my state. There are two practical problems with that, one minor and one... well, okay, the first problem is, they weigh you before you get ushered into the exam room, right? I tried to explain to the nurse that my shoes weigh five pounds apiece, but she wasn't buying it.[35]

As soon as the nurse walked out of the exam room, I quickly removed my holstered gun and wrapped it neatly into the light jacket I'd worn to the office for that purpose, setting them both under my chair along with my car keys. In came the doctor, a nice guy I've known casually for several years. I explained that my allergies were acting up again, and he asked if I knew what substances generally triggered my asthma attacks. I said, "Spring, of course—and tobacco smoke, dust and molds, and, um, please don't put this in your notes, but gun

---

35 *I've never weighed my Glock, but I know I weigh more with it than without it!*

smoke seems to be making it worse too." He nodded and finished the exam, then leaned back in his chair and said, "So tell me about your shooting—what kind of guns do you shoot?"

Well. In for a dime, in for a dollar, right? I said, "Handguns, mostly."

He said, "Cowboy action? Self defense stuff? Just plinking?"

Ah, okay. This is gun nut language! No worries, he must be one of us. So I told him that I do a lot of self defense work, and he asked about learning to shoot handguns because he was wanting to get a concealed carry permit of his own. This doctor has known my family for quite awhile, and his kids are much the same ages as mine, so eventually he asked me what I do about gun safety with a gun intended for self defense. I told him I just keep it on my hip all the time and that way they can't get to it.

He said, with some alarm, "ALL the time? In *here*?" This was a visual, ladies—I think we've all seen the male eye-wobble thing, you know, a guy's eyes running up and down your body when he thinks you're not looking, checking out the curves? That doctor did the most obvious eye wobble I have ever seen in my entire life, looking for my gun.

That was a personal experience of a time when I deliberately revealed my carry status and in the end, it turned out well. But it's quite possible to carry on-body into the doctor's office without a soul being the wiser. Of course, carrying the firearm into a medical facility is perfectly legal in my state, but it might be against the law in yours. Look up the law for yourself before proceeding merrily along.

If you carry on-body and don't have a backup concealed carry purse, bring a light jacket with you to the doctor's office. You don't have to wear the jacket if it's warm. You can just drape it over your arm. If it's downright hot, wear a loose button-down shirt over a tank top or tee shirt. You'll use the outer layer once you enter the exam room, even though you won't wear it.

> **Caution!**
>
> Metal of any type does not mix with an MRI scan. If you know you will be going in for such a scan, leave your gun safely locked in your car or leave it at home. The medical lab will probably have a locker designed for your purse and other personal belongings, but such places are generally not secure enough to entrust firearms to them.

Most doctor's visits start when you're called into the office from the waiting room. The nurse weighs you in the hallway, then takes your blood pressure and maybe your temperature after ushering you into the exam room. You can safely wear your gun during this part of the visit, because it's not her job to physically examine you no matter what your complaint is. Minor caveat: if your cover garment is heavy and long-sleeved, the nurse will probably ask you to remove it so she can get your blood pressure accurately. Be prepared for this by having a light or short-sleeved cover garment, or wear an extra cover layer underneath your heavy jacket.

There really isn't a reliably discreet way to remove the gun before the nurse has weighed you and taken your blood pressure, so if you carry on your body, you'll probably have to resign yourself to weighing a couple pounds more on the charts than you do in real life. Then the nurse leaves the room, sometimes giving instructions to undress and sometimes not. In either case, now's the time to remove your holstered gun. Don't take it out of the holster, and don't unload it. Leave the gun in your holster and take your holster off your belt.

Why *Not* Unload?

• Unloading a semi-automatic makes an easily identified noise. If anyone hears it, they're likely to come barging into the room in alarm.

• There probably isn't any safe direction in which to point the gun as you unload it.

• Loading or unloading a firearm carries with it the chance of an unintentional discharge. As long as the gun remains with its trigger covered in a secure holster, and within your conscious control, it's safe.

Now you have two choices: You can place the entire holstered gun into an empty compartment of your purse or bag. This is a great use for your concealed-carry purse, even if you ordinarily carry on body. This option might be the most secure, but unless the purse is designed for concealed carry, beware the temptation to leave the firearm there after you leave the building. A firearm in a non-carry purse is essentially inaccessible, and especially prone to "I forgot it was there!" mistakes.

If you don't have a purse or bag, wrap the holstered handgun in your jacket or cover garment, and place it carefully under the chair and out of the way. Drop your car keys on top so you don't risk leaving the office without it.

The doctor will come in and do his thing. No worries there, just don't give the game away by continually glancing under the chair. Your stuff is safe where it is as long as you are in the room.

Depending on the reason for the visit, you may have to negotiate some tricky bits now. If the doctor says, "Come on down to the other room" for a shot or some other kind of test, you're going to have to pick up that pile of belongings while making sure the gun remains completely hidden within it. Carry it in your arms as you move to the other room.

If doc says, "You can leave your things here," you'll have to pretend not to hear him (my usual ploy), or else launch into a tale about the last time you lost your car keys and how you've absolutely promised your husband, boyfriend, or insurance agent that you'll never ever let the keys out of your sight ever again. The other room will probably have a safe place to plunk your belongings where you can keep an eye on them.

Some doctor's offices have lockers where you're supposed to shove your stuff. Don't be afraid to play-act at being a fussy, persnickety person, or an airhead who is just afraid of losing stuff, in order to keep the pile with you. This takes a certain amount of chutzpah! Remind yourself as often as necessary that you are a competent, adult woman who is not afraid to look a little foolish in order to do what you need to do.

At the end of the visit, the office staff will usually give you a few minutes alone to put yourself back together. If they do not, simply carry your pile of belongings directly into the nearest bathroom and put yourself back together there.

Carrying to Church

It happened again. In the news this week, there's a bleak story about an angry, abusive man who carried a gun into a church and gunned down multiple people. He then kidnapped his children and his estranged wife, fled the scene, and killed his wife before he was taken into custody. The usual news item adds here, "The children were unharmed." Physically, I suppose that's true. Emotionally is a different matter.

As I've said in other places, carrying a gun is simply my default setting. I don't need a special, particular reason to carry in any given place. Yet, if you asked me to justify carrying in church, I would probably start by pointing at this week's headlines. The fact is, bad things can happen *anywhere,* and to *anyone,* no matter what they're doing at the time. But carrying in church presents certain legal, ethical, and practical dilemmas that merit some discussion.

Starting with the legal question: in several states, it is not legal to carry into a house of worship. In other states, there's no problem. Look up the law where you live so you can stay out of trouble. In my state, getting caught carrying in church would be embarrassing. Some church members and some pastors would not like it, so getting caught would be an awkward situation. But that's all it would be, a social faux pas.

The ethics of carrying at church

If you live someplace where it is legal to carry into church, you still must face the ethical question. Lots of people are simply weirded out by the idea of carrying into a place of worship. One friend of mine commented some years ago that she "couldn't ever" carry a gun, especially at church, because that would mean she didn't trust God to take care of her. My perspective on that is simply that wherever I go, whatever I do, I either trust God or I don't. In that sense, the inside of the church building is no different from the inside of the grocery store, my own home, or anywhere else I go.

One of the reasons I am willing to carry a gun in church is because I take the Golden Rule[36] quite seriously. If I were being stalked by an abusive ex-husband, or targeted by an insane former employee, I'd certainly want someone to step in and protect me if I were attacked in a place I'd thought was safe. As a result, I never want to be in a building full of innocent people who are being attacked, and not be able to do anything about it. For me, it would be almost hypocritical to be willing to defend my own life and my own family, and not be willing to do the same for my church family. My conscience wouldn't let me get away with that. (Of course, there are people who feel the exact opposite, and that's okay. What a boring world it would be if everyone thought all alike!)

One final comment on the ethical question. I heard a perceptive question about carrying in church awhile back. The question was simply this: If you're bothered by carrying in church, is it because you're worried that *people* might find out and then what would they think of you? Or are you worried about what *God* would think if you did it?

When I analyzed that question, I realized that my main concerns about carrying in church were not really religious. They were mostly practical and social in nature.

Practical issues

There are several practical issues that surround carrying a concealed firearm into a church building. Remaining concealed is very, very important, both because of the social awkwardness if you get caught, and also because accidentally revealing your carry status could be a distraction or a stumbling block to others in the congregation. Further, as a relative of mine puts it: "The fewer people who know I carry at church, the better. I can just see a gunman attack, and half the congregation turns around and looks at me for help! Someone might even say, 'Bob, get him!' Why not just paint a target on my

---

36   *"Do unto others what you would have them do unto you."*

body instead?"

It can be pretty hard to carry on-body in dress clothes. I'm here to tell you that it is not impossible, but it can be difficult until you get the hang of it. If you ordinarily carry your holster on your belt, you will have to find another way to tote the gun whenever you wear a dress. For my money, the best bet for on-body carry while wearing a dress is a good belly band, though it does require a friendly dress design which allows you to reach the firearm... some-how. Another option for carrying while wearing a dress is to add a boxy blazer to the outfit, and carry in a shoulder holster. I've never done this, but I've seen it done and it works pretty well for some figure types.

If instead of a dress, you choose to wear a skirt and blouse combination, you have a lot more options for on-body carry. It is possible—not easy but possible—to find skirts which have wide belt loops. If you're fortunate enough to come across one of these, you can simply carry on the waist in your usual holster with a sturdy belt. Wear it with an untucked blouse, or tuck your blouse in and add a dressy vest or sweater, or a snazzy jacket, and you're good to go.

If you cannot find a skirt with wide belt loops, all is not lost. You may simply wear a belly band around your waist, positioned so that the gun rides where it normally does while in your belt holster.

Instead of wearing dresses or skirts, you may opt to wear dress slacks. If so, your options for concealment remain nearly as unlimited as they are in more casual clothes.

Probably the most common way people "get made" is by hugging. Some sweet older lady comes up and gives you a squeeze, then gives you an odd look as she pats your waist. Arrrrgh! Now what?

Before that happens, it's worthwhile to learn how to hug without getting caught. A few tips:

☑ When someone comes up to hug you, if you're holding anything, put it in your gun-side hand. That way if your hugger does feel an unusual lump, they'll chalk it up to bumping into whatever you were carrying. Get in the habit of carrying your Bible or hymnal in your gun-side hand whenever there's a chance someone may come up for a hug.

☑ As the hugger reaches towards you, drop your gun-side hand to around her waist, and put your other hand on or around her shoulder. She will usually mirror your actions, which forces her to put her hand on your gun-side shoulder instead of near your waist.

☑ If necessary, turn your gun side slightly away from your hugger, so that the hug is more of a side-to-side action than a face-to-face one.

Final comment: although I'm not really keen on the idea of purse carry as an everyday thing, a good carry purse can be a godsend when you have to wear dress clothes. Just be certain that you never set the purse down casually, or leave it within reach of anyone else.

While Shopping

Once you accept the basic idea of carrying in public, there's really no great moral or ethical dilemma about carrying a gun while shopping. There are, however, some practical considerations worth thinking about.

The Legal Issues

Let's get the legal question out of the way first. When you receive your concealed-carry permit, the state will generally give you a list of places where carrying a gun is not legally allowed. This list of prohibited places varies a lot from one state to another. Many states (but not all) prohibit carry in bars and on school property. Some prohibit carrying at "public gatherings," but the definition of "public gathering" will change depending upon the exact wording of the law. Most prohibit carrying in and around courthouses and other government buildings. People are often surprised to find out what their state does or does not allow. And the laws about carrying into businesses open to the public are often not quite as clear as they are about carrying in other places. In some states, a "No Firearms Allowed" sign has no force unless the property owner stops you, realizes you are carrying, and asks you to leave, and you refuse. In other states, merely walking past a "No Firearms Allowed," sign is itself a legal violation. In these states, ignoring that sign is against the law. In a few states, if a business owner wants to post his property to prohibit concealed weapons, he must use a sign which has the exact wording dictated by the state. Sometimes the state even dictates the dimensions and placement of such signs. Other states have other rules, sometimes surprising ones. It isn't safe to assume that you can just carry wherever you wish, or that simply following "common sense" will keep you out of trouble. If you want to stay on the right side of the law, you must first find out what the law actually says.

Come to think of it, I guess there is at least one moral issue here after all.

A Giggle

In Texas, the legislation about guns carried onto others' property is found in the statute numbered 30-06. *No Firearms* signs are thus referred to as *30-06 signs!*

If you live in a state where "No Firearms" signs do not have the force of law, do you obey the signs or not? Personally, I obey such signs. I figure that if a business owner doesn't want my money, there's no reason for me to give it to him. But I don't get wrapped around the axle about it, and I don't stand there squinting at all the teeny-tiny fine print plastered to the window to figure out if I'm welcome or not. If they don't make the rules obvious at a glance, I probably won't worry about it.

The Practical Issues

I'm not going to bother talking about grocery shopping or shopping for shoes. You can figure out on your own that these types of shopping probably do not present any special concerns.[37] Shopping for clothes is another matter. If you're buying clothes for concealed carry, you really need to try them on while you are wearing the gun. How can you do that discreetly? How can you keep your firearm concealed in a fitting room, or keep it safe while trying on different clothes?

There's No Place Like Home...

Let's discuss the coward's way out first: you can use your own home as your dressing room. This sounds a bit odd, but actually has a lot to recommend it. At least one older lady of my acquaintance has shopped this way for many years. She explains, "With my bad knee, it just hurts too much to try on clothes at the store. At home, I have a comfortable place to sit down while trying things on. And I can take my own time without feeling rushed."

To do this, you pick out clothes in your usual size, purchase them, and take them home. Try them on at home. If they don't fit, or don't conceal the gun easily, simply return them to the store with the tags still intact.

When you try clothes on at home, you can easily find out if the clothes will work with the rest of your wardrobe, or if the garment will work with different guns or carry methods. You also have a lot more freedom to be a contortionist in front of the mirror, checking to see if the gun prints or shows in any other way. And you aren't ever faced with the awkward question of what to do with your firearm while you are half-clothed.

Obviously, this plan only works if you shop somewhere with a good return policy. And it only works if you know what your usual size is. And it only works if you live close enough to the store that going back to return stuff that

---

37 *Well, except for the question of reaching your toes without printing while trying on shoes. Take your chiropractor's advice, and keep your back straight. Oh, and keep your gun side towards a wall rather than towards the rest of the store.*

doesn't work isn't a huge hassle. But if none of these things are an issue for you, it might be the best choice—especially when you are just getting started with concealed carry, and are still in the jumpy phase.[38]

Fitting Room Basics

But let's say you're out and around, and come across a really cute outfit that just *has to* be tried on, *right now*. And you're carrying a gun on your belt. Can this really be done? Of course it can!

First word of advice: don't worry too much. You are carrying within the law. You aren't doing anything illegal or "bad." Be confident.

If possible, snag the handicapped dressing room stall. If someone in a wheelchair comes along, you can surrender it. There's almost always a bench to put your stuff on so you won't have to put it on the floor or balance your trousers and holster precariously hanging from a hook. The other plus is that handicapped stalls are usually a little bigger, so you can get at least some distance from the mirror without leaving the stall. Being able to check the mirror without leaving the stall is important because you don't really want anyone to see your firearm as you move and twist in front of the mirror to make sure the gun is well concealed.

If you cannot get into a handicapped stall for some reason, grab the one at the very end of the hallway. Fewer people will walk past your stall if it is at the end of the row, which means less chance of getting caught by a casual glance. It also means that your belongings will be more secure if you have to step out of the stall to look in the mirror.

Avoid any stall next to a mom shopping with her 3-year-old. Little kids have this amazing ability to see through walls (well, under them, anyway) and are entirely too likely to comment—loudly—about what they see. So avoid the kids if you can.

You should never take your gun out of its holster in public unless you're defending yourself. If you need to try on pants, leave the gun in your holster. Pull the holstered gun off your belt, set it on the bench, take your pants and belt off, pull on the new pants, then pick up your belt and the holstered gun and check how they fit with the new pants. Whenever I set down the holstered gun, I like to drop a piece of clothing on top of it just to reduce the risk of someone spotting it.

---

38 Incidentally, the jumpy phase does wear off, eventually. You will always be aware of the chunk of metal on your hip, but the classic "Ohmigosh everyone's looking at me!" feeling common to new permit holders does fade into the background after you've done this for awhile.

If there is no bench, I usually grab an extra piece of clothing from the rack, something I'm not going to try on. Then instead of hanging up my old jeans, I plump them on the floor with the holstered firearm inside, and toss the spare clothing on top of the pile so that no casual glance under the door can give me away. After I pull on the new clothes, I fish the gun out of the pile to make sure it will work with the new outfit.

Alternate plan: carry a tote bag. Place your holstered gun into the tote bag while you are changing.

Now for the very obvious note about security. Do not leave your firearm unattended in a dressing room, even for a split second, no matter how well you've got it smothered underneath other stuff or jammed in the bottom of your bag. The risk simply isn't worth it.

Mirror, Mirror, On the Wall...

So you've just tried on a new outfit, and it's comfortable and attractive enough that you're thinking of buying it. Now you need to check to see if it will work for concealed carry.

Pants: Check to make sure your carry belt will fit through the belt loops. If it does, and you carry inside the waistband, pick up your holstered gun and make sure there's enough room inside the waistband for both of you. With the holstered gun in place, bend over and tie your shoes. Do a couple of deep knee bends. Sit down and stand back up again. Still sure there's enough room in that waistband?

Blouses and cover garments: Place the holstered gun on your belt and adjust the garment however you intend to wear it. Stand squarely in front of the mirror. Check to make sure the gun's shadow cannot be seen through the fabric. Does the garment fit loosely enough over the gun area that you'll be able to move naturally? Are there any odd-looking lumps or bumps?

Now reach toward the ceiling like you're stretching. Does the garment ride up in a natural manner? Does the gun stay covered? Relax your arms and let them dangle at your sides. Did the garment come back down naturally, without needing to be tugged into position? Do the twist, swinging your arms from side to side. Does the garment need to be fiddled with in order to keep the gun concealed? Or does it move with you naturally? Move around a little—stretch again, scratch your back, then bend down to touch your toes. As you straighten back up, watch the mirror for any telltale signs.

The Embarrassing Questions Department

It has been said that there are no embarrassing questions... only embarrassing answers. That may be true. But if that's the case, why do we always blush when we ask the questions?

Warning: This chapter may be difficult reading for the faint of heart. Be sure to eat some chocolate before you begin. It won't make you any less embarrassed, but don't we all need a little more chocolate in our lives?

Portapotty Protocol

If you shoot very often at an outdoor range, chances are that at one time or another, you will have to deal with a portapotty while you have a gun holstered on your hip. This is risky business. Take it from someone who knows.

What's the risk, you ask? Well... a friend of mine once entered a portapotty during an IPSC match. She was carrying a Glock in a Kydex holster which had a very open front to allow faster speed draws. The Glock was unloaded, per IPSC rules. She closed the door to the portapotty, began unfastening her belt... and the firearm jumped right out of her holster and landed, KER-PLUNK, in the slime. Ewwwwww!!

Even for those of us who rarely carry in open front holsters, range portapotties pose an annoying risk of dropping magazines, speedloaders, pocket knives, flashlights, and anything else you might fasten on or near your belt while hanging out at the range. The more crud you somehow end up carrying, the more likely it becomes that whatever you're carrying can end up in the crud. To avoid that kind of nastiness, here's the portapotty protocol:

1. Close toilet lid.
2. Lower your trousers.
3. Open lid, sit down, do whatcha gotta do.
4. Stand up and close lid.
5. Then pull your trousers back up.

If the portapotty is so primitive that it does not even have a lid for the seat, you can instead turn to face it while lowering your trousers. This reduces the risk of dropping things off your belt in the first place, and improves your chances of a last-gasp save if something other than the gun does jump off your belt. Never grab for a falling gun, though—that can be dangerous.

Public Restroom Procedures

If portapotties pose problems, public restrooms do, too. There's still the risk of dropping your gun into the toilet. But there's also the added risk of getting discovered carrying while you're at it. What's a woman to do?

First and most important thing to remember: you are not breaking the law. Engrave that firmly on your conscience so that you don't make a silly of yourself. People tend to notice, in a vague sort of way, when other people are putting out emotional vibes. The stronger the vibes, the more they notice. If you're new to carrying and are not quite sure how you're going to manage this discreetly, remind yourself that you're on the sunny side of the law and have nothing to fear. Don't put off those vibes if you can help it.

Some basic tips:

- ☑ Never, ever, ever, ever take the stall next to a small child. Little kids are too likely to look under the stall and then comment (loudly) about what they see.

- ☑ Don't hang the gun on a hook or set it on a TP rack. You're too likely to walk off without it. (And don't say that can't happen to you. It can.)

- ☑ If the gun is on your right hip, try to take the stall with a solid wall on the right side while you're sitting down. If the gun is on your left hip, take the leftmost stall. End stalls have the lowest likelihood of someone peering through the crack in the door, and with a wall on your gun side you've also got a lower chance of someone spotting it from underneath the stall.

- ☑ Keep the gun in the holster if possible. That's where it belongs and that's where it's safe.

- ☑ Put your hand on the holstered gun while pulling your pants down. Don't let it flop around. Wrap your hand around the grip, the holster loop, and your belt, holding the whole thing together securely.

- ☑ Try rebuckling your belt around your knees before you sit down. This keeps the holstered gun safely above the lowest edge of the stall door. If you appendix carry, you may instead simply keep one hand on the holstered gun and hold it up while you do your business.

- ☑ Before exiting the stall, put yourself back together as well as possible. Try to avoid exiting the stall while there are other people in the common area of the restroom. As soon as you can, check your entire outfit in the mirror to be sure you have no odd lumps or other concealment challenges going on. That's always a bit easier to do if no one is around to watch you correct the problem. If you do have a problem and others are around, you can always step back into the stall to fix it.

☑ If you absolutely positively cannot figure out how to use the toilet with the gun remaining on your belt, you can instead remove the holstered gun from your belt and put it in your purse. As a rule, removing the gun from your belt is a last resort: the less gun-handling you do in public, the less opportunity there is for an unfortunate mistake.

Watch Out for Curves

Women who are not well-endowed probably won't understand this one, but... well, here's the thing. Some of us have this minor little difficulty when we draw or reholster. Sometimes, a well-endowed woman finds that certain upper-body parts might get in the way as she works with the holster, either drawing or reholstering. During the reholster, what happens is that a new shooter generally needs to see the mouth of the holster in order to reholster the gun safely. But some folks' upper body build makes it impossible to see the holster without first reaching over to pull our bosom out of the way. And some women find that the motion of the drawstroke may be obstructed if they don't hold the bosom out of the way with the other hand during the draw.

Sorry about this one. There's nothing for it but to go ahead and do that maneuver when you have to—even at the range when there are strange men around (and remember, all men are strange).[39]

As a general rule, if you do this one matter-of-factly, nobody is really going to notice. You'll only draw curious eyes if you have the vapors about it and put off those noticeable emotional vibes, or if you are awkwardly trying to figure out what to do about the problem without looking matter-of-fact. For this reason, I recommend that you begin working with your holster at home, with an unloaded gun and a safe backstop (within the protective confines of a good dryfire ritual, of course). At home, you can figure out how your body needs to move in order to complete the draw, without self-consciousness or embarrassment.

If the problem is mild, you may find that you can manage the drawstroke without encountering any difficulty, but that you'll need to do the bosom maneuver if you want to look the gun into your holster as you put it away. Don't get too hung up about this. After you look the gun into the holster enough times, eventually finding the mouth of the holster will become second nature

---

39 *So are all women. The only normal people are the ones you don't know very well.*

and you won't have to look very often unless something goes awry. This means that a lot of practice at home will prevent you from needing to move your bosom out of the way on the range very often.

While you are reholstering, whether on the range or off it, avoid having to look the gun into the holster as much as you can, but if you do have to look for some reason, make the safe choice and go right ahead. Don't give off those embarrassed vibes if you can help it—just matter-of-factly do what you need to do.

There is one time when it will always be necessary to look, and that is when there is some unexpected difficulty getting the gun into the holster. If you think you've got the right spot, but something "feels wrong" or the gun seems to be hanging up on something, STOP. Do not keep pushing the gun into the holster because it could be dangerous. Instead, bring the gun back up out of the holster and to the midline of your body, with the muzzle pointed downrange. Then look down at the holster. Make sure the holster mouth is clear of obstructions before you try again.

To help avoid getting those obstructions into the way in the first place, after each time you put the gun into the holster, you should carefully sweep the flat of your hand along your side next to the holster. Then tuck in any loose material your hand encounters. This makes sure that your shirt won't get tucked into your holster along with the gun when you go to reholster it.

So work with the unloaded pistol at home as much as you can, until you are able to draw and reholster safely without looking. Sweep and tuck after each time you reholster. And if you find yourself on the range one day with a choice between poking the muzzle of a loaded gun around your midsection blindly probing for the holster mouth, or just flopping the ladies out of the way so you can see where the muzzle needs to go... make the safe choice.

The Flasher

This one's really fun. You've signed up to take a basic handgun class designed for concealed carry. Among the topics taught in the class is how to safely draw and reholster your firearm while wearing a cover garment. So what should you wear to the range?

That's entirely up to you, of course. But if it were me, no matter what else I wore, I'd be sure to wear a nice long undershirt that tucked in very securely. Because when it is time to learn how to draw from concealment, several of the basic techniques involve grabbing a handful of cover garment fabric and yanking that garment up and out of the way, clear into the armpit if possible.

You can do the math yourself!

Dancing the Cha-Cha

Speaking of clothes to wear to the range, I hope we've all figured out by now that shooting semi-automatic firearms puts hot brass into the air around us. Actually, that's not quite true. Shooting semi-autos puts hot brass everywhere, not just into the air. Somewhere around here I've got a picture of a friend of mine with a piece of brass perched jauntily atop her ear muffs. How cute!

Not quite so cute when that same friendly piece of brass decides to snuggle up next to your skin, though. Many women have learned, to their painful shock, that hot brass is strongly attracted to women's brassieres—just as it's also attracted to male plumber's crack and to the cleft between bare toes in sandals.

Some tips:

☑ As much as is practicable, wear high-neck shirts to the range. Similarly, wear closed-toe shoes and encourage men of your acquaintance to fight crack by pulling their pants up. If you wear a button down shirt to the range, button the top button until you're done shooting.

☑ If a piece of hot brass goes down your shirt anyway, keep the muzzle of your firearm pointed downrange. Calmly set the gun down on the bench.

☑ With the firearm safely secured, then and only then may you perform the ritual Dance of Burning Flesh, sometimes called the Bra-Zillian Line Dance or the Cha-Cha. Traditionally, this informal dance is performed solely for the benefit of the dancer, not for the enjoyment of the spectators. Despite this, less-informed audiences may react with audible appreciation for the performance. It is generally considered poor form to applaud, but a quiet chuckle or even shrill whistles of approval do occur in some venues.

☑ Usually, the quickest and most efficient manner of removing the brass without actually removing your shirt is to take both hands and swiftly untuck the shirt, pulling it out and away from your body as you do so. Alternatively, untuck with one hand while grabbing the fistful of fabric centered over the brass with the other. Once the brass has been caught and isolated with the shirt untucked, open your clenched hand. With luck, the brass will drop to the ground. Without luck, it will drop straight down into your pants. Sigh.

☑ Tea tree oil works great for burns.

Oops! And Other Sticky Situations

I'll never forget the day mother made me.[40] It was shortly after I'd begun carrying a handgun for personal defense, before I'd figured out the art of giving someone a hug without giving away the secret. She and my father had offered to take my children to a movie, so the kids and I piled into our van and drove to meet them at the theater. As always, my Glock 26 rode inside my waistband in its secure holster. When I got out of the van, my mother came over to give me a hug. As she put her hand around my waist, I felt her stiffen up and pat my hip. Then she pulled away and looked at me accusingly. "What is that?"

I was caught.

As I found out, if you carry a concealed weapon very often, the odds are that sooner or later, someone you care about will discover it. The question is what to do next. How can you handle the situation with a minimum of fuss and reassure your family and friends?

Step #1: Don't lose your cool.

Sure, you're probably a little upset. After all, you didn't want to get made and even if you were planning to tell them at some point, the timing is probably less than ideal. But you don't want to give them the impression that you—a person equipped with a loaded weapon—are prone to panic.

Staying calm has other advantages, too. Getting made is really just a minor social gaffe. But a too-vigorous reaction might give your friends the idea that you're on the run from Johnny Law. This is another impression you do not want to make.

If you are in a public setting, and your reaction is very energetic, it will be noticed by everyone around you. Human beings are drawn to emotional displays. If you play it cool, you may be able to avoid at least a few prying eyes.

So take a deep breath and smile, even if you don't feel like it.

---

40 To be "made" means to have someone else inadvertently or unexpectedly find out that you are carrying a firearm.

Step #2: Say something.

Don't just stand there with your mouth flapping open and shut like a recently landed large-mouth bass. Few things make people more nervous than that. So after you smile, clear your throat and force a sound past those chilly vocal cords.

Of course, some things are better to say than others.

An example of a bad thing to say: "Ha! HA! I was planning to use that to kill everyone in the place later! What a laugh!" If all you can think of is a feeble joke about mass murder, you're probably better off to keep doing your fish imitation.

Better: "Ummmmm, oops." You may kick yourself later for your lack of eloquence, but at least you didn't make the situation worse.

Best: "It's okay, Mom, you know I'm one of the good guys." Or after your firearm jumps out of the holster and skitters across the floor, "Dang, I've been trying to teach it not to do that." Or (for the guys reading this), "Yes, but I'm also happy to see you."

A light-hearted comment often sends the meta-message that you aren't worried and that the other person shouldn't be, either. A Michigan resident named Tim was once told by a local policeman that his gun was printing. Tim smiled, readjusted his clothing, and responded, "Really? I guess now I can start it on cursive." Tim reports that the officer smiled back and replied, "Good answer."

Whatever your initial response, follow up with a calm but heartfelt apology for frightening them. After all, even though you have no intention of harming anyone, and even though you will continue to carry when and where appropriate, it's always good manners to express regret when your actions cause others to feel socially or emotionally uncomfortable.

Step #3: Answer questions without getting defensive.

This is the tricky part. You want to communicate that you are a responsible person, that you haven't lost your marbles, and that no one needs to call the police to deal with you. Depending on your relationship with the person who made you, one or all of those things might be a hard sell.

With relatives, their first concern is often whether or not you are obeying the law. "My grandmother was a bit concerned one time after she hugged my younger brother and found he was carrying concealed," says a young man who now lives in Texas. "She thought it was still illegal to carry concealed in Arizona. She didn't seem especially concerned that he was carrying, just that he do it legally."

Familiarity with your local laws stands you in good stead here. It's probably a good idea to refresh your memory about your state's carry laws from time to time, just so you will be able to deal confidently with such questions.

Some folks can be expected to react with disgust or anger. Be prepared for this, but do your best not to provoke it. If the other person is content to chew you out and then drop the issue, let them. You earned the tongue-lashing by getting caught, and your mild reaction just proves that you aren't looking for a fight no matter what tools you have on your belt.

Be prepared to deal with questions about your emotional health. "You sure do have a lot of fears," one of my relatives once told me. "Maybe you should talk to a doctor." After an accusation like this, the ideal impression to leave is that you listened seriously to their concerns, but that their concerns weren't serious. You can accomplish this by listening respectfully, while keeping your own responses light and brief.

Legal Questions

Dear Gunhilda,

I think anyone who carries a gun must be scared silly.

~ Scornful in Scappoose

Dear Scornful,

I'm not scared, silly. What do I have to be afraid of? I'm the one with the gun!

~ Gunhilda

Legal Basics: Buying a Firearm

There's absolutely no way I can tell you exactly what is legal in your jurisdiction, and what is not. There are roughly a gajillion federal gun laws in America, with another sixty kazillion state, county, and municipal laws beneath those.[41] Every time Congress meets, every time your state legislature is called to session, every time some bureaucratic committee needs to interpret and refine existing regulation, and every time an appeals court issues a new finding, the rules change. Books have a fairly long shelf life and anything I say in print about any but the most general principles is almost bound to last longer than the law does. So instead of discussing details, I intend to give you a very general overview of how to buy a gun, and then point you to places where you can find the specific information you need.

About the ATF

First, let's look at the federal agency that regulates firearm sales and purchases in the United States: the Bureau of Alcohol, Tobacco, Firearms, and Explosives (ATF). This federal bureau has a long history. Originally created in 1886 underneath a financial department that later became the IRS, bureaucratic predecessors of the ATF were responsible for enforcing Prohibition law in the 1930s. These were the famous "revenooers" of moonshine lore.

For most of the past century, the ATF was a separate department under the authority of the US Department of the Treasury. Two years after the terrorist attacks of September 11, 2001, the ATF was transferred to the newly-created Department of Homeland Security. At the same time, the old Bureau of Alcohol, Tobacco, and Firearms (ATF) became the new Bureau of Alcohol, Tobacco, Firearms, and Explosives (BATFE). Shortly after that, the abbreviation reverted to the familiar "ATF," but the agency retained the full name, "Bureau

---

41 *According to Under the Gun: Weapons, Crime, and Violence in America, using a Bureau of Alcohol, Tobacco and Firearms estimate and reported via James Wright, Peter H. Rossi, and Kathleen Daly in 1983, there are over 20,000 gun laws in the United States, including laws and regulations unique to individual states, counties, parishes, cities, towns and states.*

of Alcohol, Tobacco, Firearms, and Explosives." Under the Department of Homeland Security, the ATF received expanded powers and responsibilities, but its responsibility to oversee tax collection on alcohol and tobacco products remained with another department within the US Treasury.

If you have a question about federal firearms laws, and cannot find the information anywhere else, you can query the ATF. Before sending a letter, be sure to read the ATF's FAQ page, which is available online.[42] Remember that the ATF regulates only *federal* firearms law; your state or local laws may prohibit activities which are legal under federal law.

FFLs (Gun Stores)

Under federal law, new firearms may be sold only by businesses that possess a Federal Firearms License (FFL). These businesses are referred to in bureaucratic style as FFL dealers. The rest of us call them "gun stores." Used firearms may also be bought and sold by FFL dealers, if they wish. Not all FFL dealers sell used guns, but many do.

Although licensed by the federal government, FFL dealers also work under many local laws and regulations. They must possess business licenses, fit within zoning requirements (sometimes very onerous ones), and may only offer guns for sale which are legal within the state, county, and city where they operate. Additionally, they must observe any federal, state, and local laws, regulations, and rules which may apply to the purchase. If a waiting period applies to your purchase, it is the FFL dealer's responsibility to inform you of its duration and to enforce it.

Your FFL dealer will ask to see legal proof of your identity whenever you purchase a firearm. FFL dealers may also ask to see other personal information, at their discretion, and they are required by law to reject any sales that seem suspicious to them.

In some states, in addition to basic identification such as a driver's license, FFL dealers are required to ask the buyer to show either state- or locally-issued proof that the buyer may purchase a firearm. This may be a long-term, renewable license similar to a driver's license (such as the FOID card in Illinois) or it may be a limited-time permit good for a single purchase (such as the Minnesota Uniform Firearm Permit to Purchase). Some states, such as Massachusetts and New Jersey, even require a long-term specialized ID card *plus* a one-time permit to purchase. If your state requires purchase permits, your local FFL dealer will be able to tell you how to obtain the permission

---

42 *www.atf.gov.*

you need.

Some local jurisdictions require buyers to purchase firearm locks, show proof that they own a gun safe, or pass a test before they can buy a gun. If you are in doubt about any of these local requirements, your FFL dealer should be able to give you more information, or at least tell you where to find more information, about your local laws. If your dealer appears unable or unwilling to do this, walk away from the sale.

When you buy a gun from an FFL dealer, the dealer has a very specific set of rules and regulations he must follow. The federal paperwork requirements are very stringent and allow the dealer very little discretion. You will need to show photo ID and fill out a Form 4473. The dealer must keep this form on file at the business for a minimum of 20 years, and show it to the ATF upon request. If the FFL later goes out of business, the ATF will take possession of all the 4473 Forms on the premises.

If you are purchasing a handgun, the FFL will call in your personal information to a federal clearinghouse called the National Instant Criminal Background Check System (NICS). After giving information about the purchase to the NICS, the dealer will receive one of three possible answers from NICS: an approval, a delay, or a deny. If the sale is approved, the FFL dealer receives an authorization code which he will note on your paperwork. Delays happen for a variety of reasons which may not be immediately obvious to the buyer. Delays do not always result in a denial, so if your purchase is delayed, don't despair. The dealer will tell you when you can come back to finish processing your paperwork. A denial means something has gone badly wrong somewhere. If your sale is denied, you will want to find out the reason for it and you may appeal the denial if you believe it is not justified.

Many states require waiting periods when purchasing a handgun. If this is the case, your FFL dealer will expect you to complete all paperwork before the waiting period begins. When the waiting period is over, you will then go back to the dealer to pick up your new firearm.

Buying a gun for yourself from an FFL dealer sounds very complicated on paper, and the dealer does work under very strict and complex rules. But from the buyer's end, it is not so complicated. You walk in, select the gun you wish to purchase, and then let the dealer guide you through the paperwork and legal requirements.

Private Party Sales

While *new* firearms may only be purchased through an FFL dealer, private sales of *used* firearms are legal in some but not all states. This means that in some states, an ordinary citizen may lawfully sell a used gun to another ordinary citizen who lives within the same state.

There are many federal, state, and local regulations that apply to private party sales. Whether you are the buyer or the seller, it will be your responsibility to find out which laws apply to your sale, and to comply with those laws. Because firearms laws are complicated and punishments for breaking them are very extreme in most jurisdictions, I recommend that your first firearm purchase should be made through an FFL dealer. This is especially true if you are buying a handgun, because handguns especially are often subject to additional laws at the local level. There is no leeway in the law for mistakes made in ignorance.

Gun Shows (and that famous "loophole")

Many guns shows feature two types of sales. Most common are sales run from tables set up by an FFL dealer. These are manned by folks from the local gun store who packed up their wares and brought them down to the gun show for buyers to see. FFL dealers at gun shows must comply with every single one of the same federal, state, and local laws which apply when they operate out of their regular places of business. This includes background checks, waiting periods, and whatever extra purchases or taxes are required by your local politicians. In some states, there will even be extra requirements at the gun show that are not present when the same FFL dealer makes a sale anywhere else.

If private sales are legal in your state, and *if* the gun show's management allows, there may also be private sellers at the gun show. A private sale is not a commercial business; it is an ordinary citizen personally selling a used firearm to another ordinary citizen. There will be no private sellers at your local gun show unless your state law allows private sales in other places. Additionally, some states have passed laws forbidding private sales at gun shows while allowing them in other places. Private sellers at gun shows must comply with every single federal, state, and local law which applies to all other private sales within the same jurisdiction.

The famous "gun show loophole" so beloved of anti-firearms activists and lazy newspaper reporters is an attempt to confuse the public into believing that the already incredibly complicated laws about firearms purchases somehow do not apply to firearms which are sold in the convenient setting of a gun show. This is most emphatically not true!

If you decide to purchase a firearm from a gun show, *you must still obey every firearms purchasing law which would apply if you bought the firearm anywhere else within the same state and jurisdiction.* City, county, state, and federal firearms laws apply on the grounds of a gun show just as they do any-where else. And there may even be additional restrictions simply because you bought the gun at a gun show.

Online or Interstate Gun Sales

In most states, you may legally purchase a gun from someone who lives in a different state. But such sales *must* go through an FFL dealer. You must remember that firearm designs which are legal in a neighboring state may not be legal in your home state. Do your research before making any promises to the seller, and especially before sending any money!

To purchase a firearm from an out-of-state source, you *must* use an FFL dealer. It is not legal to purchase an out-of-state firearm without completing the FFL paperwork. It is *not* legal to ship any firearm, whether handgun or long gun, directly to a private individual in another state.[43]

You may purchase a long gun through the internet or through the mail, and then have it shipped to an FFL dealer in your home state to complete the purchase. You may also travel to a neighboring state and purchase a long gun in person from an FFL dealer there, then transport it back to your home state after you have completed the paperwork with the dealer. In other words, whether you buy in person or via the internet, if your long gun is purchased from someone who lives outside your home state, you will need to complete FFL paperwork in order to take the firearm across state lines. But sometimes you can take the gun across the state line yourself.

Federal law does not allow you to purchase a handgun in person out of state. If you wish to purchase an out-of-state handgun, you *must* have the handgun shipped to an FFL dealer in your home state to complete the purchase. You will not be able to bring the handgun across the state line yourself even if you negotiated the purchase face to face.

The way an interstate sale (such as an online purchase) usually works is that the buyer and the seller agree on terms. Then both must find an FFL dealer in their own home states. The seller's FFL dealer makes certain the sale is legal at the selling end, and then ships the firearm to the buyer's FFL dealer. Occasionally, *if* doing so is legal in both the buyer's and the seller's state, the seller may be able to ship directly to the buyer's FFL dealer and avoid using an FFL at the selling end. But an FFL is *always* required at the receiving end.

---

43 *Except for Curios & Relics—a legal term for antique firearms and rare collector's items. The rules for C&R firearms are complex, arcane, and different in nearly every particular.*

The buyer's FFL dealer makes certain the sale is legal on the buying end. The buyer must comply with all the other legal requirements of buying a gun from an FFL dealer: 4473 Form, NICS check, state-issued permission slips, additional required purchases or taxes, and any other local requirements that would apply if she were simply purchasing the firearm directly from that FFL dealer.

FFL dealers typically charge anywhere from $20 to $50 for this service, in addition to taxes and permit fees. When looking for a deal online, remember to consider the additional costs of shipping and transfer fees.

Buying a Gun for Someone Else

The rules about purchasing firearms for other people are very strict and very confusing. If you just assume the purchase is illegal unless you have specific information proving otherwise, you won't be too far from wrong.

The most important rule to remember: **It is *not* legal to purchase a firearm for someone who is prohibited by law from purchasing a firearm.** Purchasing a firearm on behalf of someone who cannot legally buy the firearm for themselves is called a "straw purchase," and the legal penalties can be very severe. If someone gives you money to buy the gun so that your name will be on the FFL paperwork instead of theirs, you are flirting with straw purchase territory. Don't risk it.[44]

Very generally speaking, it is legal to purchase gift firearms for people in your immediate family who live with you. Standard disclaimers apply, especially the bits about "varies from state to state" and "know your own local laws." Remember, handguns are often subject to additional regulations above and beyond those that affect rifles or shotguns. If you live in a state where a handgun purchase permit is required you may need to transfer title officially through the local cop shop, but most states do not require this.

The laws regarding children and firearms ownership are even more complex than the ones governing a basic gift purchase. If you want your youngster to own a gun, you're pretty much on solid ground if you purchase the firearm and retain possession yourself until the child reaches legal maturity. Whether the child can directly own or possess the firearm without your immediate presence is a much more local question. Some states permit children of any age who have parental permission to hold and shoot firearms under the supervision of any competent adult, while others require direct parental

---

44 *On a closely related note: if your new boyfriend wants you to buy a firearm for him, look him in the eye and ask him why he does not purchase it himself. The answer might be benign, but don't take anything on faith. It's not worth risking jail over.*

supervision. Still others set age limits for specific activities, with or without parental supervision.

In most states, young adults may purchase rifles and shotguns for themselves when they reach 18 years old, or handguns after age 21. Some states permit 18- to 21-year-olds to own and possess handguns, but federal law bans these young adults from directly purchasing their own handguns or from purchasing any firearm through an FFL dealer.

In most states, you may purchase a firearm for yourself, with your own money, and then later sell it to someone else either directly or through an FFL dealer. For safety's sake, unless you really know the ins and outs of the law, and are also prepared to vouch for the character of the person who wants to buy your gun, your best bet is to sell it on consignment through a licensed FFL dealer.

Where to Find More Information

If you want to know more about state firearms laws, you may contact your state Attorney General's office. Some states, especially the ones which have very restrictive laws, will also have at least one agency, and sometimes multiple agencies, responsible for writing and enforcing regulations about firearms. It is worthwhile to discover what these departments or agencies are in your state.

Legal Basics: Carry Permits

Like the laws about gun sales, the laws about carry permits vary significantly from one place to the next. Again, there's no way to give detailed specifics in a book like this. The best I can do is to give you a general overview of the concepts, along with some resources for further research.

What's a Carry Permit?

At the time of this writing, except in Alaska, Vermont, and Arizona, if you want to carry a concealed handgun, you will need a carry permit issued by your state, or by another state whose permits your state recognizes. Some states allow people to keep loaded guns in their cars without a carry permit. But as a rule, if you want to carry a handgun with you once you leave your own property, you'll need a carry permit.

Carry permits have different names in different states. In Washington state, it's a Concealed Pistol License (CPL). In Colorado, it's a permit to Carry a Concealed Weapon (CCW). In Pennsylvania, it's a License to Carry (LTC). In Texas, it is a Concealed Handgun License (CHL). "Carry permit" works as a catch-all phrase to encompass all these phrases.[45]

Not all states issue carry permits, although most do. At the time of this writing in spring 2010, 48 states make provisions for citizens to carry concealed firearms (Illinois and Wisconsin being the two holdouts). Three states (Alaska, Vermont, and Arizona) allow concealed carry without a permit. Thirty-eight states boast "shall issue" carry laws, requiring the authorities to issue permits to citizens who meet specific legal requirements. Eight cling to "may issue" laws, placing the question of whether to issue the permit at the whim of an individual bureaucrat rather than by the applicant meeting specific requirements in state law.[46]

---

45 *The usual online acronym for a carry permit is "CCW," which seems to be becoming the standard in casual use everywhere except official documents.*
46 *These numbers change rapidly. Because several states are working on changing their carry permit regulations, the numbers may be out of date even before this book sees print. The point is that concealed carry is legal nearly everywhere in the United States,*

Some states require citizens purchase a permit to own a firearm. This isn't always the same thing as a carry permit, though permission to carry might be included on the same license. In most states, ownership permits are not required.

How Do I Get A Carry Permit?

Requirements vary. Some states have simple rules, requiring the citizen pay a fee and perhaps submit fingerprints. Other states' requirements can be more complex. Typically, the state will require a training class, a background check, fingerprints, and multiple fees which go to different agencies within the state and also to the FBI for their background check.

All states require that the applicant be eligible to own firearms under federal law. Neither felons, nor involuntarily committed mentally ill, nor domestic batterers are allowed to own weapons at all, let alone carry them.

How Much Does A Carry Permit Cost?

This, too, varies. The least expensive states are Alaska, Arizona, and Vermont, where no permit is required.[47] As of spring 2010, among "shall issue" states, the least expensive permit is in New Hampshire, at $10. The most expensive may be in Colorado, which costs $152 and also requires a separately-purchased class. Among the "may issue" states, carry permits can become very expensive indeed. Issuance in these states sometimes requires sizeable donations to someone's campaign fund.[48]

In addition to the raw cost of the permit, expect to pay administrative fees. If your state requires you to submit fingerprints for a background check, expect to pay a fee to the government office which takes your prints, and another fee to the FBI for processing the prints and making sure your background is clean.

If your state requires a class, the cost of the class will depend upon how many hours of instruction the state requires, and will also depend upon the financial situation of the instructor you choose.

What is a Training Class Like?

Not all states require training classes. Of those that require training classes,

---

but sharply restricted in some places and illegal in others.
47 Both Arizona and Alaska issue voluntary permits, unnecessary in-state but often honored in other states. Arizona's carry law restricts residents without a carry permit from carrying in a few circumstances where carry is allowed for those with a voluntary permit.
48 "Gun Laws Breed Corruption," by Dr. Michael S. Brown, www.gunblast.com. "Contra Costa County Gun Permit Corruption," by Jim March, www. keepandbeararms.com.

the specific classes may be quite different. Typical are 4-, 8-, or 12-hour classes, with 4-hour classes being perhaps the most common. Some states have a very rigid curriculum laid out by law, and in these states there is little difference from one class to another. But in other states, there is no set curriculum and the content may be very different depending upon which instructor you choose.

Several states recognize NRA-certified classes, or require all classes be taken from an NRA-certified instructor. This is not surprising, as the National Rifle Association is the oldest and largest source for firearms safety training in the country.[49]

A few states require applicants to qualify for carry permits by shooting a course of fire with scored targets. These qualification shoots are usually very simple. For the most part, these qualifications do not test excellent marksmanship. They are given so the instructor can document that the applicant knows how to safely fire a gun.

Why do so many states require CCW classes, but don't require students in those classes to prove they can shoot well? To put it simply but cynically: lawmakers are often fearful that citizens will misuse firearms by shooting when shooting is not lawful, but they are not too concerned with whether or not any individual really has the skill to defend herself. Politicians need to reassure themselves that everyone applying for a permit will be exposed to laws about when *not* to use the gun and where *not* to carry it. People serious about learning how to protect themselves should seek additional training rather than relying on the required class.

Wait... Let me put that more strongly. A state-required permit class is *not* a good place to learn to how to defend yourself with a firearm. It simply gives you permission to carry a gun. If you want to learn to shoot well and safely, and especially if you want to be prepared to defend your own life, you should definitely seek out more training than you can get in the state-required class.[50]

---

49 *Founded in 1871 by Union Army veterans concerned about marksmanship ability in new recruits, the National Rifle Association provides firearms and safety training through a network of more than 65,000 instructors, more than 3,800 coaches, and more than 1,700 training counselors nationwide. As of spring 2010, NRA's Eddie Eagle program, which teaches children not to touch a firearm if they find one, has reached over 21 million children in all 50 states.*

50 *Please note that there are many good people doing good work within these programs, including many excellent instructors who bootleg as much good information to their students as they can within the limitations of the format. The best of these people will be the first to tell you that the required course barely brushes the surface of what someone determined to learn about self defense really needs to know.*

Once I Have My Permit, Where Can I Carry?

Your state law will spell that out very exactly. If you must take a class in order to obtain a permit, the class will probably cover this in some detail.

Typically, within the state you will be allowed to carry everywhere except places specifically prohibited by law. Commonly prohibited places include many government buildings, schools, bars, and sometimes hospitals and churches. In addition, some states have laws allowing shopkeepers to post their places of business to prohibit concealed weapons; frequently such signs must meet exact size or wording requirements spelled out in law. Finally, some states have quirky or unusual laws designed to keep concealed firearms out of one or two specific facilities.

The laws about where carry is and is not allowed are *very* specific to your state. Please look up the law for yourself, and do not take anyone else's word for it.

Will My Permit Allow Me to Carry in Other States?

Maybe. Most carry permits are honored by at least a few other states in addition to the issuing state. No state issues a permit recognized everywhere, though Utah and Florida's permits are both recognized in many other states. If you have a permit issued by one state, you may not carry in a second state unless the second state also honors your permit.

As with other gun laws, lists of which states honor which other states' permits are constantly changing. Several websites exist for the purpose of tracking this information, but beware: even a well-regarded and well-run website occasionally goofs or goes out of date. Your best bet is to use such websites as a starting place and general overview, but *always* double-check the information against official, legal sources before setting out.

When carrying in a state which recognizes your home state's carry permit, you must follow local laws about where carry is and is not allowed. Your own state's laws do not pertain. For example, if you live in a state where it is perfectly legal to carry into all restaurants, you might find yourself tripped up in a neighboring state by a prohibition against carry in restaurants that serve alcohol for consumption on the premises. Again, check the law directly for yourself and do not assume that one state's laws are like another!

Do I Need a Permit to Carry at Home?

Generally speaking, no. But if you live in a state with very restrictive laws, you may need a permit simply to own a firearm, including firearms you keep locked up at home.

Legal Basics: Traveling with Firearms

The Firearm Owners Protection Act (FOPA) was passed in 1986, and addressed a lot of regulatory abuses under earlier gun control laws. One of its provisions, the "safe passage" section, made it much easier to travel from state to state with firearms. Before the law passed, getting from Point A to Point B with a firearm was often a nightmare of logistics. Even if the gun was perfectly legal at both your starting point and your ending point, there was often no way to get the firearm to your destination without breaking the law. After the law passed, gun owners could travel with their firearms through areas where the firearms were otherwise illegal—provided the firearms were unloaded and not immediately accessible, and provided no extended stops were made in prohibited areas, and provided the firearms were legal at both ends of the journey. Here is the text of the relevant federal law, which is Title 18 of the US Code, Section 926a:

> *Notwithstanding any other provision of any law or any rule or regulation of a State or any political subdivision thereof, any person who is not otherwise prohibited by this chapter from transporting, shipping, or receiving a firearm shall be entitled to transport a firearm for any lawful purpose from any place where he may lawfully possess and carry such firearm to any other place where he may lawfully possess and carry such firearm if, during such transportation the firearm is unloaded, and neither the firearm nor any ammunition being transported is readily accessible or is directly accessible from the passenger compartment of such transporting vehicle: Provided, That in the case of a vehicle without a compartment separate from the driver's compartment the firearm or ammunition shall be contained in a locked container other than the glove compartment or console.*

For example, a gun owner in Virginia would be able to drive to a shooting competition in Vermont without getting arrested for passing through New Jersey or other places with prohibitive gun laws. However, the owner would need to unload the firearm and place it in the trunk of the vehicle, or in a locked box out of reach in a vehicle without a trunk, and the ammunition must be kept separate from the firearm.

In order for this section of the law to apply, the firearm *must* be legal at both ends of your journey. Be cautious about this! There are several states where it is illegal to possess a firearm without a permit from the local authorities, and several others with very complicated laws which functionally prohibit firearms. Handguns especially often run afoul of these types of laws. Do your research before you travel.

Because this law protects firearms owners during "transport" only, courts have found that a brief stop for gasoline would be acceptable. A longer stop such as spending a weekend with friends along the way would not. If you plan to travel *to*, rather than *through*, a restrictive area, this law will not protect you.

Air Travel

Many people do not realize it is legal to fly with firearms on commercial airlines. Of course, there are very strict rules, but it is surprisingly hassle-free once you understand the process.

Before gearing up to fly with your firearm, be certain your firearm will be legal at your destination. Then call ahead to check the rules for your airline. Every airline does things just a little differently than all the others, and every airport has a slightly different layout. However, TSA guidelines cover everything. According to the TSA, the key requirements for traveling with firearms as of spring 2010 are as follows:

Caution!

Whether or not you are flying with a firearm, *ALWAYS* check every pocket of your luggage to be certain none of your firearms gear snuck into them while they were stored. If you ever carry in your purse, *ALWAYS* check your purse to be sure the firearm is elsewhere before going to the airport.

- You must declare all firearms during the check-in process.
- You must keep the firearm unloaded.
- You must place the firearm in a hard-sided container.
- You must lock the container. Provide the key or combination to the security officer if he or she needs to open the container. Remain in the area designated by the aircraft operator or TSA representative to take the key back after the container is cleared for transportation.[51]

---

51 *Several companies produce locks that TSA agents can open using a master key. They're great for ordinary luggage, but you must use a non-universal lock to secure*

- You should securely pack any ammunition in packaging designed to carry small amounts of ammunition. You can't use firearm magazines for packing ammunition unless they completely and securely enclose the ammunition.[52]
- You may carry ammunition in the same hard-sided case as the firearm, as long as you pack it as described above.
- You can't bring black powder or percussion caps used with black-powder type firearms in either your carry-on or checked baggage.[53]

You'll need a suitcase with an outside lock, plus a hard-sided locking gun case to go inside the suitcase. Plan a little extra time going through security. At the counter, tell the ticket agent that you need to declare a firearm, then follow the agent's instructions. From this point, the procedure depends on the airline, but you will probably need to show the unloaded firearm to the check in agent before taking your bag to the TSA area. Someone will hand you a bright orange tag to put *outside* the gun case, but *inside* the suitcase. Make sure your locks are secure when you hand your suitcase over to the TSA, then hover in the area until they have x-rayed your bags and given you the thumbs up.

Because my locking case has a little extra room in it, I've found it easiest to partially disassemble the firearm (taking the slide off) before putting it into the gun case. This makes it obvious at a glance that the gun is unloaded.

Under TSA rules, you won't be able to carry a lot of ammunition. Plan to bring one or two boxes with you, then purchase more at your destination if you need more. If you are flying to attend a class or a match, have your ammunition shipped to your destination before you go so it will be waiting for you when you arrive.

Hotel rooms

I can't emphasize this rule enough: *check state laws before you travel.* In most states, your hotel room counts as your "domicile" for the night, which means you'll be legal to bring the firearm into your room and have it ready for defensive use. But "most states" does not mean "all states," and many places have quirky local laws. Do your research before you travel.

If you do bring your firearm into the hotel, remember hotel rooms aren't particularly secure. The same locking gun case you use when flying might be

---

firearms.

52 *Several friends of mine have successfully flown with loaded magazines placed inside magazine pouches so the ammunition was completely covered. However, some airlines insist ammunition must ride in an ammunition box. Be prepared to cope either way.*

53 *Rules found on the TSA website, www.TSA.gov. Accessed May 2010.*

used in a hotel room to secure the firearm, but of course the entire case can easily be stolen. Consider staying only at hotels which feature in-room safes for the convenience of guests, and use the safe as needed. Never leave the firearm lying around the room, either openly or hidden—and especially not during hours when cleaning services are active.

The Advanced Course: Use of Force

Among the first question many people who are new to self defense ask is, "When may I shoot a criminal?"

There are a lot of myths, misinformation, and misunderstandings in the popular culture about using deadly force. And the laws governing the use of deadly force *do* vary from one jurisdiction to another. *Look up and try to understand the laws in your own state if you are serious about self defense.* Do not just take my word, or the word of some Bubba at the gun store, or (especially) whatever vague understanding you've picked up from TV and the movies. Do some thoughtful, genuine research into the laws that affect you personally.

> ### The Basic Standard
>
> Use deadly force only when there is an immediate and otherwise unavoidable danger of death or grave bodily harm to the innocent.

A person interested in armed self-defense often finds herself walking a narrow ridge between two equally unpleasant alternatives. On one side, there is the risk of responding too soon, with too much force, or with unwarranted violence. Erring in that direction sends her stumbling over the rocky cliffs of the American legal system, where even the smallest action can have huge consequences that affect the entire life. "Better to be tried by twelve ..." as the saying goes, but anyone with an ounce of sense knows that an 8x12 cell isn't much of a life. On the other side of the ridge lies the stony valley of death or severe injury caused by responding too slowly—or by not responding at all—to a life-threatening attack.

Of the two dangers, most people rightly fear death more than they fear the tender ministrations of the legal system. And that's as it should be, but it doesn't mean you should be uninformed about or unwilling to consider the laws which affect an armed citizen. Quite the contrary! The only true victory in a dangerous encounter is to walk away with *all* of your life intact: your ability to breathe, your good health, your family's safety, and your own freedom. Anything else is a loss.

For this and many other reasons, those who are interested in self-defense should be knowledgeable about the law. You can start with an online search. Stop by www.handgunlaw.us or www.usacarry.org for handy, direct links to state and local laws. Or visit the Cornell University Law School's online legal reference site at www.law.cornell.edu. For those who prefer to do their research on bound paper, there are many options. Kevin L. Jamison, a Missouri lawyer and columnist for Concealed Carry Magazine, penned an excellent in-depth book for Missouri residents: *Missouri Weapons and Self-Defense Law.*[54] Longtime gun-rights journalist Dave Workman did a similar (but less in-depth) work for Washington residents, titled *Washington State Gun Rights and Responsibilities.*[55] Michael Martin's first book, *Minnesota Permit to Carry a Firearm Fundamentals,* discusses Minnesota law and other important concepts in an attractive, very visual layout. In Florida, the reference book of choice is the incredibly detailed *Florida Firearms—Law, Use, and Ownership* by Jon Gutmacher.[56] Similar works are available in nearly every state, and are worth seeking out.

In addition to these, on every gun owner's bookshelf should be a copy of Massad Ayoob's classic *In the Gravest Extreme.*[57] This volume (originally published in 1980 and never updated) speaks to the timeless principles which build the foundation for all defense laws common to western civilization. It provides an absolutely indispensible understanding of how the law views the armed citizen who uses deadly force, and supplies some commonsense measures an intelligent person can take which greatly reduce the chances of legal trouble following a life-threatening encounter.

Another truly excellent resource for armed citizens is the Armed Citizens' Legal Defense Network (ACLDN),[58] which provides great information about the legal realities of self defense for its members.

Finally, if after doing this research and reading the laws directly for yourself, there is anything you do not understand, make an appointment to talk to a

---

54 Kevin L. Jamison, *Missouri Weapons and Self Defense Law, Merril Press 2003. Order from 2614 NE 56th Terrace, Gladstone, MO 64119-2311or online from www. kljamisonlaw.com

55 Dave Workman, *Washington State Gun Rights and Responsibilities, D&D Enterprises. Order from D&D Enterprises, PO Box 1638, North Bend, WA 98045 or online from www.danddgunleather.com

56 Jon H. Gutmacher, Esq., *Florida Firearms – Law, Use, and Ownership, Warlord Publishing. Order from publisher at 200 N. Thornton Ave., Orlando, FL 32801 or online from www.floridafirearmslaw.com

57 Massad F. Ayoob, *In the Gravest Extreme: the Role of the Firearm in Personal Protection. Police Bookshelf 1980. Available online through ayoob.com

58 Armed Citizens Legal Defense Network, PO Box 400, Onalaska WA 98570. (360) 978-5200. www.armedcitizensnetwork.com

local lawyer and ask him to explain the state and local law to you.

Much of the material below came from Massad Ayoob, some presented in his book *In the Gravest Extreme*, or covered in detail during classes available through the Massad Ayoob Group.[59] I highly recommend Ayoob's classes to people who are serious about firearms for personal protection, as well as to those who are involved in the martial arts. If you possess the ability to kill or cripple another person, you absolutely must study the legal, ethical, and moral limits society has placed on you.

Although specific laws about deadly force vary from one state to the next, the United States has one fairly uniform standard on using deadly force which, if followed, will keep you within the law no matter where you live.[60] Rooted in common law, this standard has been used as a benchmark in law enforcement training for many, many years. It applies whether you are at home or in public, no matter what method your attacker uses to try to do you harm. When your response to the aggressor's actions falls within this standard, your position in court should be very strong.

In order to meet this basic standard, you must be able to convince a jury that you (or the person you defended) were an innocent party, and that you were in immediate and otherwise unavoidable danger of death or grave bodily harm.

Meeting the "**immediate**" part of the standard means you fight back only while the danger is actually present, not when it might be present sometime in the future or was present sometime in the past. If someone threatens to kill you tomorrow, you don't gun him down; you get a restraining order and make sure he can't find you tomorrow. If someone attacks you and runs off, you don't shoot him in the backside no matter how badly you want to. If someone leaves to get a weapon, you leave, too, so you aren't there when he gets back. You don't use deadly force unless you are in danger of getting killed right then and right there. The danger must be present at the very moment you pull the trigger.

Since you're a smart person, if you could have figured out another way to avoid the danger you would have done it. If you were in public, you probably tried to walk away or disengage. In your own home, you might have tried getting behind furniture, or barring the door, or even leaving the house.[61] If time

---

59   *Massad Ayoob Group, PO Box 1477, Live Oak, FL 32064. www.massadayoob-group.com*
60   *Some states have more permissive use-of-force laws than this basic standard would indicate, but no states are more restrictive than this basic standard.*
61   *Leaving the house is not legally necessary in any state that I am aware of, but in some circumstances it might be a good practical tactic.*

permitted, you probably called 911. The citizen who acts with lethal force must show that it was a last resort under the circumstances. But even in states where there is a "duty to retreat" from an assailant, retreat is never required unless it can be accomplished in complete safety to oneself and other persons. You need not try to outrun a bullet, or throw your helpless children to the attacking wolves.

Showing that you were the *innocent* party is also fairly straightforward in most cases. If you don't habitually get into bar brawls or yell at other people, if you've learned to deal with beggars by saying no and walking away, if you don't get involved in road-rage incidents—all of these are commonsense things your mother probably told you, and although mom probably didn't know it she was giving you sound legal advice. If you did not willingly participate in an altercation or egg it on, the court will see that you were an innocent party.

But how can you know and prove that the situation you were in was truly life-threatening, and really involved a danger of *grave bodily harm* or even *death*?

Ability, Opportunity, Jeopardy

Police are trained to answer this question by looking for three basic elements that must be present before they may use lethal force: Ability, Opportunity, and Jeopardy (often abbreviated to AOJ, or referred to as the AOJ Triad). When these three things are present, any reasonable person would believe that a life was in danger, so the defendant's legal position is very strong. But if one of the elements is missing, the defendant may have a hard time convincing a jury that shooting the attacker was really necessary.[62]

Important Definitions!

☑   *Ability* means that the other person has the power to kill or cripple you.

☑   *Opportunity* means that the circumstances are such that the other person would be able to use his ability against you.

☑   *Jeopardy* means that the other person's actions or words provide you with a reasonably-perceived belief that he intends to kill or cripple you.

---

62 See "Defending the Self-Defense Case" by Lisa J. Steele, in the March 2007 issue of the National Association of Criminal Defense Lawyers' journal, the Champion.

Any two of the elements may be present in a lot of common interactions, but the presence of only two elements does not justify using deadly force. You need all three elements together at the same time in order to justify using a firearm in self defense. This isn't as complicated as it sounds, and it is mostly just common sense.

An example of A & O, but not J: a strong young man with a baseball bat (ability) is standing within a few feet of a man in a wheelchair (opportunity). Unless the young man either verbally or physically threatens to assault the man in the wheelchair, jeopardy is not present.

An example of O & J, but not A: a very irate little girl says, "I *hate* you! I'm going to *kill* you!" (jeopardy). She is standing next to you, close enough to hit you with every ounce of her strength (opportunity). But she's only little, and she doesn't have any weapons. Ability is not present.

An example of A & J, but not O: a small female has just testified in court against a male criminal who has been trained as a martial artist and who is physically much bigger and stronger than she is (ability). As the guilty verdict is read, the criminal rages to his feet and begins threatening to kill her right there (jeopardy). But he is restrained by handcuffs and by the bailiffs. Opportunity is not present.

Now that we have defined our terms and have seen the simple overview, let's examine each of the individual elements more closely.

Ability

The power to kill or cripple another human being can be represented by a lot of different things. Most often, it is represented by a weapon of some sort: a gun, a knife, a tire iron or club, or even some improvised weapon like a screwdriver or a metal chain. This isn't a complete list! The number of items that could be used as deadly weapons is nearly infinite, and they all represent ability. But ability can be present even when a weapon is not.

If a weapon is not present, ability may be represented by something the courts call *disparity of force*. This is just a fancy phrase that means the fight would be so radically unfair and so unevenly matched that any reasonable bystander would agree that one of the participants could kill or permanently damage the other person even without a weapon. Disparity of force is figured out on a case-by-case basis, taking in the entire set of circumstances. Generally speaking, disparity exists:

- When a strong young person attacks a really old person
- When three or more people attack one person

- When an adult attacks a child
- When a healthy person attacks someone who has a physical handicap
- When a skilled martial artist attacks a non martial artist
- When one person becomes so badly injured that they are unable to defend themselves from a continued violent assault
- When a man attacks a woman

Let me repeat and clarify that last point. If an unarmed man attacks a woman, the courts generally recognize that disparity of force is present. This doesn't mean that absolutely any man in the world could kill any woman in the world using his bare hands. It simply means that if a woman is attacked by an unarmed man, she may generally assume that he does have that ability, unless something about the circumstance falls far outside the norm. Courts have found that a male attacker who goes after a female victim does not have to display a weapon in order to be considered a deadly threat to her. Unless something else about the circumstances dramatically changes the dynamic, a woman being attacked by an unarmed male may reasonably believe that he possesses the power to severely injure or kill her.

Opportunity

When opportunity is present, a person armed with a gun will be within shooting distance (up to several hundred yards, depending on the firearm). If he is armed with a blade or an impact weapon, he will be room distance or closer, with no impediments between you. He will be close enough to kill you with whatever weapon he has, or with his bare hands. And there will be nothing in the environment to prevent him from doing so.

One important thing to know about opportunity is that if the other person is armed with an impact weapon or a blade, they can possess the element of opportunity even if they are on the other side of an average household room. This is because an average adult human being can cover 21 feet of distance in about 1.5 seconds or a little less. If you have practiced on the range with a timer, you know that is just barely enough time to draw your gun from concealment and get one good shot downrange. These time frames show that an attacker armed with an impact weapon can swarm you and kill you before you are able to draw your gun, unless you begin the defensive process before he covers that distance.[63]

---

63 *From a legal perspective, you must be able to document you knew this beforehand. One way: take a class which includes "the Tueller Drill," named after its creator, Dennis Tueller. Ask the instructor if the course will include the Tueller Drill. If it does, take*

On a practical level, most criminals prefer to operate without any witnesses. If you are trying to avoid the elements of A,O,J coming into place around you, it is a good idea to be especially alert in places where a crowd is not far away, but witnesses are unlikely to follow.

Jeopardy

Jeopardy, sometimes called *intent* or *manifest intent*, is the most difficult of the three elements to articulate and the most difficult to prove. It is most often the central nub of a criminal trial. The reason for this is that human beings are not mind readers. You cannot know beyond any shadow of a doubt what another person is thinking and what he intends to do. You can only reasonably perceive his intentions based upon his actions and his words.

As with the other two elements, jeopardy is really based on the entire set of surrounding circumstances. The jury will be instructed to ask themselves whether a reasonable and prudent person, knowing exactly what you knew at that moment (and no more!), would have come to the same conclusion you did. Would a reasonable and prudent person have believed that your attacker meant to use his ability to kill or cripple you? Was your decision that the person was a threat based upon simple fear, or did his actions and/or words give you a reasonable perception that he intended to kill you? What did the other person say or do, what physical motions did he make, which convinced you that he meant to do you harm?

> **Important Concept**
>
> Jeopardy is not simple fear. Someone who "looks menacing" may in fact be an innocent person with unfortunate features. Being afraid of what someone *might* do, when they have not given any real indication that they *will* do it, does not establish jeopardy.

Jeopardy does not necessarily require a clear verbal statement that the other person is trying to kill or cripple you, and words alone are not enough to establish it. Some attacks might include a spoken threat ("I'm going to kill you!" or "See this knife? I'm gonna cut your throat..."). These types of verbal statements, along with a related physical motion, may be used to help

---

dated notes, and to keep those notes in a secure place in case you ever need to authenticate your knowledge of the danger posed by an attacker at room distance. In the absence of a class, you may be able to document your knowledge by purchasing the "Surviving Edged Weapons" video made by Calibre Press (a gory but instructional film intended for police officers in training), or by viewing "How Close Is Too Close?" by Dennis Tueller and Massad Ayoob. Both videos may be purchased online from Armor of New Hampshire. The day you watch the video, sign and date the video jacket. You may also place your initials and the date in the margins of this book after reading this section.

establish jeopardy. But jeopardy can be present even when the other person does not say a single word. For example, an intruder who climbs in through a bedroom window, brandishes a knife, and advances toward you may be showing that he intends to violently attack you with a deadly weapon. Jeopardy would be present because the intruder's physical actions clearly demonstrate his probable intent.

Jeopardy can be present even if the other person later says he was "just joking," or if it turns out the gun or knife he was threatening you with was nothing but a toy. Remember, the jury will be instructed to ask themselves whether a reasonable and prudent person, knowing exactly what you knew at the time (and no more!) would have thought the same thing you did. If the person was acting in such a way that anyone with a lick of sense would have believed he really did intend to maim or kill you, then jeopardy did in fact exist no matter what other facts might come to light after the dust settles.

Conclusion

So that's the legal reality of armed self defense: you may legally use deadly force when there is an *immediate and otherwise unavoidable danger of death or grave bodily harm to the innocent.* The individual elements that create this standard include some very complex legal doctrines, but once the key concepts are understood, the bottom line is surprisingly commonsense. You can legally use deadly force if you realistically believe your life is in imminent danger and there is no other reasonable action you can take to avoid that danger.

Now that you have learned about the elements of A,O,J and how they relate to the legal situation if you use your firearm to defend yourself, the best way to keep these items in your memory is to practice using them.

When you watch the evening news, or read a newspaper, pay attention to stories which involve criminal attacks. Are the elements of A,O,J present? Did the criminal have the *ability* to kill or cripple his victim? At what point was there an *opportunity* for the criminal to attack? Did the victim reasonably perceive that the criminal intended to kill or cripple—was *jeopardy* present? If any of the three elements were not present, what parts of the story would need to be different in order for that element to be there? What important information did the news account leave out and how could that information alter the victim's legal situation?

Get in the habit of asking yourself these questions, so that you become easily comfortable with applying the elements of A,O,J to situations which may allow the legal use of deadly force.

Legal Myths about Self Defense

Watching television and movies, it all seems so simple: the good guys always hit what they aim at, while the bad guys never do. If a good guy gets hit by a bullet, it's a minor injury, easily bandaged and soon repaired. There are never any legal consequences if a good guy uses a firearm (or his fists, or a knife, or even an improvised explosion) to defeat a bad guy. We all know that Hollywood life isn't real life, but the vividness of the screen experience means we absorb these lessons and tend to feel they reflect reality in some way. They don't!

When I first became interested in firearms and self defense, I made a conscious decision to learn from the people around me, especially people who had been shooting many years. That was a good decision, because it helped me draw from other people's knowledge as I learned to shoot. But it also exposed me to some poor ways of thinking I later needed to correct, because as it turned out, my friends and relatives watched the same great TV shows and movies that I did. My friends told me things like, "If you shoot someone on the porch, drag the body back inside." One of my relatives told me that a police officer told him to keep shooting until the criminal was dead, because "dead men tell no tales." Another told me to aim for an arm or a leg if I didn't want to use lethal force. My friends told me a lot of things! It wasn't until I began to take classes from a reputable firearms training school that I discovered just how far off-base some of the most common pieces of advice really were.

Although I have titled this chapter, "*Legal* Myths about Self Defense," some of these myths aren't really about the law. Rather, they reflect common misunderstandings about how firearms work or how human bodies react under stress. Unfortunately, these misunderstandings can and often do get good people into trouble with the legal system, and that is why they are addressed in this chapter.

The Myths

☑ If you shoot someone on the porch of your home, you should drag the body back inside.

☑ If you shoot someone inside your home, you should place a kitchen knife or other weapon in the dead intruder's hand before you call the authorities.

The Reality

No. *No.* **No.** Moving the body, or rearranging any other physical evidence that might indicate what happened, is called "tampering with a crime scene." And it is itself a very serious crime.

Tampering with evidence isn't just a criminal act. It is also an act very likely to be discovered. Investigators will definitely know you have done something to the scene, and they will (quite reasonably) assume you did so because you were trying to hide evidence which proved the shooting was a cold-blooded murder instead of an act of self defense.

If you are ever involved in a shooting, it is vitally important that you do not lie to the police. Ever! Even one little lie, if caught, can destroy your credibility. Without credibility, you will have a much harder time staying out of jail even if your actions were completely within the law. Protect your reputation for honesty by protecting the scene rather than tampering with it.

The Myths

☑ Dead men tell no tales.

☑ Shoot until the criminal is dead and you will have an easier time in court.

☑ One story, end of story.

The Reality

The problem with this type of thinking is that the law is very specific about using deadly force. Legally, you may use a firearm to defend yourself *only* as long as the threat to your own life still exists. Once the threat has stopped, you must stop shooting. It does not matter whether the criminal is unconscious, or surrendered, or running away, or dead. In each of these cases, the threat has ended and you no longer have legal authority to fire. If you continue to fire after the threat has ended, you can be charged with—and you will be *guilty of*—murder, or manslaughter, or attempted murder.

"Dead men tell no tales"... or do they? Forensic science has advanced to the point where investigating officers can usually reconstruct the entire chain of events, even without any human witnesses. Blood spatter patterns, bullet trajectories, gun powder residue, empty casings, autopsy findings, and other clues all work together to tell the story of what happened and what you were doing when the fatal shot fired. After a shooting, officers work very hard to figure out what happened and how it happened. Your chances of escaping this scrutiny are similar to your chances of winning the jackpot in the lottery: it technically could happen, but don't bet your freedom on it.

In our crowded society, criminal encounters rarely happen without witnesses. While it's tempting to think nobody else saw the attack because your entire attention was focused on the criminal, that doesn't mean there were no observers. It simply means you did not see them. Whether it's a video camera in the parking lot, a casual passerby with a cell phone videotaping from a distance, or a criminal accomplice peering through the window, others will probably witness your actions. The best way to avoid danger: decide *now* that you will do the right thing, whether anyone is watching or not.

The Myths

- ☑ I live in _____, and in this state we can shoot an intruder who comes into our home, no questions asked.
- ☑ I live in _____, and in this state we can shoot a burglar if he's on our property after dark, no questions asked.
- ☑ I live in _____, and in this state we can stand our ground and shoot anyone who accosts us in public, no questions asked.

The Reality

State laws that give the benefit of the doubt to the defender are a wonderful thing, but such laws *do not mean* no questions will be asked. They aren't a Get Out Of Jail Free card, either. If you shoot someone, you will still need to explain to the legal system what exactly happened, and why you did what you did.

Castle Doctrine laws *may* allow you as a homeowner to assume that one of the three necessary elements (Ability, Opportunity, and Jeopardy) was present, but in most cases, you will still need to show the presence of the other two elements. You must still be able to articulate why you believed your life was in danger when you pulled the trigger.

Stand Your Ground laws are even less helpful. They erase previous laws that required you to retreat if possible, *but that is all they do.* They do *not* erase the need to show how your life was in danger when you fired.

Killing a person is a very serious matter. Even a justified shoot can result in years of disturbed sleep patterns, flashbacks, health issues, and other physical and emotional manifestations of stress. It can cost every penny you own, your home, and your marriage. Pulling the trigger is simply not worth it unless you will lose your life if you don't.

The Myths

- ☑ Since I don't want to kill anyone, I could just shoot him in an arm or a leg. That wouldn't be using deadly force since I wouldn't want to kill him.
- ☑ Shooting an arm or a leg is unlikely to kill a person.
- ☑ I practice a lot, so I believe I could hit his arm or leg if I wanted.

The Reality

Shooting at someone *is* using deadly force, no matter which part of his body you aim for and regardless of whether you intend to kill him. Here is a legal definition of deadly force from the law books in Washington state, where I live:

> *"Deadly force" means the intentional application of force through the use of firearms or any other means reasonably likely to cause death or serious physical injury.*[64]

Although the exact wording of the law changes from state to state, the meaning of *deadly force* or *lethal force* remains substantially similar in most states. Shooting an attacker in self defense is an intentional use of force. Shooting someone usually causes serious physical injury, no matter where the bullet lands. Even if the shot only hits an arm or a leg, the attacker could easily die from shock or blood loss. That is why shooting someone in the arm or leg is, legally speaking, every bit as legally serious as if you deliberately shot them right through the heart. If you cannot bear the thought of killing someone to save your own life, you should not use a gun to defend yourself.

Criminal attacks usually happen very quickly and are often brutally un-expected. Under the stress of an attack, your body will go into fight-or-flight mode and will dump a massive amount of adrenalin into your bloodstream. This is good, because adrenalin will give you the physical strength and stamina to run away (if you are able to escape) or to fight back fiercely (if you cannot run away). But the adrenalin rush will also cause your hands and entire body to shake, your vision to tunnel in on the threat, and your brain to nearly stop registering input from your ears. These are all very predictable physical responses to being attacked.

Criminals aren't like cardboard targets at the range: they don't stand still,

---

64 *Definition from RCW 9A.16.010.*

they don't move in predictable patterns, and they don't play fair. They move quickly and erratically and do unexpected things.

What this means is that getting a good, solid hit under stress may not be as easy as it sounds. Nationwide, law enforcement officers who get involved in shootings have a hit ratio of only around 20%. That means that 80% of their bullets do not hit the attackers! There are a lot of reasons for this, but the important thing to remember here is that you will need every advantage you can get. For the best chance of hitting the attacker at all, you will want to aim for the very middle of the largest part of the attacker's body that you can see.

Even if you do hit the attacker in the arm or leg, marginal hits are much less likely to stop the attack quickly enough to save your life. If the attacker is drunk or hopped up on drugs, he may not even notice he's been shot until blood loss shuts his body down, which can often take five minutes or more. A lot of very bad, and very permanent, things can happen during those five minutes.

Defending yourself with a handgun isn't like the movies. Your attacker won't be blown backwards when he is hit. He may not realize he's been shot even if the hit is a solid one. Even if he takes a bullet right through his heart, it may take 30 seconds or more for his brain and body to stop working. Thirty seconds may not sound like much, but it is enough time for him to shoot an entire magazine of ammunition at you, enough time for him to fatally stab you, enough time for him to club you into brain-damaged unconsciousness.

The truth is, if you are attacked by a determined criminal, you will very likely need every advantage you can get. For your best chance of survival, you should aim for the center of the largest part of his body you can see and you should keep fighting until you know that the attacker is no longer a threat.

The Myth

☑ Learning about the law will just slow me down if I need to defend myself.

The Reality

Not knowing the law can slow you down. And it can result in physical, emotional, or legal tragedy. For example, a driver who doesn't know the traffic laws might careen through an intersection without stopping at the red light, or he might cause a multi-car pile up by screeching to a halt in the middle of the road when he actually had the right of way. Both types of mistakes, the overly aggressive and the overly cautious, are equally dangerous—and both can be prevented by learning the traffic laws.

In the same way, a gun owner who doesn't understand the rules for using lethal force might incriminate herself and endanger others by acting without regard for the law. She might shoot when shooting is not justified either in law or by common sense. Or she might hesitate on the cusp of the crucial decision, holding her fire, failing to shoot at the appropriate moment because she doesn't know she would be in the right. Both these types of mistakes are equally dangerous to herself and to others—and both can be prevented by learning the laws that apply to self defense.

The Myth

☑   I don't need to think about the law right now. If I ever need to use the gun, I'll just hire a lawyer afterwards.

The Reality

There are a lot of things you can do beforehand to reduce your legal risk and make your lawyer's job easier. You want your lawyer's job to be as easy as possible because he will bill you for every split second he spends on your case, and because even good lawyers have bad days where they get things wrong. The easier your lawyer's job, the less time you will spend caught inside the twilight netherworld of the American legal system.

First, you should know the laws in your state and have at least some vague idea of how those laws apply to you. In the internet age, ignorance of the law really is no excuse—and there are few things sadder than to see a well-meaning person spend time in jail for breaking a law they didn't even know existed.

Second, you should seek formal training from a reputable firearms instructor. This shows you take the responsibility of being an armed citizen very seriously. Take notes during the class and keep any written materials from the instructor. This paperwork may become admissible evidence, which will incidentally allow you to educate the jury about use-of-force issues (and an educated jury can save your hide). A good class gives you access to a network of people who will be on your team if you ever need to defend yourself. Your trainer may be able to testify as a material witness for you, and may have recommendations of legal resources in your area. Most criminal-defense lawyers have little experience defending innocent people who lawfully used lethal force, and thus do not understand the nuances of an effective self defense case. You will need to find, not just any lawyer, but an *appropriate* lawyer. Your firearms trainer can very likely help you do that.

Third, you should know what to do after a shooting. The most basic rule is, "Don't talk a lot." Tell the officers what the attacker did, point out any evidence or witnesses, then ask for a lawyer and *shut up.* Shutting up might be very hard to do, because adrenalin makes people chatter, and because officers are trained to keep people talking. But it's one of the most important things you can do to help your lawyer keep you out of jail.

The Myth

☑ I won't get arrested or be charged with a crime if I shoot someone, because there are a lot of gun owners where I live and the political climate here is very friendly to gun ownership and self defense.

The Reality

Living in a state where the laws are friendly toward self defense *does* give you a leg up on dealing with the legal system after a shooting. The police who respond to the shooting are less likely to be overtly hostile, for example. And they might not arrest you on the spot. [65] Then again, they might. Because the confused and bloody scene just might leave some reasonable doubt about what actually happened. And no matter how confusing the scene, the one thing that will be very obvious is that you shot someone. Even if the police do not clap you into handcuffs immediately, when the case is presented to the prosecutor's office for review, anything can happen.

If you live in a state where the political climate is *not* friendly to firearms or to self defense, it's almost a given you will be arrested and charged with a serious crime. But even in friendly climates where the prosecutor might be very sensible about self defense, you can expect to deal with the legal system for quite a while after you shoot. Expect your firearm to be taken and kept for evidence until the trials are over even if the police are sympathetic. What trials? Well, chances are that you will face a trial at some point, even if it's just a Grand Jury in a friendly state looking over the facts and no-billing you. Even if you yourself do not get charged with anything, there's your attacker's trial. If your attacker does not die (approximately 80% of people shot with a handgun survive), he will very likely be charged with attacking you. Finally, your attacker or your attacker's surviving family might sue you in civil court after the criminal trials conclude. Expect your life to be on hold, and your firearm to remain in the evidence room, until all these legal maneuverings end.

---

65 *Of course, anything can happen. The rule of thumb: if you defend yourself inside your home, you are far less likely to be arrested than if you defend yourself outside the home. But rules of thumb are not guarantees.*

Be emotionally prepared to face the worst, while hoping for the best. If you shoot someone, expect to be arrested, expect to spend some time in jail, and expect to be charged with a crime. But also—if you shoot only to defend yourself when there is no other reasonable way to avoid getting killed, expect to win in court. As complicated as the legal system may be, people who shoot in righteous self defense are rarely convicted. A realistic understanding of what is likely to happen after you shoot may help you weather the legal and emotional aftermath.

The Myth

☑ My gun is a _____, and just the sight or sound of it will make a criminal run away in fear. I won't ever have to fire it.

The Reality

Maybe, maybe not. Some criminals do amazingly brazen things under the influence of alcohol, drugs, or stupidity. While most defensive uses of a firearm do not involve shots being fired, you cannot assume that *your* criminal will be smart enough to run away when you resist.

The mere sight of a gun is not going to cause the criminal to faint! Criminals do not fear guns. They often own guns themselves, and spend their lives handling weapons of all sorts. Some criminals will run away when the intended victim brings out a gun. But it is not the gun itself that makes them run away. A criminal runs when he believes the victim will shoot and kill him if he continues his attack. If the intended victim does not show visible resolve that she will use the gun if she must, the criminal may continue his attack even though he has seen the gun.

This makes an odd paradox: people who are willing to shoot in self defense are least likely to have to do so, while someone who carries a gun just to threaten an attacker is more likely to have an attacker keep coming until she has no choice but to shoot.

The Myth

☑ You can't shoot a man for trying to rape you.
☑ A rape isn't a deadly force attack, so you can't use deadly force in response.

The Reality

Generally speaking, deadly force is justified in response to an attempted forcible rape. Deadly force is justified not because forcible rape always involves death or grave bodily harm (although it too often does), but because there is a clearly-understood threat that the rapist will kill or seriously hurt the victim if she does not cooperate. This threat of death or serious injury is present even if the rapist never says a single word to his victim, and its presence is part of what defines the crime of rape.

Further, even if the attacker assures her that he won't harm her if she cooperates,[66] a woman may reasonably believe that the rape itself would endanger her life from any of several common but deadly blood-borne pathogens. An infected rapist does not have to cut her throat to kill her by raping her; he can simply do the deed and let infection take its toll.

Whenever an attacker uses deadly force against his intended victim, his intended victim may legally use deadly force in response. In the case of forcible rape, the force used against the intended victim typically meets the legal definition of deadly force. So she may legally use deadly force to defend herself and prevent the rape.[67]

The Myth

☑ Better to be tried by twelve than carried by six.

The Reality

This myth isn't a myth. It's true! But... there are some caveats. The best outcome allows the intended victim to walk away with *all* of her life intact, not just her physical ability to breathe. For this reason, using a firearm in self defense is always a last resort. It isn't something to take lightly.

---

66 NEVER *trust a promise from an attacker. He's breaking the law by attacking another human being, and he's probably got his fingers crossed behind his back.*
67 *Lethal force expert Massad Ayoob wrote an article about this for Backwoods Home Magazine some years back. The concepts are as fresh as they ever were, and you can find the article online at www.backwoodshome.com/articles/ayoob65.html*

Safety Matters

Dear Gunhilda,

Yesterday, as I headed out the door to pick up some personal supplies, my husband asked me to grab some ammunition for our weekend trip to the range. Happy to oblige, I grabbed the items I needed off the shelf at Giant Retail Mart, then went back to the sporting goods counter to buy ammunition.

When I asked the sales lady to give me a couple boxes of ammunition, she took one look at the bottle of Midol and box of tampons already in my cart and then she turned ghost white. "Honey," she said, "are you okay?"

I didn't know what to say!

~ Flustered in Farmington

Dear Flustered,

I just hope you didn't reply, "The ammunition is for my husband."

~ Gunhilda

The Four Rules

The Four Rules

1. All guns are always loaded.

2. Never point the gun at anything you are not willing to destroy.

3. Keep your finger off the trigger until your sights are on target (and you have made the decision to shoot).

4. Be sure of your target and what's beyond.

As long as firearms have existed, there have been safety rules: "Keep your powder dry." "Don't fire until you see the whites of their eyes." "Never handle a weapon behind the firing line." Some rules applied only to long guns. Some applied only to range work, some only to field work, some only to hunting, some only to guns with external safeties, some to revolvers or single-action semi-autos or double-action only handguns. There were a lot of rules.

Colonel Jeff Cooper deserves a great deal of credit for seeing the need for truly universal safety rules, rules that would apply to all firearms at all times. He boiled down all the various rules about firearms down into just four rules simple enough that even a child can follow them, providing an interlocking safety system. Nearly everyone in the gun world has acknowledged these four rules as simple and basic and *enough*. You might not think that's a big deal, but a lot of genius went into it. Complexity is easy; simplicity is difficult. Cooper made firearms safety more simple at a time when firearms were becoming more complex. That's genius.

Why are there four rules, instead of only one? Because each one of the four rules provides one layer of safety. If you violate only one rule, the chances are that no one will be harmed. It requires a violation of at least two rules in order for any significant harm to result.

Rule One: All guns are always loaded.

Rule One means that you must always treat your firearm with the respect you would give a loaded weapon. When you follow this rule, even after you have just checked to see that your gun is unloaded, you still never do anything with it that you would not be willing to do with a loaded gun. This is the cardinal rule, and all other safety rules follow naturally from it. In simplest form, Rule One means the other safety rules *always* apply. Even when we think the gun is unloaded, we will still follow Rules Two, Three, and Four.

Rule Two: Never point the gun at anything you are not willing to destroy.

Rule Two states the first logical consequence of Rule One. No matter what you are doing with your firearm—whether you are unloading it, cleaning it, or showing it to a friend—never allow the muzzle to point at anything you are not willing to shoot. After all, if you knew for sure the gun was loaded, you wouldn't do that. Be conscious of muzzle direction the entire time you are touching the gun. If you cannot pick the gun up without allowing it to point at something that shouldn't be shot, don't pick it up. If you cannot put the gun down without allowing it to point at something that shouldn't be shot, don't put it down. Whenever you handle your firearm, think of it as a Star Wars light saber: anything it crosses will be cut in half.

Rule Three: Keep your finger off the trigger until your sights are on target.

It should take a conscious effort to put your finger on the trigger. You should never, ever, ever find your finger resting on the trigger or within the trigger guard when you didn't consciously and deliberately put it there. What is a target? A target is anywhere you deliberately point the weapon, a place you choose because you would not mind hitting it with a bullet. Never put your finger on the trigger unless you are pointing the gun at a spot you have deliberately chosen for the purpose.

It follows that in order to clean a firearm such as a Glock, which requires you to pull the trigger when disassembling the gun, you must have a safe target with an adequate backstop in your home. At the very least you must have a spot on the floor which you have deliberately chosen, a spot where your dog never sleeps. Under no circumstances would you point the gun in a random direction while pulling the trigger during the disassembly process, and especially not at your own body. If you do not have an adequate backstop, you should not put your finger on the trigger—no matter what kind of gun you have and no matter what you intend to happen when the trigger is pulled. This rule applies wherever you are and whatever you are doing, whether you are cleaning the gun, dry firing, trying out a new set of grips, or anything else.

Because the human startle reflex can overwhelm your finger muscles, never rest your finger on the trigger until you have made the conscious decision to shoot. This is especially important if you ever have to take an attacker at gunpoint. That person will be a target, by definition, but until you decide to shoot him you should not put your finger on the trigger.[68]

Rule Four: Be sure of your target and what is beyond it.

Rule Four sounds deceptively simple, but it covers a world of potential tragedies. Among other things, it means you always identify your target, and that you carefully consider the backstop—or lack of a backstop—beyond your target. When shooting at the range, you must never begin firing until you are certain that no one is lurking behind or around the targets. It isn't enough to simply hear someone call the range clear. You must look for yourself, because you are the one responsible for where your bullets land. Be sure also of the space between you and your target. Could someone come between you and what you're shooting? Be aware of the area around your target, too. If you miss your target, what other things could you hit? Pay attention!

When using a gun for self defense, you must be overwhelmingly sure of the circumstances. If you are not absolutely certain that the person you intend to shoot is an immediate, deadly threat to an innocent person, then your gun is not the correct solution to the problem. Just as a hunter must never fire at a flash of color or an unfamiliar sound, a defensive handgunner must never draw the gun unless the circumstances are certain.

Rule Four also means that every time you fire a gun in practice, you must have an adequate backstop which will stop a bullet. What is an adequate backstop? It depends on the type and power of the firearm you are shooting. A shotgun loaded with birdshot, for example, requires only a long stretch of open air before the pellets will come harmlessly to rest. But rounds from a hunting rifle can literally travel miles if they are not stopped by hitting something very solid. If you use a gun "for keeps," as in hunting or self defense,

---

68 For a more complete discussion of this point, see "Of Fingers and Triggers" by Massad Ayoob, American Handgunner, July/August 2010.

it may not be possible to have a solid backstop as you would on the range. Nevertheless, you are responsible for every shot which leaves your firearm, not only for those which hit the intended target. So you must always be aware of what is beyond and around your target.

Good hunters are always aware of the direction and angle their rounds will travel once they have left the muzzle of the gun. Many hunters prefer to fire at a downward angle, so that the shot will simply strike the ground if it misses or passes through the animal. Many will never fire at an animal silhouetted on a ridge line, because under those circumstances, missed shots will travel for several dangerous miles before coming to rest. This is wise.

For self defense, you should always be aware of the angle your shots will travel and the likelihood of hitting an innocent bystander. If you can fire at a downward or upward angle, to avoid the risk of hitting others, do so. If there is an innocent standing directly behind your target, reposition yourself if possible so that the innocent is no longer in the line of fire. You must weigh the deadly threat from the attacker on one hand against the deadly threat from your bullets on the other hand.

Always remember that you will be called to account for every round you fire, not just the ones that hit your intended target.

Who Needs Rules?

A surprising number of people need to be talked into following the safety rules, rather than instinctively understanding them. I'm not sure what drives this attitude, but if you encounter someone like that, I have two pieces of advice for you.

First: *avoid that person!* People who refuse to follow the safety rules are telling you, in the most emphatic possible form, that they don't really care whether or not they kill you by mistake. Keep yourself safe by avoiding them and their bad habits. Whether you are practicing at the range or just hanging out with friends somewhere, if someone else begins handling firearms with callous disregard for your safety, you should leave immediately. Don't argue, don't fuss, don't create a scene. Just get your irreplaceable and fragile human body out of the danger zone as quickly as you can.

Second: if the person is a loved one or someone you care about, and you really feel you need to discuss this with them rather than just moving along and avoiding them, don't try it while the firearms are out. Make an excuse to get away from the immediate danger, rather than confronting them right then and there. Plan your conversation for a time when the guns are put away and everyone feels fairly relaxed and friendly.

Some folks want to blow off one or more of the rules "because I checked it" or "because it wasn't loaded." If that's the case, try pointing out that the purpose of following the rules *all the time* is to build good habits. Good habits will carry you through the times when you are tired, or stressed, or not paying attention as well as you ought. But those good habits will only be there to help you out if you consciously and carefully build them—by following the rules every single time, even when you think the gun is not loaded. And nearly every unintentional shooting involves an "unloaded" gun.

The Cornered Cat

Dressing for
Success on the Range

Does it matter what we wear to the range? Well, yes. The issue isn't fashion—it's function. When it comes to firearms, safety trumps style, every time. The important dangers to guard against include noise damage, eye injuries, and minor burns from flying brass. (Being hit by flying brass can lead to loss of muzzle control while you are shooting.) You'll also want to protect yourself from overexposure to lead and other chemical hazards whenever you are around firearms.

Choosing Ear Protection

A lot of old timers never bothered wearing ear protection. But if you've ever had a top-of-the-lungs conversation with an old shooter, you've already realized they should have. Around one in ten Americans suffers from hearing loss. Although the most common cause of hearing loss is advancing age, traumatic injury from noise exposure—which can happen at any age—is the second most common. Doctors tell us even a single exposure to a very loud noise can cause lasting damage, including an annoying "buzz" or "ringing" in the ears called *tinnitus.*

Noise exposure is measured in decibels (dB). The scale starts at 0 dB with the softest possible sound a young person can hear. Ordinary conversations happen around 60 dB, while gunshots reach around 140 up to around 165 dB. Unfortunately, hearing damage from prolonged exposure begins at as little as 85 dB, while permanent damage can be caused by less than 30 seconds of exposure at 115 dB and above. Since gunshots typically reach at least 140 on the decibel scale, you can see why doctors warn us to protect our hearing every time we shoot or will be around others while they shoot.

To protect your irreplaceable hearing, you'll need to purchase ear protection, which comes in three basic varieties: plugs, muffs, and electronic muffs. Fortunately, good protection need not be expensive.

The government requires that hearing protection products have a Noise

136

Reduction Rating (NRR), measured on a scale from 0 to 33. The higher the number, the more protection you receive. However, the scale does not target sudden impulse noise such as gunfire. It's much more appropriate for steady noise, such as noise produced by chainsaws, jackhammers, and other heavy machinery. Because gunshots are very loud compared to these noises, we know we want to use hearing protection that has a high NRR number. But we also know the numbers aren't going to match our real world in some ways.

How Loud Is It?
0 dB - *Softest audible sound*
20 dB - *Whisper*
60 dB - *Ordinary conversation*
65 dB - *Vacuum cleaner*
70 dB - *Car engine*
80 dB - *(Discomfort and damage begins with prolonged exposure)*
85 dB - *Hair dryer*
110 dB - *Rock concert*
115 dB - *(Can cause damage with less than 30 seconds of exposure)*
140 dB - *.22 caliber rifle*
170 dB - *.357 Magnum revolver*

As this book goes to press, several government agencies plan to change how they will calculate and use NRR. In the past, NRR has been a single number, but in the future it will become a two-number range. The higher number will show the level of protection that a user achieves when the product fits properly and they use it faithfully, while the lower number will show what an average user might receive. Once this change has taken place, consumers may find it easier to understand what the label means. But as shooters, we already know we need to achieve the highest protection possible and must choose a product we will use faithfully.

Ear plugs

Ear plugs are small inserts designed to fit within the ear canal. Typically made of memory foam which expands on insertion, they must fill the entire canal in order to be effective at blocking sound. Improperly fitted or dirty plugs do not work well and should never be trusted to protect your hearing. Further, disposable plugs lose effectiveness each time they are compressed. In other words, when you take your disposable plugs out and put them back in again you can expect that they won't work as well as they do when you put them in for the very first time.

As a rule, when tested in laboratory settings, ear plugs are nearly as effective as muffs at blocking sound. Unfortunately, the real world is not a laboratory. Most people do not use and fit their ear plugs properly under everyday circumstances, especially compared to the way they use and fit ear muffs.[69]

To achieve your best possible fit, first roll the ear plug between your fingers so it becomes a slender cylinder—like making a "snake" out of modeling clay. Reach over the top of your head with one hand and gently tug your ear upward and toward the rear, which straightens the ear canal. Use your other hand to deeply insert the rolled plug so that only a small portion remains outside the ear. Hold the plug in place as you count to thirty, allowing the plug time to fully expand and fill the canal. Don't rush! Until the plug has expanded, it does not provide good hearing protection.

As a general rule, ear plugs provide better protection than using nothing at all. However, ear muffs provide better protection, are more convenient, are easier to place and remove, and are more likely to be used faithfully and properly in the real world.

Ear muffs

Held in place by an adjustable band that passes over the head or behind the neck, ear muffs block sound by covering and sealing the entire ear area, including the sound-conducting bones around the ears. They are convenient to wear on the range because you can easily pull them off and back on again without reducing their effectiveness.

As a very general rule of thumb, ear muffs provide better protection than ear plugs in the real world. But that does not mean they're foolproof! Because they are bulky and easy to remove, it's tempting to pull them off even while others are still firing. If someone fires while your ears are unprotected, it will hurt. Always be aware of what other people are doing or getting ready to do before you remove your hearing protection.

Ear muffs can lose their effectiveness in cool weather. The seal around the outer edges can become stiff and inflexible when cold, preventing it from conforming to your face as it should. To avoid this problem, store your muffs inside rather than in the trunk of your car, and look for quality materials as you shop. A leather-covered seal flexes much more consistently than plastic.

When shopping, look for quality materials. You will probably toss them into your range bag sometimes, so look for a product that can stand a little abuse. Some muffs fold for easy storage. That's great because it makes them

---

69 *The National Institute for Occupational Safety and Health (NIOSH) reducing the NRR number by 70% to estimate how effective ear plugs are in actual use. In contrast, NIOSH recommends only a 25% downgrading of the stated NRR for ear muffs. See Criteria for a Recommended Standard, DHHS (NIOSH) Publication No. 98-126. Available online at http://www.cdc.gov/niosh/docs/98-126/pdfs/98-126.pdf.*

less likely to break when you stuff them into your bag. If the product feels lightweight or flimsy to you, it probably won't hold up.

It's tempting to purchase the most slender muffs available. This may be a mistake for two reasons. First and most important, the more slender the muff, the less likely it is to provide good hearing protection. Sound-absorbing pads unavoidably take up some room that adds bulk to the muff. Second, slender muffs tend to be less comfortable, especially if you have large ears or ears that stick out a little. Look for a cup that snugs over your ears without squishing or folding, and you'll be more comfortable whenever you shoot. (You might even have enough room left over that you won't have to remove your earrings!)[70]

As you pull your muffs into place, give them a little wiggle to be sure they seal completely and seat firmly. Your protective eyewear can interfere with the seal, so take a moment to be sure it doesn't.

Even well-rated ear muffs that fit well don't always provide enough protection for your hearing. For this reason, several government agencies recommend that shooters double up on hearing protection, using *both* muffs *and* plugs.[71] This works so well at protecting us from outside noises that it can become a problem: using both plugs and muffs, you may not be able to hear other shooters, or range commands, or instructions from safety officers. For this reason, if you decide to double up on ear protection, I strongly recommend you purchase electronic muffs rather than standard (passive) ones.

Electronic muffs

What are electronic muffs? Sometimes called "active hearing protection," electronic muffs protect the ears just as regular muffs do. But they also feature a tiny microphone which amplifies ordinary sounds so you can hear what's going on around you while you wear them. The microphone shuts off far faster than your ears can sense the sound when a shot fires, so they provide good hearing protection without interfering with your ability to hear range commands and other important sounds.

As with so many other things in life, with electronic muffs you get what you pay for. Or rather: you *don't* get what you don't pay for. Prices for electronic muffs as of spring 2010 range from around $40 up through around $300. At the lower end of the market, the amplification often sounds tinny,

---

70   For people shooting long arms, look for a thick muff with a "cutaway" on the lower edge, so the muffs do not interfere with the long gun stock. Only choose slender, less effective muffs if you absolutely cannot get the fit you need with thicker, higher rated ones.
71   For the NIOSH recommendation, see www2a.cdc.gov/hp-devices/huntershooters. html.

fake, and difficult to understand. And the microphones tend to cut out un-necessarily for long periods of time. They work, but not nearly as well as the more expensive varieties.

When shopping for electronic muffs, look for a "fast attack time" and a "fast recovery time" in a muff which fits you well. Most important, be sure that the basic muff provides good hearing protection. The best electronics in the world will not protect your ears if placed inside a poorly-insulated cup.

To keep the electronics working well, always toss a small desiccant pack into the cups when you fold the muffs for storage. You can purchase desiccant packs of silica gel wherever other types of sensitive electronics are sold, or order them online, and they will definitely extend the life of your muffs.

The last word about hearing protection

To protect your hearing, wear ear protection the entire time you are at the range. Always choose hearing protection that fits your body in the best possible way. Buy only from a well-known company and avoid purchasing generic or off-brand products. And if you ever walk off the range with your ears ringing and your head pounding, toss out the gear you've been using and move up to something more solid.[72]

Choosing Eye Protection

I'm a great believer in eye protection. A few years back, I was standing next to a friend who foolishly fired a low-speed round at a tree stump. The round bounced off the stump and came whistling back, striking my friend in the forehead. Fortunately, the bullet did not penetrate his skull. But it did tear an opening in the skin and give him a goose egg just over his right eye. If it had struck an inch lower, he would have been blinded for life.

Eye protection—safety glasses or safety goggles—shields your eyes from bounceback, flying brass, and other hazards on the range. And yes, you need true safety glasses, even if you already wear prescription eyeglasses. Regular eyeglasses do not provide impact protection, and may even shatter when struck.

Look for "High Impact" eyewear that provides good coverage around the sides of your eyes. Sideshields help protect your eyes regardless of whether you face downrange. They also guard against flying brass. Sometimes a person shooting a semi-auto will "catch" a piece of hot brass when it comes out

---

72 See also *Preventing Occupational Hearing Loss, A Practical Guide. DHHS (NIOSH) Publication No. 96-110. Available online at http://origin.cdc.gov/niosh/docs/96-110/pdfs/96-110.pdf.*

the side of the firearm. If the brass gets caught behind your eye protection by coming in from the side or top, it can really hurt. It can even blister your eyelid. Good sideshields help prevent this hazard.

If you ordinarily wear prescription lenses, you have two choices. You can purchase eye protection designed to wear over regular glasses. Although awkward, it works well enough for most purposes. However, if you end up shooting a lot, you may want to purchase prescription safety glasses. Surprisingly, in many states prescription safety wear costs less than ordinary prescription eyewear. For those distracted by distortion from multiple lenses, prescription safety glasses can be a godsend.

You can buy tinted safety wear or stick with clear lenses. As a general rule, I prefer clear lenses because that's what I'm most likely to be wearing if I need to shoot in self defense.

Protection from Flying Brass

Flying brass can't seriously harm you. The worst it can do is leave a small blister on your skin. Big deal, right? Well, yes. It actually can be a big deal. When a shooter receives a sudden sharp pain in a tender place, she may do something unfortunate with the firearm—like wave it around, or throw it down, or even point it at herself or others in her haste to get away from the pain.

Hot brass can land behind your eyewear, causing blistered eyelids or upper cheekbones. To prevent brass getting in from the top, wear a hat with a brim so the brass will bounce away from the top edge of your lenses. Wear eye protection with sideshields, too.

Brass loves to snuggle into female cleavage. It's also drawn irresistibly to the waist gap at the back of blue jeans, especially low-riding ones. To protect against these problems, wear a high-collared shirt and tuck it in.

The hot-foot dance caused by brass landing on top of bare toes can be just as dangerous as the cha-cha dance caused by brass landing inside the clothing. If you'd rather sit that dance out, wear closed-toe shoes on the range, and save the cute strappy sandals for the ride home.

If, despite all these precautions, a piece of brass finds its way to a tender place, **put the gun down** (safely!) before dealing with the burning sensation. After all, it's only a little piece of brass. The worst it can do is leave a little blister... unless you panic and respond inappropriately.

Minimizing Lead Exposure

Exposure to lead can be harmful to your health. We heard in school that

Rome fell because the emperors drank lead-sweetened wine from lead goblets. Lead in the bloodstream makes people go crazy, and toward the end most of the emperors were indeed crazy, so Rome fell because of lead poisoning. Right? Actually, Rome's fall can be traced to a gajillion things (and some serious historian is probably grabbing her keyboard *right now* to tell me about them). But too much lead did play a tragic role. Similarly, many potters suffered from lead poisoning before people realized it wasn't a good idea to use lead in ceramic glazes. High lead levels can kill just as surely as any other form of poisoning.

Lead can affect nearly every organ and bodily function. Because it affects many different body parts in different ways, the symptoms can be confusing, especially at mild levels. Symptoms include an odd taste in the mouth, abdominal pain, headache, anemia, depression, personality changes, and irritability. In children it can cause hearing loss, stunted growth, and learning or behavior disorders. Adults can suffer from neurologic problems such as confusion, weakness, pain, or tingling in the extremities. Severe lead poisoning causes seizures, coma, and death.

Avoiding lead exposure takes a simple commitment to good hygiene along with some basic safety practices. We don't need to get all panicky about this easily-controlled risk, but in view of human history, we do need to take it seriously. The more you shoot, and the more time you spend on the range, the more careful you should become about your lead exposure.

Where does lead come from?

As a bare lead bullet moves down the barrel of the gun, small amounts of lead become superheated and vaporize into the surrounding air. This creates a cloud of lead dust. Although this cloud expands only three to five feet from the shooter, it settles on clothes, hair, hands and face. It also falls on the surrounding area. The floors and walls of indoor ranges get very dusty, and most of that dust comes from vaporized lead.

The primer, which produces the spark that allows gunpowder to burn, typically uses lead styphnate as a basic component. Although lead-free primers are available, most ammunition uses lead-based primers. Even ammunition that uses non-lead bullets often uses regular primers. Fortunately, primers are really a minor source of lead exposure for most shooters. You'll need to pay attention to this source if you learn to reload your own ammunition, or if you begin handling fired primers for some other reason. But for those who simply shoot, it isn't a major source.

Cleaning the firearm also exposes the shooter to lead. As the bullet traveled down the barrel, parts of it melted and clung to the inside of the barrel. This lead must be dissolved and removed during the cleaning process, so scrubbing the barrel often creates more lead exposure.

How do we avoid it?

Now that we know how we are exposed to lead, we can find ways to avoid it or reduce our risk. But first we need to know a few more things about lead. First, lead is a toxic metal. It has no known beneficial effect. It isn't like zinc, or iron, or cobalt, where a tiny amount might be helpful but a larger amount becomes dangerous. It's always bad. Once lead gets into the human body, it tends to stay for a long time. Exposure to lead is cumulative. It adds up on you. Because lead doesn't do anything good even in tiny amounts, and because it stays around for a long time, you should avoid exposure whenever possible. But because lead is a common element and present nearly everywhere (whether you are a shooter or not), it will not be possible to entirely eliminate exposure to it.

Lead on your skin isn't a cause for worry by itself, because you can't absorb lead through your skin. However, lead that gets into your stomach or lungs can be very harmful indeed. Lead on your skin can easily travel to your hands, then to your lips, then to your stomach. So you can limit your exposure by washing your hands and face after you've been to the range.

To limit exposure to airborne lead, shoot at outdoor ranges where air circulation isn't a problem. If you must use an indoor range, choose a well-ventilated range that circulates the air *away* from the shooters. If you feel air blowing toward your face on an indoor range, that's not good. The air movement should flow toward the targets.

Shooting jacketed bullets—bullets covered with a thin layer of a metal such as copper—reduces your exposure in two ways. First, it keeps lead out of your lungs on the range, because the jacket material prevents the lead from vaporizing as the bullet travels down the barrel. Second, it reduces your exposure to dissolved lead when you clean your firearm, because the jacket material prevents melted lead from coating the inside of the barrel. Using jacketed bullets on well-ventilated ranges can significantly reduce your exposure.

You may choose to purchase only lead-free ammunition, but be aware this can be expensive. When lead-free ammunition isn't available, choose jacketed bullets whenever possible. And of course, you can't control what ammunition other people shoot while you are at the range. That means no matter what ammunition you use, you will need to take steps to remove lead from yourself and your clothing when you are done shooting.

Cleaning up

The first step is simple: wash your hands and face after shooting. Never eat, drink, or smoke at the range. After washing your face and hands, blow your nose to remove any trapped lead dust. I keep a supply of baby wipes in my range bag to provide an immediate clean up when I'm done shooting. Then when I get home, I scrub a bit better, using cool water and lots of soap. You can buy special lead-removing soap at many gun stores or online shooting supply places.

If you shoot at indoor ranges, consider keeping a spare pair of "shooting shoes" boxed up in your car. You can pull these shoes on before you go into the range to shoot, and then take them off before you get into your car. This avoids tracking lead dust from the range home to your own carpets, especially important if you have small children.

Avoid cleaning firearms inside the house. Take them out to the garage for cleaning. If that's not possible, avoid some exposure by using a splatter-reducing product such as the MuzzleMate from Accu-Fire.[73] Be scrupulous about cleaning up after you've cleaned up: place a disposable pad and lots of absorbent newspapers under your work area, and throw everything away when you're done. Clean the area as well as you can.

Yikes...

Whew! That's quite a collection of worries and hazards, isn't it? It sounds overwhelming when we lay it all out. But now that I've finished making it complex and worrisome with all the details, let me make it simple again: wear closed-top shoes and a high-necked shirt to the range. Use eye and ear protection that works for you, and wear a hat. Wash your hands and face when you're done. And don't talk back to your mom.

---

73 *Accu-Fire Inc., PO Box 121990, Arlington, TX 76012. www.accufireproducts.com.*

Safe Storage

Three types of people challenge your ability to store firearms at home: children, the criminal, and the clueless. Of these, children often create the most worry, and understandably so. But the other two groups represent threats of equal concern. If you want to be sure nobody else uses your firearm—whether accidentally or purposefully—to do harm, you need to find a way to store your firearm securely when you are not using it.

What Doesn't Work

One afternoon when my children were very small, I walked into the kitchen during naptime and found our redheaded two-year-old sitting on top of the fridge. He had used the kitchen drawers stairstep-fashion, then precariously balanced the toaster on top of the breadbox so he could use them as stepstools.[74] Without saying a word, the kid convinced me that to secure something from small children, you need to do more than simply place it "up high where the kids can't get it." Children usually grow faster, learn earlier, and get into more trouble sooner than their parents ever expect. Certainly if you had asked me the day before if my little darling could so easily scale Mt. Amana, I'd have laughed at the thought.

Another strategy doomed to ignominious failure: hiding stuff. Probably every parent in the history of western civilization has hidden Christmas presents from their children. But is there a child, anywhere, who *never* found the goodies? Try asking that question of young adults at a holiday gathering, and the stories you'll receive—*if* their parents aren't listening—will curdle your eggnog. If the kids know it's in the house, and they want to find it, they will. And if they don't know for sure that it's there? They'll still poke around, explore, snoop... and deny everything when Mom gets home.

Hiding firearms from thieves works just as poorly as hiding them from children. "The bad guys know where you hide guns," points out Marty Hayes

---

74 *He had his reasons: we often hid the bribe candy in a cabinet above the refrigerator. If the smoke alarm sounded, every child who beat me to the front door got a piece of candy.*

of the Firearms Academy of Seattle, a longtime police officer. "People put them in mattresses, or tuck them up inside the crawlspace door. They put them in the hideaway bed. The criminals know all those places." Indeed. A friend of ours once lost several thousand dollars worth of firearms when he left his house briefly during the day. The thief or thieves—they were never caught—slipped in, grabbed firearms from various hidey-holes throughout the house, and left before our friend returned.

What about the clueless? Surely hiding guns should work to secure them against the well-intentioned but bumbling guest. So one would think. But how many guests sneak a peek into the medicine cabinet when the host isn't looking? If they spot it, they'll handle it, and if they handle it, tragedy could result. Check out this forum post, for example, from an online discussion board in the firearms community:

> *What an eventful evening this has been so far! Here's the story: I had some coworkers over for some drinks and a BBQ this evening. Put the loaded Kel-Tec and Kimber up in a cabinet in the kitchen thinking nobody would ever find them. One of the guys gets hungry for some snacks and starts rooting around, finds the Kel-Tec and pulls the trigger. It launches a 9mm 124 grn +P Gold Dot through my cabinet and through the outer wall and into a banister on the staircase going upstairs. I know it's my fault as much as his and I feel like a complete idiot.[75]*

For all these reasons, hiding firearms—whether up high or not—does not serve to secure them from unauthorized access. You need something more certain.

Budget Woes

Not everyone who can afford a firearm finds it easy to purchase the accoutrements, however. Some budgets stretch, just barely, to cover the gun and an occasional box of ammunition, with precious little left over for "extras" such as solid training and secure storage devices. What's a poor gun owner to do?

Here's what *not* to do: shrug and give up. Even the tightest budget has some options. They might not always be the best and most desirable options, but they do exist.[76] A little later, we'll discuss affordable options and low-cost

---

75   Originally posted at http://forums.1911forum.com/showthread.php?t=42916 and shared elsewhere on the web. Used with author's permission.
76   My beloved grandma, not long before she died, looked me in the eye and said, "Kathy, that's one thing I wish my mother had taught me. Nobody told girls this back

measures you can take to secure your firearms. But please don't tune me out before we get there; you might find that the higher-end products aren't as far out of reach as you thought. And it's always best to know the ideal before looking for a compromise.

Full-Size Safes

When most people think of a "gun safe," they think of those huge, refrigerator-sized metal boxes that weight about a bajillion pounds and take up several feet of floor space. And those are certainly viable options for people with more than a few firearms, especially if some of those firearms are long guns rather than handguns. Costs for these full-size safes (as of spring 2010) run from around $500 up through many thousands of dollars, depending on the size, brand, and available options.

For the beginning gun owner, with only one or two handguns to secure, a full-size safe really isn't needed. If you do decide to shop for a full-size safe, first think about where you will put it and how you will get it home. Explore shipping and delivery options as part of your purchase, because moving a full-size safe is a nontrivial job. Look for good fireproofing so you can store documents inside as well. Be aware that even most full-size safes need to be bolted in place to be truly secure.

Finally, when you do need to move up to such a safe, buy the very largest one you can afford. If the gun bug has bit you hard enough that you need a full-size safe, you'll need more room in it before long.

Smaller Safes and Boxes

While you might not need a full-size safe yet, a smaller safe could make perfect sense. We're talking here about containers just large enough for a handful of handguns, at most. These smaller boxes come with a variety of options, and range in price from around $30 to $300 or a bit more. They also vary by intended use, with some designed for mounting in a vehicle, others for travel, and others for use at home. Many include features allowing the user to securely mount the container to two or more different locations—such as against a closet wall at home and on special brackets installed in the trunk of a car. Once mounted, the container becomes more secure than its size would suggest.

Here are a few points about some commonly-available options.

Combination locks vs. keys vs. biometrics. You might forget the com-

---

then, but you need to know this: you always, always, always have choices." Who am I to doubt her?

bination in a moment of stress, and opening a combo lock tends to be a bit slower. However, keys get lost too—and are all too easily found by the wrong person. Keyed locks are also somewhat easier to defeat than combination locks of the same price range and general quality. Biometric safes, which "read" fingerprints to allow access, have not yet advanced to the point where they can be trusted with a human life; they still occasionally misread the print, denying access when you need it most. Use these types of locks only on safes which secure non-defense firearms.

One nice feature available on GunVault-brand products: a combination lock designed around placing a human hand on top of the safe. Place your hand in the raised outline, then press buttons in a known pattern to access the safe. Once practiced, it's fast and intuitive—and it can be done in the dark without any need to see numbers or find a key.[77]

Cables vs. bolts vs. brackets. The most common way to defeat a small safe happens when a thief simply picks up the entire safe, firearm and all, and walks away with it—taking it elsewhere to open at his leisure. So a small case isn't secure unless affixed to some stationary object: a wall stud, the frame of the vehicle, an architectural element in the house, the floor. For this reason, manufacturers include cables, bolts, or brackets on these products, and your lockbox simply isn't secure unless you use them.

Cables probably provide the most flexibility, especially for a container you will use in your car or while traveling. The cable can be locked around the seat of your car, enabling you to easily slide the box under the seat and back out again while keeping it attached firmly to the vehicle. In hotel rooms, the cable can be wrapped around a bed leg (if the bed is bolted to the floor as it often is) or another element in the room. Unfortunately, a cable lock can never be as secure as bolts or even brackets.

Bolting the box in place works well for permanent installations, and may provide the most security. To improve matters still further, place the box somewhere with limited side space so it becomes difficult to use a pry bar on it.

Brackets provide a nice balance between the flexibility of a cable and the security of bolts. With these products, you choose two or three locations to install permanent mounting hardware—such as a closet in your home, somewhere in your vehicle, and perhaps somewhere at work if you own your own business. Then you can easily move your "permanently mounted" box from one location to the other, unlocking the case to access wing nuts or other

---

77 GunVault, *www.gunvault.com*. *(877) 869-8373.*

hardware that allows you to make the change quickly and easily. Using this option provides good security in known locations.

Regardless of the mounting option you choose, you must keep your small box out of sight. A thief who knows of its presence will still find it much easier to defeat than a more secure full-size safe. If it's in a vehicle, affix it inside the console or trunk, or slide it under the seat. At home, choose a closet or other confined area to get the box out of sight and reduce the risk from pry bars.

Cable and Trigger Locks

If you have a choice between using a cable or trigger lock, or using nothing at all—use the lock! Such on-gun options do provide good security against accidental or negligent use, including access from children and the clueless. However, they do nothing to secure your firearms against a thief.

Of the two, cable locks have a decided safety advantage, because messing around near the trigger of an "unloaded" firearm simply asks for trouble. When using a cable lock, you begin by removing the magazine and locking the action open; it simply isn't possible to properly install a cable lock without unloading the firearm. Trigger locks, on the other hand, can easily be installed on loaded firearms although doing so is patently unsafe.

The Safest Storage of All

Although fast-access safes exist, a gun locked securely in a good safe will never allow truly immediate access; you must first get to the safe, then open it, before you can address the trouble. But if you need a defense gun at all, you will need it in a big hurry and no one is going to warn you in advance that you will need it. So you need to store the defense gun in a way that you can get at it very fast, but also without any chance of the children, the criminal, or the clueless getting their hands on it. The most secure option for doing that also happens to be the very quickest: you can keep the gun on your hip, loaded.

That's the decision I made several years ago. It sounds radical, but really was not. My husband often worked late, coming home after midnight. Our home is many miles from the nearest police station. In the event of a criminal invasion, it seemed likely I would be alone with the children when it happened, and the police would probably not arrive until the action was over. I wanted a firearm for home defense, but most of the ways to secure it seemed either too slow, or not secure enough. So I decided to carry my pistol almost all the time, even at home.

A handgun under the conscious control of a responsible adult may be considered safely secured from the children, the criminal, and the clueless. If I were unwilling to carry a gun on my hip at home, I would certainly get one or more quick-access safes which are specifically designed to store defense guns, and practice opening those safes until there was literally no way I could ever forget the combinations under stress. And if I weren't willing to do at least that much, I would not have a loaded gun in the house.

Finding Your Firearm

Dear Gunhilda,

I usually carry a .40 S&W, but lately I've been thinking about moving up to a .45 ACP. Why can't I get the guys in the gun stores to show me anything but .25s and .32s?

~ Undersized in Umatilla

Dear Undersized,

Try wearing a fake mustache when you shop.

~ Gunhilda

Gun Store Miss Adventures

When a woman purchases her first defensive handgun, she begins a personal journey that is often exciting and frequently bewildering, and it usually provides a few unexpected bumps and thrills along the way. Sometimes her journey starts with a traumatic event; more often, it is the outgrowth of life changes both big and small, or the doing of friends or family who urge her to set foot upon the path to determined self defense.

Facing such a life change, entering an unfamiliar subculture, and dragging along at least a little emotional baggage, it is no surprise that a woman in search of her first firearm might feel a bit overwhelmed the first time she steps into a gun shop. "My first steps into a gun shop seven years ago were with fear and trepidation. I knew I didn't belong there and had no business walking up those threadbare astro-turfed steps," admits concealed-carry permit holder Stephanie Cáceres. "I walked in with my eyes averted hoping no one would address me because I sure didn't know what I was going to say to them."

That's not an uncommon feeling for a woman entering such an unfamiliar world. It might even be the norm.

With a little help from my friends ...

When women reminisce about purchasing their first defensive firearms, friends and family often figure prominently in the stories. This is not surprising, since women are usually social creatures. Nor does this dynamic stop with the purchase of a gun; women are perhaps more likely than men to go to the range with friends than by themselves, and more likely to seek out social shooting events. The wonderful reality here is that good friends can often ease a new shooter's induction into gun ownership, and make that first gun-shopping experience much less traumatic.

After a home invasion left her battered, bruised, and feeling vulnerable, Cassandra, a pediatric nurse in Tennessee, called some friends in law enforcement for advice. "I called them thinking they'd tell me pepper spray or martial arts classes because they all knew how I felt about guns, but all of them said,

'We're going to teach you how to shoot. We're going to get you over this fear and you are going to own a gun.' It took several months to heal up from the attack, and then to get past the fear of guns, but I did it."

"They brought me lots of guns," says Cassandra of the friends who helped her. "I shot everything, just everything you can imagine. I had a lot of things to deal with and I needed to figure out what I was comfortable with, what fit my hand and what I was willing to practice with. They really helped expose me to a lot of different handguns." By the time she was ready to purchase her own firearm, she felt confident enough to make her own selection. "And then," she adds with a laugh, "my friends bought me a gun-warming gift—a bright purple range bag that I just love. And a box of ammo, and a cleaning kit."

Too much help?

Many women have discovered that even if they have a husband or friend willing to do the research legwork or even purchase a gun for them, it pays off to do your own shopping anyway. "My husband bought me my first gun," says Jennie van Tuyl, a gun owner in Washington. "We learned the hard way that one needs to be involved in the shopping for her own gun. I decided I needed a gun that fit my hand better and was easier to conceal." Many women could sing along on that chorus. The well-meant gift gun that ends up gathering dust in the back of the safe is very nearly a cliché. Almost as trite is the gun purchased by a loved one while the woman comes along as a silent partner rather than an active participant.

People behind the counter often feel frustration at this turn of events. Tamara Keel, former sales manager at Coal Creek Armory in Knoxville, Tennessee, says, "You know it just annoys me so much to have to elbow the man out of the way to make the sale to her. She's got to want the gun for herself and it's got to be what she wants, or it's just going to end up getting shoved into her nightstand drawer anyway." No matter how tempting to let someone else drive your handgun purchase, you are more likely to be happy with the end result when you drive the process yourself.

Bumps in the road ...

Christine Cunningham tells about her first handgun purchase: "The first store we went into, although it was obvious that I was looking at the guns in the counter, the guy working there ignored me and asked (my husband) Grant what he'd like to see. When it was pointed out to the clerk that I was the one looking for a gun, he gave me a very patronizing look, and then pulled out a snubnose .38 special, and said, 'Well, she might be able to handle this.' I still believe that my instant dislike of revolvers at that time was due to his attitude, and it took several years before I overcame that. When I said that I wanted a semi-auto instead, he then pulled out a very small .22 for me to see, and then turned away and ignored any further questions."

Even a professional who has worked within the firearms industry for many years is not entirely immune to such treatment. Tamara Keel wryly comments, "I had walked into a gun store, and my pockets were really flush. I was after an expensive 1911. I walked in and I stood at that counter for probably a good 30 minutes. The guys behind the counter milled back and forth, talked to each other, joked around with each other. They were helping guys who walked up on either side of me. I was standing there, literally with a roll of hundred dollar bills in my pocket, and they just did everything they could to ignore me. I finally walked out and never did buy anything from them. They're out of business now."

"You're going to love this one," longtime handgun owner Diane Walls told me. "I just went to the gun show last weekend. We were looking at mostly collectibles in a display case and there was this little tiny .22 revolver that was quite small and rather elderly looking. The guy behind the counter said, 'That's just the thing for a little lady like you. You could put birdshot in it and pop your husband in the butt when he acts up!'"

While there is no shortage of women who tell similar stories, this kind of treatment isn't the norm. A more typical, though less memorable, shopping story: "I had a very nice experience buying my gun," says Jennie van Tuyl. "Bill and I went to Bullseye in Tacoma [where] a woman who works there... made it a fun experience for me. I had learned what I liked and did not like from shooting other people's guns." Other women praised their own local gun shops for taking extra time with them on their purchases, explaining firearm function and offering extra goodies—everything from discounts on holsters, to free range time, to cleaning kits, to invitations to join classes and shooting leagues. When shopping for a gun, it is worthwhile to seek out and support such shops.

What's a woman to do?

Stephanie Cáceres admits, "In retrospect, I know that any 'little lady' treatment I thought I received was either imagined or self-inflicted. The owner's wife and daughter both work at the shop.... I know that I myself promoted the initial 'helpless damsel in distress' aura because I *was* in distress and I *was* feeling helpless."

Gila Hayes, of the Firearms Academy of Seattle, has some advice for women who fear facing discrimination when shopping for a handgun, or who feel overwhelmed by the task. Do your homework first, she suggests. "You could think, 'I'm a woman trying to do this in a man's arena, poor me, I just know I'm going to get treated badly,' and you could give up. Wouldn't it be better, though, to think, 'I know this could be challenging, so in advance I'm going to read everything I can, learn the vocabulary, and I'm going to find someone who knows about guns who will answer my questions.' Then you need to keep at it until you get the information you need and until you get explanations you can understand."

Along the same lines, former gun salesman Larry Correia says, "You need to know what you're looking for. Even if you don't know what brand or type, walk in knowing what you will want to do with that gun—what you're buying it for, whether it's for carry or for home defense or for a combination of things. Be confident, and don't let the salesman boss you around."

This process of doing your research may very well take you to several gun stores until you find a good match, but the time invested in it is also time spent developing relationships and resources that will serve you well in the long run.

Like each of the other women I talked to when writing this chapter, Cassandra says she has had both good and bad experiences in gun stores, but she prefers to emphasize the good. "Some gun stores just go out of their way to support women shooters. We should really reward that kind of good behavior." And on that, I think we can all agree!

How to Choose a Firearm

Shopping for your first firearm can be exciting, overwhelming, confusing, frustrating—or pure fun. It all depends on how much homework you've done beforehand and what expectations you have when you walk into the gun store.

To improve your chances of having fun while shopping, let's first talk about trade offs. Every firearm provides a balance between desirable features. Despite ad slogans to the contrary, no firearm offers perfection or suitability for all tasks. Picture the trade offs as a type of seesaw, with the balance point between competing features a moving variable depending on the user's needs. For example, carrying a concealed handgun feels best when the handgun weighs very little. So place *light weight* at one end of the choices seesaw. But at the other end of the same seesaw, *shooting comfort* sits. That's because smaller, lighter guns always provide more recoil than their heavier counterparts—and also because as the firearm's size shrinks, so do the number of comfort features that will fit on it without increasing its size or adding extra weight.

What's that got to do with shopping fun? It's like this: if you enter the store with unrealistic expectations, you're bound for disappointment. But a balanced understanding of what's possible helps keep your expectations in check and reduces frustration.

What do you need?

The first question any sensible salesperson will ask is, "What are you looking for today?" Of course, when you enter the store, you won't necessarily know which models you're after. But you should be able to explain how you intend to use the firearm and which features you like.

If you'd like to purchase a handgun for learning to shoot, that's a very different mission from finding a handgun for concealed carry. The ideal learning handgun features gentle recoil, soft springs, easily-reached controls, excellent sights, a long barrel and a full grip. But the ideal carry gun requires light weight, a solid caliber, minimal controls to reduce snagging, and adequate sights—all in the most compact package possible. The ideal features appropriate to a good carry gun usually produce stiff springs, harsher recoil, and a reduced grip size, all drawbacks to avoid on a learning gun. With these starkly competing needs, finding a dual-purpose gun often becomes a frustrating search for contradictory goals.

Here are some features and their polar opposites. Your pre-shopping homework: choose your own ideal balance between these opposites, keeping the purpose of the firearm in mind.

Opposites

Light weight —	**Heavy weight**
More pleasant to carry	*Less felt recoil*
Easier to hold on target	*More pleasant to shoot*
Short barrel —	**Long barrel**
Easier to conceal	*Easier to shoot accurately*
Lighter weight	*Easier to shoot at long distance*
Short grip —	**Full grip**
Easier to conceal	*More comfortable to shoot*
Can fit small hands better	*Holds more ammunition (semi-auto)*
Short slide —	**Long slide**
More compact for carry	*Softer springs = easier to rack*
Small overall size —	**Full size**
Easier to conceal	*Easier to control muzzle direction*
Cuter	*More complete features*
Snag free controls —	**Larger controls**
Smoother draw	*Easier to reach*
Less wear on skin & clothing	*Faster to manipulate*
Stiff trigger —	**Light trigger**
Reduced risk of mishaps	*Easier to shoot well*

Although at first glance it may appear that one size always works better than the other, this isn't true. The "goodness" or "badness" of the size really depends on your goals when you purchase. If you aspire to acquire a handgun that will always be with you, you can probably cross full-size handguns off your shopping list. On the other hand, if you aim to become an accomplished shooter, avoid small guns, because a tiny little handgun will definitely impede your progress. And if your purpose includes *both* concealed carry *and* learning to shoot, consider purchasing a dedicated firearm in the appropriate size for each task.

Counting the cost

You can realistically expect to spend a minimum of $400 on a concealable defensive handgun, up to roughly twice that amount.[78] Budget another $200 for accessories such as a solid belt and a holster, ear muffs, good eyewear, spare magazines or speedloaders, a range bag, and cleaning supplies. Nearly all accessories may be purchased some time after you've bought the gun, but eye protection and ear protection won't wait. Targets, range fees, and ammunition are an ongoing expense. Some calibers are more expensive than others, but no matter which caliber you choose, the cost of ammunition will soon rival the cost of the gun itself. If money matters to you, factor in the cost of ammunition while shopping for your firearm.

Semi-automatic or revolver?

You will find vigorously enthusiastic proponents of both firearms types everywhere gun owners hang out. Read and learn as much about this as possible and listen to what people say. As you evaluate the arguments, ask yourself what kind of gun owner you intend to be. Will you practice regularly? Will you learn to shoot well and run the gun safely? Will you clean your firearm regularly? Every gun requires some level of knowledge, but some guns are more complex than others.

Do not allow yourself to be swayed by generalities that may not apply to you personally. For example, a lot of old timers still believe women do not have enough strength to run the slide of a semi-automatic handgun and will tell you not to get a semi-auto because of that. But if you know you can run a slide, there's no reason to let yourself be swayed by this particular argument—though of course you might choose a revolver for other reasons. Keep what applies to you and throw the rest away.

Neither revolvers nor semi-autos are perfect for everyone. Each has unique strengths. Would you be surprised to hear that choosing between them might create a trade-off? The right choice for you depends on your personal priorities. By definition, your personal priorities are *personal.* You're the only one who can set them in the ideal order for your life and lifestyle. But here are some factors you might consider:

Ammunition: Semi-automatics usually carry more ammunition, and they are easier to reload. While no one really envisages fighting off a horde of invading zombies, you may need to shoot a determined attacker multiple times before he goes down. And he might have buddies. A revolver will often allow the user to load two different types of ammunition (such as .38 Special and .357 Magnum). This allows greater flexibility, because you can choose a

---

78 Guesstimate based on firearms prices as of spring 2010.

soft-recoiling round for practice while choosing a hard hitter for defense.⁷⁹

Budget: When shopping, it is easier to check out a used revolver than it is to inspect a used semi-auto without firing the gun. Revolvers are also less likely to suffer non-obvious problems that affect function.

Cleaning: To clean a revolver, you don't need to disassemble it. But you must learn how to take the semi-auto apart and put it back together in order to clean it properly. However, once you've learned that, it's usually faster and easier to clean a semi-auto than it is to clean a revolver.

Ease of use: Revolvers have fewer moving parts than semi-autos. But a semi-auto is less complicated than a washing machine or a car, and every normal adult in America can understand both of those complex machines at least well enough to run them.⁸⁰

Hand strength issues: Conventional wisdom says racking the slide of a semi-automatic takes a lot of hand strength. It isn't always quite that clear-cut. I've met many women who couldn't manage a double-action revolver trigger but easily learned to rack a semi-auto slide once shown the correct technique. If hand strength (or the lack of it) troubles you, try both types of firearms before ruling either out.

Recoil: All other things being equal, a semi-automatic generally produces less perceived recoil than a revolver of equal weight and power. That's because the slide movement absorbs some of the energy.

Reliability: Comparing modern, quality semi-automatics with modern, quality revolvers, there's no appreciable difference in reliability. However, if you choose a semi-automatic, you will need to learn how to clear a misfeed and a doublefeed. These malfunctions happen only to semi-automatics. Revolvers rarely experience a simple malfunction such as these. If a revolver fails to fire, there's a simple cure: pull the trigger again. But if pulling the trigger a second time does not cure the problem, it may be necessary to take the gun to a gunsmith. Revolvers rarely choke, but when they do it often

---

79 *To be fair, you can choose different rounds for defense and practice with a semi-auto too. But not to the same extent that a revolver allows.*
80 *Though a few people always like to pretend they can't. Not that we're bitter about that.*

requires the help of a trained professional.

Sights: Semi-automatics often (but not always) have the advantage here. A lot of revolvers have low-contrast sights which are little more than nearly invisible bumps on the front of the gun. Of course, that problem isn't unique to revolvers, nor are all revolvers like that. But you definitely need to consider the sights when evaluating a gun for its self defense potential.

Choosing a caliber

Ammunition does cost money. If you want to learn to shoot safely and well, you will burn up lots of ammunition. If you are reluctant to shoot because of the cost, you won't practice as much as you ought. So take the cost of practice into account as you are shopping for a gun.

Most knowledgeable firearms instructors will tell you that good defensive handgun calibers are bracketed by .380 Auto at the lower end and .45 ACP at the upper end. Within those upper and lower limits, you will find many different calibers and a huge selection of firearms. Unless you have a strong reason to do otherwise, try to choose a gun that falls between those parameters.

Small calibers usually launch more comfortably than larger ones. But not always. The firearm design affects how we perceive both recoil and noise. For example, a straight-blowback .380 ACP design often produces more unpleasant recoil than a larger caliber launched from a different design. Try to fire lots of guns in different calibers before making decisions about your preferences. Some people cannot sample firearms because they can't find a rental range in their area. If this applies to you, I suggest limiting your choice to either a .38 Special (revolver) or a 9mm (semi-auto). Both fuel many different guns, both fall solidly within the defensive handgun power bracket, and both are easy on beginners.[81]

How much ammunition should the gun carry?

The larger the firearm's capacity, the more difficult it becomes to conceal. In a semi-auto, the more ammunition it can hold, the larger its grip becomes; this can be a decisive point for folks with smaller hands. On the other hand, if you do need to use the gun to defend yourself, it seems rather unlikely that you'll be standing there at the end of the encounter saying, "Darn it! I wish I hadn't had quite so much ammunition!" Look for a happy medium.

---

81 *To take full advantage of this recommendation, avoid superlight handguns and stick to mid-weight or full-weight ones.*

Safeties

Shopping for a semi-auto, you might wonder if you want an external, manually operated safety. My carry gun does not have one, because as a newcomer watching experienced shooters, I saw that even skilled people sometimes missed flicking the safety off when they were rushed. For safety, I decided to pour my energy into training rather than rely on a mechanical device that could fail. Some of my friends carry guns with external safeties because they like the extra security. How strongly you feel about this question might help you narrow down your prospects.

Triggers and Actions

Triggers and actions relate to each other in an interesting way. The type of trigger pull you prefer will often tell you which type of action to choose.

Double Action Only (DAO)	=	*Medium to heavy pull*
Double Action/Single Action (DA/SA)	=	*Heavy pull (first shot)*
		Light pull (subsequent shots)
Single Action (SA)	=	*Light pull*
Striker-fired	=	*Medium pull*

While shopping, ask permission to dry fire, pulling the trigger without any ammunition in the gun (be sure to check and double check that the gun is unloaded). Dry firing lets you check how different triggers feel to you. Pull the trigger very, very slowly and pay attention to how it feels. You'll probably have to pull the trigger more than once, perhaps five or six times, before you are satisfied you have felt what you needed to feel. And you will need to feel the triggers on several different types of guns before you really grasp how these differences work. But the education you can give yourself doing this is very valuable, and doing this homework means you will probably save a great deal of trouble by picking a firearm that suits you well.

Testing a trigger

When dry firing, how far does the trigger travel before you hear the click of the hammer fall—a short distance, or a long one? Is the trigger's movement stiff and hard to move ("heavy"), or is it easy to pull ("light")? Can you feel crunchy bits of mechanical movement happening inside the firearm while the trigger is moving, or is the trigger pull smooth? Does the way the trigger moves feel the same throughout its journey, or is it heavier toward the end of the pull?

Try lining the sights up on a small spot in your safe direction, and pull the trigger again. Can you easily keep the sights lined up while the trigger is moving? Or is the trigger so heavy that you pull the sights off target because you must strain to move the trigger? Do you think you would be able to pull the trigger again and again and again, fifty or more times in a row, to practice shooting this gun? Or would your finger wear out before you were able to do that?

For those with weak hands, a heavy trigger often becomes a big problem. I have worked with shooters who literally could not keep the sights aligned with the target while pulling the trigger. I have met people who could not fire a heavy trigger fast. I have even seen people who could not pull a heavy trigger three times in a row. Nobody needs to endure such struggles. The way to avoid them? Choose a firearm with a trigger pull suited for your hand strength.

Trying on a Gun

Before you plunk down your hard-earned money for a handgun—especially a defense handgun—you need to make sure it will fit your hand.

First, check by sight and by feel to be sure the gun is unloaded. For semi-automatics, remove the magazine and run a finger into the magazine well to make sure it is empty. Lock the slide open and look in the chamber. Then run the tip of a finger into the chamber to be sure it's empty. Visually check the chamber again before you close the slide. For revolvers, open the cylinder and visually count the holes. Then run your finger over the holes and count them again by feel. Count them again before closing the cylinder.

Now that you've unloaded the gun, you're almost ready to check its fit. First, a tip: do not cock double-action revolvers or DA/SA semi-automatics, because doing so moves the location of the trigger in relation to the rear of the gun. That means the trigger is not in the same place it would be when you first pick up the gun. You want to know how the gun will fit when you grab it in a hurry—not how it fits under ideal conditions.

Now, with the gun pointed in a safe direction that includes a safe backstop, put the first crease of your trigger finger on the trigger. Do not use the tip or the pad of your finger. *Without pulling the trigger back,* wrap the rest of your hand around the gun to get a good, one-handed firing grip. Now look at how the gun fits in your hand.

A Perfect Fit

If the gun's backstrap firmly centers in the web of your hand, midway between your thumb and forefinger, the gun fits your hand perfectly. A correctly-sized gun lines up perfectly with the bones in your forearm. The recoil will push directly into the web of the hand and be transferred along the long bones of the arm, allowing a strong and natural grip without strain.

Small Gun

If your hand has a lot of extra slack, with your trigger finger curving out from the side of the gun (so that you would be able to put a large portion of your trigger finger through the trigger guard if you wanted to), then the gun is small for your hand.

A small gun still lines up well with forearm bones. And small guns are rarely too small for effective shooting, so don't let this deter you if it's otherwise suitable. Unless you find the gun radically undersized, you can easily adapt. But you will need to pay special attention that you don't get too much of your finger on the trigger while firing.

Too Large

If you cannot center the gun's backstrap in the web of your hand, midway between thumb and forefinger joints, the gun is too big for you. A too-large gun does *not* line up nicely with forearm bones, and the recoil directs itself into the thumb joint rather than into the web of the hand.

Provided you can reach and use all the controls, you can probably work with a slightly large gun. You can try scootching your hand around just a little, so the backstrap rides slightly off-center while your finger is on the trigger. Or—on guns where this is an option—you might have a gunsmith install a shortened trigger, which will reduce the distance between trigger and backstrap.[82]

However, if you find the gun uncomfortably large for your hand, the recoil will drive into your basal thumb joint when your finger rests on the trigger properly. A really oversized gun prevents a secure hold and it will probably be painful to fire a lot of rounds as the recoil batters the base of your thumb. Even if it doesn't hurt, it can cause joint problems and isn't worth it in the long run. You will need to look for a different gun.

Reaching for controls

After checking for grip fit, also check to be sure you can reach *and use* all the gun's controls.

---

82 *If you do this, be especially aware of whether you can reach all important controls. Changing the reach to the trigger does not change the location of other controls.*

- **Thumb safety:** You *absolutely must* be able to flick the safety off with the thumb of your firing hand. If you cannot flick the safety off with your firing hand, that's a deal-killer.
- **Slide Lock / Slide Release:** You *must* be able to lock the slide back without extreme effort. To do this, you must be able to keep a solid grip on the gun while lifting up on the slide lock lever with your dominant thumb. It is okay if you need to shift your hand a little so you can reach the lever. But it is not okay if you need to shift your hand so far that you cannot lift up on the slide lock *and* run the slide at the same time.
- **Magazine release:** You *should* be able to press the magazine release with your dominant thumb without losing your firing grip. If you cannot, that's bad but you may be able to work around it. Try scootching your hand around so you can reach. If you absolutely can't, even after practice, that's a deal-killer.
- **Decocker:** You *should* be able to reach the decocker. But you can use your non-dominant thumb if you need to.

Just as you would try on a pair of shoes before buying them, if it is at all possible, try to fire the gun or one like it before you purchase. Many gun stores and ranges have rental guns. While rental fees can be expensive, paying such fees can often save considerable money in the long run because of the mistakes thus avoided.

Parting shots

As you can see, there are lots of variables to think over, and some of the variables are very personal. Don't get discouraged at what seems to be a complicated process! As you consider and research the questions above, you will soon find a type of gun that you gravitate toward. That will make it much easier when you walk into the store to make your final selection, because you'll find that the formerly bewildering array of guns behind the counter has resolved itself into a manageable collection of specific firearm types that you can consider at your leisure.

And shopping will be fun.

Holsters and Concealed Carry

Dear Gunhilda,

Our son left for college this morning and in cleaning out his room I found an old audio tape which featured the songs of a really annoying purple dinosaur. When our son was a toddler, he forced us to listen to that tape in the car all the way from Dallas, Texas to our new home in Minot, North Dakota.

Should I take the tape to the range with me? If so, which gun should I use? I have a 9mm handgun, a .22LR rifle, and a 20-gauge shotgun.

~ Vindictive in Vacaville

Dear Vindictive,

No flamethrower?

~Gunhilda

What's a Holster For, Anyway?

The key to evaluating holster safety is to first understand the purpose of a holster. What is a holster designed to do? Why do we use them? Once we've understood the holster's purpose, understanding the elements that create a safe or an unsafe design becomes a lot easier.

To keep the firearm secured

Holsters serve several purposes. First and foremost, the holster keeps the firearm safely secured. The specific manner in which this security is achieved will vary from holster to holster or from carry system to carry system, so don't get too hung up on specific design features. Focus instead on the primary goal: to keep the firearm secured.

Ideally, once the firearm is placed within the holster or carry system, there should be *no way* for the firearm to unexpectedly discharge—whether by the user's wayward finger or by external happenstance. As a general rule for modern firearms, this means the trigger and the entire trigger guard area *must be* enclosed or encased, and the material surrounding the trigger must be sturdy enough to prevent outside activity from moving the trigger. This is true no matter which type of carry system is used. If the gun is carried in a pocket, the trigger *must be* protected from external movement just as surely as it would be if it were carried in a belt holster. If it is placed within a purse, the trigger must remain as protected as if it were in an ankle holster. Allowing the firearm to float around loosely within an oversized compartment, with trigger uncovered and vulnerable to pressure from keys, pens, coins, and other detritus, is simply asking for trouble. It is much safer to choose a carry method which allows the firearm to ride in stately isolation within a sturdy enclosure which prevents external pressure from reaching the trigger, and which holds the firearm in essentially the same orientation until we choose to retrieve it.

With the trigger covered or otherwise protected from external influences, we know that the firearm will remain a safe and inert object as long as it remains within the holster. But how do we know that the gun will remain within the holster until such time as we deliberately take it out?

For standard belt holsters, one simple test of whether the holster meets this design requirement is the *tip test*. To perform this test, take an unloaded gun. Check to be sure it is unloaded, and unload if necessary. Remove all ammunition from the room and check the gun again to be sure it is still unloaded. Then place the unloaded gun into the holster, securing any straps or retention devices, and hold the holster a few inches above a soft surface such as a couch or bed. Slowly tip the holster upside down and shake gently. Does the gun fall out or does it stay where it should? If the gun falls out of the holster when the holster is tipped upside down and gently shaken, that holster does *not* meet this primary holster purpose of holding the gun securely.

Obviously, not every carry method can be checked with the simple tip test. But for most on-body carry methods, it is a good place to start.

If the tip test is not readily viable for your carry method, try a more active approach. First unload the firearm using the procedure above, then place the firearm into your holster or carry system just as if you were preparing to carry it as normal. Now, do some calisthenics. Do a few jumping jacks. Jog in place. Touch your toes. Do a somersault, even. Get down on the floor and roll around a little, as if you were wrestling with someone. (Got a dog? They love this part!) Does the firearm remain securely in place or is it working its way out of your holster or carry system? Remember, in many situations where activity dislodges the firearm, you won't be able to put a steadying hand on the gun to prevent it from working its way completely out and falling to the ground. If your holster or carry system does not keep the gun where it should be with no extra help from you, it fails this test.

For those who read the paragraph just before this one and shook their heads, figuring that they would never be all *that* active anyway, remember that children and grandchildren often expect their adult cohorts to play with them, to bend over to comfort them, to reach down and help untie the knotted shoelace. Even an ordinarily sedentary person might be coaxed into a short

---

A SAFE Carry System

- ☑ Securely holds the gun.
- ☑ Accomodates every feature of the firearm, so that retention straps or other controls do not interfere with the proper function of safety devices on the gun.
- ☑ Firmly protects the trigger with materials that are rigid enough to prevent external pressure from moving the trigger.
- ☑ Encloses the trigger and entire trigger guard area.

but vigorous sprint when the family dog is headed toward the street, or when scurrying to catch up with a young family member toddling toward danger. And finally, if a criminal grabs you from behind, will you remain in a calmly upright position, or would you perhaps become a little more active in your quest to free yourself and access your firearm? For these reasons and many more, holsters must be designed to hold their firearms securely in place.

To keep the firearm comfortably concealed

Although many holsters are designed for open carry on the range or in the field, our subject here is concealed carry. For us, one of the primary purposes of the holster is to help us keep the gun hidden from prying eyes.

There are two basic ways that a holster can do this. First, the holster can ride underneath the clothing so it becomes *literally* invisible to others. Belt holsters may feature strategically-placed belt loops to help bring the gun more tightly to the waist; they may be designed to allow the user to tuck a shirt over the top of the grip; they may be designed to cant the gun or to ride slightly higher on the beltline so that the cover garment needn't be overly long. Together with sensible clothing choices, such holsters become invisible and keep firearms invisible to others.

The other way a holster or carry system might keep the gun concealed is to make the carry system *functionally* invisible through effective camouflage. For example, a purse or waist pack can usually be seen by others. But a well-designed carry purse can conceal a pistol compartment. Similarly, if the waist pack effectively matches the circumstances in which it is carried, others' eyes slide past without truly seeing what they are looking at. The gun remains undetected even though the carry method hides in plain sight.

When we choose a holster or carry method which is uncomfortable, concealment becomes more difficult. It is human nature to fidget or scratch, to fiddle with the thing that's making us uncomfortable—and every time the user's hand is drawn to the firearm, others' eyes are drawn right along with it. If the carry method is uncomfortable enough, the gun will be left at home despite our best intentions. For this reason, comfortable concealment is a crucial aspect of holster or carry system design.

To keep the firearm accessible

When shopping for a new holster, most of us ask ourselves, "How well can I *carry and conceal* my firearm with this holster?" As soon as we can tote the gun around with us, we're satisfied. This makes good sense because, after all, carrying and concealing the firearm is our everyday experience. If the carry rig is uncomfortable or poorly concealed, we notice it and take pains to correct it. But when we ask that, another crucial question gets overlooked far too often. That question is, "How well can I *access and use* my firearm with this holster?" After all, an otherwise-excellent holster which holds the firearm securely, fits comfortably, and allows us to easily conceal wouldn't be excellent at all if we couldn't get to the gun when we need it.

While it is true that trade-offs will nearly always be present, that doesn't mean they're not trade-offs. In search of the perfect, comfortable carry method, people tend to forget that the whole reason they're putting up with that lumpy, heavy, uncomfortable bulge is so they can *use* it if necessary. If you've compromised on carry methods or equipment to the point where the gun is no longer readily accessible, to where you cannot realistically practice with the setup you actually use, to where drawing the gun involves bodily contortions worthy of a Houdini and requires more time than it takes for the cops to arrive, you might as well get that troublesome lump off your body and leave it in the safe. If you've compromised to the point where the gun you carry has shrunk to little more than a piece of jewelry, a miniature talisman against evil which has little effective power and which is too tiny to practice with, you might as well sprinkle fairy dust on your shoulders to ward off criminals.

To test for ready accessibility, unload the gun as previously described. Enlist the help of a friend. Pick a safe direction—one that would definitely stop a bullet. Clap your hands (this forces you into a good start position) and then draw your gun. Have your friend start counting at the sound of the clap. Your draw should be smoothly complete before two seconds pass. You should be able to do this from both standing and seated, wearing the clothing you ordinarily wear, with your carry rig set up as you ordinarily wear it. No cheating!

The purpose of a holster is to safely secure the firearm, to comfortably conceal the firearm, and to keep the firearm readily accessible for rapid use. Any holster or carry system that meets these requirements is a good one. Those which fall short on any one of these crucial considerations should be avoided.

Holsters & the Four Rules

The other day, I received an intriguing question in my email. In a nutshell, my correspondent wanted to know, "How can the Four Rules apply while the gun is holstered, since many holsters seem to point the weapon in unsafe directions?"

The second of these Four Rules is the crucial one here: "Never point the gun at anything you are not willing to destroy." This rule applies every time you pick up, hold, or put down a firearm. While you are holding the gun, you never deliberately or cluelessly let it point at stuff you don't want holes in. But what about muzzle direction when you are not directly holding the gun?

A gun, by itself, is inert. There is no rational reason to fear a loaded gun lying on the kitchen table as long as no one is touching it.[83] Gun shop customers do not need to

> ### The Four Rules
>
> 1. All guns are always loaded.
>
> 2. Never point the gun at anything you are not willing to destroy.
>
> 3. Keep your finger off the trigger until your sights are on target (and you have made the decision to shoot).
>
> 4. Be sure of your target and what's beyond.

worry about a gun of unknown state (loaded? unloaded?) which is behind a gunshop counter, no matter which direction the gun is pointed, as long as no one is touching it. An untouched firearm is only a *thing*. It is not a living creature with a mind or a will of its own.

The risk comes when humans enter the picture. Because humans are prone to accidents and mistakes, the gun must be pointed in a safe direction whenever human hands touch it. If you cannot pick a firearm up without pointing it in an unsafe direction (or if it is already pointed in an unsafe direction), you should not put your hand on it. If you cannot put a firearm down without pointing it in an unsafe direction, you should not put it down. This is necessary because the mixture of human hand and unsafe direction can cause bad stuff to happen.

Muzzle orientation really doesn't matter *while the user's hand is not on the gun.* A gun held securely inside a trigger-covering holster, which is not being handled by a human being, is as safe and inert as one which is lying on the table untouched. But notice the italics. The real danger comes when the gun is being placed into, or withdrawn from, the holster, because that is the point at which human hands get involved in the process. With some holsters, such as a dropped and offset outside the waistband holster worn on the point of the hip, it takes a near-determined effort of will to cover oneself with the firearm. Yet this sort of rig isn't easily concealed and thus isn't practical for those who

---

83 *Please note the exception! If there is a possibility of children, the criminal, or the clueless picking the gun up, it's not safe just lying there. But as long as none of those pesky and unpredictable human beings come on the scene, the gun isn't going to do anything on its own.*

want to carry a concealed firearm.

With care, the risk of pointing the gun in an unsafe direction during the process of getting the gun into or out of its holster can be greatly minimized. This deliberate action takes a very conscious effort of will, and should never become a matter of complacency. One example of minimizing the risk would be the careful process of safely holstering and unholstering with a shoulder holster. Most smart folks I know who carry with one of these rigs make a conscious effort to raise the left elbow while drawing with the right hand. This moves the brachial artery away from the risk of inadvertent discharge.[84]

> **Important!**
>
> Any time you must come close to violating one of the Four Rules, let that be a red flag to slow down and pay special attention to all the other rules.
>
> The safety rules should be so engrained in your habits and thoughts that it should take a deliberate, conscious act of the will to do anything near the line.

Another example: Since I carry my inside the waistband holster in the appendix carry position, I never reholster while sitting down. If I did so, the gun's muzzle would be pointed directly at my femoral artery while I handled the gun—a dangerous combination! So I'm very conscious of where my trigger finger is while I am reholstering, and hold my trigger finger far outside the trigger guard. I put my right leg slightly to the rear, suck my gut in, and lean back slightly while reholstering. This allows me to angle the muzzle away from me during the process. I'm always very conscious of the risk while reholstering, and never reholster in a hurry.

The combination of human hand plus loaded gun is dangerous. Every carry method allows the gun to point at stuff you don't want shot, and there's simply no way around that fact. For safety's sake, remember that if the gun is pointed in an unsafe direction, *you* must never be the one doing the pointing.

For more detailed information about safe holster use, including photos of safety challenges and solutions, visit the Cornered Cat website and read the "Safety Matters" articles in the Holster section.[85] If you are uncertain whether you have been using your holster safely, contact a qualified instructor to talk about specific concerns.

---

84 *It does not, however, reduce the danger to people standing behind or to the left. Always be aware of your surroundings as you draw.*
85 *See www.CorneredCat.com. Follow the links from the main index to the Holsters section.*

How Do I Hide This Thing?
An Overview of Options

Holster designs fall into two wide categories: on-body and off-body. On-body holsters allow you to carry the firearm underneath your outer clothing, while off-body designs allow you to tote it in a purse, pack, or other device. There's some slight overlap between the two main categories.

Off-Body Carry	On and Off: Pocket Carry	On-Body Carry
Purse	*Pants or Shorts pockets*	*Ankle Holster*
Fanny Pack or Waist Pack	*Jacket or Vest pockets*	*Belly Band*
Daytimer or Briefcase	*Jacket or Vest with built-in holster*	*Belt—IWB Holster*
		Belt—OWB Holster
		Bra Holster
		Kangaroo Pouch
		Shoulder Holster
		Thigh Band
		Undershirt Holster

Off-Body Carry

Carrying off-body, in a purse or a pack, sounds great at first. In theory, no wardrobe adjustments will be needed, and if you need to enter someplace where firearms aren't allowed, you can discreetly lock your bag in the car. But off-body carry creates significant trade offs you need to understand before you make a commitment to carry in this manner.

No matter how careful and dedicated you are, off-body carry cannot secure the firearm as well as on-body carry. Purses, packs, and daytimers often get set down and occasionally forgotten. If you ever leave your bag where another person can access it, the odds are very high that you will be "made"— that is, that other people will discover you carry a gun. This can range from embarrassing to disastrous, depending on where you are and who found out.

Off-body carry can be much more socially awkward than carrying on the body. Few people make a habit of carrying a pack with them literally *everywhere* they go—even to walk from one room to the other. When visiting a friend's home, for example, most women set their purses down somewhere, and don't think of it again until it is time to leave. If a firearm is hidden within the purse, leaving it casually lying around like this is simply not an option, but continually keeping your purse slung over your shoulder or balanced on your lap is likely to earn you an odd look.

Purses, bags, and packs are also frequently targeted by thieves. In some situations, the best survival tactic might be to simply hand over your belongings and be a good witness. But since most people are not willing to simply hand a firearm to a known criminal, carrying a firearm inside the purse limits your choices.

Furthermore, at a single glance, many criminals will recognize a concealed-carry waist pack or purse for what it is. Those who do might decide to look for easier prey, but if they instead decide to attack, the element of surprise may not be on your side.

Drawing the gun from most off-body options is usually very slow, and sometimes prone to fumbly-fingered mistakes. A properly designed waist pack, or a purse which holds the firearm in a vertical orientation, is an exception to this general rule. And, of course, regular practice can help you draw faster. But even a well-practiced purse or pack draw will never be as fast as drawing from an on-body holster carried near the waist.

Purse

Safety Issue

If you carry in a purse, you *must* use a dedicated compartment which contains the gun, the gun only, and only the gun. If there's other stuff in the same compartment, you could end up with a lipstick tube levering the trigger back and firing an unintentional shot when you sling the purse over your shoulder.

Probably the most common off-body carry method for women, purse carry has a lot going for it. Certainly a lot of women do not believe there is any other way they can carry a gun. It involves minimal changes to the way you're already living your life. You don't have to buy new clothes or figure out how to make your existing wardrobe work with an altered waistline. Most women already carry a purse, and putting a gun in there doesn't usually feel like a hugely invasive change. Furthermore, when dressed up for church or a party, there often really-and-truly *isn't* anywhere else to reasonably hide a gun except in a purse. Concealed carry and female dress clothes can be a very awkward match. But do you really want to dance while carrying your purse? If not, where will you leave it, and will the person you leave it with be aware there's a gun inside?

The best purse for concealed carry has been specifically designed to tote the gun. Such purses have dedicated compartments, often with adjustable, built-in holsters intended to hold the gun securely in the correct orientation. They usually have wide, sturdy straps so the added weight of the gun won't dig into your shoulder and destroy your nerves. The gun compartment often allows discreet access, allowing the carrier to get her hand onto the grip of the holstered gun (while walking through a parking lot, for example) with no one the wiser. Some of them even allow the user to lock the gun compartment separately with a clever little padlock built into the zipper.[86] More about this in a later chapter.

Waist Pack (Fanny Pack)

Let's get the fashion issue out of the way right up front. If you're wearing a waist pack, you have to wear the right clothes to go with it. Waist packs don't work with dress clothes. They don't belong in most offices and they look horrible with many everyday outfits. Waist packs work well in vacation areas, especially while wearing tourist-y clothes or exercise clothes… and that's really about it.

But waist pack carry has a lot going for it. It's very comfortable. It's more secure than most other methods of off-body carry. With the pack attached to your body, you're unlikely to set it down and walk away. It's also less socially awkward, because it isn't unusual to continue wearing the waist pack even while walking around indoors. Out of all off-body carry methods, a properly designed waist pack provides the quickest access to the gun if you need it in a hurry, and is least likely to create fumbles with the gun while drawing. That's a big plus.[87]

Good features to look for include:

- Light padding where the gun nestles against the tummy-side panel. This increases comfort and reduces floppiness.

---

86 *It's a good idea to fasten that clever little padlock if you set your purse down while you're inside your sister's home playing with her children. But it could be a safety issue of a different sort if you forget to unlock it when you leave, and then need the gun in a hurry to save your life.*

87 *Note that a standard waist pack, one not designed for concealed carry, does not share this advantage. It's slow and awkward and might even be dangerous.*

- Adjustable elastic or hook-and-loop straps in the gun compartment, to secure the gun in the orientation you prefer. This prevents internal flopping, and allows you to draw without fumbling.

- Fast-access zipper cord(s) allow the user to rip the entire pack open with a single movement and access the gun very quickly. Packs without this design feature are much slower in use.

- Ability to set up for either left-hand or right-hand access. Even those who are not currently ambidextrous are only one sprained wrist away from needing a weak-hand carry method.

- An extra, non-gun compartment for other stuff. If you have bulges in your pockets where you are toting wallet, keys, cell phone and other junk, you really give the game away. Try to keep this in perspective, though. Avoid bulky packs more than a few inches thick.

Daytimer or Briefcase

Slow. Awkward. *Very* likely to be in the wrong place if you need it in a hurry. But it's the only way some folks feel comfortable carrying a gun to the office. For lawyers or others who continually enter and exit secured buildings, it can work... provided there's somewhere safe to lock it up.

As with other methods of off-body carry, look for a product with a dedicated gun compartment which has adjustable straps to carry the gun in a stable and predictable orientation. The dedicated compartment isn't just a safety feature to prevent your ballpoint pens from nestling in the muzzle. It also serves to prevent accidental exposure when you need to open it up and use it as an actual daytimer. When considering a purchase, make sure the product you're looking at will do that part of the job properly, too.

Final caution: don't set that thing down, *anywhere*, unless the area is truly secure from all three Cs: children, the clueless, and the criminal.

On and Off: Pocket Carry

Properly speaking, pocket carry qualifies as on-body carry. However, carrying in a jacket or vest pocket has more in common with off-body carry than with the other forms of on-body carry because it is so easy to set your jacket down and become separated from your weapon.

Pocket carry is generally very convenient. During winter in colder climates, many people find they can draw much more quickly from an outer coat pocket than they can from a belt holster hidden underneath several layers of clothing. And during a hot summer, carrying in a shorts pocket while wearing a tank top can be much cooler than wearing the extra layer of cover garment most other forms of on-body carry require.

Except for those who habitually wear very baggy clothing, a pocket carry gun usually has to be quite tiny. And this leads us to the primary problem with pocket carry, a triple whammy: tiny guns usually come in marginally effective calibers, they are not often easy to shoot, and few people enjoy shooting them. Shot placement is important with any size weapon, but critically so in smaller calibers. In order to get good shot placement, you've got to get good at shooting your weapon. And in order to do *that*, you've got to spend time on the range. What this all adds up to is that if you want the convenience of carrying in a pocket, you will need to dedicate yourself to spending lots of time on the range getting good with a tiny gun which you may not enjoy shooting.

Because guys tend to wear looser pants than girls do, pants-pocket carry usually works considerably better for guys than it does for gals. A lot of women's pants don't even have pockets, and many of those that do feature vestigial pockets that are not deep enough to conceal a firearm. Because men tend to be wider at the waist and narrower at the hip, men's pants tend to fall loosely from the waist, creating a void where the firearm can ride without printing. But women tend to curve outward through the hip and upper thigh, making it difficult to conceal a firearm riding in a pants pocket. Of course this depends on your body type and preferred clothing style, but most women find it very difficult to carry in a pants pocket. Fortunately, jacket-pocket carry works equally well for both sexes.

Does pocket carry require a holster? Absolutely yes—unless the pocket itself is designed for secure concealed carry, such as those from CCW Breakaways.[88] Many companies produce holsters for pocket carry. A pocket holster disguises the outline of the gun, protects the gun from damage, holds it in a predictable and stable orientation so that drawing is easier, and most important, covers the trigger and trigger guard area to prevent negligent discharges.

A chilling story that was on the news a few years back: a young dad went to the movie theater on a weekend afternoon to catch a flick with his kids.

> **Safety Issue**
>
> If you carry a concealed handgun in a pocket, unless the pocket is specifically designed for secure concealed carry, you *must* have a pocket holster or other device to cover and protect the trigger.

---

88   At the time of this writing, however, the company was not producing pants in women's sizes. CCW Breakaways, PO Box 190, New Cumberland, PA 17070-0190. (717) 774-2152. www.CCWBreakaways.com.

He was carrying a handgun in his jacket pocket, an ordinary pocket without a retention strap, without a trigger guard, and without a pocket holster. He set the jacket on the seat next to him during the movie, and when the movie was over, he reached over to pick up his jacket. As he picked up his jacket, his finger or a piece of the material caught the trigger, and the gun fired. The bullet struck him in the abdomen, severely injuring him, and barely missed the head of a six-year-old who was standing behind him. Was this an accidental shooting? It was not. It was a *negligent* shooting, which happened because the young man was carrying his handgun in a dangerous manner. If you carry in a pocket, you need to protect the trigger. That's all there is to it.

Shirts, Vests or Jackets with built-in holsters

Several companies make shirts, vests, or jackets which have built-in holsters. Usually these holsters are located inside the front panels so that they can be easily accessed simply by reaching in to the front near the zipper or buttons, as one would reach for a wallet. Many of these designs are quite attractive, but remember that stylish is in the eye of the beholder.

Safety Issue
When drawing from a concealment vest or jacket, be extremely careful not to allow the muzzle to point at your own brachial artery. Lift your non-dominant elbow out of the way as you draw.

One motorcycle rider of my acquaintance frequently carries his sidearm in a black leather concealment vest he purchased from Coronado Leather. It works very well for him because when someone steps off a motorcycle, observers truly expect to see the black-leather "biker look." Because it's an expected part of the image, no one looks twice. That's a successful concealment rig!

One possible issue to consider is the weight of the gun. Because the gun will generally be carried in the front panel, most of its weight will be distributed along your neck and shoulders when you wear a vest or jacket with a built-in holster. If you are already prone to neck tension, this may not be the carry option for you. Fortunately, several companies—such as Concealed Carry Outfitters—produce vests which carry the weight of the gun directly beneath the arm; this eliminates neck strain and makes it quite possible to comfortably carry even a heavy gun.[89] The downside of this position, however, means that some folks find it difficult to draw when the gun rides on the non-dominant side of the body.

---

89 *Concealed Carry Outfitters, 1505 Cobblestone Drive, Lincoln, CA 95648. (916) 672-8721. www.concealedcarryoutfitters.com.*

It can be very hard to find a wearable product that really fits your body. The size, shape, and length of your torso—including the shape of your bosom—will affect how easily you are able to conceal a firearm in a holstered clothing product worn on the torso. This goes double for products that place the firearm high underneath one arm.

Additionally, and in common with all off-body carry methods, you must make provision for what to do with your gun-toter when you are not wearing it. If you take your jacket or vest off, you *must* carefully consider where you set it down and who will have access to it. Be aware that even a well-designed jacket or vest which is not being worn and has a gun inside it should never be handled roughly lest a mishap result.

On-Body Carry

No matter how attractive off-body carry might seem, carrying on the body has definite and indisputable advantages. First, no matter what happens, you know the gun will be with you when you need it. Even if you carry your purse with you *nearly* everywhere you go, there is still the chance that your purse, and the gun inside it, might be sitting on a chair clear across the room if you need it in a hurry. Most on-body carry methods are more quickly accessible than most off-body carry methods. If you need to pull the gun out in a hurry, you are less likely to fumble when drawing from a belt holster than you are when rummaging through a pack or purse. Worse, if your pack or bag has a built-in lock, there's just the off chance you locked it at your last stop and forgot to unlock it. Carrying on-body is generally more secure than off-body carry methods. Because the gun is strapped right to your own personal body, you will surely notice and prevent anyone from accessing it without your permission. There's very little chance of children, the clueless, or the criminal getting into it without your knowledge.

The chief drawback to most forms of on-body carry is that it can be very uncomfortable to wear a gun everywhere you go. While it's tempting to recite Clint Smith's dicta here ("A gun is supposed to be comforting, not comfortable"), few people are willing to make the commitment to carry a gun when it is not comfortable to do so. The comfort factor can be improved by choosing the proper gun, by selecting a quality holster, and by careful choice of clothing.

Hmmm, let me repeat that last bit, a little more forcefully: if you choose the wrong gun and carry it in a poor quality holster, you *will* find on-body carry to be too uncomfortable to keep up for very long.[90]

Ankle

Holsters designed for ankle carry usually require the gun to be placed on the inside of the non-dominant ankle. Thus, a right-hander would carry on the inside of the left ankle, while a lefty would carry on the right ankle. Ankle holsters are often padded for comfort, because there is so little natural padding on the body in that spot.

For those who simply don't want to fiddle around with belt holsters, and who don't want to worry about cover garments, ankle carry sounds like an attractive option. Because they generally already have a lot of gear carried on the beltline, ankle carry is frequently chosen by police officers who need to stash a back-up gun. Because a gun carried on the ankle cannot possibly get tangled in a seat belt, people who do a lot of driving often find that ankle carry works well for them. Possibly the chief benefit for ankle carry is that it requires only a minimal wardrobe adjustment: wider pant legs which are slightly longer than normal. Except perhaps for a spare sock, it doesn't require any additional layers of clothing.

One important consideration when choosing a gun for ankle carry is that it must be resistant to dirt and grime. Snubby revolvers are ideal for this work. Even so, the gun must be cleaned with obsessive regularity to be certain it will not be clogged with gunk when it is needed. Remember that the gun cannot weigh much, unless you want to develop a permanent tilt to one side. It should also be very small, for the sake both of comfort and of concealability. Concealability in ankle rigs can be more of a factor than most folks realize. The pant legs should be wider and slightly longer than normal, so they do not ride up when you sit down. Even with longer pants, it may still be necessary to avoid crossing your legs at the knee, because that will often reveal the holstered gun. For quick access, wider pant legs are a definite necessity. Wide pant legs also help concealability, because it is very hard to explain bulgy, bulky ankles. Because of the concealability issue, many folks who carry in ankle holsters get in the habit of wearing three socks: one on the non-holster side, and two on the holster side. The undersock provides padding, while the oversock is pulled up to cover most of the holster leaving only the gun's grip exposed.

Drawing from an ankle holster can be very difficult. The easiest draw is

---

90 *Think of it like buying a pair of shoes. Wearing poor-quality shoes that don't fit you is far more uncomfortable than wearing good-quality shoes that do fit properly. In both cases, you know you're wearing shoes, but good shoes don't hurt while bad shoes make your feet feel terrible.*

accomplished while sitting down, an important point for those stuck behind a desk for the majority of the day. It is impossible to draw from an ankle holster while walking or running away from a developing situation, and very difficult to draw from an ankle holster while grappling. However, if you have been knocked to the ground but the assailant is *not* already on top of you, ankle draw is fast and intuitive.

From standing, the usual ankle-draw technique, developed by master firearms instructor Massad Ayoob, works like this for the right-handed shooter. First, take a big step forward with your left leg, or a big step to the rear with your right leg. Drop your rear end so you're in a deep crouch with your feet staggered. Grab your pant hem with your left hand and yank it up out of the way. Reach over with your right hand and get a firing grip on the gun, unsnapping the retention strap as needed.

> **Cowards Take Note!**
>
> You cannot draw from an ankle holster while you are running away.

You can fire from the crouch, which is fastest, or quickly stand as you fire. Avoid kneeling unless you are behind cover. If you aren't behind cover, you may need to run in a hurry and getting out of a kneel can be fatally slow.

Belly Band

I have to say this right up front: I love belly bands. What's a belly band, you ask? A belly band is a wide, stretchy piece of elastic with a built-in holster and often an extra pocket for a spare magazine. It usually features a hook-and-loop closure, and is designed to be worn around the waist or lower torso.

Belly bands allow you to wear your gun on your body even when your pants don't have wide belt loops to hold a gun belt. They're a very flexible option, allowing you to place the gun anywhere on your torso that works with your clothing and figure type. For those already accustomed to carrying a gun on the hip, carrying in a belly band can be a very comfortable change of pace. A belly band can provide a remarkable degree of wardrobe flexibility. It can be worn underneath dressy officewear, something difficult to do with a traditional belt holster.

For women especially, having a belly band in the closet brings back a lot of options that would otherwise be lost to on-body carry. Want to wear tight, hip-hugging jeans? Or dressy polyester office slacks? You can wear your belly band wrapped around your mid-torso under a short-cropped but loose tee or sweater.

Want to wear a skirt that doesn't have belt loops? Wear your belly band and position it exactly where your belt holster would have put the gun.

Want to wear a dress with your belly band? That gets a little more problematic. Yes, it can be done. I've done it many times. Unfortunately, belly bands provide so much flexibility in where you place the gun that it is easy to get carried away and place the gun somewhere you wouldn't be able to draw from. You can carry under a dress... but can you draw from there? Perhaps, depending upon the dress style. Or perhaps not.

Possibly the most important factor in belly-band concealability is the size and shape of the handgun. Small, flat handguns are more easily concealed than larger ones. Revolvers tend to lend themselves more to this form of carry than all but the slimmest semi-autos. Something about the revolver's irregular shape mimics the natural fall of clothing over the human body.

Comfort can be a factor when wearing a belly band. The hook-and-loop material can be itchy. An undershirt definitely helps. In hot weather, I sometimes wear a plain tube top underneath mine. This avoids putting any extra layers of clothing anywhere else, but still gives a nice cushion from the itchies.

Safety Issue

When drawing your handgun from a belly band, take excruciating care that nothing (including your trigger finger) gets inside the trigger guard, because the gun will very likely be pointed at important body parts during the drawing process.

It is impossible to safely place the gun into your belly band while you are wearing it. Instead, take the band off, tuck the firearm into its pocket, and *carefully* place the band around your torso.

Belt Carry

Carrying the gun on a sturdy belt around the waist has long been the preferred method for professional gun-toters. There are two basic methods of belt carry: outside the waistband, commonly abbreviated OWB, and inside the waistband, or IWB.

There are four things you really need in order to gracefully manage belt carry. First, you need an appropriately-sized firearm. Second, you need a safe holster. Third, you need a way to attach that holster securely to your body: a good, sturdy belt. And finally, you need an attractive "cover garment"—that is, clothing that covers the holstered gun and doesn't look too weird.

Remember to budget for a quality holster, because a good holster can make all the difference between successful and unsuccessful attempts at carrying a firearm. While you can find a cheap, collapsible holster for as little as $15, it is really, *really* worthwhile to look for something with at least some semblance of quality. What makes a quality holster? Well, the most important thing a holster does is hold the gun securely. If the holster doesn't do that, it's not a quality holster no matter how much they're charging for it.

Some holsters have soft, collapsible mouths. These holsters are dangerous because it is literally impossible to put the gun into a collapsible holster without holding the mouth of the holster open with your non-gun hand. This means that while putting the gun into the holster, the muzzle will point at your hand. Not good! The floppy mouth is also risky for another reason. It can sometimes fold down and be caught inside the trigger guard while holstering. If you purchase one of these types of holsters, be extremely cautious to the point of paranoia any time every time you holster the gun.

Now about the belt. I'm not sure of this, but I rather suspect that the belt itself is the biggest wardrobe change women have to make in order to carry on the waist. You really-and-truly cannot comfortably or securely tote a belt holster without a good belt to put it upon. A good belt means one that is both wide and stiff. The belt must have some rigidity in order to provide a stable place for the gun to ride.

I strongly recommend that women with curvy figures purchase *contour-cut* belts, which tend to be a lot more comfortable for most. Ordinary, straight-cut belts make a straight line when they are laid out on the table in front of you, while a contour-cut belt makes a gentle U shape which allows it to conform much more comfortably to female curves. The shape also eliminates that annoying back gap so common with straight belts and other clothing that doesn't quite fit an hourglass figure.

When carried on a narrow belt, holsters tend to flop around, twist your clothing into weird shapes, and just generally drive you right up the wall—especially when the holster's slots do not match the belt width. Yet wide belts often look odd with dress clothing. Consider purchasing a tapered belt, which will narrow in the front to accomplish a dress-belt look without sacrificing stability.

The final sine qua non of successful belt carry is a good cover garment. That's such a large topic that we'll cover it on its own later. For now, just remember that OWB requires a longer cover garment than IWB, that prints cover better than solids and darks cover better than lights, and that every piece of clothing you wear has to look like something you would ordinarily wear. One final comment about your cover garment: please remember you don't have to wear ugly clothes in order to hide a gun. Pretty clothes work just as well.

Belt—OWB (Outside Waist Band)

Generally speaking, carrying on the belt outside the waistband is usually more comfortable than carrying inside it. You can easily keep the gun away from your skin, and you don't have to find pants an inch or two bigger in the waist to make room for the gun. OWB is also generally easier to draw from, because the grip is more accessible to the hand. The gun often comes free more easily, because the only tension holding the gun in the holster is the tension which the holstermaker designed it to have. In contrast, unless the IWB holster is very stiff, it can be partially collapsed by pressure from the belt and pants waistband.

Concealment is the chief concern with OWB carry. Because the gun and holster are entirely outside the clothing, the cover garment must be significantly longer than it needs to be when the gun is carried IWB. Furthermore, if the cover garment flops open, there's no hope that you can nonchalantly pass off a partially-glimpsed grip as something else such as a phone or PDA; when you are carrying OWB, whatever anyone sees will very likely *look* like a gun.

> **Comfort Tip**
>
> A belt holster needs a good, stiff belt in order to work right. Whenever a formerly comfortable holster starts moving around or otherwise acting weirdly uncomfortable, it's usually time to replace your belt.

Although many knowledgeable instructors advise against it for various reasons, if you live in a state where openly carrying a firearm is legal, you might occasionally want to wear your gun openly and without a cover garment. Open carry works best with an OWB holster because you are less likely to inadvertently cover the gun. When you open carry, you must use a holster with a thumb break or other device designed to prevent other people from grabbing your gun out of its holster.

For a range holster which is not intended to be concealed, I recommend women purchase a dropped and offset OWB holster, perhaps in Kydex for speed and ease of maintenance. A dropped holster places the bulk of the firearm below the waistband, while an offset holster allows the butt of the gun to ride away from the body rather than hugging closely to it. Both of these features together work to promote better all-day holster comfort for women, who often have a narrower waist than either hip or rib cage and thus are often subject to pain where the muzzle end drives into the hip or the butt end drives into the tender ribs. Lowering the bulk of the gun and edging the grips away from the body thus dramatically improve comfort. The only drawback is that dropped and offset holsters are not concealable, no how no way, in any known universe.

Belt—IWB (Inside Waist Band)

Right now, my personal favorite IWB holster is a holster made by Ted Blocker Holsters as part of a (heavily modified) "LFI Rig" set.[91] The reason I love this holster is, in part, because it is tuckable, a feature I consider darn near indispensible for my lifestyle and carry methods. Tuckable means that the gun rides on your belt, inside your waistband, like any other IWB holster. But because of the manner in which the holster loops are shaped, it is possible to tuck your shirt tail in between the outer side of the gun and the inner part of your waistband. The gun will be completely hidden by your regular clothing, with only the holster's attachment loop visible on the belt. In the case of my much-beloved modified LFI Rig, even the belt attachment is invisible, because the belt features a soft loop lining on the side facing my body, while the holster features a Velcro-type hook-covered tab where it faces the belt.[92] As you can imagine, these two factors—tuckable holster and invisible belt attachment—together open up a world of clothing options that would otherwise be closed off by the choice to belt carry.

I prefer to wear my IWB holster in the appendix position, which places the firearm in front of my strong side hip. Wearing the gun in the appendix position requires a closed-front cover garment unless you've got a tuckable holster, but the gun does not get driven into either hip or ribcage as it often does when worn on or near the hip. Another advantage is that, when seen from front or behind, a woman wearing her firearm in the appendix position can still have a nice waistline curve.

Many women, particularly those with a less noticeable hourglass shape, prefer to carry just behind the hip in a holster that features a deep *cant* (the angle at which the gun rides on the belt). Many people have a nice little flat spot immediately behind the hip, and behind-the-hip holsters take advantage of that, while a deep cant allows a more comfortable draw and helps avoid the whole "gun driven into hip and ribs" problem.

Probably the biggest issue in purchasing a gun for carry IWB is how thick the gun is. Put very simply, the thicker the gun is, the thicker your waist will look unless you dress carefully around it. You'll need to shop carefully in order to avoid that problem.

Around the holiday season, I have occasionally found myself looking sad-

---

91 *Ted Blocker Holsters, 9438 SW Tigard St., Tigard, OR 97223. (503) 670-7972. www.tedblockerholsters.com.*
92 *VELCRO ® is a registered trademark of Velcro Industries B.V.*

ly at my summer jeans and then at my handgun. "There's not room enough in these jeans for the both of us!" the gun seems to remark. Too, too true. If you're going to carry IWB, you have to buy jeans which are an inch or two bigger in the waist than you normally would. Unfortunately, ladies' jeans are designed to fit a certain waist/hip ratio. If you purchase jeans larger in the waist, it is quite possible they'll be baggy in the rear. Try slipping over to the men's department to purchase guy jeans for yourself instead. Men's jeans are proportionately bigger in the waist and narrower in the rear end than women's jeans, and that's just what you need in order to fashionably conceal an IWB pistol while avoiding the dreaded baggy-butt problem. Another possible solution, assuming the men's department jeans give you too much room in the waist or not enough in the rear, is to purchase ladies' jeans with stretchy fibers in them. That little bit of extra "give" can make all the comfort difference in the world.

The gun can abrade delicate skin when worn IWB. Simplest solution: get in the habit of wearing a lightweight undershirt to provide a mild cushion between yourself and the gun. You can also add a layer of soft padding to the backside of your own holster. There's at least one company out there, Kramer Handgun Leather, producing holsters which have a layer of back padding already built in.[93] Finally, if your firearm has sharp edges or rough spots, you can take it to a gunsmith and request a "melt job" which will improve matters somewhat even without a cushioning layer between yourself and the gun.

Bra Holsters

When I first began researching concealed carry, I believed bra holsters were 98% Hollywood fantasy. But I've since come to believe that it actually can be a viable carry method for some women. For instance, here is what an online correspondent, Holly, had to tell me about her favorite carry method:

> *"I was reading on your page that you don't think too much about carrying in your bra. I've carried a KelTec P-11 and P32 behind the underwire behind my left breast for several years in cool weather with no discomfort. Maybe we just have different comfort levels. [My husband] got a clip that screws into the right side of the frame, just below the slide. It allows you to clip the pistol onto your belt, pants waistband, pocket, or bra."*

93 *Kramer Handgun Leather, PO Box 112154, Tacoma, WA 98411. (800) 510-2666. www.kramerleather.com.*

Following Holly's advice, I did very much the same thing when one of my sons got married. I was unwilling to carry in my purse that day (who would watch my purse while I danced?), and unwilling to leave the firearm at home (we would be the last ones in the building cleaning up after dark). So I sewed an elastic pouch into my bra strap directly beneath my left armpit, where my little KelTec rode securely and discreetly with its trigger safely covered.

As a practical question, it makes sense that a woman would want to take advantage of the weight-bearing harness she already wears to help carry the weight of the firearm. The draw would be similar to any other undershirt or shoulder holster carry method, but you'll usually snake your hand down the neckline to access the firearm. No chance of putting your hand discreetly on the firearm in advance of the draw.

Kangaroo Pouch

A kangaroo pouch straps around your waist and rides in the front of your pants below the waistband. It comes in variants from different companies under different brand names; the most well-known are SmartCarry and Thunderwear.[94] All variants are supposed to ride low on the hips, with the elastic belt riding over your tucked shirttail.

This works well for guys, because guys' pants tend to be a lot more baggy in the crotch than women's pants, and strangers who notice a bulge in the front of a guy's pants are generally too polite to comment on it. Because women's pants tend to be snug in the spot the gun will ride, this type of carry doesn't work really well *with pants* for most women. But here's a secret: these holsters work pretty well with skirts. And the nice thing is that because the entire holster and gun are below the waistband, you really won't need a special cover garment to carry this off. Another handy factor: when you carry in a kangaroo pouch, an unexpected hug from a friend won't reveal your secret.

Take care not to *clunk* when you plunk yourself down onto a hard wooden pew (or any other hard surface, of course), especially in a quiet environment such as a church. Don't ask me how I learned this.

Other factors to remember include accessibility and draw speed. To draw, you snake your hand into your waistband, so you need to have a fairly loose waistband to make it work. If you wear one of these underneath a tight waistband, it will be very difficult to draw in a hurry. And regardless of how your

---

94 *SmartCarry from Concealed Protection 3, Inc., 940 7th Street NW, Largo, Florida 33770-1112. (727) 581-7001. www.smartcarry.com. Thunderwear from Defense Security Products, 3-01 Park Plaza, Suite 108, Old Brookville, New York 11545. (800) 830-3057. www.thunderwear.com.*

waistband fits, you'll find it quite difficult to draw from a kangaroo pouch while seated. Check out how it will work for you at home with an empty gun before venturing out in public.

Shoulder Holsters

I have heard, from more than one source I consider reliable, that shoulder holsters are comfortable. You couldn't prove it by me. Up until this very year, I had found every one I'd tried on to be quite uncomfortable in different ways. Every body shape is different and this just underscores that it's a bad idea to set your heart on any carry style or holster design that you haven't tried for yourself, no matter who recommends it. Despite my own lack of success with shoulder holsters, I know several women who have them and love them. These women all cite comfort as a number-one reason to love shoulder holsters, along with concealability under dressy business clothing and easy access while sitting.

The simplest way to conceal a shoulder holster is underneath a boxy blazer or swing jacket. That makes it an ideal choice for business clothing, but with one caveat: you must be certain that the straps will never be visible as you move around. This requires some time in front of a full-length mirror as you bend and twist to be certain those straps will stay hidden with the outfit you've chosen. The other concealability issue you may encounter with a shoulder holster is that if the gun is held horizontally rather than vertically, and you are fairly thin, you may find that the gun tends to poke out in front or in back. If this is the case, you may be better off searching for a vertical holster design.

Incidentally, one of the nice things about shoulder holsters is that they practically require you to carry extra ammunition, simply to balance out the weight on both sides. That a reload can be carried so easily and concealed so naturally is a pleasant bonus.

Thigh Band Holsters

When we talk about a thigh holster for concealed carry, we're not talking about the soldiers' method of carrying openly in a sturdy plastic retention holster buckled around the thigh. Rather, a concealed-carry thigh holster is a type of modified belly band, a wide piece of elastic with a gun-pocket sewn into it. Like a garter, a thigh holster wraps around your upper leg underneath a skirt or dress.

The problem with a thigh-band holster is that it can be uncomfortable, and it definitely requires—how do I put this delicately?—a body shape that does not include thighs that rub together. Those who fit this description may find that a thigh holster allows you to be discreetly armed even while wearing dress clothes.

To keep the band from slithering down your leg and suddenly turning into an ankle holster, you need to wear a support strap. It works like this: around your waist, under your clothes, you wear a thin strappy belt.[95] Then you hook one end of the support strap to your belt and the other end to the thigh band to anchor everything in place.

Many thigh holsters don't have a retention strap to secure the firearm inside the gun pocket, but they really should. If you're handy with a sewing machine, just attach a small strip of Velcro[96] loops to the outside of the holster, then stitch one end of a short elastic strap to the opposite side of the holster. Sew a small piece of Velcro hooks on the loose end of the elastic strap. To use this device, place your firearm into the thigh band as usual, then slap the Velcro end of the elastic strap into place over the top of the gun. This retention strap should secure the firearm inside the holster so it won't come out unless you take it out.[97]

In use, you'll want to avoid crossing your legs unless you've worked out in advance whether or not the firearm will "print" or will remain discreetly concealed with the particular outer clothing you've selected. You may need to experiment a little by moving the gun higher or lower on your leg, or rotating the band around your leg, before you find the ideal spot for the gun to ride.

Safety Issue

When drawing from a shoulder holster, NEVER point the weapon at your upper arm. To get your upper arm and the vulnerable brachial artery out of the way, raise your non-dominant elbow as you draw. See the process in pictures at www.CorneredCat.com.

Undershirt Holsters

Similar in function to a shoulder holster, an undershirt holster places the firearm directly beneath the user's arm. And just like a shoulder holster, an undershirt holster requires you to wear a good cover garment. But unlike a shoulder holster, the cover garment can be as simple as a button-down blouse or any other type of shirt you would wear over an undershirt. There's one

---

95 *Yup, like a garter belt.*
96 *VELCRO ® is a registered trademark of Velcro Industries B.V.*
97 *I'm pretty sure my lawyer would want me to put something here, so I did. Please flip back to the first pages of the book and read the disclaimer.*

caveat, however: your cover shirt *must* allow you to easily access the firearm so you can draw it if you need it.

The construction of the holster pocket varies from brand to brand, though not as much as one might expect. Look for varieties that offer a removable retention strap. You won't need that strap with every firearm, but because the elastic holster pockets are sized to accept a range of firearm sizes, the retention strap will probably be needed whenever you carry a smaller gun. To check whether the strap will be needed or not, unload the gun. Unload it again. Check to be sure it's unloaded. Then place the firearm into the holster pocket as usual, without your cover shirt in place, and bend down to tie your shoes. If the gun falls out of the pocket, you need a retention strap.

These types of holsters vary wildly in concealability and comfort, depending on the material of the base shirt. The mesh type feels cooler in summer weather, and allows a greater variety of cover garments. However, the mesh type suffers from a lack of stability. Because the base material moves around, the holster tends to sag and gap, flop and shift, even with lightweight firearms. Undershirt holsters built on compression shirts are more stable, but they often create a different problem. Not every woman finds the compression effect a flattering one. "It's that uniboob look," says a very anonymous but well-endowed friend. "A compression shirt works great when you're exercising, or for thin people, but if you've got anything up top it squishes things and gives you a shape that just looks weird when you're not at the gym." Those who are more slender or less endowed won't have the same complaint.

As with all shoulder holster types, you need to have pretty good upper body flexibility to manage an efficient draw with an undershirt holster. Be sure to keep your upper arm away from the muzzle during the drawstroke, lifting it out of the way to avoid crossing your brachial artery with the muzzle. Reholstering can be very difficult, too. Avoid the temptation to use the muzzle of the gun to wiggle into the elastic opening, since this invariably points the gun directly into the body core. Instead, curl your left arm up, elbow lifted high, to hold the holster mouth open as you insert the gun with your right hand. Did I mention that this type of holster does require some upper body flexibility?

Wrapping Up

So there you have it, an overview of holster options from A to U.[98] As you can see, there really are quite a lot of possibilities. That can be overwhelming at first! Fortunately, in use it's not that difficult: you need one basic method

---

98 *Someone needs to invent a holster type that begins with a Z, that's all I've gotta say.*

that works the majority of the time, plus one or two "special occasion" options hiding in your closet for the rare times when your basic method won't work. To simplify, don't worry too much about special cases and your toughest concealment challenges at first. First things first! First find something that will work for you 80% of the time, then commit to filling in the gaps by sampling other methods for the tough tasks.

If you are unsure where to start, I strongly suggest starting with on-body belt carry, which has become the standard and most common carry method for many good reasons. Don't reinvent the wheel if you don't have to. Move on to trying other options only after giving belt carry a fair chance to succeed. You might be pleasantly surprised to discover how simple it really is.

Straight Talk About Curves

If you decide to carry in a traditional belt holster, the chances are that you will need to hunt a little harder to find a holster that works for you than your male counterparts do. Why? Well, this shouldn't come as a total shock to anyone, but guess what: men's bodies and women's bodies are shaped differently. My husband is shaped like a piece of celery. Straight up and down. His best friend has an apple-shaped torso. Plenty of guts, but no hips. Lucky men. A man can hide a gun nearly anywhere on his body and it'll disappear. Me, I'm shaped like an hourglass. One of my best friends is shaped like a pear, another is more like ... well, curvy celery. Thin everywhere, but like every other woman I know, her figure still has a certain flair to it.

As many women have discovered, the curvier you are, the more painful it can be to hold an unyielding chunk of metal firmly against your waistline. Faced with this simple biological fact, a lot of women simply give up on the idea of carrying a concealed handgun on the belt.

Good News! Up until recent years, few holster makers were producing designs specifically intended to work with a female figure. But we live in a golden age. Today, if the holster hunt is difficult, it isn't because there are no good choices. It is because there are so many choices that picking between them can be overwhelming.

There are good reasons to carry on the beltline, though. Security and ease of access are the two biggies. For me, it just didn't seem a good idea to put a deadly weapon into the purse I kept losing. The draw from a holster is considerably smoother and more predictable than one from a purse, and there's also the comparative hassle of carrying a big, heavy purse instead of a small, lightweight one. Finally, if you want to attend a class or shoot in competition, you will probably need a belt holster, no matter how you ordinarily carry your firearm.

Let's define the problem first. The problem is that women have curves, and guns do not. The more pronounced a woman's curves are, and the longer the gun is, the more difficult it becomes to find a holster that is both comfortable and concealable. Both ends of a straight piece of metal held securely against a curved waist will be driven into delicate flesh.

Approaches to solving this problem fall into two main categories: those which move the gun away from the waist, and those which move it away from the hip. Commonly, a workable design will use one choice from each category.

Getting the gun off the waist

A high-ride design raises the holstered gun so that more of it rides above the belt, and thus avoids pulling the gun into the waist curve. It is comfortable, stable, and easy to conceal, but with so much of the gun above the waist, drawing can be very difficult for the short-waisted or those with shoulder flexibility issues. A high-ride holster often works well for a woman with a long torso.

Lowering the holster also gets the bulk of the gun off the waist. Comfortable when worn, a dropped holster design makes the gun very easy to draw. But the lower the gun rides, the more difficult it becomes to find a cover garment long enough to cover the muzzle end. A dropped holster design often works well for a high-waisted woman, or for one with a short torso.

High-ride and dropped holsters have one thing in common: how well they work depends somewhat upon where your pants put your beltline. It would be counterproductive to wear a high-ride holster with hip-hugging jeans, for example.

Dropped holsters often include a feature called offset, which pushes the top half of the holstered gun out away from the body so that the grips are no longer driven into the ribcage by leverage from the muzzle end. The benefit of this is that it smoothes out the curve, but it also adds bulk to the waistline and can make you look fat or lumpy when concealed. Designs which combine drop with offset work very well for open carry. If you are looking for a range holster these are two features well worth considering.

Holster makers use the terms "rake" or "cant" to describe the angle at which the gun will be rotated on the belt. Designs which do not have any rake are called "straight drop," which means the muzzle will be pointed straight at the ground when you are standing. A holster with an extreme rake is one which holds the gun at a sharp angle, usually with the muzzle toward the rear. The chief benefit here is that the muzzle end is up and rotated away from the curviest part of the waist, so the grip end is no longer being driven into the ribs by leverage.

Moving the gun away from the hip

Because a woman's curves are usually most pronounced at the hip, the other primary set of carry solutions each involve moving the gun around the belt and away from the hip. There are four main methods of doing this: cross-draw, appendix, behind the hip, and small of back.

Cross-draw and appendix carry both move the holster to the front of the body, to the area between belly button and hip. The difference is that a cross-draw holster is carried on the non-dominant side with the gun's grip pointed forward, while appendix carry is on the dominant side with the grip toward the rear. Both are best used with short-barreled firearms, and either may be combined with a tuckable holster for better concealment. Of the two, appendix carry is slightly more concealable because your clothing is less likely to catch on the butt of the gun as you move around. Couple appendix carry with a tuckable holster, and you've got a fairly concealable combination that is also quite comfortable for many women.

Cross-draw carry is often recommended for people who need to drive a lot, because of all belt carry methods it is least likely to get tangled in your seat belt. Cross-draw is also a good choice for anyone with shoulder mobility issues. But while appendix carry is often acceptable for classes or competitions, cross-draw rarely is.

There's a lot of territory behind the hip, but when holster makers refer to carrying behind the hip, they usually mean immediately behind the hip, snugged into the back of the iliac crest. Combined with a moderate to severe rake, the flat spot just behind your hip can be an ideal place to conceal your holster. Moving the holstered gun even farther to the rear, so that any part of it is held over the spinal column, creates two safety issues. The first is that if you ever fall on top of your holstered gun, there is some chance of spinal damage. How significant the risk is will depend upon a lot of factors, but it bears mentioning. The other safety issue is that it is nearly impossible to draw from a small of back holster without sweeping a wide area behind and around you. For this reason, small of back carry is rarely allowed in CCW classes or on crowded ranges.

Nearly all of the above approaches may be combined with at least one other to give a workable design for different body types. For example, a woman with a long torso and an athletic figure might prefer a holster which has a high rise and a moderate rake, and carry it behind the hip. Another woman, petite and with an hourglass figure, might find that she can carry forward of the hip in a dropped holster with a slight muzzle-forward rake.

The important thing to remember is that if one design doesn't work for you, there is almost certainly another one out there which will, if you are just stubborn enough to keep looking for it. Here's to success!

Should I Carry in My Purse?

This was a difficult chapter to write, and I've hesitated to include it for fear of discouraging other women from carrying a gun at all. However, it's my firm belief that even the timid are better served by learning everything they can before making up their own minds. So I have set down my concerns quite plainly here, but I don't know you or what practical carry challenges you face. As a competent adult, you will draw your own conclusions about these issues, and you are the one who must live with the consequences of whatever choices you make. While I've tried to be as objective as possible, I'm not a fan of off-body carry as a daily thing. Of course, we all know that sometimes there are no other viable choices, but I have a sneaking suspicion that most women who carry in a purse do so simply because they have never given on-body carry a serious chance. Below, you'll find plain talk about the benefits and drawbacks of carrying a concealed handgun in a purse. The sections are alphabetized because what's most important to me may not be as important to you.

Clothing

Clothing might be the biggest reason many women prefer purse carry. And it's true enough that carrying in a purse involves very little wardrobe adjustment. Oh, you might have to get used to the idea of carrying a large purse rather than a tiny one, and surrender the idea of carrying a purse with a designer label, but that's really about it. No wardrobe angst required, except on the days or in the places you might ordinarily choose to travel without a purse.

But before you decide that *only* purse carry will work for you, I want to tell you a dirty little secret. As an avid people-watcher I believe that roughly 95% of the outfits I see on other women would work for concealed carry.[99]

---

99 *Obviously, this varies according to time of year, the age of the women, and the region of the country. During a summertime visit to California's central valley, I observed that the proportion of women who could be carrying underneath what they were already wearing had dropped to around 85%. That's still overwhelmingly high, but not as high as the 95+% I see in the Pacific Northwest.*

Fond of tight, skimpy shirts and classic bootcut jeans? Guess what—that's a great ankle carry outfit. Most office pants work well with ankle holsters too. Love shrug sets? If the cardigan hits the waist, it can conceal a behind-the-hip holster; if the cardigan is short, the outfit will probably work well with a belly band. Whether you love crafty vests, pretty blouses, boxy blazers, or cozy cotton sweaters, the chances are that with a little determination and creativity, you *can* wear a firearm on your body without altering your wardrobe nearly as much as you fear.

When it comes to fancy dress clothing, carry methods do get harder to find (though surprisingly, not entirely impossible with a little work). In some dress clothes, a carry purse might really be your only viable option. But unless you wear your party clothes twenty-four hours a day, chances are that you have other choices most of the time.

Expenses

If you decide to carry in your purse, it's an excellent idea to purchase a quality holster purse. Carrying in a normal purse *isn't* very safe. And it's so slow to access that it simply should not be done if you can possibly avoid it. On the other hand, a holster purse will typically set you back at least $100, often up to $300.[100] Purpose-designed carry purses often cost as much as a good leather holster, *plus* the cost of a high-end leather purse. Some companies offer less expensive purses, and with the rising popularity of concealed carry we hope to see more of these affordable options soon. But for now, that's the reality.

In contrast to this, as of spring 2010 you can expect to pay around $100 for a custom leather belt holster, or $50 to $75 for a Kydex one. Nylon holsters can be found for as little as $20, but these are not recommended for serious every day use.

Firearm selection

When carrying on-body, you'll want to select a handgun with the smallest overall dimensions you are able to shoot comfortably and accurately. Size is usually the limiting factor. Provided you have a sturdy belt designed for the task, there's little difference between a heavy gun and a lighter one which has the same overall dimensions. Not so when carrying in a purse. For a purse, the overall size doesn't matter much, but you'll notice every ounce. So when choosing a firearm for purse carry, the most important issue becomes the gun's weight.

---

100 Ballpark figures as of spring 2010.

Keep in mind, though, that heavier guns produce less recoil and are more pleasant to shoot—and regular practice is crucial for safety's sake. If you are recoil-averse, you may want to avoid purse carry just so you can comfortably carry a slightly heavier handgun.

With a carry gun in your purse, be aware that you'll be tempted to set the purse down more often than you otherwise would, or to leave it behind on short errands. You already know that the gun cannot save your life if it isn't with you when you need it, and that there are safety issues to consider whenever you set the purse down. So if you go this route, consider in advance what you will do on occasions when the purse becomes too heavy to tote comfortably.

Safety issues—unintentional discharges

Whether you decide to go the regular-purse route or to carry in a holster purse, be aware that literally *nothing* else can share a compartment with the gun: not your lipstick, not the car keys, not a piece of paper. Even a double-action revolver can get caught in all the other clutter when it's dumped into a crowded purse, with messy and perhaps disastrous results.

In the news awhile back was the tragic-comic story of an off-duty police-woman who dropped her purse in a crowded fast food restaurant. The gun fired, and while no one was hurt, great pandemonium ensued. The police of-ficer panicked and fled the scene, leaving her purse behind. Someone called 911 to report shots fired. When other officers arrived at the scene, they found their co-worker's newly-ventilated purse on the floor, with her driver's license and all her other identification still in it. Oops.

Safety issues—security and gun retention

It can be very socially awkward to treat the gun purse with the respect it must be treated. When embarrassed, people tend to disregard the safety rules "just this once," making understandable excuses for themselves. But "just this once" is all the time it takes for an unexpected tragedy to strike. And "just this once" has a nasty tendency of turning into an ongoing bad habit.

To put a human face on this, few women keep their purses literally on their laps the entire time they are visiting friends. Most of us toss our purses casually over the back of the chair when eating out (with the attendant risk of walking away without it). We shove our purses underneath our desks when we get to work, and don't think about them again all day. We plunk our purses into the shopping cart in the grocery store, then turn away to pick out toma-toes. But it literally only takes a split second for a purse-snatcher to do his thing—and even less than that for a child or grandchild to get into your purse when mommy's not watching as carefully as she ought. **There is literally no safe place to set a gun purse down if it is not locked up.** But physically holding onto your purse all the time will definitely earn you some odd looks from your friends. You must be prepared for this fact, and consider ways to cope with it.

While it is easy to think, "Oh, that won't happen to me," there are enough horror stories out there about this that it really gives one pause to think. For instance, in Half Moon Bay, California, a woman was being stalked by her ex-husband. Her danger was acute enough that she managed to score a concealed-carry permit (in California!) and routinely carried in her purse. One day, she absent-mindedly walked out of the grocery store without her purse. The manager reached into her purse to get her phone number, spotted the gun, and called the police. Now the woman is facing a legal nightmare: charged with a crime for leaving her firearm behind, she cannot have firearms anywhere near her until her case is settled, and her name and picture were plastered all over the local papers. Her previously-private address has become a matter of public record. This is no way to avoid a stalker.

Speed of draw

Drawing from a purse can be difficult. If the purse isn't designed for concealed carry, or if you're carrying it incorrectly, you may find yourself rummaging through it with your head down at the very moment when you most need to have your head up and scanning for trouble. Other objects in the purse can slow you down, too. I vividly remember watching a friend work with her carry purse on the range one afternoon, and her acutely frustrated expression when the contents of her overstuffed purse defeated her efforts to draw quickly. Remember, it isn't enough simply to have a gun with you. If you're going to use the gun to save your life, you have to be able to get to it. The thing to keep in mind is that if you need the gun at all, you will very likely need it in a hurry.

Regardless of how you decide to carry your firearm, you absolutely *must* practice getting the gun out, so that you will be able to do it as efficiently as possible if you ever really need it. And you must practice doing this under realistic conditions. For purse carry, that means you'll need to practice with all the other stuff you routinely carry in your purse along for the ride.

The practical difficulty of this is that it is hard enough to find a range that allows people to practice drawing from the holster. Finding one that allows drawing from a purse might be an impossible mission. But practice is critical.

If you cannot find a range which allows it, you can always practice drawing an *unloaded* firearm at home, provided you have a safe backstop and follow the safety rules.

The Bottom Line

Despite the negatives I've listed in this chapter, sometimes you'll face the choice of either carrying in your purse, or not carrying at all. Or you might look at your life and decide that you would rather not make the changes that on-body carry requires. That's okay. Just choose a good purse, practice often, and take care to protect it well. Commit yourself now to doing whatever it takes to stay safe.

How to Choose a Carry Purse

Lately I've been looking at lots of purses.[101] I've handled concealed carry purses from established names like Galco[102] and Coronado,[103] from less well-known but equally experienced mid-sized makers, and from tiny little startup companies. Women interested in purse carry benefit from many more choices than were available just a few short years ago.

As a rule, I don't believe purse carry is an ideal primary carry method. There are just too many possible ways it can go wrong. But there are times and places where purse carry—and only purse carry—makes sense. For this reason, I believe that every woman who carries a gun should have at least one holster purse in her wardrobe as a *secondary* carry method, ready for use in those rare circumstances where on-body carry won't work.

Further, many women simply will not carry unless they can carry in their purses. That's understandable, because although on-body carry offers real advantages, carrying the firearm in your purse certainly works better than not carrying it at all. Since so many people do choose to carry in their purses, whether occasionally or regularly, we need good, solid information about this common carry method.

Design Considerations

Concealed carry purse designers have it tough. They need to create purses that:

- conceal the existence and purpose of the gun compartment;
- reduce the risk of a purse snatching;
- assist the user to maintain positive control over her firearm at all times;
- minimize the slow draw and difficult access compared to other carry

---

101 Disclaimer: all companies mentioned in this chapter sent me at least one purse for review purposes.
102 Galco International, 2019 West Quail Avenue, Phoenix, Arizona 85027. (800) 874-2526. www.usgalco.com.
103 Coronado Leather Company, 1059 Tierra Del Rey, Suite C, Chula Vista, CA 91910. (800) 283-9509. www.coronadoleather.com.

methods;

- ease purse weight and lessen shoulder strain;
- allow users to choose different sizes and shapes of firearms with internal holsters that securely hold different firearms; and
- please women looking for fashionable choices.

That's a tall order, and purse designers meet these challenges in different ways. For example, considering the dangers of a purse snatching, one designer produces crossbody styles with metal-reinforced shoulder straps. Looking at the exact same issue, another designer uses plain straps and suggests women avoid crossbody purse styles. The first company wants to protect customers from losing the firearm to a thief. The second company wants to protect customers from wrestling with a thief over the purse.

Which is correct? They both have valid points and good reasons for their decisions. Different designs work for different circumstances, and every woman has her own priorities. So I cannot tell you which of these choices is right for you, in your circumstances, based on your own priorities. I can only describe the features and the reasons the designers chose them. When there is a fundamental difference in perspective between designers, you'll have to decide on your own which of these perspectives best addresses your own priorities.

Gun compartments

While many ordinary purses have a simple compartment of a size that *could* be used to hold a firearm in a pinch, a purse designed for concealed carry does much more. Such purses feature an internal holster designed to hold the gun securely while safely covering the trigger guard. This keeps the gun in the same orientation at all times and prevents it from sliding around. When the user reaches for the gun, the muzzle will be pointed in a known direction and the grip will present itself naturally to her hand. She won't have to fish around for the grip while hoping to avoid accidentally finding the trigger. The holster compartment allows fast, comfortable access. Some designers place a premium on discreet access, too.

Typically, the gun compartment rides near the center of the purse, with an opening at one end. But other layouts exist. Some purses allow top access into the gun compartment. In such cases, the end user must ask herself whether she will *ever* absent-mindedly unzip that compartment while reaching for her wallet. It's not really a safety concern, since you're unlikely to draw the gun in such circumstances, no matter how absent-minded you might otherwise be.

But letting others see the firearm could cause a scene that ranges from mildly embarrassing to financially catastrophic.

The gun compartment liner must be sturdy because it is the weak point of any bag, destined to fail long before good leather or quality zippers give way. The liner, together with the surrounding walls, helps support the weight of the firearm so it does not slide around within the purse. Such movement can make the grip difficult to find under stress. It can also make the gun difficult to draw because it is distracting. A loose or flimsy liner can even become entangled with the holster in extreme cases. For this reason, as you shop for a carry purse, always look for a sturdy liner and stiff gun compartment walls.

Accessing the compartment

Almost universally, purse designers have chosen to use zippers to seal their gun compartments, although it is possible to find designs which seal the compartment with Velcro.[104] These hook-and-loop style closures have one significant advantage over zipper closures: they are *much* less easily spotted even by someone who knows what they are looking for. As an example, I was in the room at the Firearms Academy of Seattle one spring as a group of women were discussing holster purses and passing examples around the room. When an older purse with a hook-and-loop closure was passed around, four different women examined it before anyone was able to identify the entry point or find the gun compartment. On another occasion, an online friend of mine told of having her purse pawed through by a security guard who never spotted her concealed weapon although he did confiscate her water bottle.

The negative side of the hook-and-loop style closures is, of course, that getting into the compartment will always make that distinctive *rrrrrriiiiip-pppp* sound. For those whose defense plans include slipping a stealthy hand inside the gun compartment, this can be a deal killer.

Whether the concealed carry compartment features a zipper closure or a hook-and-loop closure, some women find that the edges of the zipper, or the hook side of the hook-and-loop, will irritate their hands when they reach

---

104 *Errr, excuse me. I meant to say, "... with a hook-and-loop style of closure." Velcro, of course, is a brand name and not all such purses would be designed around that particular brand of hook-and-loop closure. Just to please any trademark attorneys reading this, I also am careful to put "adhesive bandages" rather than Band-Aids on my children's owies, and I've never, ever xeroxed a paper for the boss.*

VELCRO® is a registered trademark of Velcro Industries B.V., Band-Aid® belongs to Johnson & Johnson, and Xerox ® belongs to the Xerox Corporation.

into the compartment. There is little to be done about this, but women who have thin or sensitive skin may want to choose a larger purse, which is more likely to have a generous gun compartment opening that will be kinder on the hands.

To lock or not to lock

Many concealed carry purses feature a locking zipper to secure the gun compartment (hook-and-loop openings, of course, can never be locked). On the surface, this seems like a grand idea and it might even be a lifesaver in some circumstances. For example, on overnight visits to family or friends who have small children, the locking purse offers a readily-available means of securing the firearm from inquisitive younglings while you are asleep.[105]

Zipper locks create a few risks, however. A woman might lock the firearm compartment and later forget to unlock it. Or a woman who isn't quite comfortable with the notion of carrying a firearm might habitually leave the compartment locked, making it impossible to get the gun quickly when she needs it. She might even leave the unlocked purse where a child can access it, thinking it was locked when it really wasn't. The presence of a lock always adds a layer of complication into the owner's defense plans ("Is it or isn't it?"). And in all of these cases, a lock-related memory lapse could have truly catastrophic consequences.

If you choose a purse with a locking zipper, be especially wary of these factors to avoid falling into dangerous habits.

Internal holsters

Because guns come in different sizes, the internal holsters in concealed carry purses are usually required to handle a wide variety of firearms. Designers have addressed this need in different ways. Coronado Leather, for example, produces a "holster" made entirely of elastic and hook-and-loop material. It is designed to be wrapped securely around the outer portion of the firearm and then snugged into place with the hook-and-loop ends before being placed within the compartment. Once fitted, the holster retains its shape and the gun can be withdrawn and replaced at will. The design provides a custom fit for each type of firearm and securely retains the gun without a retention strap. But because guns come in different sizes, it does not entirely cover the trigger guard in all circumstances.[106] Other makers have addressed this same con-

---

105 *Although of course you will still want to keep the purse out of sight and out of reach.*
106 *The gun compartments in Coronado purses feature walls that are stiff and sturdy,*

cern by providing a loose-fitting bucket of soft leather, often with an elastic retention strap, or by offering internal holsters in different sizes to fit different firearms.

Many internal holsters—those attached with a hook-and-loop system—easily let the user swap them from one purse to another. With these designs, you can position the holster at different angles or depths to suit yourself and your firearm. However, this is not always the case. Some makers stitch their internal holsters into the liners of the carry compartment. This sacrifices flexibility, but might make the holster a little more secure.

Some internal holsters include a separate retention strap that attaches either directly to the holster or to the inner wall of the gun compartment with a hook-and-loop fastener. These retention straps vary in design, but the easiest to use are "pull-through." A pull-through strap holds the gun securely in place but allows the user to free the firearm with a single swift jerk. Retention straps without a pull-through design must be freed by hand before the gun can be drawn, which slows down the already-slow process of getting the gun out.

Oh, by the way, there's a little secret for adjusting holsters that attach to the interior walls of the gun compartment with hook-and-loop material: place your *unloaded* firearm into the holster, then wrap a piece of paper around the outside of the holster before sliding it into the compartment for the first time. The paper will prevent the hooks on the holster from mating up with the loops on the interior wall until you've positioned the gun where you want it to be. Once the holster is properly positioned, simply slip the paper out of the way and the holster will immediately grab its spot on the wall of the compartment.

Shoulder straps

There are at least two schools of thought about shoulder straps on concealed carry purses. You need to understand what the choices are and why they matter, because your purse selection will dictate your defense tactics to some degree.

Some concealed carry purse designers, such as Gun Tote'n Mamas,[107] have chosen to reinforce their straps with a metal cord. If you examine the strap carefully with a knowing eye, you may spot the internal cord, but it isn't obvi-

---

so the firearm's trigger and trigger guard are very definitely well-protected when it is within the purse. But the elastic construction of the internal holster does not, by itself, provide that protection in every circumstance—only in most circumstances.
107 *Concealed Carry Handbags by Gun Tote'n Mamas, 1303 Shermer Road, Northbrook, IL 60062. (847) 446-0700 Ext. 204. www.guntotenmamas.com.*

ous. The cord helps defeat the slash-and-grab purse thief. Because there is a firearm within the purse, the reasoning goes, the user has to hold on to her purse at all costs. Purses with this reinforced strap will be worn crossbody for added security. With or without a reinforced strap, crossbody carry has some real advantages. For instance, it makes it much easier to gracefully retain the purse in situations where a woman with a different type of handbag might look awkward holding onto it.

But because it's not obvious that the strap has been reinforced, a thief who planned to slash through the shoulder strap and grab the purse as he fled is not deterred from trying it. He is only prevented from succeeding. So the user might get tangled up with a knife-armed thief in a struggle over her purse, and because it is a crossbody design, she will not be able to easily dump the purse in order to escape unharmed.

Does this mean reinforced straps are a bad idea? Not at all. It simply means that a woman who buys a purse with reinforced straps should understand her choices and master some basic hand-to-hand skills. She should practice drawing from various awkward positions so she can deal with this type of problem. How extreme is her risk? Probably not high. Most purse snatchers will not have plans to stay and fight if the purse does not immediately rip free. The added security from the reinforced strap that prevents a purse snatcher from getting the firearm might be worth this trade-off for a prepared woman who has a plan.

On the flip side, a woman who opts for unreinforced straps must understand that her choice puts her firearm at risk from a slash-and-grab purse snatching. By the way, although many concealed carry purses are designed to be worn crossbody, by no means are all designed to be used this way. Hobo, tote, knapsack and many other handbag styles are also available. And many companies produce purses with adjustable straps so the user can tailor the strap length to suit herself. Styles with shorter straps, of course, place the owner at risk of losing a firearm from a standard purse snatching, not just from a slash-and-grab type. They also make it more likely that you'll set the gun down when you shouldn't. Again, when selecting a purse you'll need to decide which of these practical concerns take priority for you, and choose your style and your strategy accordingly.

One more strap-related note: because concealed carry purses are almost always heavier than is comfortable, a wide shoulder strap makes a huge difference in comfort. If you can find wide straps that are also padded, so much the better.

Left, right, or ambidextrous?

As left-handers know all too well, most of the world is designed for the convenience of right-handers. Concealed carry purses are no exception to this rule, and most concealed carry purse designs work well *only* for right hand access. Making matters worse, several companies claim their purses are ambidextrous but a lot of times when this claim is made the companies are—how shall I word this gently?—*lying through their teeth.* There are exceptions: I want to give a special shout-out here to Gun Tote'n Mamas, a company that obviously put a lot of thought into making truly ambidextrous designs that really do work as well for left-handers as they do for right-handers. Thank goodness there's still some truth in advertising!

A right hander usually carries her concealed carry purse on the left shoulder, or crossbody with the bag landing on the left hip. The gun compartment zipper faces toward the front of the body where the right hand can easily reach it. You draw by stabilizing the purse with your left hand while yanking down the zipper (or ripping open the hook-and-loop) with your right hand. Then you get a firing grip on the gun before pulling it out of the gun compartment. Although similar to the draw from a crossdraw belt holster, purse draw is much slower because the compartment must be opened before the drawstroke can begin.

Most purses are designed to have a decorative side facing away from the user's body as the purse is carried, with a plainer side facing toward the user's body. The outer face will almost always have added design elements such as extra pockets, fancy zippers, or other features, while the inner face will usually be entirely plain or nearly so.

As a result of these two facts—the way a concealed carry purse must be used, and the typical purse style which provides only one decorative face—concealed carry purses are almost universally *backwards* for the left-hander. If you carry the purse on your right shoulder with the decorative face outward, the natural method for a lefty, the access zipper faces to the rear where your dominant left hand can't reach it. If you wear it unnaturally on your left shoulder, the zipper will face forward and the decorative side will face out, but there's no easy way to get a firing grip with the left hand with the purse on the left shoulder. You might carry the purse zipper-forward on your right shoulder, which makes it possible to access the gun left-handed—but then the decorative face of the purse will be toward your body and the ugly plain side will face the world. Ugh.

Besides all that, designs with sewn-in holsters always place the holster and retention straps to suit the right handed user, not to suit the lefty. And yet the companies' literature often claims that the purse is "ambidextrous." After all, you *could* swing the purse around and get in there left handed—if you were a contortionist, or didn't mind habitually carrying your purse ugly side out!

So my advice to left-handers looking for a concealed carry purse is that you look *very* carefully at the actual designs. Do not trust the literature or website verbiage, which almost universally mislead or outright lie to the left-handed consumer. Instead, *look* at the photos and design sketches to visualize how you would use the product as a left hander. If you cannot figure out how it could work, steer clear and purchase a purse that you know will work for you.

Some ways the purse makers have addressed the handedness issue is to make extremely plain purses without a decorative face (many makers); to design pass-through gun compartments with a zipper at either end (Gun Tote'n Mamas); or to create left-handed and right-handed versions of the same purse style (Ladies Protection).[108] These solutions are worth pursuing, and we hope to see many more of them.

As a general rule, if you are purchasing a concealed carry purse as a backup method or alternative carry device, you'll probably want to purchase an ambidextrous design even if you are not left-handed and even if you do not consider yourself ambidextrous. The added flexibility of ambidextrous capability means that the purse could also function as your everyday holster if you ever become injured in your dominant hand, wrist, arm, or shoulder—exactly the sort of circumstance a backup carry method would be intended to cover.

Size matters

One of the complaints frequently heard about gun purses is simply this: "It's too BIG!!" Although purse size styles change with the changing seasons, most women have a preferred handbag size that they'll return to whenever possible. Since that preference isn't always for the large or oversized, it pays to shop carefully.

Fortunately, concealed carry purse makers have finally addressed this concern in recent years. Several companies specialize in small purses suitable for carrying smaller firearms. Unfortunately, using a smaller purse means you'll be carrying a smaller, more difficult to shoot handgun, one which may not be comfortable to practice with or powerful enough to do the job you need it to do when you need to do it. And a smaller purse almost always features an

---

108 *Ladies Protection LLC, PO Box 1432, Lebec, CA 93243. (661) 993-7160. www. ladiesprotection.com.*

uncomfortably small opening to the gun compartment, more likely to abrade the hand and also much slower and more awkward during the draw. For this reason, be wary of purses that seem too small to be true. They might also be too small to be useful.

At the other extreme, an oversized purse tempts you to overload it with too much weight. Larger purses make room for a full-size firearm, easier to shoot, but full-size guns weigh more than the tiny pocket wonders ideal for smaller purses. The added weight tempts the user to set the purse down often, increasing the risk that it will be left somewhere inappropriate or that the firearm will not be in reach when needed.

When shopping online, pay special attention to the measurements given in the catalogs. A lot of catalogs don't provide background details to give a sense of size or perspective in their product photos, but nearly all of them provide measurements. If you're in doubt about whether the purse dimensions listed in the catalog will work for you, get out a ruler and a large piece of paper and trace out an approximation of the purse on the paper using the measurements given in the catalog. Is it too small? Too large? Or just right for your purposes?

A question of fashion

Finally, we get to the question most women ask first, "Is there such a thing as an attractive concealed carry purse?" My answer to this is an emphatic YES. Just a few short years ago, there were very few choices, and the designs—while attractive in the classic sense—were fairly boring and uniform. Not so today! These days, whether your style is classic or modern, sporty or flirtatious, trendy or more staid, you should be able to find a concealed carry purse that suits your fashion sense and your lifestyle.

On-Body Carry for the Fashionable Woman

"Here's the problem I have with concealed carry," a friend confided to me one day. "I want to look like a girl, not like some guy wearing oversized baggy clothes with an untucked tee shirt and jeans four sizes too big. There just isn't any way for a fashionable woman to carry on-body, is there?" Sometimes it seems so, I told my friend. Fortunately, the situation is not nearly as dire as it might seem at first. Women who want to dress attractively and still be prepared to defend themselves do have some good choices.

A complete on-body concealment system requires four things:

- a firearm of the appropriate size,
- a safe holster,
- a secure method of attaching that holster to your body, and
- a good cover garment.

Each of these four components is *equally* important, and together they make a complete carry system. Far too many people focus on only one of these elements, neglecting the other three, and then are surprised when they cannot comfortably conceal the firearm. A great many people purchase successively smaller and smaller firearms, not realizing that the difficulty they are encountering is actually due to the poor holster types they've been choosing. Or they frantically purchase one holster after another, failing to understand that without a solidly secure way to attach the holster to the body (typically a stiff belt) even the best holster will be uncomfortable and fail to conceal the firearm adequately. Each element must work with the others to create a complete concealment system.

And that brings us to a discussion of cover garments. On the range, an acceptable cover garment might be a ratty old oversized sweatshirt, or the baggy untucked tee shirt that so distressed my friend. But few people go through their day to day lives wearing nothing *but* country-casual clothes. Most of us go to an office, or out on the town, and we want to be attractive when we do. So what do everyday cover garments for women look like?

Better than you'd think! Surprisingly, women's styles are actually *more* conducive to on-body concealed carry than men's styles are... once you let go of your prejudices.

For example, a quick thumb-through of the spring 2010 catalogs shows me that this summer, many women will be wearing baby-doll halter tops with empire waists. A lot of these styles sport extra ruffles and flourishes, too. So if consumers follow the catalogs (sometimes they don't), we'll probably be able to wear belt holsters along with slim jeans or shorts. The summery, flowing baby-doll halter top will run long enough and loose enough in the waist to function as a cover garment. That's ideal for on the waist carry.

Sheer fabrics appear to be going strong, too. Can a lace-crocheted cardigan vest help concealed carry? Surprisingly, yes it can. Here's how: wear a long, snug tank. Pull the tank layer down over the gun to cover it. You may have a visible lump. Not to worry—toss the lacy cardigan over it. That breaks up the covered outline beautifully, and the gun vanishes.

Although these specific styles will undoubtedly change even before this book sees press, they should serve as an example of the type of thinking you'll need to do in order to stay fashionably armed. Look for fashion elements that accommodate potential carry methods, rather than bemoaning what you *can't* do. For example, when bellbottoms are in style, shirt styles usually shrink to show bare bellies or cling to cleavage. Difficult to carry on the waist in such circumstances, isn't it? But those wide-legged pants mean we can conceal an ankle rig even while wearing body-skimming tops that would never hide a belt holster. When skinny jeans are the rage, shirt styles will almost invariably change to accommodate carry up top. It's almost never fashionable to wear clothes that reveal *everything*, and the parts that aren't revealed are the parts you focus on for concealed carry.

That's an important point and worth repeating: when you want to show off one part of your body, simply conceal the firearm somewhere else. You'll never be happy trying to hide a handgun on a body part you enjoy revealing.

Growing up, we all learned that vertical stripes or dark colors can help you look more slender. Older relatives told us to wear a slip with a light-colored skirt, and friends pointed out that nylons might make you look tanned but sometimes look wrong for the outfit. This is the type of knowledge women new to concealed carry need to develop: what fabrics best cover a firearm? What should we avoid? Are there any styles that actually help us look *better* when we're carrying a firearm than when we're not?[109]

---

109 We will know we have arrived as a special interest group the day someone finally develops a really excellent girdle-based holster.

Here are a few of my own observations from many years of carrying a firearm. Please note that every rule has an exception. Occasionally you'll come across an outfit which seems to defy all the rules but works well anyway. Thank goodness!

Fabrics and Prints

Prints generally offer better firearms concealment than solids, because they can disturb the outline of the firearm to prevent it from printing. Random patterns seem to work better than repetitive patterns such as stripes or plaids. Sometimes such repeating patterns actually emphasize the lump you're trying to conceal.

Dark colors usually conceal the gun better than light ones. If you wear a light color you will have to make sure the gun doesn't show in various types of lighting. If the gun doesn't hide well underneath the blouse material in all lights, but the blouse works well otherwise, consider adding a layer and tucking the gun beneath an undershirt.

Fabric with some body to it works better than flimsy, wispy stuff. If you have a thin blouse that *almost* works, add a little body by ironing it with starch.

Blue Jeans

The problem with blue jeans is that the "right" waistline changes dramatically and often. One day, everyone happily wears jeans that fall comfortably at their natural waists; the next, low-cut jeans are the rage and anyone with a natural waist gets laughed at for wearing "mom jeans." Four inches of rise, five inches, eight inches, six inches... back to four. Or even three. How low can you go? Of course it's all a ploy to make us buy more clothing, but let's face it: it works!

When it comes to concealed carry, those moving waistbands cause serious problems. A holster designed to fit below the waistband doesn't work well when there's no real estate below the waistband where it can hide. A high-ride design can only be worn so high before drawing it hits your armpit. And that's just how it goes. For this reason, when you're thinking about buying a new pair of jeans—perhaps since the "right" waistline moved again while you were mopping the kitchen floor or something—take the holster and firearm with you as you shop. You'll never know if that new waistline will work if you don't try it with the holster in question.

More prosaically, guys sometimes tell each other to buy the next size up when they start carrying concealed, especially in the waistband (IWB). But that trick rarely works well for women. Instead, head over to the guys' department and snag jeans there. Guys' jeans are bigger in the waist and proportionately narrower in the rear than women's jeans, creating a little extra room for a gun carried IWB while hugging the curves the way jeans should.

Speaking of hugging the curves, if you can find jeans with stretchy fibers in them, you'll find IWB carry much more comfortable.

Casual Slacks

Shopping for casual slacks presents all the challenges faced when shopping for jeans, plus one more: a lot of women's slacks simply don't have belt loops. And of those that do, the loops are often vestigial or decorative, not functional elements intended to help you use your clothing to secure a practical belt.

Right now, this season, I've had some success finding sturdy twill pants with useful waist features. If you do find some you like that work well for you, stock up! They'll be gone next week for sure.

If you can't find slacks with belt loops, do the next best thing and position a belly band so the gun rides exactly where it otherwise would. The draw remains comfortably familiar, and your ordinary tops and blouses will provide the same concealment you're used to.

Dress Slacks

Although at first glance it might seem that dress slacks would create even more problems than casual slacks, this needn't be true—in part because the more tailored look demanded by most offices serves to keep dress slack waistline designs from becoming too outré. You can nearly always find belted dress slacks if you look for them.

Some years, dress slacks tend toward the loose and flowing, in which case ankle carry seems the natural response. When the look becomes severely tailored, consider adding a business jacket and using a shoulder holster or undershirt-based style.

Blouses, Sweaters, and Tops

To experiment with styles on the cheap, take a trip to the local Goodwill store or do the flea market/garage sale thing. You can purchase a wide variety of clothes to experiment with in the privacy of your own home. Once you've found some basic shapes that work reasonably well for you, your trips to the full-price retail outlets will go a lot more smoothly because you'll eliminate most of the guesswork before you get into the dressing room.

Until you learn where your own limits are, you will probably want to buy blouses one size up from your usual. If you're petite, consider shopping in regular sizes for blouses, because the slightly-longer lengths might work better—especially if you carry outside the waistband (OWB) and need longer cover garments. Similarly, if you like man-styled oxfords or other unisex styles, remember the clothes in the men's department have a little more length and may suit your purposes better.

Sweaters usually work very well for concealed carry, but they have to be the comfy-cozy-bulky type, rather than the thin clingy type. Cardigans are great, shrug sets not so great. But sometimes you can make a shrug set work well if you own a belly band and have a generally straight posture.

Skirts and Dresses

Belly bands work great for skirts. Any blouse or top that works well for concealment with jeans will usually work just as well (or better) with a skirt and a belly band positioned near where the gun normally rides when it's on the belt.

A skirt with wide belt loops is worth its weight in gold. It's worth scouring the stores until you find one or a dozen that will work for you. Such a skirt makes it entirely possible to wear your normal holster and belt combination along with blouses and tops you would ordinarily wear with slacks or jeans.

When positioning your belly band or undershirt holster beneath a dress, carefully consider how you will draw the firearm if you need it. Can you reach it through the neckline? Will you pull the skirt up for access? Practice this, cautiously, with an *unloaded* firearm during your regular dry fire routine.

A kangaroo pouch holster (such as SmartCarry) often works well with skirts and dresses. With a skirt, you draw from the waistline just as you would with pants. When wearing a dress, the draw becomes more than a little immodest—but what do you care? We're talking about *saving your life* here... and if you shoot accurately enough, the criminal won't survive to tell anyone about seeing your underwear.

Conclusion

So there you have it. Although at first it might seem impossible to carry on-body while maintaining your own sense of style, facing the challenge with a little creativity and a sense of fun can help provide solutions.

Beyond the Handgun

Dear Gunhilda,

If an attacker tries to take my gun away
and use it against me, what should I
do?

~ Worried in Willows

Dear Worried,

Pull the felon repulsion lever. You
should find it just underneath your
trigger finger.

~ Gunhilda

The ABCs of Ammunition

Choosing a good ammunition for your handgun can be a confusing and frustrating process. Fortunately, once you understand what you're looking for and why it matters, the process gets a lot easier. Please trust me on this one: this isn't something you need to agonize over. It's just one more thing to learn something about. Once you have the basics down, it won't feel nearly so overwhelming.

About Ammunition Shopping

In many gun stores, ammunition is stocked behind the counter—either by law or by shopkeeper choice. If that's the case, you will need to tell the person at the counter what you want and he or she will hand it to you. In other places, however, you'll have to find your own ammunition, possibly buried in the midst of an overwhelming selection. Here's how to simplify the trip.

First, ammunition comes in the following major categories:

- Handgun
- Rifle
- Shotgun

Each of these ammunition types usually has its own division within the ammunition section. But sometimes handgun and rifle ammunition might be stocked together because there is some overlap between the two. If you are after .22-caliber ammunition in a store which stocks handgun and rifle ammunition separately, look in the rifle section first.

Once you have found the handgun category, it gets easier. Store owners usually stock their ammunition by caliber, from smallest to largest. So you can usually find .25 or .32 ammunition at one end of the section and .45 or larger ammunition at the other end, with .38 and 9mm and .40 calibers somewhere near the center.[110]

Once you've found the caliber you're looking for, you need to know that

---

110 *Remember that cartridges which begin with a period—such as .25, .32, .38, .40, .45—are fractions of an inch, while the ones which end with mm are measured on the metric scale.*

there are two basic types of handgun ammunition: practice or target loads, and self defense or hunting loads. Practice rounds generally cost less than self defense rounds, because rounds intended for self defense usually feature higher-quality components and require precision workmanship. Practice ammunition usually arrives in larger boxes of 50 or 100 rounds, while self defense ammunition is usually offered in smaller 20-round boxes. This size cue should help you tell at a glance which type of ammunition you've got your eye on.

When shopping for practice rounds, buy the cheapest ammunition you can find that offers "jacketed" bullets; that is, bullets with a thin layer of copper or another metal over a lead core. Look for boxes labeled *FMJ* (full metal jacket) or *TMJ* (total metal jacket). The difference between these two is that a full metal jacket covers only the front part of the bullet, while a total metal jacket covers the entire bullet including the base.[111] Both are good choices. Using jacketed bullets will greatly reduce your lead exposure and will also make it much easier to clean your firearm when you are done shooting.

If your firearm barrel has standard rifling (check your owner's manual), you may choose to practice with less-expensive bare lead bullets rather than jacketed rounds. I don't recommend this because of the dramatic increase in lead exposure both while shooting and while cleaning the gun later. And perhaps I haven't been clear enough about the amount of work that goes into cleaning a leaded-up barrel: it's a major and annoying pain in the backside, and not worth it. But that's your call based on your own priorities.

Safety Issue

Never shoot bare lead bullets through a Glock or other firearm with polygonal rifling inside the barrel. On these types of barrels, bare lead bullets can dangerously increase the internal pressure.

As a general rule, buy American-made ammunition only. Many foreign brands—especially those which use steel cases—will foul the firearm much worse than American ammunition does. Why make more work for yourself than you have to? Many also smell terrible when fired, creating a somewhat unpleasant shooting experience.

There's one more exception to the "buy whatever's cheapest" rule for practice ammunition: *never* buy or shoot ammunition someone else has reloaded. Buy only factory rounds from a known company with good quality control. Although they may seem a good deal at first, reloaded rounds such as those purchased from an individual at a gun show offer no quality control and may

---

111 *You won't be able to see the bullet's base. It's covered by the case.*

even damage your firearm.[112]

So that's the briefing for practice ammunition: buy what's cheap, with a few caveats. But before you select your self defense ammunition, you will need to understand a little bit about bullet shapes and a little bit about what you need the bullet to do.

Bullet Shapes

Ammunition manufacturers create different-shaped bullets to do different things. For instance, practice rounds marked "wadcutter" or "semi-wadcutter" punch very tidy holes in cardboard or paper targets. The tidy holes make it easier to see where each individual bullet landed when shooting in competitions. Roundnose bullets (the traditional bullet shape) cost little to manufacture and feed very nicely in semi-autos. But—although both have been used for such purposes—neither of these shapes is designed specifically for self defense.

What's a bullet to do?

In order to understand what bullet shape we need for self defense, we first need to understand what we want our ammunition to do. Here's the goal: you need a cartridge that stops your attacker quickly. The more quickly you stop him,[113] the more likely you are to survive his attack. It doesn't matter what happens to him *later*, after the attack is over. It only matters that he stops, right here and right now. For this reason, you can safely ignore anyone who says to you, "Plenty of people have been killed by (insert favorite round here)." Someone who says that has missed the point, because the single most critical factor for defense ammunition is whether the attacker STOPS. It will give you no joy to know that he died a week after he killed you. You need to stop him immediately, *before* he can do whatever-it-was he was planning to do to you.

Breaking it down still further, there are two basic ways to stop an attacker: 1) he stops because he decides to stop, or 2) he stops because he is physically incapable of continuing. Door Number One offers the most common way firearms stop criminals. The vast majority of the time when firearms are used in self defense, nobody has to fire even a single shot. Of those times when shots are fired, a lot of times the "fight just goes out" of an attacker who actually has very minor injuries. Thank goodness.

Unfortunately, that's not something you can count on. Although the at-

---

112 *"Damage your firearm" is a euphemism for "cause the gun to shatter into pieces while you are shooting it, endangering bystanders and possibly sending you to the hospital for hand surgery."*
113 *Or her! Criminals come in both sexes and all ages.*

tacker may quit when you display your weapon, the situation becomes far more dangerous for you once he discovers you are armed—especially if you hesitate. You must be determined to follow through. Discovering that his intended victim is armed, or even getting ineffectually shot, will almost certainly frighten him, but what he *does* as a result of being frightened... that's up to him. Some people become angry, aggressive, violent, and downright vicious when frightened. A very determined person can keep fighting (and keep trying to kill you) despite very bad injuries. You might get one of those. So never plan on the mere display being enough to stop the attack. Never plan on a minor injury making him quit. Hope for it, but don't plan on it. Plan to keep going until he is really down and count it as a happy bonus if he stops before that point.

So now let's look behind Door Number Two: stopping the attacker by making it physically impossible for him to continue.[114] To stop an attacker quickly, the bullet needs to hit something important and it needs to carry enough energy to damage or destroy that thing once it gets there.

Put even more simply and brutally, it is the attacker's brain you need to stop. To do that, you can either intimidate his brain or incapacitate it. To incapacitate his brain, you can hit the brain directly or you can instead hit the brain's supply and command lines: the oxygen and blood that the brain must have in order to continue directing its attack on you, or the major nerves that carry its commands to the attacker's muscles.

Hitting the brain directly doesn't work as well in real life as it does in the movies. In the movies, good guys always hit what they aim at while bad guys always miss. In real life, the outcome doesn't depend on which side you're on. And in real life, the attacker's brain hides inside a small, rapidly-moving bunker with an effective aim point about the size of a tangerine from most angles. If you miss by a few inches when aiming for the brain, you've missed the attacker entirely. Missing the attacker generally means you hit something or someone else, possibly someone you love. And it means the attacker keeps coming.

In contrast, hitting the brain's supply system—the heart, lungs, and major blood vessels—works more reliably. If you aim for the center of the attacker's

---

114 *This doesn't necessarily mean "dead," by the way. Please don't think I'm using euphemisms here! Stopped means stopped. And that's all it means. An unconscious attacker has been stopped. A paralyzed attacker has been stopped. A disarmed attacker who cannot re-arm himself has been stopped. Remember: it does not matter what happens to the criminal after the attack stops. It only matters that the attack stops as quickly as possible and that you—the innocent person—get home safely to the people who love you.*

chest, a miss by a few inches in any direction will still hit the attacker rather than endangering bystanders. And you have a fairly good chance of disrupting those supply lines. The attacker's brain, starved of the oxygen and blood it needs to continue the fight, will allow his body to collapse so you can escape.

Reaching the goal

And that brings us back to bullet shapes. The brief discussion above helped us understand the things we need our defense ammunition to do. We need ammunition that helps us damage or destroy important tissue deep in the chest. The ideal bullet shape will help you hit the structures you need to hit, and will also do enough damage to disable the attacker once it gets there.

Of course your choice of target and your ability to hit where you aim makes the most significant difference as far as what gets hit. However, the larger the bullet diameter, the better chance you have of hitting something important. A near miss with a small bullet might turn into a decent hit with a larger one. Further, bigger wounds bleed faster. The faster the blood loss, the faster the attacker will lose consciousness and stop his attack on you. So you want to make a big hole in the attacker if you can.

Although some major blood vessels run close to the surface, most lie buried near the body's core. The heart beats deep within the center of the chest, between the lungs and slightly to the left of the sternum. The aorta, the vena cava, the thoracic artery and the pulmonary artery—the largest vessels in the human body—nestle close to the heart. To strike these structures from many angles, you need a round that penetrates twelve inches or more. If the bullet isn't going fast enough to reach this depth, it may not ever touch the vital organs, or have enough power to incapacitate them if it does.

Generally, the larger the bullet's caliber, the more difficult it becomes to control the firearm that launches the bullet, especially when shooting rapid multiple shots. As with so many other things in life, finding the "best ammunition" involves balancing many different factors. Many people shoot small calibers more accurately, but stopping an attacker often requires a large-caliber hole. So researchers began looking for ways to make smaller bullets behave like larger ones.

Further, a fast-moving bullet penetrates more deeply, and thus is more likely to reach the important structures. However, the faster the bullet moves, the more likely it becomes that the bullet will go completely through the attacker and hit innocent others. So researchers also looked for a bullet shape that would "put the brakes on" once it reached its target. If the bullet were going fast enough when it hit the brakes, they reasoned, it would reach the important structures but stop there.

Researchers thus needed a bullet that would act larger than it really was, and one that would reliably stop when it reached its target. What if they could create a bullet that would actually change shape? One that behaved one way (like a small bullet) when fired, but a different way (like a large one) once it hit the target? Thus was born the hollowpoint bullet, a bullet designed specifically for defense use.

Picture a traditional bullet with its round nose. Now, scoop out the end of that nose, hollowing out a small hole on the point of the bullet's nose. That's a hollowpoint—a bullet with a hollow point at its nose. Add some refinements, such as scored grooves around the rim to help the bullet change shape when the time comes, and you have the ideal bullet for stopping an attacker. This shape helps achieve several important goals for defensive ammunition.

When the hollowpoint bullet hits a solid target, pressure from the impact forces the bullet to open, curling back from its dimpled nose almost like a banana peel. It spreads out into a mushroom shape and becomes much larger in diameter than its nominal caliber. This allows the bullet to make a much larger hole in the attacker than it otherwise would. Although a small caliber will never have the mass that a larger one does, the hollowpoint shape allows bullets of all sizes to function much more efficiently than traditional bullets of the same diameter.

Safety Note

Never fire ammunition of the wrong size for your gun. Most firearms have the correct ammunition type stamped on the frame or barrel. If yours does not, don't guess. Take the gun to a gunsmith or to the gun store from which you purchased it, and have an expert measure the chamber.

As the hollowpoint bullet opens up, its new shape also puts the brakes on the its velocity, allowing it to slow and stop within the attacker's body. Think of it as a parachute which slows the bullet's descent into the body cavity, helping it remain safely contained inside its intended target.

Are hollowpoint bullets "more deadly" than other types of bullets? Yes—and no. Yes, each individual bullet does more immediate damage than bullets that are not designed for self defense. However, because the hollowpoint shape does its job more efficiently than other bullet shapes, the attacker tends to stop sooner—and that, in turn, means attackers shot with hollowpoint bullets get shot fewer times, on average, than attackers shot with other bullet types. They are thus *more* likely to survive with prompt treatment, because they have been shot fewer times. Of course you will continue to shoot until the attacker stops, and you will not have time to pause and assess the effect of each shot! Every situation is different, and there's no way to tell in advance how many bullets it might take to stop any individual attack. But as a general rule, attackers stopped with hollowpoint bullets receive fewer shots and are more likely to survive with prompt medical care. Hollowpoint bullets are thus safer for the attacker than other bullet shapes.

Further, because hollowpoints open up and generally stop within the body of the attacker, hollowpoints are safer for witnesses and bystanders. The bullets penetrate the attacker's body, but are less likely to reach beyond that and hit innocent others.

And finally, because the attack can be stopped more quickly, hollowpoint bullets are safer for you. Stopping the attack remains the crucial goal and hollowpoints help you reach that goal more quickly than other types of bullets.

The majority of law enforcement agencies in America use hollowpoint ammunition because it is safer for the officers, safer for witnesses and bystanders, and even safer for assailants. So whenlooking for defensive ammunition for yourself, do what the police do: look for a hollowpoint bullet in a round designed for self defense. If anyone questions your choice, tell them that all the reasons that make hollowpoint ammunition ideal for law enforcement also make it the best choice for civilian self defense.[115]

Weight a minute...

Bullets come in different weights, measured in grains. The higher the grain (gr.) number, the heavier the bullet. Generally, weight improves penetration but also slows the bullet's flight. If the bullet isn't going fast enough when it hits, the hollowpoint might fail to open and do its job. For this reason, I suggest purchasing a mid-weight bullet in most calibers, which provides a balance of desirable features. For example, 9mm bullets might be offered in 115-gr., 124-gr., and 147-gr. sizes. By choosing the middle weight, the 124-gr. bullet, you select a bullet with enough mass to do the

> **Rimfire**
>
> Ammunition with the primer located in the bottom rim of the case. In casual conversation, *rimfire* often refers to the .22 Long Rifle cartridge or to guns which fire it.

---

115 *If you live in a jurisdiction that prohibits hollowpoint ammunition to ordinary citizens, find out what your local police use when they are off-duty and use that. If even their off-duty choices are off-limits to you, consider using a larger caliber than you would otherwise choose and select a fast-moving roundnose instead. And lobby to change the unreasonable law which limits you to a less safe choice for personal defense.*

job but also enough speed to open up when it arrives on target.

Caliber Confusion

Calibers are confusing. Don't allow anyone to make you feel stupid if you don't intuitively understand this stuff, because there's nothing intuitive about it. Generally speaking, caliber refers to the size of the bullet a gun will fire, and also usually refers specifically to the bullet's diameter or to the bore size of the gun that fires it. But due to all sorts of vagaries in the ammunition-manufacturing world, the nominal caliber designation isn't always the actual bullet diameter. Nor is the bullet diameter the only factor that matters, as we will see in the discussion below.

Sometimes caliber is measured on the imperial scale, by decimal fractions of inches. Other times it is measured on the metric scale, usually in millimeters. In either case, the first number you see doesn't provide all the information you need in order to know if the ammunition will work in your gun. Sometimes, instead of one simple number, the ammunition size and type will be represented by two groups of numbers. In such cases, the first number usually indicates the bullet diameter, while the second number often (but not always) represents the length of the cartridge, measured from base to case rim.

Centerfire

Ammunition with the primer located in a small cup at the bottom center of the case.

Caliber numbers (such as *9mm* or *.45*) are usually followed by words or letters to create the complete name of the cartridge (9mm *Luger* or .45 *ACP*). These letters are as important as the caliber number. They often represent a brand name or an abbreviation for the name of the company that first introduced the round. Sometimes they provide more information about the cartridge in some other way. For example, ammunition designed for semi-autos generally differs in shape from ammunition designed for revolvers. Using only the caliber number, without the added letters, some semi-auto and revolver rounds seem identical.[116] But a closer look shows dramatic differences, and that they fit different types of guns.

Below follows a whirlwind tour of some common calibers and cartridges. It is not a comprehensive list, merely a quick overview of some caliber-related facts that might interest a beginning or intermediate shooter. To help you

---

116 Such as .380 and .38, for example. Mathematically, there's no reason to throw the 0 onto the end of the .380 round. But it serves to help distinguish the .380 ACP (semi-auto) from the .38 Special (revolver).

easily use this section as a reference, I've listed the calibers from smallest to largest.

.22 Calibers

Starting with the lowly .22, then, let us begin. These three .22 rounds are all rimfires. The most common .22-caliber round is the .22 Long Rifle, which is often abbreviated .22 LR. Don't let the word "rifle" in the name confuse you, because this ammunition fires from both handguns and rifles. When someone talks about shooting a .22, they usually mean .22 LR. This ammunition is plentiful, easy to find, and very inexpensive. It has very little recoil and isn't as loud as many other cartridges so it is very comfortable to shoot. All of this makes it an ideal round for beginners who wish to learn to shoot well.

Next up—but actually a step down in power—we have .22 Short. The bullet diameter matches the .22 LR, but the bullet gets placed in a shorter case with less powder. Years back, shooting galleries used rifles chambered in .22 Short at carnivals and county fairs.

The **.22 Winchester Magnum Rimfire (.22 WMR)**, often called .22 Magnum or .22 Mag, may fire from handguns or rifles. Slightly larger in diameter than .22 LR or .22 Short, its long case holds more powder, giving the round a little more punch than .22 LR. A revolver chambered for .22 Magnum will accept a .22 LR round, but these are different calibers, and it is dangerous to fire .22LR in a gun designed for .22 Magnum.[117]

.25 ACP and .32 Calibers

Less powerful than the .22 calibers, the **.25 Auto Colt Pistol** (.25 ACP or .25 Auto) provides the next step up in diameter. If you're looking for a defense round, stay away from this one. Although this centerfire round is quite common in inexpensive handguns, it does not produce enough power to do that job. Of the .25 Auto, firearms great Jeff Cooper once quipped, "Carry a 25 if it makes you feel good, but do not ever load it. If you load it you may shoot it. If you shoot it you may hit somebody, and if you hit somebody—and he finds out about it—he may be very angry with you."[118]

The **.32 ACP or .32 Auto** was among the many cartridges developed and popularized by John Moses Browning and the Colt Company back around the turn of the last century. In Europe, this round is called the 7.65mm Browning.

---

117 *Some single-action revolvers (and a few rare double-action types) allow the user to convert a .22 Magnum revolver to fire .22 LR ammunition. Such conversions are perfectly functional; the caution applies to firearms designed to fire only .22 Magnum ammunition.*

118 *Jeff Cooper's Commentaries, Vol. 4, No. 14 (December 1996).*

Although often used in lightweight pistols, especially those small enough for pocket carry, most firearms instructors say .32 ACP does not produce enough power for dedicated self defense.

Designed for revolvers, the **.32 H&R Magnum** round was introduced in 1983. It isn't the same thing as .32 ACP. A handful of firearms manufacturers produce revolvers chambered for the .32 H&R Magnum.

Are .38 Super and .380 Auto the same thing?

No. Although both fire from semi-auto handguns, .380 Auto has an overall length of slightly under an inch, while a .38 Super cartridge measures over an inch.

The *Really* Confusing Calibers: .38, .357, & 9mm Rounds

With the **.380 ACP or .380 Auto**, we enter the realm of truly confusing caliber facts. Remember that the cartridge numbers often, but not always, indicate the diameter of the bullet? The .380 Auto is one of the exceptions. Its bullet actually measures .355" (9mm) in diameter. Because its bullet diameter measures 9mm, but the cartridge's overall length measures shorter than other 9mm ammunition, .380 ACP is sometimes called 9mm Short. Other names include 9mm Kurz (kurz means short in German) and 9mm Corto (Corto means short in Italian). It's also sometimes called 9mm Browning because its inventor was John Moses Browning. The .380 ACP round is widely believed to be the minimal round acceptable for self defense, and it was the favored police round throughout Europe for most of the 20th century.

Another round in this size class is **9x18mm Makarov**, often simply called 9x18. This one was pretty rare in America until a few years after the breakup of the USSR, but has become more familiar to American buyers with the popularity of Makarov pistols. Lengthwise, the 9x18 falls about halfway between the .380 ACP and the more common 9mm Luger, but it performs most similarly to the .380 ACP. A confusing factoid: although the 9x18 is called a 9mm round, it is really not 9mm. Its bullet is slightly larger than 9mm, measuring .364" rather than the 9mm-equivalent .355".

Despite the incredible number of cartridges which fire bullets 9mm in diameter, most of the time when someone refers to 9mm, they mean the very common 9mm Luger round, so named in honor of its inventor, Georg Luger. Other names for this same round include 9mm Parabellum (9mm Para), or 9x19mm, or 9mm NATO. The 9mm Luger often costs less than other self defense rounds. More powerful than the anemic .380 ACP, like the .380 ACP it easily lends itself to small, easily-carried firearm designs. It remains widely used in police work throughout the world, and also represents one of the most popular concealed carry calibers.

To avoid further confusion, I'm not even going to talk about the **9mm Largo** cartridge, a Spanish round rarely seen in America and sometimes referred to as the 9x21. Just be aware that it isn't the same thing as the 9mm Luger.

We haven't yet left the realm of the 9mm calibers. Next up: the **.357 Sig**, a young cartridge first introduced in 1994 and designed by Sig Sauer[119] in partnership with Federal Ammunition.[120] Created to fire in semi-automatic handguns, it mimics the ballistic performance of .357 Magnum revolver ammunition. Despite its name, the .357 Sig does not use .357" diameter bullets, but rather uses 9mm-equivalent .355" bullets.

A semi-auto round introduced in 1929 and popular for many years, **.38 Super Auto (.38 Super)**, was steadily diminishing in popularity and perhaps on the edge of extinction when a new shooting sport called IPSC revived it and gave it a place in history. Now it ranks once again among the most popular cartridges. Competition shooters love .38 Super because it provides power nearly equivalent to .45 ACP, but with lighter recoil and magazine capacity more typical of 9mm. Despite the name, .38 Super does not fire .38" bullets. The bullets it uses measure .355" or .356".

Designed for revolvers, **.38 Special** might boast of being the most popular revolver cartridge ever produced. Despite the name, this caliber actually uses .357" bullets. While any short-barreled revolver may be called a "snubby" by aficionados, most folks immediately think of a .38 Special caliber revolver when they hear the word snubby. As with many other rounds, the .38 Special comes in standard and +p variants. The .38 Special has a long history, which means many revolvers chambered for this round were produced in the days before modern metallurgy. These older revolvers cannot handle the more powerful ammunition called +p (think, plus power) which became available in the early 1970s. As a result, older .38 Special revolvers should fire only standard rounds, avoiding ammunition marked +p. Even some modern revolvers, most notably the super-lightweight alloys, are not designed to handle large volumes of +p ammunition. If in doubt, read the owner's manual or call the manufacturer before using ammunition marked +p.

119 *SIG SAUER, Inc., 18 Industrial Drive, Exeter, NH 03833 (603) 772-2302. www. sigsauer.com.*
120 *Federal Cartridge Company, 900 Ehlen Drive, Anoka, MN 55303-7503. (800) 831-0850. www.federalpremium.com.*

The nice thing about the **.357 Magnum** round is that revolvers designed to fire it can also fire .38 Special ammunition.[121] Gun owners who purchase a .357 Magnum revolver can use less-expensive .38 Special as a practice round, while reserving more powerful and more expensive .357 Magnum rounds for self defense. Be aware, however, that repeatedly firing .38 Special ammunition through your .357 Magnum frame requires a special emphasis on regular, deep cleaning. Otherwise, a ring of lead residue will build up within the chambers. If enough rounds are fired between effective cleanings, the residue may become so stubborn as to be considered permanent, and its presence will prevent the ability to chamber the longer .357 Magnum round in that revolver.

.40 and 10mm Calibers

The **.40 S&W** and **10mm Auto** cartridges aren't identical, but have an interesting shared history. The idea of using a bullet in measuring .40 inches or 10mm in diameter for a semi-automatic cartridge had been around for many years, but it wasn't until 1983 that a commercial version of the 10mm appeared. And it was another five years after that before handguns designed to fire it became widely available. Around the same era, many law enforcement agencies—including the FBI—issued 9mm Luger weapons to their departments. After a disastrous shootout in Miami, the FBI decided they needed a more powerful round, and chose to issue 10mm Auto. However, FBI administration soon came to believe the 10mm was too much gun for many of its agents. For this reason, the FBI looked for a round that would put less powder (and thus less power) in the long 10mm cases. In part because of the FBI's search for a less-powerful 10mm, Smith & Wesson introduced the .40 S&W cartridge in the early 1990s, using a shorter case but a bullet the same diameter as the 10mm Auto. This allowed pistols chambered for the .40 S&W cartridge to be smaller than those designed around the 10mm Auto. As soon as the .40 S&W was introduced, the FBI adopted it and many other law enforcement agencies swiftly followed suit. Today the .40 S&W may be the most commonly used

> **ACP?**
>
> ACP means "Automatic Colt Pistol." You'll find it used to designate many different cartridges designed by the Colt Firearms Company.

---

121 *Modern .38 Special firearms will not chamber .357 Magnum. However, some older, inexpensive .38 Special revolvers still available on the used market have chambers bored all the way through, making it possible to insert a .357 Magnum round into these guns. These older firearms were not designed to cope with the stronger pressure of the modern .357 Magnum round.*

police round in America.

.44 Calibers

These rounds fit revolvers. First came the **.44 Russian,** a very old cartridge developed back in the 1870s by Smith & Wesson for the Russian Army under the czars. Initially developed as a black-powder round, it successfully made the transition to smokeless powder and today is very popular for Cowboy-Action Shooting.

Introduced around the turn of the last century, the **.44 S&W Special** (commonly called simply .44 Special) uses a longer case than the older Russian round. When carried in a compact revolver, .44 Special can be a good choice for concealed carry. Like the .44 Russian, .44 Special is also very popular in the Cowboy Action sports.

"This is a **.44 Magnum,** the most powerful handgun in the world... Do you feel lucky, punk?" Despite the claim in Clint Eastwood's famous lines, the .44 Magnum (its full name is .44 Remington Magnum) never was the absolutely most powerful handgun cartridge. However, it's a very powerful round and its popular mystique makes it even more so. Though an excellent hunting round, .44 Magnum isn't tailored for self defense: difficult to shoot rapidly, the bullet can pass through the intended target to hit innocent passersby.

.45 Calibers

No matter what the old guys in the gun shop tell you, .45 Auto or .45 ACP will not send an assailant flying across the room if you hit him in the pinkie finger. It is, however, a very good defense round which makes satisfyingly large holes in the target. First developed by John Moses Browning for the Colt Company around the turn of the 20th century, .45 ACP became one of the most popular and successful rounds ever invented. In part this is because of the tremendous continuing popularity of 1911-pattern pistols designed to fire .45 ACP. Even though there are 1911 variants which fire other calibers and even though there are many other handguns designed around the .45 ACP cartridge, the .45 ACP and the 1911 pistol are closely linked in the minds of most shooters.

Introduced just a few years ago, the .45 GAP or .45 Glock round mimics the ballistic performance of .45 ACP, but launches from smaller, more concealable pistols. To achieve this, it uses a shorter case than the .45 ACP. Guns sized for .45 GAP often fit shooters with small hands better than guns sized for .45 ACP.

An old round designed for revolvers, the .45 Colt (sometimes incorrectly called the .45 Long Colt) remains popular today. In fact, it is the oldest centerfire handgun cartridge still in regular use. Commonly found at Cowboy-Action games, several more modern revolvers can launch it too. The round is not the same as the .45 ACP: the case is longer and has a higher volume, making it potentially a more powerful round.

.50 Calibers

The .50 calibers fall outside the realm of reasonable defense weapons, mostly because of controllability and follow up speed. These really aren't for beginners in any case. The only thing it seems necessary to point out here is that the **.50 AE** (or .50 Action Express) designed for use in hunting handguns is radically different from, and weaker in power than, the **.50 BMG** round designed for rifles. The.500 Magnum S&W, a hunting round, fits revolvers chambered in the same caliber class, but packs considerably more power than the shorter .50-caliber semi-auto rounds.

Lighting the Night

Like cockroaches, criminals love darkness—and for much the same reason. Darkness hides them from the view of those who would otherwise stop their foul activities. For us, darkness creates an unavoidable challenge. Even in well-lit cities, black shadows lurk around the corners of our lives. Fortunately, technology provides great tools for coping with low light. From the incandescent light bulb to florescent tubes, scientists long labored to bring humanity out of smoky, poorly-lit caves into the dazzling brightness of modern life. Facing the same challenge, the self defense industry produced useful tools for people eager to protect themselves.

Unfortunately, human-made products can fail. So these tools don't erase our need to learn how to cope with darkness. They simply make the job a little bit easier—when we have them with us, when they work, when the batteries remain alive. When the lights go out, we still need to defend ourselves. For this reason, if you're serious about protecting yourself, you'll need to learn how to shoot in poor lighting conditions without modern tools. When such tools are available, you can use them. But when they aren't, you won't be dead in the dark.

Choosing a Flashlight

A flashlight provides the simplest form of portable lighting. At the flick of a switch, a smooth beam of cool light floods the area, lighting your path and illuminating the darkness.

The first and most important feature to look for in a flashlight? Presence. You can have the greatest flashlight in the world sitting on your nightstand at home (and you should), but if it's not in your hand as you walk through a shadowy parking lot, that flashlight doesn't meet your needs. It cannot light your way if you don't have it with you.

Hear me out on this one, please. Although you've probably never considered carrying a flashlight with you on a daily basis, a handy light can keep you out of many uncomfortable situations. And once you try keeping a light readily accessible, you'll constantly surprise yourself by wondering how you ever lived without it. Whether it's lighting your footsteps on treacherous ground, illuminating the shadowy figure approaching you in a parking garage, making you more visible to oncoming traffic as you walk, or helping you find the cell phone that slid under the seat of the car, you'll find a million uses for this indispensible tool once you've started carrying it.

In order to keep the light with you, you'll want to find something small, lightweight, and sturdy. It needs to readily cope with getting banged around in the bottom of your purse and it needs to tolerate getting dropped on occasion. To meet these basic requirements, you want an LED bulb rather than a conventional one which doesn't stand up well to abuse. If you might occasionally want to drop the light into a pocket, look for a light driven by a single battery rather than multiple batteries. A pocket clip provides a nice touch, too.

Simple presence puts you well ahead of the lighting game. But for self-defense, you'll want a few other features. Look for a light that provides:

- At least 65 lumens of illumination.
- Good throw. Look for a flashlight that throws a bright, tightly-focused beam at least three car lengths.[122]
- One touch to full light. Avoid lights that require you to cycle through dimmer options before reaching full brightness. You may need full brightness *immediately.*
- Easy off. Avoid lights that require you to cycle through several options before allowing you to shut off the light. You may want to *immediately* get the light off.
- Rear switch. "Tactical" flashlights offer a rear switch rather than (or in addition to) a side switch for the simple reason that you may need the light *immediately.* A side switch can roll away from your thumb, making it necessary for you to hunt it down before activating it. A rear switch remains in the same place at all times.

Do you need a light with a "DNA sampler"? That depends on your goals and your dedication. This scalloped front edge (bezel) provides a vicious striking surface for dealing with an attacker. Unfortunately, it also provides a vicious surface for tearing up your purse, your hands, and your clothing when you carry it.

Now, about batteries and battery life. The state of the art changes con-

---

122 *For this reason, look for "tactical" or "defense" lights rather than "utility" lights. Although they can be equally bright, general-purpose lights usually throw a broader, softer beam.*

stantly with flashlights, and LED lights in particular have evolved rapidly in the past several years. As a general rule, specialty batteries based on lithium, lithium-ion, or other chemistries run longer with less dimming than standard alkaline batteries do. However, in modern LED lights this difference no longer reaches the extreme. So for practical purposes, choose a flashlight run by batteries *you* find easy to replace. Whether that's an alkaline battery or a lithium battery or some other type will depend on your own circumstances. If you regularly shop online, you can easily add specialty flashlight batteries to your online shopping list. But if you're committed to shopping at physical stores, you may want to stick with commonly available alkaline batteries rather than longer-lasting specialty ones.

Finally, a word about cost. With flashlights as with so many other things, you get what you pay for. Although a $2 light from the hardware store might light your way, to get the specialty features most helpful for self-defense, expect to pay $50 or more.[123]

Weapon-Mounted Lights

Time for me to admit a bias. I am not a fan of weapon-mounted lights for defensive handguns in most circumstances. Yes, I realize they are increasingly popular and that I'm swimming against the tide of common opinion. But there are good reasons to avoid these lights. First a definition: a weapon-mounted light is a type of flashlight that affixes to the underside of your firearm. It adds bulk and weight, two factors that present problems for concealed firearms. It also alters the shape of the firearm, making it difficult to find a suitable holster. But although these drawbacks can pose a significant problem, being poorly suited for concealed carry, they aren't the reason I oppose such lights even on home defense handguns.

A light's primary purpose is to help you identify your target. But if use a weapon-mounted light for that purpose, then you point that light—and the firearm it's attached to—at people who might be good guys rather than bad ones. Remember Rule Two? "Do not point your gun at anything you are not willing to destroy." Following this rule becomes much more difficult when armed with a light-bearing firearm. Hanging a light at the muzzle end of a deadly weapon does not turn the deadly weapon into a flashlight. It turns it into a deadly weapon with a flashlight attached to it. It is surprising the number of people who forget this, or never realize it in the first place.

For long guns, typically used from an ensconced position after the homeowner has gathered her family together and all known good guys are securely

---

123 *Guesstimate based on prices as of spring 2010.*

in place behind her, a weapon mounted light may make good sense—especially since few people can wield a long gun one-handed. But for a handgun, which you may use as you travel quickly through the house to gather family and usher them to the safe room, hanging a light on the end of the gun means you will be tempted to point it at flimsy, interior walls as you move. Or at unidentified shadows that might turn out to be sneaky but beloved teenage children. In an already high-stress situation, when any sudden noise or movement could result in a startle discharge, pointing the light—and thus the muzzle—in directions that may include loved ones could create a tragedy.

Rather than affixing a light to your handgun, store the handgun alongside a good flashlight. Use the light to clear your way and identify your target, and keep the firearm free for use as a firearm alone.

Night Sights

What are night sights? These bright dots of glow-in-the-dark material allow sights to shine in poor lighting conditions. Some night sights consist of tiny tubes of tritium, while others use painted dabs of phosphorus to get essentially the same effect. The tritium tubes provide brighter and much more consistent visibility.

Night sights make a great addition to any defensive pistol. To use them most efficiently, get in the habit of making a tiny pyramid or triangle with the sights when shooting in low light, rather than lining up the three dots in a row. This works well because when the gun's silhouette isn't readily visible, it's surprisingly easy to get the single dot of the front sight dramatically to one side of the two rear-sight dots rather than centered between them. Habitually placing the front sight just a little high cures this problem—as does selecting night sights with different colors for front and rear.

Lasers and Laser Grips

A laser uses "Light Amplification by the Stimulated Emission of Radiation." That's the official acronym. On firearms, lasers work as alternative sighting devices to put a bright dot on target. Manufacturers offer many different types of lasers for different types of firearms, mounting on firearms in different ways. Each type has its own advantages.

Rail-mounted lasers attach underneath the barrel of a handgun equipped with built-in guide rails. They cannot be used on firearms without rails. They do not affect either the grip size or shape, but they do change the gun's weight and balance. Rail-mounted lasers are the most easily-installed type of laser sight. However, those with short fingers may find the control switch too far forward for easy access, and most shooters will discover that reaching forward to activate the control switch slows down the shot. These bulky lasers rarely fit available holsters, making them less than ideal for concealed carry.

Guide rod lasers replace the handgun's factory guide rod with an aftermarket laser unit, which fills the normal function of the guide rod while it also functions as a laser sight. As with the rail-mounted lasers, you activate a guide rod laser with your trigger finger just before firing, which definitely slows your shooting. Guide rod lasers do not change the balance or weight of the pistol, and do not alter the exterior of the pistol in any significant way. They do not require specially-fitted holsters.

Laser grips, primarily produced by the Crimson Trace Corporation,[124] build the laser into specially-designed plastic or rubberized grips. Activated by a pressure-sensitive pad, laser grips provide a fast and intuitive supplement to standard sights in low light conditions. Laser grips sometimes alter the feel of the gun in your hand. Some models affect the shape of the firearm enough to require a specially-designed holster, but most do not.

Laser benefits

Laser grips work light-years faster in the dark than any other sighting system. That make it far easier to hit multiple targets, especially when you and the targets are also moving. Under stress, lasers let you do what you instinctively want to do: keep your eyes on the threat. You can shoot from contorted, awkward positions while hiding behind irregularly-shaped cover and still hit what you want to hit.

Training tips

Some shooters fear using a laser will draw the bad guy to their hiding place. Fortunately, good light discipline takes care of this problem. Train yourself to relax your grip or flick the switch off when your muzzle isn't on target, using the laser *only* when you are in the very act of firing the gun. Never activate the laser until you are sure of your target and are raising the gun to fire.

Lasers shine in the dark. In full daylight, the dot often vanishes to uselessness. Because it will not be visible in all circumstances, you must continue to practice with your regular sights. Lasers provide an addition to regular sights, not a replacement for them.

Batteries sometimes die. To best manage battery life, keep two sets of batteries. Use one set for practice, and the other for carry. Replace your carry

124 *Crimson Trace Corporation, 9780 SW Freeman Dr., Wilsonville, OR 97070. (800) 442-2406. www.crimsontrace.com.*

batteries twice a year, at the same time you replace smoke alarm batteries and set clocks for Daylight Savings Time.

You may find yourself thinking the bad guy will see the red dot on his chest and surrender immediately. But he might not even see the dot. If he does see it, his response is not within your power to control. He might surrender meekly. Or he might lunge for you in a rage. In either case, you should never point your firearm at anyone you are not emotionally and legally prepared to shoot. The laser exists as a *sighting device*, not as an intimidation tool. Activate it only during the split second it will take you to aim and pull the trigger

Now That You Have Your Gear

Dear Gunhilda,

What do you call the dance a lady does
when hot brass finds her cleavage?

~ Blistered in Biloxie

Dear Blistered,

Depending on the style, it's either the
BRA-zilian line dance, or the Cha-Cha.
If you'd rather sit that dance out next
time, consider wearing a high collar at
the range.

~ Gunhilda

Gun Cleaning 101

Gun cleaning is one subject I hesitate to address, because gun owners often express very vehement opinions about it. I'm not eager to gore anyone's sacred cows, so let me just say this: this chapter explains **a** way to clean handguns, not **the** way to do it. If you or someone you love has a different way of doing things, that's okay. As long as the gun gets cleaned well enough that its function remains absolutely reliable, it's all good.

When to Clean

Beginners often ask, "How often should I clean my gun? Do I need to clean it every time I shoot it?" That depends. With a target or practice gun, you can probably allow the crud to build up a little bit before cleaning it, though it's usually easier to remove the crud immediately.

Back when buffalo roamed the plains, everyone shot black-powder rifles. In those days, all firearms required immediate cleaning, because black powder was (and is) such a corrosive substance that it would ruin the gun if left in the barrel. Modern powder is not corrosive, so it cannot damage your firearm if it gets left in the barrel for awhile. Fouling *can* and often *does* affect reliability, however. Because crud can slow down the slide, dirty semi-automatic firearms might fail to feed or to eject a spent case. Uncleaned revolvers may bind up, making it difficult or impossible to pull the double-action trigger because the cylinder isn't turning easily. Dirty firearms do not run as reliably as their well-cleaned and properly lubricated counterparts.

To avoid such problems, clean your defensive handgun immediately after every trip to the range, no matter how many shots you fire. Since you will be betting your life on the function of your gun, avoid fouling-related problems by keeping it as clean as you can.

Why Clean Your Own Gun?

Many of us women live with men who are perfectly willing to clean our firearms for us. If that's the case, why should you do it yourself? Cleaning your own gun helps you become familiar with how your gun works. Although the mechanical function of the gun may not be fascinating to you, it's still a good idea to know how it works. That way, if it ever stops working, you will have a solid idea of what went wrong and whether you will need a professional to fix it. Taking the gun down and putting it back together again on a regular basis helps you develop confidence in your gun-handling skills. This confidence carries over to how you handle the firearm on the range and in real life. Cleaning your own gun allows you to visually inspect all the inner pieces of your gun, so that you spot the signs of wear and tear and are able to replace worn pieces before they break on you. And let's be honest: men aren't always a permanent fixture in women's lives. If he runs off to Tahiti with that bimbo from his office tomorrow, it's one less thing for you to learn once he's gone.

The Basic Cleaning Kit

> **Tip**
>
> Never use a bronze brush with copper solvent. The brush will fall apart.

To begin your gun-cleaning adventures, I suggest you purchase a simple all-in-one kit from the gun store. As time goes on, you will gradually find your own preferred products, filling in your kit with other tools and supplies. Until you get to that point, these basic kits provide a great starting place. Inside a basic cleaning kit, you will usually find:

- ☑A bottle of solvent, such as the popular classic Hoppe's No. 9[125]
- ☑A bottle of lubricating oil
- ☑A rod
- ☑A jag (attaches to the end of the rod)
- ☑A patch holder (attaches to the end of the rod)
- ☑Patches

In order to complete your cleaning kit, you must purchase a bore-cleaning brush which attaches to the rod in your cleaning kit. Although some kits include the brush, the brush usually has to be purchased separately because they come in different sizes for different calibers of guns. A 9mm bore brush is too small to effectively clean the bore of a .45 ACP firearm, for example, while the .45 ACP bore brush will not even fit within the barrel of the 9mm gun. So make sure you get the correct size of brush for your gun. Everything else in the kit will be interchangeable, so once you have your 9mm kit, if you want to clean a .45 ACP, the only thing you need to purchase is another brush in the

---

125 Hoppe's is pronounced hop-ease. It's produced by Bushnell Outdoor Products. (800) 423-3537. www.hoppes.com. There are lots of other solvents and cleaners on the market, but Hoppe's is probably the most well-known.

correct size.

Plastic, stainless steel, and bronze brushes are available. For basic cleaning, the brush should be made of bronze rather than of nylon or stainless steel. The only reason to switch to a nylon bore brush is if you are going to be using a separately purchased, super-powerful solvent designed to dissolve copper fouling, because bronze brushes will also be dissolved by such solvents. In all other cases, bronze brushes are far easier to use than nylon, and will get the gun cleaner with less hard work on your part.

Stainless steel bore brushes have the opposite problem. Unlike nylon, which is generally too soft to do a good job, the metal in a stainless steel brush can be as hard as the metal in the bore of a firearm. This means that a stainless steel brush would damage the barrel if the brush ends were bristly. In order to avoid this problem, manufacturers of stainless steel brushes use a slightly different design from the nylon or bronze brushes, so stainless steel brushes are looped rather than bristly. Unfortunately, this design just doesn't clean as well as good old fashioned bristles do, so you get a double whammy with these— the stainless steel brush is so hard that it might damage your barrel, but it still doesn't clean as well as a bristly brush made of the softer bronze.

After a few uses, you will run out of the kit-supplied cleaning patches. When that happens, you can go out and buy more store-bought patches. Or you can simply make your own by cutting similar-sized squares out of old cotton tee shirt material. If my kids haven't outgrown or otherwise destroyed enough old tee shirts when I need new patches, I usually just purchase "new" old tee shirts from the local garage sales for a quarter apiece. Yes, I am a cheapskate.

Other Cleaning Supplies

There are other supplies you may want to have on hand. Some of these are simply nice to have, while others come close to being essential. Most of them can be found lying around your house.

☑**A toothbrush.** You can purchase a specially-designed scrub brush in the same basic shape; some of those offer a skinny row of bristles at the opposite end from the main brush. If you don't need the skinny end, a plain old toothbrush will do just as well.

☑**Q-Tips.** I mean cotton swabs; the brand name isn't important.[126] Some people hate them for cleaning because they can leave lint behind if you're

126 *Q-tips® is a registered trademark of Chesebrough-Pond's Inc.*

not careful. I love them, and I avoid leaving lint behind by being careful.

☑**Pipe cleaners.** Don't get craft-store pipe cleaners, which are usually made of nylon or some other non-absorbent and not so useful material. Genuine pipe cleaners are made of cotton and are designed to clean awkward small spaces; you can usually find them in the big-box stores in the same check-out stand where cigarettes are sold. Some pipe cleaners have flecks of bristly-brush nylon interspersed between absorbent cotton fluff, and these are very cool if you can find them.

Girl Stuff

To protect your fingernail polish, wear nitrile gloves while gun cleaning.

☑**Cleaning rags.** You can get by with only one rag, but you will probably want a handful. You can specially purchase shop rags made for the purpose, or just use hand-sized squares of old cotton tee shirt material or an old dish towel you aren't going to use in the kitchen anymore. Try to avoid using anything too linty. Expect to stain these rags. They can be washed and re-used, but the oily stains will probably be permanent.[127]

Safety Gear

Wear safety goggles whenever you are working with gun-cleaning solvents. Even the not-so-toxic types are dissolving some very nasty stuff which can damage your eyes. As you run the bore brush in and out of the bore, the cleaning goop is going to spray around—just as if you ran a finger across the bristles of a wet toothbrush. A few years ago, when I first got into firearms, I accidentally splashed a bit of solvent onto my prescription glasses. The plastic lens was immediately etched deeply by the cleaning stuff. I was so thankful that it wasn't my eye!

To reduce splatter, and to reduce the amount of lead getting flung around the area as you clean, consider using a cleaning shield such as the MuzzleMate from Accu-Fire.[128] Whether or not you use a splatter shield, if you clean the gun indoors you will need a way to keep any spilled or dripped solvents from destroying the finish on your furniture. I use several layers of newspaper, laid out on top of a large plastic garbage sack. When my gun cleaning chores are done, I crumple up the newspaper and the icked-up disposable patches, then

---

127 *Don't ick up your washing machine or set your dryer on fire by doing something foolish when you clean your solvent rags. You can wash them entirely by hand. Or you can rinse them first, wash them separately, and air-dry rather than tossing them into the dryer.*
128 *Accu-Fire Inc., PO Box 121990, Arlington, TX 76012. www.accufireproducts.com.*

flip the plastic bag inside-out to catch the whole mess. Turning the bag inside-out neatly places any spilled solvent on the inside of the bag, thus trapping the smells a bit better. To avoid lead contamination in your home, dispose of the bag immediately, then clean your cleaning area well using good soap and lots of fresh water.

While you clean the gun, you will need a way to keep the solvent off your hands. To some extent, this problem could be solved by purchasing some of the newer, high-tech solvents which tend to be a bit more hand-friendly. However, no matter how "non-toxic" the solvents themselves might be, they are still dissolving some pretty nasty stuff that is better to avoid getting on your hands. They will also dissolve your fingernail polish. So get yourself some gloves. I use gloves made of nitrile, not latex. Latex gloves are cheaper, but they tend to fall apart before the cleaning is done, which defeats the purpose. Nitrile gloves hold up to the solvents and since I began using them, I've never again ruined a fresh manicure while gun cleaning. (Stuff the guys just won't bother telling you!)

Gun Cleaning and the Four Rules

There's a tragic story in the news this week about a man who was cleaning a firearm, and accidentally shot and killed his own son. Although the article doesn't mention what type of gun he used, the usual online chatter has already begun. It's all the gun's fault, of course. A faulty design, no doubt, probably one of those which require the user to pull the trigger as a preliminary step to disassembling the gun. But this mishap wasn't the gun's fault. In order for this tragedy to happen, the man in the news had to violate not just one, but *all four* of the safety rules. So let's discuss: how do you clean a gun without violating the Four Rules?

Rule One means that when you pick your gun up for the purpose of cleaning it, you treat it with every ounce of respect you would give it if you knew for certain that it would fire if the trigger were pulled. This first rule says that the other rules always apply, even to an "unloaded" gun we are getting ready to clean.

Rule Two means that as you carry your gun to the cleaning area, and once you begin the process of disassembling the gun, you maintain constant awareness of where the muzzle is pointing. Just because you are preparing to clean the gun does not mean that it is no longer a gun.[129] Rule Two means that you

---

129 It stops being "a gun" and becomes "a collection of gun parts" once you have disassembled it to the point where it can no longer launch a bullet. A gun is a bullet-launcher. Once it's in pieces, it can't launch a bullet and is thus no longer a gun.

never point the firearm at your dog, your left hand, your firstborn child, or at the expensive widescreen TV you cannot afford to replace.

Rule Three means that if your firearm requires you to pull the trigger before disassembling it, then even after you have removed the magazine and made sure the chamber doesn't contain a live round, you *still* do not put your finger on the trigger until you are pointing the muzzle at a target. Never put your finger on the trigger unless and until you are pointing the gun at a deliberately-chosen spot where it would be okay for a bullet to land.[130]

Rule Four means that when you choose that spot, you must remember that regular walls, doors, floors, and windows do not stop bullets. If you need to build a solid backstop in order to have a safe place to disassemble firearms in your home, do so.

The Process

> **Tip**
>
> Don't contaminate your solvent bottle! Just drizzle a little bit of solvent out of the bottle wherever you need it. Avoid dunking dirty patches or used brushes.

Start by unloading your firearm. Open the cylinder or lock the slide open and check by sight and feel to be sure it is really unloaded. *Always* remove all ammunition from the room while you are cleaning the gun, because otherwise it is just too easy to make an absent-minded (but noisy) blunder. Get the ammunition out of the room so you will have to mentally change gears before you can reload the gun when you are done cleaning it.

Now you will need to disassemble your firearm. For a semi-auto, remove the slide and separate it from the frame. You'll also remove the barrel and at least one spring. For a revolver, you'll usually want to remove the cylinder. Check your owner's manual for instructions about how to disassemble the gun for cleaning. If you purchased your gun used, or if you've lost your manual, you can usually download a new manual online from the manufacturer.

Once you have a pile of parts sitting in front of you, grab the rod and put a patch-holder on the end of it. Thoroughly wet the patch with solvent and run it through the barrel a couple of times, then leave the wet patch attached to the rod and resting inside the barrel to soak for awhile. Set it aside so the solvent can do its work on the barrel while you clean the rest of the gun.

---

130 Remember the key point: *minor property damage is okay. Sucking chest wounds are not.*

I like to give the frame of the gun a quick once-over with a solvent-wetted rag before getting to work on the detail areas. Drizzle a little solvent on the toothbrush and scrub the dirty areas of the gun. For a semi-auto, pay special attention to the area around where the firing pin pokes out and to the feed ramp (the area where the round enters the chamber). Use cotton swabs and pipe cleaners to get into the smaller areas of the frame, wiping everything down and refreshing your solvent as needed. Scrub the frame and then all the other pieces, leaving the barrel for last so it gets as much soaking time as possible.

> **Lost Owner's Manual?**
>
> If you have lost your owner's manual, surf past the manufacturer's website. Most offer free downloads of product manuals. If that doesn't work, pick up the phone and call the company. Or use a search engine to see if another owner has put a copy somewhere on the web. Even old, used firearms have manuals!

For a revolver, after wiping the gun down, wet your bronze brush and scrub each of the cylinders thoroughly. If you fire .38 Special ammunition through a revolver which can also shoot .357 Magnum, scrub the chambers especially well to remove the ring of material which builds up in front of the chambered rounds. Scrub under the star at the back end of the cylinder. Pay special attention to the breechface, too.

To clean the barrel, run your wet patch up and down inside the barrel a few more times. Now drizzle a little solvent on the bronze bore brush. For a semi-auto, insert the brush from the breech end (not the muzzle end) of the barrel; for a revolver, you'll have to run it in from the muzzle end. In either case, be very careful to avoid rubbing the cleaning rod against the crown—that is, the area immediately around the muzzle end of the gun. The bore brush will need to go all the way through the barrel and come out the other end before you will be able to reverse it and bring it back. Don't try to move the brush up and down inside the barrel, or it will get stuck! Run it completely through, then reverse directions. After you've scrubbed the barrel with the bore brush, run a clean damp patch through the barrel. It should come out covered with grimy, messy, sloppy, oily black sludge. That's fine. Now dampen a fresh patch and run it through, then repeat your brush-scrubbing process. Finish by running a wet patch through the barrel, then a dry one. You are done when a dry patch comes out "clean." To answer the most common question beginners ask at this point: unless you are obsessive, the final patch doesn't have to come out perfectly clean. Mostly clean is good enough.

Wipe the frame down and dry everything that you can reach. Do the same for all the parts you just cleaned.

Now you will need to apply some lubricant. How much lubricant you will use, and where you put it, really varies from one firearm type to another. For example, a Glock likes to be mostly dry with just a little oil in a few key spots, while a 1911 generally runs best with plenty of oil nearly everywhere. Consult your owner's manual to find out where to put the lubricant on your firearm. Never use more lubricant than the manual recommends, and never put it anywhere except the recommended spots.

Once you have oiled the gun, you will need to put it back together. Again, consult the owner's manual for the details. After you have your gun reassembled, choose a safe direction—one that would definitely stop a bullet—and dry fire a few times. Does everything feel right? Does the slide run properly? Does the trigger feel like it did before? If you have any doubts, get a knowledgeable friend to look over your work, or box the firearm up and take it to a gunsmith for a checkup.

Once you are satisfied that the gun is working properly, don't reload immediately. Instead, leave the action open, set the gun in a safe spot, and clean up your cleaning area. Get all of your gun cleaning work done before you reload. and when you do reload, say aloud: "This gun is loaded. This gun is loaded. This gun is loaded." Take time to consciously pay attention to what you are doing, and use your voice to help focus your attention on the changed status of the firearm. Never reload the gun until you have mentally shifted gears away from cleaning it.

Shooting Basics

Astute readers will notice that this chapter is very simple. There's a reason for that: I strongly believe that firearms instruction belongs on the range. Print is a very poor medium for teaching or learning physical skills. There's just too much that can go too drastically wrong. So I have limited myself to describing some of the most basic fundamentals of defensive firearms use, with an emphasis on helping newcomers understand why they will need to learn these basics.

These instructions focus on techniques for self defense shooting. If you are interested only in target shooting, especially in any of the high-accuracy, high-concentration distant-target sports, you will be better served looking elsewhere for information about how to hold and use the firearm.[131]

You may wonder why I suggest using self defense techniques even in casual practice. Does it really matter whether we use a grip appropriate for self defense when we are just plinking? Why use a defensive stance on the range, when we can easily shoot relaxed and upright? Here's the deal: just as you might choose to keep a firearm available "just in case" you ever need it, it's important to keep good habits available "just in case." If you make a habit of using techniques appropriate for defense even when shooting casually, those techniques will come naturally under stress. On the other hand, if you get sloppy or lazy in practice, good defensive techniques that might otherwise see you though the crisis will not be available. Good habits must be practiced faithfully so they will be there when we need them.

Get a Grip

Shooting success begins with a good grip. A good grip means you are holding the gun in the safest possible manner. You will not be damaged by

---

131 *Because precision shooting and self defense shooting are very different, be wary of shooting advice offered by well-meaning strangers. Most shooters use target shooting techniques, and are unfamiliar with the unique requirements of defensive handgunning. The crucial differences are not always obvious to the uninitiated, but they do exist and they do matter.*

the slide activity of a semi-automatic, or by the hot gases coming out of the cylinder area of a revolver. Held properly, the gun will not twist in your hand, causing unexpected (and painful!) strain to your hands or wrists. A good grip helps you shoot fast and accurately, while a poor one can slow you down even if you are doing everything else right.

When firing a semi-automatic handgun, a solid grip allows the firearm to function at its best. Because semi-automatic parts move while firing, the pistol's reliability depends on a solid, nearly immobile platform. You provide that platform with your solid grip and stance.

A good defense grip is strong and secure, so that a close attacker will be unable to wrest the handgun away from you. This grip must allow you to shoot quickly and to rapidly re-align your sights after shooting. It must enable you to fire at moving targets, possibly while you are also moving. And it must be secure enough to allow you to do all of these things without relaxing or readjusting your hands in any way between shots. If you ever need to use the firearm to defend your life, you will be tense—so when practicing for self defense, you must learn to get your hits with your muscles tense and the firearm held as firmly as you can manage.[132]

Trigger finger and hand placement

Proper hand placement begins with the trigger finger. Although precision target shooters often use the pad, defensive shooters usually place the distal joint on the trigger. Old-time revolver shooters called this joint the "power crease," as they found it gave them more strength to pull the heavy trigger typical of double action revolvers. For our purposes, we find that using the power crease gives us the best possible balance between precision (found toward the finger's tip) and strength (found toward the finger's base). This increased strength translates to increased speed during follow up shots, a critical skill for self defense.

For those who use a Glock-style trigger, with its trigger safety lever, placing the power crease on the trigger also improves reliability, because doing so guarantees you will activate the safety properly. On these types of triggers, using the tip of the finger creates a risk of missing the trigger safety lever when you are stressed or in a hurry.

---

132 Some say you must grip the gun with "60% strength in the weak hand, and 40% in the strong hand," or other precise mixes of tension and relaxation. These techniques work well in games, where competitors learn to shoot in a state of relaxed tension. I do not believe they will hold up well under life-or-death stress, where tension is a guarantee but relaxation will be a bit more elusive.

With the unloaded gun pointed in a safe direction, find your best shooting grip by placing your power crease on the trigger.[133] Then wrap the rest of your hand naturally around the gun, placing the web of your hand high on the backstrap. A high hold helps reduce muzzle flip to allow fast follow up shots. On a semi-auto, the web of your hand should snug into the gun's tang. On a revolver, your hand should be high on the grip but not so high that you lose leverage for pulling the heavy trigger.

Except for your now-straightened trigger finger, keep your fingers snugly together on the grip, and do not allow them to spread out. Your middle finger should snug tightly against the underside of the trigger guard, with all your other fingers pressed with equal snugness against each other on the grip. If the gun is too small to allow all your fingers to ride together on the grip, simply curl your pinky finger under the magazine butt plate while keeping your other fingers together. Keeping your fingers together increases your gripping strength. It also improves repeatability, a crucial aspect of shooting consistently.

As soon as you have found your best grip, learn to pick up the firearm with your dominant hand, keeping your trigger finger straight and your hand already adjusted to allow the trigger finger to land where it needs to land when you begin shooting. Always pick up the gun with that good firing grip, so that you will not need to scootch your hand around later in order to reach the trigger properly. Make a habit of picking up the gun as if you were going to fire immediately.

Thumb placement

Most competition shooters use a thumbs-forward grip, which places the thumbs alongside the frame and pointed toward the target while shooting. This works especially well for shooters using handguns with 1911-style thumb safeties, as many competition shooters do.

Unfortunately, the thumbs-forward grip sacrifices two things important to defensive shooters. First, it weakens the overall strength available to hold the gun. You can see this simply by making a tightly clenched fist with your thumb up or forward. As you curl your thumb down, you can feel the remainder of your grip become stronger. Holding the gun as securely as possible is one of the primary goals in defensive shooting; you *don't* want to risk having

---

133 Note that this is only to find your proper grip. Once you have found your proper grip, get in the habit of picking the gun up with your trigger finger far outside that trigger guard.

the gun snatched out of your hand by a close-in attacker.[134]

Shooting with your thumbs forward sacrifices your ability to shoot rapidly with one hand without rearranging your grip on the gun, particularly when shooting smaller handguns tailored for concealed carry. In order to make fast, consistent shots one-handed, you need a bit more stability than you can get with your thumb pointed forward.[135] You never know when your non-shooting hand might be needed for other important matters such as holding onto a toddler, pushing an older child down and to safety, keeping track of an adult loved one, holding a door shut or shoving it open, or any number of other critical tasks. And this is quite apart from the possibility of becoming injured during the encounter so that you only have one uninjured hand with which to shoot. For these reasons, one-handed shooting often becomes a critical skill for defensive handgunners even though the preferred shooting style uses two hands.

Revolver shooters, especially those shooting small frames, should be wary of the thumbs-forward grip for another reason: there's a risk of getting your leading thumb into the area alongside the cylinder gap. The cylinder gap allows hot gases to forcefully escape, which means that getting your thumb alongside that area risks burning and permanently damaging it. For this reason, when shooting a revolver, it's best to habitually curl the thumbs downward, away from the risk.

For all these reasons, I believe that the older, thumbs-curled grip is more appropriate for self defense in most circumstances. It allows you to grip the gun in the firmest possible way, provides extra stability when shooting one-handed, and guarantees your thumb will never get into the cylinder gap area when shooting revolvers.

However, the stronger thumbs-curled grip does not work well for all shooters and all types of handguns. If the firearm is very large or very small for your hands, you may need to use the thumbs-forward grip. If that is the case for you, simply learn to run the gun well and bask in the knowledge that

---

134 *I strongly recommend taking a class in firearm disarm and retention skills, which will give you more options for coping with a gun grab. Habitually using a very firm grip buys you a brief time window, increasing the odds of surviving the immediate threat so you can fire or use an appropriate retention technique. It doesn't solve the entire problem by itself.*

135 *Although you can shoot one-handed with your thumb pointed forward, you don't get maximum stability and speed. As a general rule, as the firearm becomes smaller and lighter, the more crucial it becomes to wring the maximum amount of recoil control out of your shooting technique. Full-size, all-steel firearms such as those used in competition provide a great deal of recoil control simply by being what they are. But these are not typically used for concealed carry.*

you are using the same grip preferred by competition shooting champions worldwide.

Wrists and hand tension

Grip the gun firmly while shooting. In addition to providing a brief window of security during a gun grab, a firm grip helps hold the muzzle steady if you snatch the trigger. You will train to avoid snatching the trigger, but it's very likely to reappear under the extreme stress of a life-or-death encounter. Further, when shooting with a relaxed hand, shooters often pull the gun off target by "milking"—that is, by tightening the rest of the hand sympathetically as the trigger finger moves. Good training will help you overcome this bad habit, but a very firm grip on the gun prevents it from developing in the first place.

Both hands contribute equally to holding the firearm securely. Although many target and competition shooters have discovered that keeping the firing hand relaxed improves precision accuracy, you want to mimic the type of muscle tension produced under extreme stress.

Keep your wrists straight and firm. This allows the energy from the fired shot to be cushioned by your arm bones rather than stressing your tendons or even painfully wrenching your wrists.

Bad Grip Habits to Avoid

While you build good habits to see you through a life-threatening encounter, avoid creating bad habits that can slow you down, cause you to miss, or increase your risk of injuring yourself while you practice.

The teacup grip

Some shooters use what we call a "teacup grip" or the "cup and saucer hold." Gripping the handgun normally with the shooting hand, they place the non-shooting hand underneath the magazine—almost as if it were the saucer for a teacup.

From a defense shooter's perspective, the chief problem with this hold is that the non-dominant hand provides absolutely no assistance in recoil control for rapid shots, and little assistance in retaining the gun if necessary. Because it is very difficult to hold the non-shooting wrist straight in this position, it also increases the chances of straining or spraining the wrist while shooting.

The sole advantage of the teacup grip is that the non-dominant hand does give additional support to the lifting muscles in the dominant arm. This means that if you ever need to hold someone at gunpoint for an extended period of time, you may want to bring your arms closer to your body, relax your elbows slightly, and allow your hands to fall into the teacup grip. Just remember it isn't best for shooting or for hanging onto the gun if you are in a fight for your life.

Non-dominant finger on front of trigger guard

Placing the non-shooting trigger finger forward to ride on the front of the trigger guard accomplishes nothing. It improves neither recoil control, nor strength, nor accuracy. It lessens the gripping strength of your non-shooting hand, which in turn weakens your entire grip. There's another reason to avoid doing this: it's dangerous. When shooting some small firearms with short barrels, the forward finger can easily be shot or damaged by the gases which escape from the end of the barrel. This isn't a factor with every firearm design, of course, but habitually placing your finger forward really increases the risk that you will thoughtlessly place that finger forward on a firearm where it *is* a factor.

Wrist brace

Sometimes you will see an old-time revolver shooter using the wrist-brace grip, with the non-dominant hand firmly wrapped around the wrist of the shooting hand. It is not necessary to reinforce the wrist in this fashion, and doing so prevents your non-shooting hand from doing other good stuff like helping to hold the gun securely. By the way, if your wrists hurt while shooting, there's a good chance that you are not holding them straight but are instead crooking them while firing. The solution isn't to put your other hand up to hold your crooked wrist still. Instead, learn to fire with your wrist straight.

More important, getting into the habit of holding a firearm in this way can be very dangerous. If you try it with a semi-automatic, either deliberately or out of thoughtless habit, you'll painfully discover *why* it's such a bad idea.

Thumb behind slide

Some new shooters feel the need to wrap both hands entirely around the gun, placing the non-shooting thumb atop the shooting hand at the back of the gun. Don't do this! *Never* allow the thumb of your non-shooting hand to rest behind the slide of a semi-automatic.

When a shot is fired, the slide moves very quickly toward the rear, and then is driven forward again by a powerful spring. If you put your thumb in the path of the moving slide, you're likely to slice your thumb open. You may even need stitches. Avoid this danger by always keeping your non-dominant thumb on the same side of the grip as your dominant thumb.[136]

Choose a Stance

"Over the years I have concluded that certain body and hand positions are helpful to deliver better and quicker hits, but if a student chooses to disregard my teachings it is all right with me, as long as his results are good." —Jeff Cooper [137]

"Stance" is the word shooters use to refer to body position while shooting.

There are literally dozens of minor variations for each of the common handgun shooting stances. This is because every body on the planet is different from every other body. What works well for you may not work quite as well for the person standing next to you. If a particular stance works well for someone whose basic body shape and proportions are similar to yours, it's possible that the same basic stance will work well for you, too. But because your body is not identical to theirs, you will probably still have to tweak the stance a little to make it *your* stance.

Some shooters choose to make stance something like a religion: you must use a particular stance, or you're not really a shooter. Please do your best not to listen to the dogmatists. Each stance has its own strengths and weaknesses. After you have tried them all, you will probably realize that one stance works best for you. That's good, but you also need to be familiar with them all, and able to get good hits from each one.

If you ever need to use this stuff for keeps, the chances are that you will not use any particular foot position—you'll be running, or crouched behind something, or ducking. That doesn't mean you "aren't using a stance." Remember, stance just means your body position while shooting. Even without considering what your feet are doing, you still hold the gun in a particular way (probably the way you have practiced most often). Your arms are either straight or bent. Your grip is either firm or loose. Your upper body is either squared to the target or it's not. All of these things together make up a stance.

The three basic defensive handgun stances are Weaver, Chapman, and

---

136 *At least one revolver instructor teaches students to place the non-shooting thumb behind the gun, atop the shooting hand, when shooting small revolvers. I think this can easily lead to a bloody injury when the shooter picks up a semi-auto and uses the now-familiar technique.*
137 *Jeff Cooper's Commentaries, Vol. 14, No. 1. January 2006.*

Isosceles. Weaver and Chapman are named after the men who first popularized them, while Isosceles is named after the triangular shape made by the shooter's arms and upper body. All three stances have been used both in competition and on the street, and each has its own strengths and weaknesses.

Weaver

Jack Weaver was a Deputy Sheriff in the 1950s when he began standing this way in competition. A young Jeff Cooper quickly adopted Weaver's stance, and later popularized it at his shooting school, Gunsite. The Weaver stance was a truly radical departure from the way things were done at the time. Until Jack Weaver came along, most handgunners held the gun with one hand and fired quickly from the hip, or from the shoulder while sighting down the extended arm. Few held the gun with both hands, and few used the sights.

In the Weaver stance, the upper body is slightly bladed in relation to the target rather than squared towards it. Both elbows are flexed and pointed downward. The strong-side arm is slightly straighter than the weak-side arm. The shooter pushes *out* with the gun hand, while the weak hand pulls *back* toward the shooter. This produces a push-pull tension, the chief defining characteristic of the Weaver stance.

Weaver depends on muscle strength rather than skeletal support for recoil control. Because women tend to have less upper-body musculature than men do, Weaver tends to be slightly more popular with men than with women.

While many women have no problem with Weaver, women who are very well-endowed may have difficulty achieving stability in this stance, because getting good stability in Weaver requires your elbows to point directly downward rather than out to the sides as you shoot. The very well-endowed can find their endowments getting in the way, while the merely buxom can find the stance uncomfortable because the non-dominant elbow tends to squish sensitive areas. If this is a factor for you, you may be able to fix the difficulty by straightening both elbows slightly more than the average Weaver shooter does. Or you might fix it by sweeping your elbows in from the side as you get into the stance, rather than bringing them straight down.[138]

To engage targets off to the side in the Weaver stance, simply bend one elbow more sharply to bring the gun around. Many shooters have found that Weaver is the most flexible stance for working in tight quarters, and for engaging targets in multiple directions.

---

138 *If you use the second technique, you should still end up with your elbows pointed downward. Bringing your elbows in from the side as you get into position sweeps the problem areas toward the center, away from where your elbows need to be.*

Cross-dominant shooters—that is, people who are right-handed but left-eyed, or left-handed but right-eyed—often have difficulty shooting well in Weaver, particularly when shooting fast. Because of the body mechanics necessary to get the cross-dominant eye squarely behind the sights, these shooters tend to do best in Isosceles. Because of those same body mechanics, shooters whose hands fit the gun perfectly often do best in Weaver, particularly working at high speeds.

Chapman (Modified Weaver)

The Chapman stance is named for Ray Chapman, another shooter who had a great influence on the styles handgunners use today. Chapman adopted Weaver's stance, but changed it just slightly. Using the same push-pull tension which defines the Weaver, the Chapman stance straightens the gun side elbow and locks it in place. Assuming a right-handed shooter, the right arm is punched straight out, while the left elbow is bent and the left hand pulls firmly back to provide tension. As a result of this change, Chapman gets its stability from both muscle and skeletal support. This makes it a little more friendly than Weaver for those who lack upper-body muscle strength.

In Chapman as in Weaver, the bent elbow flexes *downward* rather than out to one side. This provides a stable, repeatable platform that places no strain on the wrists. If you find that your non-dominant wrist gets sore when shooting either Chapman or Weaver, chances are that you are not pointing your elbow directly downward.

Because the ideal Chapman stance involves sighting directly down the shooter's dominant arm, cross-dominance remains an issue in Chapman just as it is in Weaver. Occasionally, you will find a left-eyed person who shoots right-handed Chapman by turning her head sharply to rest on her bicep, allowing her left eye to sight along her right arm. Sighting along the right arm works well for a right-eyed shooter, but for a left-eyed shooter it cuts the field of view into a very narrow area. Given that tunnel vision is likely to be a problem anyway, narrowing your visual field in this way can be dangerous because it may prevent you from seeing the attacker's friends or the arriving police. You need the widest field of view you can achieve.

Isosceles

While the Isosceles stance had been around for several years, it did not really become popular until some young upstarts named Brian Enos and Rob Leatham started using it to win IPSC competitions in the early 1980s.

In Isosceles, the arms are straight and the gun is positioned directly in front of the shooter's center line. Seen from above, the position of the arms in relation to the upper body produces the triangular shape which gives the stance its name.

There are two basic variants of the Isosceles stance. In Traditional Isosceles, the feet are parallel and pointed toward the target, the knees are straight, and the entire body is upright. This is an acceptable range stance, but this variant does not provide the flexibility, easy recoil control, and speed of movement required by self defense shooters. If you are practicing for self defense, you will want to use the Modern Isosceles stance instead.

In Modern Isosceles, the feet are roughly shoulder width apart, with the gun-side foot slightly to the rear of the off-side foot. Both knees are flexed and the entire body leans slightly toward the target. The shoulders are closer to the target than the hips, and the hips are more forward than the knees. The shoulders are rotated forward and the head, rather than being upright, is vultured down behind the sights. The entire body thus has an aggressive appearance, and is poised to move quickly if necessary. Picture the way the human body looks when it is getting ready to run or to fight, and you have a good idea of how to build the lower foundation of the Modern Isosceles stance.

In either Isosceles variant, the skeletal system provides most of your recoil control. Rather than actively controlling the recoil using muscle strength as in Weaver or Chapman, Isosceles shooters passively control recoil by absorbing it with their entire bodies.

To engage targets to the side, think of your upper body as the gun turret on a tank. When you need to point at a target to the left or right of the original one, pivot your entire upper body smoothly to aim at the new target. When the angle becomes too steep for this, try flowing into a Weaver stance to bring the gun around a bit farther, or drop one hand to shoot one-handed—or simply move your feet!

Isosceles stance works well for those with eye dominance issues because the gun easily aligns with either eye from the center position. Turning the head *very* slightly, or tipping the gun *very* slightly off the perpendicular, brings the left eye into perfect alignment when the gun is held in the right hand. Because the stance centers the firearm along the shooter's centerline and avoids sighting directly down one arm, Isosceles works especially well for those shooting firearms slightly too large for their hands. It also tends to provide the most solid platform for those with weak hands.

The Isosceles stance tends to bounce the gun a bit when the shooter moves. Relaxing the arms slightly, so the elbows are not locked out, reduces the jarring but lessens the skeletal support necessary for rapid recoil control in this stance.[139]

Faux Isosceles

I made up this phrase and you won't find it anywhere else that I know of. But... some women will just bend over backwards in order to shoot. I think the reason so many do this is because a woman's center of gravity is a lot lower than that of an equal-statured man. Where most men can hold a heavy gun out in front of them without strain, some women have difficulty doing so for long. There's probably some counter-balancing going on, too. Since women have proportionately less upper body strength than men do, and because there are those curves hanging out in front, bending far backwards causes the lifting muscles to do a little less work. Finally, many new shooters are somewhat afraid of the gun, and so you see them doing this to get their faces farther away from it.

There are three problems with this bent-over-backwards stance.

First, it just looks goofy. If you want to be taken seriously as a competent shooter, it's good to look the part. Looking as if you're afraid of the gun does not help much in the "take me seriously" department.[140]

Second, it's not stable. It might be good enough for slow, controlled target shooting, when you're shooting light loads and the speed of follow-up shots really doesn't matter. But if you're practicing for self defense, you should strive for a more solid foundation. You must be ready to move in any direction at any time, which means keeping your weight balanced on the balls of your feet. If you make a habit of getting your upper body weight back, you *will* land on your backside when you need to move quickly with gun in hand. That's bad medicine.

Finally, bending away from the gun sacrifices the body language of confident control. If you ever need to use the firearm to defend yourself from a criminal attacker, you will want every possible advantage you can get! By aggressively leaning into the firearm, your body language positively shouts, "I MEAN IT." This by itself may save the day.

---

139 *Competition shooters, who tend to shoot heavy guns with light-kicking loads, often instruct people to avoid locking their elbows in the Isosceles stance. But a defensive shooter, who often carries a light gun with hard-kicking loads, usually needs the improved control and reliability offered by locked-elbow skeletal support.*
140 *Yeah, I know it's not about looking cool, but about getting the job done. But there's something tremendously discouraging about shooting well and only getting (negative) attention for the way you stand while doing it!*

Other Stances

While Weaver, Chapman, and Isosceles are the dominant triumvirate of defensive handgun stances, there are many other handgun stances familiar to shooters worldwide.

Shooting from the hip is sometimes called the "Speed Rock" or "Shooting from Retention." Although some may suspect that this position and others like it allow shooters to blaze away without knowing where they will hit, these positions actually use alternative alignment techniques to get on target without using the sights. Done properly, these alternative techniques can be quite fast and surprisingly accurate at close ranges. However, they do tend to fall apart as distances increase.

Until Jack Weaver started using two hands in the Leatherslap competitions in the southern US during the 1950s, most handgun shooters used the one-handed Bullseye stance. They stood upright, with the non-shooting hand tucked into a pocket or just dangling straight down from the side. They turned sideways to place the gun side toward the target, sighting casually down their arms as they fired.

Modern defensive shooters do not use the Bullseye stance. Rather, when shooting one-handed, they thrust the gun directly from the front of their bodies, just as they do when shooting two-handed. The non-shooting hand is clenched into a fist and pulled up sharply to ride just beneath the pectoral muscles. Because of the body's sympathetic nervous system, clenching the weak hand provides an increased measure of strength to the strong hand. The position also mimics the body's natural response to an injured limb, bringing it in toward the chest. Finally, anchoring the non-dominant arm in this way provides extra stability while shooting, and prevents shooters from allowing their non-shooting hand to drift in front of the muzzle while preparing to shoot.

Sighting Basics

Marty Hayes, owner of the Firearms Academy of Seattle, is fond of telling new students the one and only real secret of accurate marksmanship. Are you ready? Here it is, the secret of accurate shooting: **"Your sights must be aligned with the target at the moment the hammer falls."**

That's it. That's the entire secret of accurate shooting. Everything else you hear about—grip, stance, smooth trigger press, follow-through—all of these are just detailed ways to ensure that your sights are in the right place when the hammer falls. If your sights are lined up with the target when the shot goes off, you will hit the target. If they aren't, you won't. By understanding how sights are designed to work, using them appropriately, and working the trigger smoothly, we can guarantee good hits.

Sights come in a variety of configurations. There are three-dot sights, bladed sights, U-shaped sights, V-shaped sights, dot-the-i sights, peep sights, and on and on in nearly infinite variety. All of these different mechanisms are designed to assure that shooter holds the gun so that the shot lands neither to the high nor low, and neither left nor right. When the muzzle of the firearm (represented by the sights) lines up with the target at the moment the shot breaks, the bullet will hit the target.

Understand front and rear sights

No matter how the sights are configured, the front sight should be centered in relation to the rear sight. If the rear sight is a vertical line, for example, simply place the front sight directly on top of it, as if you were dotting an *i*. Otherwise, center the front sight within the notch, square, or vee of the rear sight. Keep an equal amount of light on either side of the front sight. This will keep your shots from going to the left or right of where you aim.

Except in the case of "dot the i" sights, hold the top edge of the rear sight exactly level with the top edge of the front sight. This prevents your shots from hitting high or low.

Some sight designs, especially those with a large front sight and small rear sight, will tempt you to "bury" the front sight while shooting. This will cause your shots to go a bit low. Pay special attention to keeping the top edge of the front sight in line with the top edge of the rear sight until you have become very familiar with using these types of sights.

> ### Who Needs Sights?
>
> Your sights (and thus the muzzle of your gun) may be perfectly aligned with the target even if your eyeball is not behind them, which is why a well-practiced shooter may easily hit the target while pointshooting from the hip at close distances.
>
> But when shooting for accuracy rather than pure speed, especially at longer distances, you must use your eyes to be sure that your sights are aligned correctly.

Where to put the front sight

Now that you have the front and rear sight in the correct relationship to each other, where do you place the front sight in relation to the target?

Most handguns will have their sights adjusted to provide either a *combat hold* or a *target hold*. Those phrases answer the commonly-heard question, "Do I put my front sight in the middle of the bullseye, or at the bottom of the bullseye?"

Guns sighted for a combat hold require the shooter to place the front sight directly over the center of the target. Guns sighted for a target hold achieve greatest accuracy placing the front sight at the bottom edge of the bullseye. Generally speaking, handguns appropriate for self defense use the quicker but less precise combat hold, meaning that you will simply center the front sight on the spot you want to hit.

Consider Mel Gibson's advice to his son in the movie *The Patriot*: "Aim small, miss small." When you are faced with a large target, pick a small area within that target upon which to center your shots. For instance, when looking at a cardboard IPSC target, rather than aiming for "somewhere in the center," try to hit the triangle which makes up the top part of the capital A in the A-zone.

Always remember that the correct placement of the front sight on the target must happen at the same time as the front and rear sights are held in the correct relationship to each other.

Where to focus

No matter which sighting system your handgun uses, you should learn to keep your eyes focused on the front sight the entire time you pull the trigger, and during follow-through after the shot goes off. Physiologically, it is simply not possible for the human eye to focus on a near object and a far object at the same time. This means that when your eye is focused on the front sight, the target will be blurry. And when your eye is focused on the target, the front sight will be blurry. Some people (mostly young folks) can switch their focus back and forth rapidly enough to fool themselves into thinking that both are in focus at the same time, but it's not true. Only one or the other is in focus at any given time.

What all this means is that you will need to decide which is more important to have in sharp focus: the large target, or the tiny front sight. If you want to shoot accurately, you need to really see what that tiny front sight is doing. And that is why shooting instructors always tell their students to look at the front sight.

If you are prone to missing high, you may be shifting your focus from the front sight to the target at the last possible moment before the shot goes off. When you shift your sight to the target, it's very common for the muzzle to rise slightly in response—just enough to make the shot land high rather than in the center of the target.

What about that wobble?

It is normal for the sights to wobble a bit when you are holding your firearm on target. Accept that fact. The wobble is a normal event, and it happens to every shooter. Human beings are not machines! Nobody can hold a firearm with machine-like stillness and immobility. The wobble will always be there.

Sometimes the wobble will be worse than other times. As humans age, our hands naturally become a little more shaky. After a few swallows of tea, coffee, or caffeinated soda, most people experience slightly shaky hands (though most of us never notice this apart from the range). And when there is a lot of adrenalin in your system—for instance, when shooting in front of someone you want to impress, or for points in a match, or under the significant stress of a deadly force encounter—hands will always shake. It's just a fact of life.

So what to do about it? First, admit that you *do* shake. Don't try to force yourself not to do it. You must accept the wobble and pull the trigger smoothly while the wobble is happening. If instead you fight it or try to snatch the trigger back during that brief, absolutely perfect moment as your front sight trembles across the center of the target, your shots *will* go low. Don't say I didn't warn you! Instead of snatching the trigger back at the magic moment when the sights are absolutely, totally, perfectly aligned, try this: smoothly increase pressure upon the trigger while keeping the sights aligned on the target as steadily as you are able.

By smoothly increasing the pressure on the trigger while keeping the sights lined up as steadily as you are able, you assure that you will hit the target when you fire.

Fixing the Flinch

We've all done it. Mysteriously misplaced holes appear in the target. The holes are low, below the bullseye, and usually fall left of the centerline. What in the world could cause that?

A flinch happens when your muscles clench suddenly in anticipation of the shot firing, yanking the muzzle of the gun downwards and off-target at the last possible moment. It can be made worse by firing without adequate hearing protection, or by firing large-caliber guns with unexpectedly solid recoil, or by firing guns that just don't feel good in your hand. Every shooter on the entire planet has dealt with a flinch at one time or another. There are no exceptions. It's the one universal experience all shooters share.

Sometimes a habitual flinch can be created with just a single negative experience. I've met more than one woman whose first exposure to shooting was when a jokester relative handed her a full-power .357 Magnum, or a 12-gauge shotgun loaded with 3 1/2-inch full powered slugs, and told her to pull the trigger without warning her what to expect.[141] Such a rough introduction to the shooting sports can create seriously negative opinions about shooting, and often leaves an enduring flinch.

Since every shooter has dealt with a flinch, most shooters have some method of coping with a flinch when one develops. It's worth listening to experienced shooters at the range, and finding out what works for them. The only "solution" I would warn you away from is the non-solution of mechanically adjusting your sights so that the gun hits high and right when it is fired by someone without a flinch. That's a range trick, not a solution.

Diagnosis

Diagnosing a flinch is not difficult. Sometimes you can feel yourself getting ready to flinch—that clenched, quivery feeling in your muscles right before the shot fires—provides the telltale sign. Or perhaps you find yourself trying to yank the trigger during the brief, magic moment when your sights

---

141 *Such behavior is not funny. It is malicious.*

are perfectly aligned exactly in the center of the bullseye, rather than steadily increasing the pressure on the trigger while holding the front sight as centered on target as possible, without worrying too much about minor wobble. But by far the most certain way to diagnose a flinch is to fool your muscles into believing that you are about to fire live ammunition, when in fact you are going to dry fire the gun.

In order to diagnose and cure your flinch, if you have a semi-automatic handgun, you will need to purchase snap caps or dummy rounds. These are inert ammunition-shaped objects you can put into your gun. They are the same size and shape as your regular ammunition, but usually come in bright colors so they may be easily distinguished. When a snap cap is loaded into your semi-automatic handgun and the trigger is pulled, all you will hear is a *click*. Snap caps are not live ammunition. They cannot fire, nor will they cycle the gun's action.

This works best if you have two or three magazines. Fill each magazine with a couple of live rounds, a snap cap, a little more live stuff, another snap cap, and so on. Randomly mix the number and order of snap caps compared to live rounds. If you only have one magazine, have a friend fill it for you while you look elsewhere. If you have two or more magazines, fill them yourself and then shuffle them around so you do not know which one is which. Using these specially-prepared magazines, on the range when the firing line is hot, simply load your firearm as you ordinarily would.

To accomplish the same task with a revolver, you can either randomly mix snap caps in with live ammunition in the cylinder, or you can randomly leave a few empty holes where ammunition would ordinarily go. Before you close the cylinder, close your eyes and gently rotate the cylinder. Close the cylinder without looking, so you do not know how the ammunition is lined up in your gun.

Now your firearm is loaded partially with real ammunition and partially with fake ammunition which will not fire. The next step is to fire the gun. Line your sights up on the target, focus on the front sight, and steadily increase pressure on the trigger until the shot fires with a bang. When you get to a snap cap, instead of a bang you will hear a click. And if you have been flinching, you will graphically see the muzzle end of the gun take a deep dive instead of remaining steady as it should.[142]

---

142 *This is also a good time to practice clearing a misfeed, a task often called Tap, Rack, (assess and) Bang. When you encounter a snap cap or any other failure to fire in a semi-automatic handgun, tap the magazine sharply into the firearm to be sure it is firmly seated, rack the slide to clear the non-functioning ammunition out of the way, assess the*

Having diagnosed the problem, it's time to write the prescription for curing it.

Prescription: Dry Fire

The first and most important method of dealing with a flinch is lots of dry fire. What is dry fire? Dry fire is going through the motions of firing the gun when there is no ammunition in it. You can do this at home as long as you have a safe backstop and as long as you follow every single one of the rules for safely dry firing a gun. If you are uncertain whether you can safely dry fire in your home, **DON'T**. You can always safely dry fire on the range. There is no rule that says you must always use ammunition at the range. It is perfectly safe and acceptable to dry fire there instead. No one will be surprised, because good shooters often dry fire at the range as one part of a regular practice routine.

Just as if you were firing live ammunition, you will grip the handgun properly, align your sights carefully, and slowly increase pressure on the trigger until the trigger's break point is reached. You will keep your eye glued to the front sight and will continue to hold the trigger to the rear *without lessening your finger's pressure on the trigger* for a full two seconds after the trigger has been completely pulled.

Safety Note

Never allow your snap caps to get mixed in with your defense rounds. That could be Very Bad.

As you focus sharply on the front sight during dry fire, you may notice that your front sight wobbles a bit. This is normal and expected, not something to worry about or fight against. If you watch the front sight for awhile, you will see something interesting: no matter how badly your hand is shaking, the area on the target that is actually covered by your "wobble zone" is really quite small. As long as your trigger pull is smooth, every single shot will fall within that very small wobble zone close to the center of your target. But if you try to snatch the trigger back to get an absolutely perfect shot during the brief moments when your front sight wobbles across the exact, perfect center of the bullseye, your shots will land very low and much farther away from the center.

Do not try to muscle the wobble away. The more you clench up, the worse the wobble becomes. And don't try to race against it by snatching the trigger back. Simply increase the pressure on your trigger while accepting the wobble for the normal phenomenon that it is.

---

target to be sure it still needs shooting, and pull the trigger again to make a bang.

Even though you have accepted this normal wobble of the front sight, remember that you are still trying to hold the front sight as steady as you humanly can. Don't allow it to dip or sway as a result of your trigger pull. If you find your trigger pull also pulls the sights out of alignment to the right or to the left, adjust the amount of trigger finger you have resting on the trigger. Grip the firearm firmly so your non-trigger fingers cannot sympathetically tighten and "milk" the pistol while you are pulling the trigger.

As you pull the trigger, you may be able to feel the tension within the trigger mechanism increasing so the pull feels heavier as the trigger gets farther back. Do not allow this to slow down the rate at which the trigger is traveling to the rear. Instead, pull the trigger at the same speed during the entire process, increasing the pressure upon it steadily until the trigger breaks to the rear with a sharp click.

Never think about the trigger's break point, or about the shot firing. Let the hammer fall surprise you, every time. In order to keep themselves from thinking about the trigger break and to allow the trigger break to come as a surprise, many folks find that chanting "front sight front sight front sight" helps keep their minds from trying to anticipate the shot.

> **Shooting Tip**
>
> Especially when using a firearm with a heavy trigger, grip the gun very firmly. This helps avoid pulling the gun off target while pulling the trigger.

This is an important step: after the trigger has broken to the rear, do not take your finger off the trigger for at least two full seconds. Keep the sights steadily on the target and continue holding the trigger completely to the rear while you count one-one-thousand-two-one-thousand. Try to dry fire for five minutes every day or so.[143]

Prescription: On the Range

On the range, try to do exactly as you have practiced in dry fire. Get the sights lined up on the target, focus sharply on the front sight, and gradually increase pressure on the trigger. Do not think about the shot firing. Do not try to grab the magic moment when your sights are completely and perfectly centered on the bullseye. Instead, accept that the front sight will wobble a little, and concentrate on holding as steady as you can while you put increas-

---

143 *And don't try to make up six missed days in a marathon session. This is self-defeating, as your attention will not remain at optimal levels throughout an extended practice time. Stick with short, sharply focused sessions.*

ing pressure on the trigger. If you need to chant "front sight front sight front sight," do so. Anything to keep your mind from anticipating when the shot will fire. Let the shot be a surprise to you.

Practice good follow-through. After the shot goes off, continue holding the trigger completely to the rear while you line the sights back up and focus sharply on the front sight. Count one-one-thousand, two-one-thousand while you hold the trigger to the rear. Then and only then, release the trigger and allow it to come forward.

If you feel your muscles getting ready to flinch, take a deep breath. Then safely unload your firearm, and practice dry-firing until you have settled down. Or try this: consciously relax every muscle in your body except the ones you need in order to shoot safely, and go back to dry firing until you feel ready to try shooting live rounds again.

Checkup

After you have fired live ammunition for awhile, it's time for a checkup. Mix snap caps in with your regular ammunition just as you did for the initial diagnosis. This time, you are simply going to shoot the gun and keep shooting it. Since you have been doing so much dry fire, you know exactly what the sights should look like when you pull the trigger on an unexpected snap cap— it should look and feel exactly as it does when you were *expecting* to dry fire.

By the way, it's embarrassing to find that muzzle dipping downwards so dramatically when you come across a snap cap while firing. The only cure I've ever found for that embarrassment is to conquer the flinch.

Back at home, set up your safe dry fire area again. You need to practice dry firing some more. This time you are going to do something different: you're going to try balancing a coin on the front sight while you dry fire.[144] Lay a penny across the top of the front sight, then dry fire as usual. Align the sights, focus on the front sight, and steadily increase pressure on the trigger while keeping the coin balanced on top of the front sight. Can you keep the coin there throughout the entire trigger pull? Practice until you can do it, then practice until you can do it every time without fail. Make a game of it: instead of using a penny, use a dime. Get a roll or two of dimes. Every time a dime falls off, pick it up and put it into your penalty jar—then get out a fresh dime. Bonus! When the jar is full, you can use the contents to purchase ammunition or professional firearms instruction only. (No cheating ...) Continue to regularly practice dry fire, especially when you cannot get to the range for awhile.

---

144 *Not on edge! Lay it flat.*

Follow-Up Care

Now that your flinch is under control, you should take your snap caps to the range with you from time to time, to check on your progress and to prevent the flinch from returning full force. Remember you will need regular dry fire practice, too.

Most shooters have recurring bouts of flinch trouble. This isn't unexpected or unusual. It only means that it is time to focus on the basics once again. And now you know what to do about it when it happens to you.

Running a Semi-Auto

The basic skills to run a semi-automatic handgun, or any other type of firearm, come naturally to no one. Rather, they must be learned, preferably taught by a competent shooter. Fortunately, a semi-auto is no more complex than any other tool we use regularly: simpler than a motor vehicle, easier to use than a washing machine, less complex than the computers and DVDs and mobile wireless devices we regularly take for granted.

Or as my friend Tamara Keel puts it:

> *Somewhere in America today, a woman is going to operate a door-knob, lock a deadbolt, operate an alarm remote, and operate a door handle. She will then operate an ignition switch and a seatbelt latch, manipulate clutch and gas and brake pedals while simultaneously rowing a gear selector and working a turn indicator switch. Arriving at her destination, she will manipulate all these controls again in reverse order, walk into the gun store, and be told by some bright spark with a barely-room-temperature IQ: "These automatic pistols have too many complicated controls on 'em, honey; whatchoo need's a revolver."*[145]

Previous generations of gun owners passed shooting instructions along to their children (usually to their sons) when the children were so young that when they grew up, they had no conscious memory of the time they didn't know this stuff. They thought they knew it "naturally" and so they reasonably assumed that any adult who needed instruction in the basic skills *had to be* a bit dim. But accurate shooting and firearms manipulation are learned skills, not inborn traits—and you can learn them just as easily as the children of earlier generations did.

How to Rack the Slide

"My wife can't always rack the slide, so even though she wants a semi-auto, I am going to insist she gets a revolver."

---

145 *Tamara Keel on the View from the Porch blog, www.booksbikesboomsticks.blogspot.com.*

"I like my revolver okay, but I'd sure like to try a semi-auto. Problem is, I can't pull the slide back."

"I can almost pull the slide back, but not far enough to lock it open."

"I'm not strong enough to do the slide ..."

If I had a nickel for every time I have heard variations on that theme, I'd be a wealthy woman today. Despite this, it is my contention that healthy adult women who really-and-truly cannot be taught to rack a slide are extremely rare. I'm almost tempted to say there are none at all.[146]

A lot of men who have shot for years never learned how to rack a slide without using a lot of muscle. They have not learned the easiest techniques, because they haven't needed

> ### A Dirty Little Secret
>
> Racking the slide is not about strength. It is all about technique.

to. As a result, when these men become informal instructors for their female loved ones, they don't know what to do if a woman can't just muscle the slide back in the same inefficient way many men do. Soon these men become convinced that "Women just can't ..." And their female loved ones buy into that, thinking of themselves as too weak to run a modern firearm.

It is true that a lot of women cannot rack a slide simply by muscling it through. There's no shame in this! A woman's strength is usually centered in her lower body and particularly in her legs, rather than in her upper torso and arms. But there are techniques that work with a woman's strengths, rather than against them. If you struggle with the slide, probably the biggest hurdle to overcome is the belief that you're not strong enough to rack the slide and that racking the slide is a matter of brute force. *It is not.* Technique matters far more than muscle. If you have difficulty, don't give up. You can learn this.

Some people are reluctant to be aggressive in handling the firearm. They want to baby it, trying to move the slide slowly or gingerly. Please believe me on this one: there is *very* little you can do with your hands to damage this piece of modern metal. The gun is designed to cope with extremely high pressures from the inside, and the slide is designed to travel far faster than you will ever be able to move it. The springs inside it are built to cope with far more energy than you'll ever produce with your hands. You cannot hurt the firearm by moving quickly.

Finally, some women are afraid the slide will bite them or otherwise hurt their hands. A gruff instructor might just growl, "Get over it," but maybe that's a little harsh. If you are afraid of the slide and its movement, I suggest you

---

146 Note the word "healthy" in the preceding sentence. Arthritis, current or past injuries, and other joint or muscle problems all take their toll.

ask a knowledgeable someone to show you the internal parts of your semi-automatic and educate you about exactly what each part is doing and why it is doing it. Then pay special attention to the instructions below so you learn where you can safely place your hands during the process. With your hands placed correctly, you are less likely to get pinched or poked when you move quickly. Finally, if there are any sharp or pointy edges on your firearm, consider asking a gunsmith to gently soften the offending corners.

A Note about Safety

Let us start by discussing safety. The very first rule in learning to rack the slide is that **all other firearms safety rules still apply.**

Human hands have a sympathetic grip reflex. When one hand clenches, the other hand often closes along with it. When part of the hand closes tightly, the rest of the hand wants to close just as tightly. This can be a problem because your trigger finger will be affected by this reflex. As you grasp the slide, your trigger finger will want to join the other fingers of your grip hand as they tighten, and will often curl right into the trigger guard and onto the trigger. Especially if racking the slide is difficult for you, you must consciously prevent your finger from curling onto the trigger while you work the slide.

> **Danger!**
>
> *NEVER* allow the muzzle to sweep people on your left. Keep the muzzle pointed downrange at all times, moving your body in relation to the gun if you need to change your grip angle.
>
> *NEVER* allow the muzzle to point at any part of your own body while you are working the slide. Do not point it at your left elbow, your abdomen, or your knees.
>
> *ALWAYS* keep the muzzle pointed downrange!

It can be difficult to remain aware of muzzle direction while your mind and hands are learning this new skill. But for safety's sake, you must always be conscious of the direction the gun is pointed, just as you must every other time you handle a firearm. Even though it may be difficult, it is very important that you never point the firearm at anything you are not willing to shoot.

Occasionally, you will encounter people who cluelessly or deliberately point the firearm at their own abdomens or at their weak-side forearms and elbows while they are racking the slide. Please do not be one of these people! Be aware of your muzzle direction at all times, and keep your own body parts away from the line of fire.

Practice racking the slide with a carefully-checked *empty* firearm until you are able to do the task with confidence. There's no reason to race ahead to working with live ammunition until you are certain you have mastered the skill and can do it safely.

Positioning Your Hands

First, get a good grip on the butt of the gun with your firing hand. This grip should not be too different from your normal shooting grip, except that your trigger finger stays far outside the trigger guard. If you index it along the frame, make sure it is high on the frame so the sympathetic grip reflex doesn't cause problems.

With your dominant hand on the grip of the gun, your non-dominant hand is free to grab the slide. You can grab the slide in one of two basic ways. Since every human hand is different, you will need to try both and figure out which one works best for you.

Overhand grasp: The overhand grasp is the strongest technique for most people. To use this technique, assuming you are right-handed, hold the gun in a firing grip with your right hand, with your trigger finger indexed along the frame far outside the trigger guard.

Take your left hand off the gun and hold it up in front of your face: palm flat, fingers straightened together, and thumb pointed back toward you.

Now, with your thumb still pointed toward you, place the heel of your hand on the slide serrations behind the ejection port. Keep your fingers together as you wrap them over the top of the slide to land on the other side, and grip the slide firmly with your fingers and the heel of your hand.

Slingshot grasp: The slingshot grasp tends to be less strong for most people. I include it here simply because it is sometimes needed when working with the smallest of small handguns. To use this technique, again assuming you are right-handed, hold the gun in a firing grip with your right hand, with your trigger finger indexed along the frame far outside the trigger guard.

Take your left hand off the gun and hold it up in front of your face. Fold your fingers over with your thumb sticking out, as if you are hitchhiking.

Now tip the gun over toward the left, so that the gun is horizontal or even a little upside down.[147]

Keeping your hitchhiking fist together, place the horizontal gun into the pocket between your hitchhiking fist and thumb, so that the back of the slide lands in the web of your hand. Bring your thumb down on top of the serra-

---

147 *Yes, just like you see the "gangstas" do on TV and in the movies.*

tions behind the ejection port and squeeze hard. This is the slingshot grasp, so called because you are now pinching the slide just as if it were the sling of a slingshot.

Hand placement—some dangers to avoid

Avoid turning the slingshot grasp into a weak pinch with the fingertips. Use as much of your hand as you can manage, making use of the strength of a fist rather than the weakness of your fingertips.

When using the overhand grasp, be sure that your hand is placed behind the ejection port, which is the part of the gun from which the empty shell casings come out. You should never cover the ejection port while there is still a round in the chamber. One reason is because covering the port can prevent the chamber from being emptied when you rack the slide, and may even cause a jam. But the more important reason not to cover the ejection port is that doing so can be dangerous. If the primer is punched while you are struggling with the slide—rare but not impossible if your firearm has a protrusive extractor or ejector—the shell casing is likely to split and the full force of the round may detonate in the palm of your hand. This could be messy and uncomfortable.

Be extremely aware of your trigger finger as you prepare to move the slide. Is your finger far outside the trigger guard? Is it high on the frame of the gun? Keep it there! Don't let it drift downward alongside the trigger guard, or the sympathetic grip reflex will create problems.

So grasp the grip of the gun firmly with your shooting hand, index your trigger finger high on the frame, and grasp the slide firmly with your non-shooting hand. Do not cover the ejection port.

Moving the Slide

Now that you have positioned your hands, you need to find a position for your arms and body that will maximize your strength and allow you to move the slide efficiently. Human beings tend to be strongest at the midline, with hands fairly close to the body. When you extend your arms straight out, you lose some of that essential strength. Similarly, you don't want the gun too far to one side or the other. Just bring it back to your center, somewhere around and just above your belly button near your midline. Keep the gun pointed downrange at all times. From this point, you have two choices.

Method One is simply to drive your gun hand sharply forward while holding the slide firmly in place so that it does not move with the gun.

When I say to drive the gun forward sharply, that is exactly what I mean:

you want a quick, explosive movement of the grip hand, punching it out and away from your body. The movement is sudden, fast, explosive. You may pull back slightly on the slide while this is happening, but "pulling the slide back" is not the goal. The goal is to **punch the gun forward** while the slide stays still. *Do not think of it as pulling the slide back, but as punching the gun forward.*

Method Two is harder to describe with the written word than it is to perform on the range. In this method, you anchor your dominant elbow to your dominant hip, and then quickly rotate your entire hip and lower body to punch the gun forward while holding the slide in place with your non-dominant hand.

This one works really well because it recruits your strongest muscles, those in your legs and lower body, to do the work of moving the slide for you. But in order for it to work, you must punch the gun forward fast and hard.

Let the slide slam forward

Once you have punched the gun so far forward that the slide has traveled all the way to its rear, you will need to let go of the slide so it can go forward on its own. To load the gun reliably, the slide needs to move forward under its own spring tension. It needs to SLAM forward.[148]

Some people have a hard time letting go of the slide after getting it back. They let their slide hand travel forward with the slide, intentionally or unintentionally slowing it down. This is called "riding the slide" and it is a very bad habit because it keeps the gun from functioning reliably. In order to avoid this bad habit, create the good habit of simply opening your hand when you feel the slide hit its rearmost point. If necessary, slap yourself on the shoulder with your slide hand as the gun hand continues to travel forward. This will keep your slide hand from reflexively traveling forward with the slide. Remember: the slide needs to travel forward on its own. If you "help" it forward, you may create a jam.

Once you have figured out how to move the slide briskly and decisively, practice the motion a few times (don't wear yourself out!) before you move on to the next step.

Locking the Slide Open

At this point, you may be saying, "Wait a minute. I can move the slide okay. I just can't get it to lock back!" Have no fear—there's a secret, easier

---

148 *If you are not loading the firearm, but instead want the slide to close on an empty chamber, you can lower the slide gently by hand. But to rack the slide when loading, you must allow the slide to close itself without softening its fall in any way.*

method to doing that, too.

To lock the slide to the rear, you will be doing the same series of motions that you did above when you moved the slide. However, before you punch the gun forward, you are going to shift your grip hand around just far enough that you can lift of up on the slide stop lever *during the entire time* that the slide is in motion. The reason you are lifting up on the slide stop lever the entire time is that it takes a lot of strength to hold the slide to the rear while you fumble around looking for that annoying little lever. So you instead will explosively punch the gun forward with the lever prepped to slip into place when the slide gets to the right point.

CAUTION!

No matter how much you may struggle with the task, NEVER put your finger on the trigger or inside the trigger guard while racking the slide.

You should be aware that semi-automatic slides can be retracted up to an inch farther back behind the slide lock point. You are not bringing the slide to its rearmost point, but only most of the way there. That is another reason to put upward pressure on the lever while racking the slide: you won't have to struggle to hold the slide back while moving it back and forth looking for the magic spot. With upward pressure on it, the stop lever will slip into place, locking the slide as soon as the slide reaches its lock point.

If you absolutely cannot find a hand position which allows you to reach the slide stop lever while punching the gun forward, it may be time to consider personalizing your gun by installing slimmer grips, getting a grip reduction, or even purchasing a different gun whose grip size is more suited for your hand.

For Lefties Only

Left-handers have some special challenges when it comes to running guns designed for right-handed people. This is nothing new for us lefties, since by the time any lefty reaches adulthood, we've all had years of practice at overcoming such challenges. Although it can be discouraging at first, remember that this problem is not impossible. It's just one more adaptation to a right-handed world.

If your firearm is not truly ambidextrous, but you are running it left-handed, here is what you will need to do in order to lock the slide back. Hold the gun with your left hand, with your trigger finger indexed along the frame far outside the trigger guard.

Now take your right hand off the gun.

Tip the gun over toward the right, so that the gun is horizontal or even a little upside down.[149]

Hold your right hand with the palm flat and fingers straightened together, with your thumb sticking straight out. Now look at your palm.

Take the fingertips of your right hand and place them together on the serrations on the *right* (underneath) side of the firearm near the back of the slide. Now wrap the rest of your right hand over the top of the slide, ending with the heel of your hand firmly gripping the slide and your thumb pointed toward the muzzle. Use the muscle at the base of your thumb to firmly grip the slide on the thumb side, so your thumb can still wiggle just a little.

This grip should enable you to reach and engage the slide lock lever with your right thumb when the slide is back.[150]

To retract the slide, just like the right-handers do, you will drive the gun quickly forward with your strong hand. Don't think of it as "pulling the slide back," but as "punching the gun forward." Practice this motion a few times before you try to lock the slide.

To lock the slide open, punch the gun forward. Then use your right thumb to pull up on the slide lock lever when the slide reaches the sweet spot. You might have to work a little bit to find that spot.

You may need to move your hand forward or rearward on the slide to find the optimum hand placement that will work well for you so your thumb can reach the slide lock lever when the slide is retracted. If you cannot pull up on the slide stop lever with your right thumb without partly covering the ejection port, that is okay *as long as you have first checked that there is no round in the chamber*. First drop the magazine and rack the slide several times, making sure there is no round in the chamber. When there is no magazine in the gun, and no round in the chamber, it is not unsafe to cover the ejection port while you lock the slide open.

Be careful not to get the meat of your hand pinched within the port if you need to lower the slide from this grip.

You *can* do this...

Although working the slide can be a challenge for many novice shooters, the challenge can be mastered with a little determination and willingness to experiment. If after reading the instructions above you still have difficulty,

---

149 *Yup. Just like the "gangsta" movies.*
150 *Note that the lever will be near the base of your thumb when the slide is forward, but as you pull the slide you will become able to reach it with the pad or tip of your thumb.*

find a competent female instructor and ask her to show you how she does it. Do not get discouraged, and do not give up. You CAN do this!

To Load the Semi-Auto

To load a semi-auto, you first fill the magazine with fresh rounds, then get the magazine into the firearm, and finally rack the slide briskly. Immediately engage the safety if your gun has one, and decock if you are running a double action pistol with a decocker. That's all there is to it.

Always keep the muzzle pointed in a safe direction as you are loading your pistol. If you absolutely cannot rack the slide without pointing the muzzle at your own left elbow, you should not be running a semi-auto. Learn to do it safely or move to using a revolver.

Many people have difficulty getting rounds into the magazine, especially the last few rounds. The stiffer springs of double-stack magazines can create particular trouble in this area. If you're one of these people, don't despair! Several companies make great tools that can help. Try an UpLula universal magazine loader, learn how to use it, and don't look back.[151]

Important Safety Reminder

If you struggle with the clearing process, be *very* conscious of your gun's muzzle direction at all times. Do not allow it to point at anything you are unwilling to shoot. Although the gun cannot fire while the doublefeed is in place, it can fire an unintentional shot the moment the magazine comes free.

ALWAYS keep the gun pointed in a safe direction with your fingers far away from the trigger and outside the trigger guard.

To Clear a Misfeed

Although a misfeed is simply a subtype of the larger category of malfunctions called "failures to fire," a misfeed is by far the most common cause of a failure to fire. Misfeeds often happen when a round of ammunition fails to enter the chamber as expected. Because there is no round in the chamber, the gun cannot fire.

Failures to fire can also be caused by faulty reloads or otherwise poor ammunition which does not react as expected when the primer is struck. In some cases, the fault may lie within the mechanics of the firearm: worn springs or dirty firing pin channels may not allow the firing pin to strike the primer as hard as it must be struck in order to fire the round. Whatever the cause, when you pull the trigger nothing

---

151 See www.maglula.com for company contact information. At the time of this writing, the product was widely available through Brownell's, Midway, and other retailers.

happens except a very disconcerting *click*.

Getting a new round into the chamber so that your gun works again only takes a second or two, but you must do it in the right order. The phrase to remember is **Tap, Rack,** (assess and) **Bang.**

Step One: Tap

Tap the bottom of the magazine firmly upwards with the base of your palm. You are doing this because one of the most common causes of a misfeed is a magazine that is not completely seated. If the magazine is not firmly in place, when the slide comes forward it will slip right over the next round, failing to pick it up for chambering.

You must tap the magazine into place first, *before* you rack the slide.

Step Two: Rack

If the previous round of ammunition was a dud, it will be ejected at this point. As the slide comes forward again, it will pick up a good fresh round from the top of the firmly seated magazine.

Yank the slide back quickly and decisively. No matter how aggressively you move the slide, you cannot hurt the gun in this way. When the slide is fully to the rear, simply let go of it. Do not lower it by hand because that can cause another misfeed. Instead, simply let go of the slide and allow it to fly forward again under spring tension.

Don't bother to tap the magazine again after you rack the slide. There's no point. Either you firmly seated the magazine on step one, or it's too late now. In order to work, these steps have to be done in the correct sequence.

After you rack the slide, allow the slide to slam forward on its own. Resist the temptation to help it along. Do not rest your hand on the slide, and do not allow your hand to follow the slide forward.

Step Three: (Assess and) Bang

Look at your target. Does it still need shooting? If so, pull the trigger. *Always* check your target before blazing away at it. If you ever do this in real life, the bad guy could have grabbed a hostage, run away, or surrendered in the amount of time it took you to clear the malfunction.

Clear a Doublefeed

A doublefeed happens when two rounds try to enter the chamber at the same time. Because there is not enough room for both, the gun locks up with the slide partially to the rear. You cannot fire until you have cleared the problem. A doublefeed may happen because the extractor did not yank the old case out of the way as the slide moved back, leaving the spent case in the chamber as the slide on its return journey tried to stuff a new round into the same space. Another common cause of a misfeed: the shooter tried to clear a misfeed but forgot to tap the magazine into place first before racking the slide. Oops.

Learning to clear a doublefeed can be confusing at first. The steps must be done in the correct order, and it is easy to lose your place until you understand what it is that you are doing and why you are doing it. Do not get discouraged! With repeated practice, it becomes much easier.

It may help you to think of this process in these terms: when the gun jams and tap-rack doesn't work, you should vigorously unload the gun, briskly rack the slide several times, and reload. That's all we're doing in the steps below.

Step One: Tap, Rack...

Upon experiencing any malfunction, immediately begin the procedure for clearing a misfeed. You are doing this because a misfeed is the single most common type of malfunction, and because your hands are faster than your eyeballs at diagnosing what is wrong. So even though Tap, Rack won't do anything to clear away your doublefeed, don't omit this step in practice. It's important for diagnosing the problem under stress or in the dark—two factors you might someday find yourself dealing with if you need to use the firearm "for keeps."

Step Two: Lock the Slide Back

Even though it appears the slide is already locked back, it is not. It is being held back by the rearward cartridge. This means there is a lot of pressure holding that cartridge in place. Since the cartridge is still attached to the magazine, it will be very difficult to remove the magazine until the pressure is relieved by locking the slide back.

Some people who have super-strong hands (or weak gun springs) can omit this step. Personally, even though I have really strong hands, I find it so much easier and more certain that I will never skip this step in practice—because when it really matters, I may not be able to do the next step if I skip this one.

Step Three: Strip the Magazine Down and Out

Hit the magazine release and yank the magazine out of the gun. The magazine is held in place by a lot of tension when there's a doublefeed in place. It's going to be a little stiff to pull out and you may have to yank on it *hard*. Don't be afraid to manhandle it a little. Guns are very strong and there's not a lot you can do with your hands to hurt them.

Glock owners: be careful not to block the opposite side of the magazine release during this step.

Step Four: Rack, Rack, Rack

Once the magazine is out, briskly rack the slide *at least three times.* The doublefeed was very likely caused by a stuck, stubborn case that did not want to be extracted from the chamber. So a single rack may not clear it out. Rack it at least three times.

Step Five: Insert New Magazine

Don't put the old one back in if you can help it, because there's a chance that it was the cause of your woes. And even though you may feel flustered at this point, be sure to seat the magazine firmly. The last thing you need is to start this cycle over again!

Step Six: Rack the Slide

This puts a new round into the empty chamber. Be sure to rack the slide good and hard, allowing it to slam forward on its own. If you ride the slide or soften its fall forward, you can set up yet another malfunction. So rack it hard and let it do its thing without help.

Step Seven: Assess

Even if you are well-practiced, you may have taken ten seconds or more to clear the doublefeed. You might have taken a lot more than that, especially if you had difficulty getting the magazine out. In that amount of time, the situation may have changed substantially. If you were doing this "for keeps," there's a chance your attacker ran away, or grabbed a hostage, or moved behind concealment.

Take the time to check! Do not get in the habit of blazing away without checking your target first.

Step Eight: Bang

If your target is still there, and still needs to be shot, shoot it.

To Unload a Semi-Auto

To unload the semi-auto, first remove the magazine from the gun by pressing the magazine release. Always let an empty magazine fall to the ground, so you don't get in the habit of slowing yourself down fiddling with the empties. Full magazines should be treated with a bit more care, but don't waste time with the empty one. On most defensive pistols, you'll find the magazine release on the left side of the gun near the base of the trigger guard, but some European-style pistols feature a magazine release found near the butt of the gun.

1. *After* removing the magazine, rack the slide. Rack it two or three times, watching to see that the round in the chamber has ejected.
2. Now lock the slide open.
3. With the slide locked open, look down into the ejection port to see if you can see all the way through the bottom of the magazine well to the daylight on the other side.
4. Look in the chamber. Can you see the telltale brass glint of a loaded round?
5. Poke a finger into the magazine well. Is anything in the way?
6. Poke your pinky finger into the empty chamber. Make sure there's no round lurking there.
7. Look again at the magazine well and chamber, being sure they are really empty.
8. Close the slide and put the gun away safely.

This process sounds obsessive because it is. There's nothing wrong with obsession when it comes to staying safe around deadly weapons!

Checking the magazine well and the empty chamber with our fingertips as well as our eyeballs allows us to be certain the firearm is unloaded, even in the dark. Furthermore, we use the multiple layers of checks—locking the slide back, looking twice, *and* using fingers to check again—because semi-automatic pistols have a notorious habit of hiding a round in the chamber when they are supposedly "unloaded." Sometimes tired or distracted people do things out of sequence, racking the slide and then dropping the magazine. Sometimes the ejector fails to remove the chambered round when the slide is racked. For these reasons, we need multiple layers of safety when unloading any firearm.

Make a habit of checking the gun very thoroughly with your eyes and your fingertips every time you pick up the gun, every time you are handed the gun, and every time you unload the gun. Do it so often that it becomes an ingrained habit that will carry you through and perhaps even save the day when you are tired, or stressed, or not thinking clearly.

Running a Revolver

Running a revolver is supposed to be simpler than running a semi-automatic handgun. And it is—usually. But there are still things to learn. Starting the process with the idea that you won't have to learn anything sets you up for a dangerous failure. Because using a firearm around other people necessarily puts them in danger if you use it incorrectly, when you purchase a defense gun, you are also purchasing the obligation to learn how to use it safely and well. There are no firearms—none!—which can be effectively used without practiced skill. This goes for revolvers as well as for semi-autos, for shotguns as well as rifles. Although the learning curve might be less steep with some guns than with others, it takes work to master even the "easiest" firearm.

The smaller the revolver, the more difficult it becomes to shoot well.[152] But even the smallest revolver can be mastered by someone determined to learn. Here are some ideas to get you started.

To Unload and Reload

To unload and reload the revolver, you will need to open the cylinder and swing it out from the side of the gun. Begin by holding the revolver in a firing grip with your right hand, with your trigger finger indexed along the frame far outside the trigger guard.

Take your left hand off the gun and hold it up in front of your face, palm flat, fingers together, thumb sticking out. Now curl your entire hand into a C shape, with your fingers still together.

Bring your C-shaped left hand up underneath the trigger guard of the revolver, so that your thumb holds the left side of the cylinder and your fingers (still together) press against the cylinder's right side.

To open the cylinder, use your right thumb to move the latch on the left-hand side of the gun. Some models need the latch pushed forward, while others require the latch to be pulled to the rear. If you need to scooch your right

---

152 *This goes for semi-automatics as well. Tiny, lightweight guns are difficult to shoot well and safely. They are properly the province of expert shooters, not good guns for beginners.*

hand around in order to manipulate the latch, that's just fine—your left hand has a good grasp on the gun now anyway.

At the same time as you move the latch with your right thumb, press the cylinder toward the left side of the gun (the side where your thumbs are). This should make the cylinder "pop" open to the left.

As the cylinder pops open, wrap as much of your left thumb around the cylinder as you can, holding it securely. You can now take your right hand entirely off the gun, since the gun is held securely in your left hand.

Without altering your grip on the cylinder, turn the firearm so that the muzzle is pointed directly up, toward the sky.[153] You will notice that the top end of the cylinder has a rod coming out of it. This is the ejector rod.

Take your right hand and hold it with the palm flat and fingers together. Turn your hand so it is horizontal.

Flipping it Shut?

To avoid straining delicate parts of the gun, never "flip" or "slap" the cylinder closed. Simply close it gently but firmly with your hand.

Using the fat, solid part of the heel of your right hand, press the ejector rod smoothly all the way down. Do this only once, smoothly and briskly.

If the gun was loaded, you will see and feel the empty cases drop out of the back end of the cylinder when you press the ejector rod. Notice that this emptying technique guarantees that your hands are entirely out of the way to allow these cases to fall to the ground, so they won't get hung up and slow down your reload. Notice, too, that with the gun held vertically during this process, you are very unlikely to create a jam in your revolver by getting debris or even a shell stuck underneath the star.

Now, still keeping your left thumb wrapped securely around the cylinder as much as possible, point the muzzle directly at the ground. Anchor the butt of the gun against your belly button.[154] Note that your left thumb will keep the cylinder from moving during the next steps.

With your right hand, grab your fresh ammunition and insert it into the cylinder. You can feed your rounds in one at a time, or you can use a speed-loader to feed all 5 or 6 rounds in at once.

As soon as the cylinder is full of fresh ammunition, bring your right hand

---

153 *This is safe because your fingers have replaced critical firing parts of the gun. The gun could never fire with the cylinder out.*
154 *Anchoring provides a felt index, which will allow you to keep your eyes on the threat instead of staring at your own hands. It also makes it possible to easily reload in the dark if necessary.*

smoothly back to obtain a firing grip on the revolver, with your trigger finger far outside the trigger guard. At the same time, use your left hand to close the cylinder, pushing it closed with your thumb while cushioning it with your fingers. If you used a speedloader, just let it fall to the ground during this step.[155]

Give the cylinder a little wiggle-turn to be sure it is closed and latched. When it is in place, it will not be able to turn. If you can turn it, keep turning it until it clicks into place.

Now slide your left hand smoothly into its firing grip as you bring the gun up to the target. You are ready to shoot.

To Check That the Revolver Is Unloaded

Always check to be certain the revolver is really unloaded before you put the gun away. Here's how:

1. Open the cylinder as described above.
2. Point the muzzle toward the sky and press the ejector rod with the heel of your right hand, ejecting any empty rounds.
3. Point the muzzle at the ground and look at the cylinder. Are there any rounds or empty cases still inside?
4. Run your right index finger across the holes, counting each one as you go. Are the holes all there? Are any holes missing?
5. Look again. Can you see clear through each and every hole?
6. Close the cylinder and put the gun away safely.

This process sounds obsessive because it is. When people are under stress or in a hurry, they find it surprisingly easy to miss seeing things they weren't really expecting to see in the first place. And one of life's most unpleasant little surprises is discovering one round lurking inside a revolver you believe you unloaded. So don't get in the habit of just glancing at your revolver before putting it away. *Really* look. Look twice and count the empty chambers to be sure they're all there.

Oh, and please—*please*—don't be one of those people who thinks they can "check" a revolver by glancing in from the side without even opening the cylinder. That's plain foolish! Check the revolver very well every time you pick it up or set it down, even if you believe it's already unloaded. This will build a good habit that can carry you through times when you're tired or stressed and not paying attention as well as you ought.

---

155 *Research has shown that, under stress, people generally do things the same way they did them in practice—even if they meant to do otherwise. So let the empty rounds fall and let the speedloader fall. Don't practice wasting time.*

To Decock the Hammer

Safely lowering the hammer without firing the revolver requires some co-ordination, but it's an important skill for many reasons. Here's how:

1. Point the gun in a safe direction—one that would definitely contain a bullet and cause no damage to any person or thing you are not willing to shoot.
2. Keep a solid firing grip on the gun with your dominant hand.
3. With your trigger finger far outside the trigger guard, securely pinch the hammer using your non-dominant hand. This pinch should place the pad of your thumb slightly *forward* of the front surface of the hammer so that if the hammer slips you may catch or cushion its fall.
4. With the hammer securely pinched, gently pull the trigger. You will feel the hammer release as you do so. Lower the hammer just slightly and remove your finger from the trigger.
5. With your finger far outside the trigger guard, gently lower the hammer the remainder of the way.
6. Your hammer may stop at the half-cock position. If so, repeat steps 4 and 5 until the hammer releases again. As soon as it has released, take your finger off the trigger and out of the trigger guard.

Why remove your finger from the trigger while lowering the hammer? Simple: if the hammer slips and your finger is on the trigger, the gun will definitely fire. If the hammer slips and your finger isn't on the trigger, it is much less likely to fire.

Coping with a Heavy Trigger

Custom revolversmith Grant Cunningham writes:

> *Mastering the double action pull takes time, dedication, and practice; that's just a fact of life. The nice, light, short trigger pulls on autoloaders are much easier to become proficient with, which is part of the reason they are popular.*[156]

Modern, double-action revolver triggers usually provide a lot of resistance to the shooter's finger. Placed on a trigger scale (a device for measuring the

---

156 Grant Cunningham, *The Revolver Liberation Alliance* blog, www.grantcunningham.com.

amount of pressure the trigger requires before the shot will fire), most weigh in around twelve to fifteen pounds. That's a lot of pressure to provide with just one finger, especially given that the shooter mustn't allow the muzzle to waver during the process.

To overcome the difficulty, shooters take several different approaches. Perhaps the most common approach is to cock the hammer on firearms so equipped. This converts the double action into a single action, lightens the trigger pull weight, and reduces the distance the trigger must travel before the shot fires. Unfortunately, cocking the hammer before each shot creates several dangers with a self-defense firearm (more about that in a bit), so that's not an option open to us. Some shooters use both index fingers to pull the trigger, which works moderately well as an emergency measure but can hardly be considered a long-term solution. Finally, there's the option of taking the revolver to a gunsmith to lighten the springs, or lightening them yourself. Unfortunately, several pragmatic concerns limit the extent to which you can lighten the trigger on a defense gun, especially since double action revolvers mechanically require a certain amount of tension in order to function reliably. So this solution, too, has its limitations.

Why not cock the hammer?

For those uninterested in self-defense, cocking the hammer while shooting makes perfect sense. But for a defense gun, it's a dangerous act.

First, cocking the hammer takes time—time you may not have to spare when attacked. This may not matter for the initial shot, but for second and subsequent shots it can slow you down quite a bit.

Second, if you cock the hammer and the attacker immediately surrenders, you cannot righteously shoot him. But holding the intruder at gunpoint using a firearm with a superlight trigger means that avoiding an unintentional discharge becomes much more difficult.

Further, in such a situation, massive amounts of adrenalin will flood your body, making fine motor control very difficult. But safely lowering the hammer without firing the gun requires fine motor control.

Cocking the hammer gives you a superlight trigger, good for shooting—but it also opens you up to an enthusiastically wrong prosecutor pursuing charges for manslaughter with the "theory of the case" that the shooter actually lied about defending herself, and instead claimed self-defense after *accidentally* shooting the *victim* with her *hair trigger!* While it's possible to defeat such claims in court, it's a lot less expensive to avoid them in the first place.

Scientists tell us that the actions we habitually perform in practice nearly always return under stress—even when we don't intend them to. Since you'll want to avoid cocking the hammer during a life-threatening encounter, don't practice cocking the hammer on the range. Instead, shoot the revolver using the double action trigger, and learn to use it well.

Trigger job

There's a mechanical limit to how much a double action trigger can be lightened without affecting the gun's reliability and speed of reset. If you choose to lighten the trigger of your double action revolver, be sure your chosen gunsmith understands that you intend to use the firearm for self defense, and thus that your most crucial concern centers on *reliability.*

Fortunately, smoothing out the trigger often helps improve a shooter's results, even in the absence of significant lightening. Getting a gunsmith to smooth and soften the trigger pull often provides the needed boost and makes a previously-difficult double action revolver a joy to shoot. But those mechanical limits might also limit your ability to enjoy this benefit to the full.

So what's the answer?

Although our society loves the quick fix, sometimes the quick fix won't do the job we need. In the long run, if you shoot a double-action firearm, you will need to increase your hand strength to manage the task efficiently and well. Just as a rower needs to regularly exercise her arm muscles to build up her strength for the task, a double-action shooter needs to regularly exercise her trigger finger.

Dry fire. The simplest way to improve your hand strength is to faithfully dry fire the double action revolver. Every day, using a safe dry fire routine, point the unloaded revolver in a safe direction and pull the trigger an increasing number of times with the sights aligned on a chosen target. Be sure to practice with each hand, just in case you ever need to fire using the "wrong" one.

Exercise equipment. Musicians, climbers, and weightlifters often use rubber balls, tensioners, and other devices to increase their hand and finger strength. For our purposes, take a look at multi-key devices (such as the GripMaster)[157] intended to allow the user to exercise each finger independently of the others. Take care not to overdo it when first starting out. Faithful, gentle exercise works better than enthusiastic fits and starts.

---

157 See www.gripmaster.com.au. GripMaster products are widely available through sporting good stores and online retailers.

Practice Time!

Dear Gunhilda,

What's the best firearm and technique for shooting zombies?

~ Zombiefied in Zellwood

Dear Zombiefied,

Shooting 'em ain't the problem. It's cleaning 'em you've gotta worry about.

~ Gunhilda

Practice Doesn't Make Perfect

Here is a secret to effective practice:

Practice doesn't make perfect. Practice makes *permanent*.

If you practice doing something wrong 3,428 times, guess what? On your 3,429th time, you are going to do the wrong thing. You will have permanently engraved the wrong action into your habitual responses.

This means we can't get lazy when we practice. It might be easier to neatly collect revolver brass instead of briskly dumping it as we reload, but if the goal is to learn to do a quick reload under pressure, we're better off to dump the brass and pick it up later. It's often easier to yank the trigger roughly than it is to pull it smoothly—but if we want to learn to shoot accurately, yanking the trigger will not get us where we want to go.

This also means that it's a good idea to learn the fastest, smoothest way to do something *before* you start doing that thing a lot. There are a lot of old guys out there who have literally spent years practicing an inefficient reload or a dangerous holstering technique. These poor guys have to erase years of habits before they can learn better shooting techniques and safer gun handling skills.

If you consider yourself a beginning shooter, please consider this carefully: right now, you have the perfect opportunity to begin with a clean slate. If you find a good instructor and learn to do it right in the first place, you can save yourself literally years of fighting bad habits.

It's worth thinking about.

Incidentally, there's another, more popular "practice doesn't make perfect" saying in the firearms training community. This one goes:

Practice doesn't make perfect. *Perfect* practice makes perfect.

That's true as far as it goes, but I don't think it goes far enough. Because you are a human being, and because human beings make mistakes, you will *never* be perfect in practice. And that's okay.

Just don't repetitively practice doing everything entirely wrong.

Dry Fire Safety

When you dry fire, you go through all the motions of firing your gun, including pulling the trigger, without using live ammunition.

Dry fire can prevent the development of a flinch, or cure an existing one because it removes the stimuli of the shot going off. Dry fire is usually more convenient than going to the range, and it is a boon to shooters on a limited budget because it allows you to practice without spending money on ammunition. You can build thousands of repetitions attaining perfect sight alignment, perfect trigger squeeze and perfect follow through without the expense of firing thousands of rounds. Dry fire allows you to learn a smooth, safe draw stroke without the danger of an accidental or negligent discharge while you are learning.

> **Important!!**
>
> The Four Universal Rules always apply, even while dry firing.

But there's one nasty little drawback: dry fire is very dangerous. Many, if not most, accidental shootings among good shooters are caused by someone dry firing in a dangerous manner—while distracted, or while overtired, or while failing to follow all the safety rules. If you doubt that dry fire is dangerous, run a search for the words "negligent discharge" on any internet gun board, and see how many tragedies and near-tragedies happened while dry firing.

Dry firing can be done safely. It is not inherently safe, but it can be done safely. In order to be safe, there are specific rules you must follow, every single time, without exception. Those who cannot habitually follow the safety ritual should never dry fire at all. But those who are willing to learn and carefully follow the rules can dry fire in perfect safety.

Too many people become complacent and chuck the Four Rules out the window simply because they need to get some dry fire practice in. Foolish! The purpose of dry firing is to engrain certain physical habits into your memory—so deeply engrain them that your body will automatically behave that way under stress. You do not want to engrain poor safety habits. Dry firing without following the Four Rules is worse than not dry firing at all, because it accomplishes the exact opposite of its intended purpose.

Dry Fire and the Four Rules

Rule One, "All guns are always loaded," means that the safety rules ALWAYS apply, including while you are dry firing. Never do anything with an "unloaded" gun that you would not be willing to do with a loaded one. Some people believe checking the gun's status means you can treat it like a toy—that you can point it at your friends to pose for a picture, or at your training partners for disarming practice, or at a flimsy interior wall for dry fire. That's a foolishly bad idea that kills a certain number of people every single year.

Rule Two, "Never point the gun at anything you are not willing to destroy," means when you choose a direction for dry fire, you must choose a direction in which you would be willing to fire a loaded weapon. Don't point it at your dog, at the big-screen TV you can't afford to replace, at a friend, or at an heirloom vase. Point it at something that would result in only minor and acceptable property damage if the gun were loaded.

> **Note**
>
> The word "willing," as used or implied in the first two rules, does not mean you really *want* to shoot your subfloor, or that you have a burning desire to blast that bucketful of dry sand all over your bedroom carpet. It only means you are aware that your other safety measures may fail, and you are willing to sacrifice these things if you make a mistake. It means you reasonably believe that only minor property damage—not physical or emotional tragedy—will result if you err.

One reason people dry fire is to learn **Rule Three, "Keep your finger off the trigger until your sights are on target."** This rule must be contained not just in your thinking brain, but in your body's physical response to holding the gun in your hand. It should take a conscious effort of will to put your finger on the trigger. You should never, ever, ever find your finger resting on the trigger or within the trigger guard when you didn't consciously put it there. Keep your finger out of the trigger guard until your sights are on target. But what's a target? A target is anywhere you have deliberately chosen as the best place for a bullet to land in a given situation. It can be a piece of paper, a criminal intruder, or a falling steel plate. It can be a particular spot on the living room floor, a thick stack of phone books, or a painting hung on a basement wall. The important thing is that the target is deliberately chosen. Never put your finger on the trigger, for dry fire or for any other reason including disassembling the gun, until you have deliberately chosen the best place for a bullet to land in that situation.

Rule Four, "Be sure of your target and what is beyond it," means you will not point the gun at a flimsy interior wall which you know would never stop a bullet, or at your own reflection in the bathroom mirror. You won't dry fire at the TV. Instead, you'll set up a useful target with a safe backstop. If you cannot set up a safe backstop in your home, you must not dry fire there.

Steps to Safe Dry Fire

Below follows one safe dry fire ritual. It is a ritual because it must be done the same way every time. Doing it the same way every time means that this safe behavior will become habitual behavior. Such habitually safe behavior may help prevent a tragic goof if an interruption happens or your attention wanders. Good habitual routines like the one below can help build redundant layers of safety into your firearms handling skills.

1. No interruptions! Turn the ringer off the phone and lock the front door. If you are interrupted, re-start your ritual beginning at step #1. Don't just pick up where you think you left off.
2. Unload your gun.
3. Check that the gun is unloaded. Check by both sight and feel. Lock the action open, then run the end of your pinky into the empty chamber to be sure there's a hole there. If you have a revolver, run your finger across the opening to each chamber in the cylinder. Count the empty holes to be sure you touched them all.
4. Get all the ammunition out of the room and out of sight. I even go so far as to lock the door to the room where the ammunition went so it takes several steps to get the ammunition back together with the gun.
5. Choose a safe backstop, one that will definitely stop a bullet. If you cannot find a reliable backstop, you must not dry fire.
6. Tape a target to your backstop. Do not dry fire directly at anything that will remain in the room all the time. Put up a specific target and take it down when you are done.
7. Check again, by sight and feel, that the gun is still unloaded. Don't skip this step! Guns can be sneaky and sometimes load themselves when no one is looking. Every time the gun has been out of your hands, check it again when you pick it back up.
8. Dry fire. Make it short and sweet—less than ten minutes, tops. As soon as your mind wanders, stop immediately. That's a sign that you are not paying attention to what you are doing, and is a prime red flag for safety.
9. Take the target down immediately, before reloading the gun. Never

leave the target in place. That way you won't be tempted to take "just one more dry fire shot" at it, forgetting that you reloaded the gun. Put the target away, out of sight, before you get the ammunition out of the other room and before you reload.

10. Lock your gun out of reach, or get out of the practice room. Or both. Stay out of the area and away from the firearm until your conditioning to pull the trigger in that room has worn off and been replaced with conscious thought.

11. When you do reload the gun, say aloud, "This gun is loaded. It will fire if I pull the trigger. This gun is loaded." Say it three times, and say it out loud. This brings your brain front and center while loading the gun, and helps cement the end of practice time in your mind.

Backstop Ideas

If you dry fire a handgun in your home, you need to be prepared in case your gun ever loads itself when you are not paying attention. This means you will need a backstop which would stop a handgun bullet. You must be certain that an unintended shot could not possibly do any harm other than minor property damage.[158]

What will stop a handgun bullet in the average home? Not an interior wall. Not a standard exterior wall unless it is made from solid brick. Not the couch, not the TV, not the front door. It's surprising the number of things that *won't* stop a bullet. In fact, you can pretty much assume that nothing works as a safe backstop unless you have tested it for yourself. With that thought in mind, read the list below as "things to test for yourself" rather than as absolutes. Before reading any farther, and just to please my lawyer, please taken another look at the disclaimer at the front of this book. You, and you alone, are responsible for every shot that leaves your firearm. So you, and you alone, must be certain that your backstop is sufficient for the caliber you use at the distance you shoot.

With that in mind, here are some ideas for creating home backstops suitable for dry fire. Try:

☑ A two-to-three-foot thick stack of phone books, positioned with the books' faces toward the shooter. For convenience, you could place these phone books inside a cardboard box, to be pulled out for dry fire and put away out of sight at other times.

☑ A brick fireplace—but stand back to avoid potential ricochets.

---

158 *And embarrassment.*

☑ The cement wall in your basement (ditto ricochet potential).

☑ A very crowded bookshelf, with no airspace between books, using the long end. Do not dry fire straight into the spines of the books. Instead, aim at the bookcase end, so an unexpected bullet would travel the entire length of the bookshelf before coming to rest somewhere between the pages.

☑ A bullet-resistant vest, hung on the wall.

☑ A five-gallon bucket of sand. This could be disguised inside a decorative basket, with a fake houseplant such as a silk-leaved ficus tree plunked inside the sand bucket. Such a contraption is a handy place to point your firearm when you must load, unload, or disassemble it (especially in the case of Glocks and other designs which require you to pull the trigger during the disassembly process).

Obviously shooting any or all of these things could easily damage property. The bulletproof vest, for example, would subsequently be useless. Replacing the books would be a drag. Undinging brick or cement walls is difficult; getting sand out of the carpet is nigh unto impossible. But minor property damage is acceptable—uncontained bullets are not.

Do You Need Professional Firearms Instruction?

First-time students at the Firearms Academy of Seattle[159] often tell me, "Wow! I just didn't know how much there was that I didn't know!" Sometimes they'll say, "I thought I was a pretty good shooter... until I came here." Or they'll say, "Gosh, I never realized how much there is to think about with this stuff." These students make it clear that the firearms training industry has generally done a poor job educating shooters about *why* they need professional training.

The problem is compounded greatly by state-required classes for concealed carry permits, which many people think of as "real training." These classes can provide good information, but their primary purpose isn't to train the students how to defend themselves. On the contrary, state-required classes exist to assure political leaders that people who acquire a CCW permit in their states will not endanger the public.

As a lifelong autodidact,[160] I was a bit taken aback the first time a friend suggested to me that I might benefit from professional firearms training. "Good grief!" I thought. "This stuff is not rocket science. Why can't I just teach myself, or learn from books and videos?" Fortunately for me, I took my friend's advice anyway.

Why not learn from a book?

Books can be a great way to impart philosophical points (see *The Art of War* by Sun Tzu; *Principles of Personal Defense* by Jeff Cooper). They can give the reader practical and tactical concepts (see *Guns, Bullets, and Gunfights* by Jim Cirillo; *Stressfire* by Massad Ayoob; *Teaching Women to Shoot* by Diane Nicholl and Vicki Farnam). They can address specific social considerations and give a good overview of the process of becoming a responsibly armed

---

159 *The Firearms Academy of Seattle, PO Box 400, Onalaska WA 98570. (360) 978-6100. www.firearmsacademy.com.*
160 *Definition? Let's just say that the autodidacts reading this will go look up the word, but nobody else will.*

citizen (see *Personal Defense for Women* by Gila Hayes). They can explain legal issues (see *In the Gravest Extreme* by Massad Ayoob) and ethical questions (see *Shooting Back* by Charl Van Wyk) and address physiology and sociology (see *Into the Kill Zone* by David Klinger). They can help prepare you to deal with the aftermath of using deadly force in self defense (see *On Killing* by Lt. Col. Dave Grossman).

But the written word is a very limited medium, especially when it comes to teaching physical skills. Take, for example, this description of how to do a back fall:

> *Squat down with your feet at the edge of the mat and your*
> *back facing it. Cross your arms over your chest, tuck your chin*
> *down... Curl your spine outward. Then gently allow yourself to tip*
> *backward, keeping your arms crossed and your head tucked. When*
> *your shoulders are against the floor, allow your arms to open up*
> *and slap your palms down on the floor on either side of your butt.*[161]

There's nothing wrong with the description. It's crystal clear to anyone who has ever seen a back fall done. But someone who has never seen a martial artist perform this basic skill will be left with many unanswered questions: at what angle are the arms supposed to slap out? How does the timing work? Short of actually seeing the task performed, the inexperienced reader will have a difficult time properly doing it. More important: when you try it for the first time, you receive no feedback to tell you whether you did it right.

Ah ha!, some of the more astute readers are thinking, *then what about seeing it on video?*

Learning from videos

It's a lot easier to learn a physical task from watching a video than it is to learn the same task by reading a description in a book. You can actually see the action and watch the timing of the events, seeing how one motion flows into the next and then into a third. And, as with a book, there's the wonderful, wonderful advantage of being able to stop the action and think about what you've just seen. You can rewind the video to the spot where you got confused, or slow it down enough that you can clearly see what is going on and have time to assimilate each step before moving on to the next. In some ways, videos are better than real life. But videos are not terrifically portable.

---

161 *Self defense for Women: Techniques to Get You Home Safely, by Elizabeth Pennell.*

Typically, you watch them in the comfort of your own home, absorb as much information as you can, and then take that information (however much of it you've absorbed) out to the range with you. If you're missing a piece that you need to know, you have to go home and watch the video again in order to get it. More likely, you'll just guess and fill in the gap, *thinking* that you are doing what the video suggested.

A video cannot give you feedback about what you are doing. This is huge! Not long ago, another instructor and I were talking about a course he was assisting with. "Rough day!" he confided. "One guy pointed a gun at me—TWICE. The first time I didn't see what led up to it. Got there as quick as I could and redirected the muzzle. Gave him the stink eye and the full chewing out. He apologized, felt bad, promised he wouldn't do it again."

"So what happened the second time?" I asked.

"The usual..." Deep sigh. "He simply did not have the faintest idea that he was bringing the muzzle around to point behind him every time he reached for a fresh magazine. Honestly did not. Just a complete failure of self-awareness."

Experienced shooters and intelligent people often have a hard time believing how much they need this honest and direct feedback from a skilled observer. But everybody *does* need it—and the longer the shooter has practiced without formal training, the more desperately they are likely to need this feedback as it relates to both safety issues and shooting techniques.

When I first began working out of a holster, I thought I was doing pretty well with it. Maybe I wasn't as fast as others, I reasoned, but at least I was doing everything safely. Or so I thought. Right up until a professional firearms instructor stood next to me and said, "Hey. You just pointed the muzzle at your own hand." I did? I hadn't even been aware of it! Similarly, I have in turn stood next to students who were totally oblivious to their own major safety violations, everything from pointing the firearm at their own abdomens while racking the slide (yes, really), to sweeping the person next to them, to casually leaving their fingers on the trigger. When caught, the universal response is honest bewilderment: "I did? I didn't even notice!"

And that's just for gross and obvious safety issues. Shooting skills are even more prone to this type of personal blindness. One of the most powerful tools a good instructor has in the toolbox is a little trick called the "exemplar drill." Most instructors know that no matter how carefully they describe a good, smooth, steady trigger press, a certain number of their students simply cannot wrap their minds around the concept. You can describe it, write about it, show video of it, demonstrate it, talk them through it—and all too many folks will still not get it. So with the exemplar drill, we stand next to the student, have them place their sights on target and their fingers on the trigger without pulling it. Then the instructor comes alongside and carefully puts a trained trigger finger over the student's trigger finger, tactilely demonstrating what a good and correct trigger press actually feels like, the steadily increasing pressure until the shot finally breaks and a good solid follow through after the shot fires. It's a great tool. And it's a necessary tool, because sometimes words and even example just aren't enough.

I'll never forget the first time I stood next to a student and did an exemplar drill with him. It was like watching a light bulb go on over the student's head. He turned to me in amazement. "But that's what I *thought* I was doing before!" he exclaimed.

Nor is this dynamic unique to trigger press alone. Whether it's a sloppy and fumble-prone drawstroke, a pattern of movement which guarantees a stumble with gun in hand, or an awkwardly slow method for clearing a malfunction or reloading, every shooter has blind spots. These problems can be corrected easily when spotted by an experienced observer, but are very unlikely to be corrected by the shooter who is not aware of them in the first place.

Benefits of professional training

Good instructors incrementally build skill upon skill, technique upon technique, until the students are blowing the centers out of the targets much faster and more accurately than they ever believed was possible. Attaining this increased skill level is accomplished *not* by simply shooting a lot of ammunition, but by building a solid foundation first, and then shooting that ammunition with a purpose and a plan.

Good instructors force their students to learn and then to practice skills the students aren't already good at when they come into the class. This counters the natural human tendency to over-learn the stuff we already know, while neglecting the stuff we need to learn.

There isn't enough time in one lifetime to make all the mistakes yourself. While any given instructor might directly discover or invent a solid technique to solve a specific shooting problem, the best instructors have learned from many other good people who have done the same thing and then compared notes. This means that the solutions Jeff Cooper found in his heyday are still being passed along; that the lessons Jim Cirillo taught the world did not perish with him. It means that the way Jack Weaver stood to shoot, and the tweaks that Ray Chapman gave to Weaver's stance are still being taught and refined by others. The Hackathorn Rip, the Bill Drill, the Ayoob Wedge, and the El

Presidente are all easily available to the serious student, even in classes where these techniques or practice routines have been discarded in favor of newer ones. Dennis Tueller's famous drill is run in dozens of schools. But *you* needn't attend a dozen different schools to be exposed to this body of knowledge, because professional instructors talk to each other and learn from each other. They filter through a tremendous sea of distilled experience so they can pass the best ideas straight down to their students.

Learning directly from a professional trainer provides another little-advertised advantage. Students who have attended a professional school often have access to resources available only through that school: secure email lists, private forums, assurances of personal help if legal problems arise, referrals to trusted lawyers and expert witnesses and trauma counselors after a deadly force event. These valuable resources are usually available *only* to people personally known to (and trained by) the professional who offers them.

Finally, there's one more huge advantage to attending a professional firearms training school: it's fun! As one woman said to me not long ago, "Well, I absolutely needed to take a real vacation for myself this year. It was a choice between going to Disneyland or getting some training... and training sounded more fun."

What shall we learn?

Most people believe they are already safe gun handlers. Many do not believe they need to be taught the first and most basic lesson most instructors stress: the ability to safely manipulate a firearm. But those who haven't had a class from a competent instructor often overestimate their abilities in the safety department.[162]

Safe gun handling includes the

What's to Learn?

☑ Safely use the firearm

☑ Reload efficiently

☑ Shoot accurately

☑ Shoot quickly

☑ Draw from a holster

☑ Shoot multiple targets

☑ Shoot one-handed

☑ Shoot moving targets

☑ Shoot while moving

☑ Shoot in low light

☑ Learn to think with gun in hand

---

162 *In a series of studies reported in the December 1999 Journal of Personality and Social Psychology (Vol. 77, No. 6), researchers Justin Kruger and David Dunning examined the idea that the least skilled people often have the highest perception of their own skills. The study is titled Unskilled and Unaware of It: How Difficulties in Recognizing One's Own Incompetence Lead to Inflated Self-Assessments, and it won an Ig Nobel Prize in 2000. It's also a very funny read, if you like that sort of thing.*

ability to load or reload your firearm quickly. This one might sound silly; after all, what are the odds of needing to reload in a hurry? Are we going to take on a horde of invading zombies by ourselves? Doesn't seem likely. Yet this skill is simply a subset of safe gun handling. If you cannot easily load your firearm quickly, without pointing it at any important body parts, and without losing muzzle awareness, then you have not yet completely internalized how to handle your firearm safely. And if that is the case, you may negligently shoot yourself or a family member if you ever need to handle your home-defense firearm under the extreme stress of a home invasion.

Accurate shooting is usually next on the syllabus. A fellow who opines that if he were engaged by a criminal at 15 feet he would simply "fire in the direction of the target" is not only at risk from an attacker—he is a risk to everyone around him. You are responsible for every bullet that leaves your firearm, not just the ones that hit the intended target. (An aside: Most people are unable to judge distances at all, let alone to do so accurately under stress. That poor fellow might surprise himself someday by trying to shoot at someone who is a lot farther away than he has ever tried to shoot at the range.)

Firearms instructors show their students how to bring the gun out of its holster and onto target quickly. How fast is fast enough? How much time would you have to draw and fire if you were attacked? When a student asked defensive firearms instructor John Farnam that question, Farnam famously replied, "The rest of your life." While the answer sounds flippant, it cuts right to the heart of the issue. You do not know, in advance, how fast you will need to be. But you should learn to become as fast and as accurate as you can.

There is another reason to learn how to draw and fire quickly: a fast draw is a smooth draw, and a smooth draw is a safe draw. Not everyone will need to draw fast, but everyone with a holster should be able to draw safely. A smooth draw brings the gun out of the holster without fingering the trigger, it doesn't get tangled up in the clothing, and it doesn't point anywhere it shouldn't on the way up. A smooth draw is a safe draw.

What about shooting multiple targets quickly and well? Do we really need to learn to do that? Yes. While being attacked by a herd of rampaging criminals might seem a bit far-fetched, few criminals attack when they think the odds are even. Criminals like to have the odds in their favor when they attack. If you don't look like an easy target, a lone criminal will probably pass you by, but a gang of criminals working together might consider you fair game. As Marc MacYoung puts it, "Bad guys have friends, too."

Another subset of quick and accurate shooting is the ability to shoot well with only one hand. This looks like a show-off range trick, but in real life, you may not be able to use both hands to fire your weapon. Maybe one hand will be carrying a small child, or keeping a grasp on a larger child so you know where she is. Perhaps it will be fending off a close attacker, or shoving the door shut while an assailant tries to open it. Or perhaps, heaven forbid, one hand will be disabled in the initial attack. If you carry a gun for self-defense, you should know how to safely draw and use the weapon with either hand alone.

Moving targets are fun and challenging on the range. They really catch the students' attention and they appeal greatly to the Walter Mitty fantasy guys. But that's not why good classes include moving targets. Quite simply, good classes include moving targets because in real life, criminals do not just stand there and imitate a piece of cardboard; they move. If you are unable to reliably hit center mass on a moving target, you are not yet prepared to deal decisively with a living opponent.

Similarly, while it appeals to wannabe warriors to shoot while their feet are moving, that's not why good classes teach students how to do so. Instructors teach students how to shoot while moving because anyone with half a brain will be running for cover when a criminal attack happens. If you carry a weapon, you owe it to yourself and everyone around you to learn how *not* to shoot the innocent grandmother putting her groceries in her car on the other side of the parking lot while you boogie to cover and get away from the bad guys.

Most criminal attacks happen in the dark. Of course a good class will teach you the most obvious tactic: turn on the lights and equalize the environment if you can. But if you cannot turn on the lights, it's really a good idea to be sure you can hit the bad guy instead of the innocent bystanders.

"We don't need no stinkin' tactics."

It's surprising how many people malign learning good tactics. Undoubtedly this is because "tactical" is such a joke online. On chat boards, people post the most amazingly convoluted, idiotic scenarios, stuff that could never possibly happen in real life in a million years... and then everyone is surprised when the ensuing discussion is silly and stupid.[163]

A tactical firearms class teaches students how to think about and solve life-threatening problems. Such a class might teach students how the physical body reacts under stress, and then how to *use* the body's stress reactions rather than simply endure them. Students might practice making shoot/no shoot decisions with realistic three-dimensional targets, first under the mild stress of a timer and later under more extreme types of stress.

---

163 *But if we ever get attacked by mutant zombie bears while armed with any one firearm produced before 1963, by golly, we'll all know what to do!*

If you could figure out how to win a fight without getting hurt, why wouldn't you do it? Learning good tactics just means learning how to do what you want to do (survive!) with the least amount of damage to yourself and to the people you love. The trainer's goal is to teach the students how to think on their feet to solve these types of problems.

By the way, every single criminal attack is a tactical problem, whether you're armed or not. Even if the intended victim is unarmed, she still must decide how to react and what to do in order to survive. Carrying a gun gives you more options, but the most important tool you carry will always be the one between your ears.

Money matters

If your budget has kept you out of classes, there is a way to train for nearly free. You can get together with one of the nationally-known traveling trainers, and be the one to organize a class for that person to teach in your area. If you are the organizer, you will generally be allowed to participate in the class at no cost or at a very reduced cost, and since you organized it, you know in advance that the training will suit your work schedule and your vacation plans. You'll schedule the class close enough to your own home that you will save on travel expenses too. It will still cost you money for ammunition, but you would be buying ammunition anyway—and ammunition fired in classes is purely beneficial whereas ammunition fired off in undirected range play sometimes isn't. Organizing a class is serious work, and it's not for everyone. But if money is the only thing keeping your from getting advanced training, this route is well worth considering.

How to Find an Instructor

Looking for a firearms instructor whose teaching matches your learning style might not be quite as difficult as finding a life mate, but it's probably a little harder than just finding a date for Saturday night.

One reason for this is that firearms instructors don't exactly advertise. You'll rarely find an instructor directly through print or radio ads (though you might find one through the pages of a firearms magazine). The yellow pages are worth a try, and so is a Google search. But for the most part, firearms instructors rely on word of mouth to reach potential students.

What Type of Class Do You Need?

The first step, before doing anything else, is to define the type of class you want to find. There are a wide variety of classes aimed at specific types of students. There are classes for law enforcement, classes for beginners, classes for target shooters and competitors, and many more. There are big classes and small ones, co-ed classes and women-only classes, classes taught entirely in the classroom and classes taught only on the range.

Sorting out this muddle of possibilities is going to take a little effort, but it can be done once you know a little about class types.

Familiarization Class

A familiarization class is a basic, entry-level class which is designed simply to get people familiar with firearms terminology, the simple mechanics of how firearms work, and the safety rules. This type of class is usually very inexpensive and occasionally even free. It will often be taught by a part-time instructor or volunteer, and usually will be very short, often only a few hours. Some of these classes are spent entirely in the classroom rather than on the range, but if shooting is included, it won't be a whole lot of shooting—maybe 50 rounds or so. Equipment requirements for this type of class are minimal or non-existent, and instructors often supply everything needed, sometimes even including firearms.

State-mandated Carry Class

Not every state requires classes. In those that do, remember that these classes are not designed to teach the student how to protect herself. Politicians pass laws requiring these classes because they want to know that people who obtain carry permits have been exposed to the state laws governing concealed carry and will not use guns unsafely. That's *it*. The purpose isn't to teach people to protect themselves, but simply to make sure they won't harm innocent others once they have their carry permits.

Having said that, there are a lot of really good CCW instructors out there, and a state-required class from an excellent, motivated instructor can indeed teach you some of what you need to know in order to defend yourself. But if that happens, it's a happy bonus. You should never count on it happening because it's not what the required class is designed to do. I hate getting political here, but one reason I'm wary of state-required classes is because going to such a class often gives people the impression they've now been "trained" and have learned as much as they need to know about self defense. Most often, that is simply not true.[164]

Although both familiarization classes and state-mandated concealed carry classes can be a good first step, neither teaches people the skills most likely to be needed in self defense. These baby steps are necessary, but they are not enough for someone learning to protect herself.

Sport Class

These are often associated with IDPA or IPSC, and may be advertised as a way to "improve your scores." These usually have super-high round counts, often 1000 rounds per day or more. These types of classes consist mostly or entirely range work, with little or no lecture time. If lecture is a part of the class, lectures will focus on shooting techniques and game strategy, and won't include discussion of defensive firearm use at all.

---

164 *Again and to be clear: training is good. That's why I'm against laws requiring classes: because the existence of state-required classes encourages the dangerously false idea that a very brief, cursory class will provide everything you need to learn about this vital topic. Raising bar for state-mandated training requirements would not improve matters, because that becomes burdensome to people in crisis and people with financial challenges. A single mom being stalked by a psycho ex should not have to delay protecting herself until she can budget for bureaucratic niceties. She should be able to legally carry to protect herself the very day she learns her life is in danger, then get more training as her time and budget allows. Far too many people with limited budgets currently face the unsavory choice between either being able to buy the necessary tools of self defense, or being able to pay government fees allowing them to protect themselves legally. The more regulations we put on carry permits, the worse this problem becomes.*

Sport classes are great places to develop smooth gun-handling skills and speed, but because the recommended gear will usually be sport-specific and not necessarily appropriate for concealed carry, you may find after a class like this that you've gotten really quick at grabbing for gear you aren't wearing. Similarly, those interested in mindset issues or legal and ethical questions find that such classes do not address those needs.

Self Defense Class

A defensive firearms class may teach students how to use handguns, shotguns, rifles (carbines), or all three, but the most common type teaches handguns only. One or two day formats are probably the most common, because they fit so nicely into a weekend, but some classes run for a very full five or six day week. They often feature a mix of range time plus classroom time, with lower-level classes having slightly more classroom time than upper-level ones. Sometimes homework will be given, such as required reading before the class or a test at its conclusion. Topics may include legal doctrines about deadly force, handling the aftermath of a shooting, developing a good defensive mindset, and more.

On the range, a defense class focuses on defensive shooting skills, often at short distances, using firearms and gear appropriate for concealed carry. Many will be run "from concealment," meaning the instructor expects students to have a cover garment to work with. Human-shaped silhouette targets, or cartoon pictures of human beings, are often used. Round count will vary according to the school's instructional philosophy, but will rarely be as high as in a sport class.

Finding Possibilities

Once you decide which type of class you want, it's time to start gathering leads to instructors and schools in your area. Firearms stores, gun shows, and shooting ranges are a good place to start. A full service gun shop which includes range facilities is likely to have an instructor associated with it, but don't overlook smaller stores where the folks behind the counter may be able to tell you about local classes. Don't know where the gun stores are? Walk your fingers through the local yellow pages because the odds are there are a lot more stores in your area than you realized. Look under "Guns," "Rifles," and "Firearms." Don't bother calling pawn shops. These might be good places to get a deal on a gun, but a pawn-shop proprietor isn't likely to know much about the shooting world. You can do a lot of your research on the phone, but you might have better luck in person, because in person you can check the bulletin boards and counters. Look for flyers, business cards, or brochures offering classes.

Next call: your local cop shop. The local police very often will have leads to nearby firearms instruction which is not otherwise advertised. Similarly, if your state has a training requirement, the police department or sheriff's office will probably have a list of state-approved instructors in your area. Many instructors who teach the state-required classes also offer advanced self defense classes, so don't overlook this source.

> **Important Tip!**
>
> Don't ask anyone but the instructor about women's classes, even if that's what you're looking for. Just ask who might provide classes. Third parties often do not know exactly what an instructor offers, and may erroneously cross a name off your list.

If you do your research via phone, remember that at this point you are just after names and phone numbers of potential instructors. Any details you get from third parties are going to be fuzzy and might be outright wrong. Unless it is obvious that the person on the other end of the line has some personal experience with the instructor, take all details with a grain of salt. Just get the name and contact information, and move on.

When calling a gun store, club, or range, ask first whether they themselves offer instruction, then whether they know anyone who does. Finally, ask if they know someone else you can call who might know someone who teaches classes.

Researching shooting schools online isn't as easy as it sounds. For one thing, far too many professional trainers still aren't quite up to speed on this whole "welcome to the early '90s" internet phenomenon. But once you have a school or instructor name in hand, you'll probably be able to Google the specific name and get useful links and reviews.

Narrowing down the choices

Now it's time to call the instructors and figure out if they are offering what you need. Make the phone call even if you think everything you need to know can be found on the instructor's website, because absolutely nothing takes the place of that personal contact. Here are some questions you might want to ask.

☑ **Do you have a few moments to chat about your class?**

This isn't just common courtesy. You'll get better and more complete answers if the instructor isn't rushed for time and can concentrate on your questions rather than pondering how to get you off the phone without being rude.

☑ **How long have you been teaching? How often do you do classes?**

Both of these questions will give you a feel for how much instructional experience the person has had. You shouldn't write off someone who teaches classes only occasionally, but if they seem fuzzy about their answers here, you may want to look elsewhere because that's a tip off that they aren't very serious or professional about what they're doing.

☑ **How many students in your classes, on average? What kind of instructor-to-student ratio do you aim for?**

A private class, working one on one with the instructor, might sound ideal, but it may not be comfortable for you if you are very shy. Further, although personal attention can be wonderful, when working individually, some instructors tend to gloss over points that would otherwise be well-covered by a prepared class lecture. At the other end of the scale, high student numbers often become a safety issue. The more students are on the line, the more coaches and assistants are needed to keep the students safe.

A good rule of thumb: in a beginning class, you should have one instructor or coach for every two to three students during the actual live-fire portion of the class. Avoid classes where an instructor will supervise more than three new shooters at the same time. As classes become more advanced, it becomes possible for one instructor to safely watch much higher numbers of students, so these numbers apply only to classes for beginners.

☑ **Do you work with other instructors or have assistants helping with your classes?**

An instructor who has gathered a team of people around him, rather than being a Lone Ranger, is usually more professional and probably has more teaching experience. A team can also handle larger classes more safely than an individual is able to manage.

☑ **How many women do you usually have in each class?**

Unless you are prepared for it and not blindsided when you walk in, it can be daunting to discover you're the only female student in a large group of guys. The answer to this question may tell also you how comfortable the instructor is working with women, and gives you a general idea about whether other women have been comfortable working with him.

☑ **What topics do you cover in class? What would I need to bring with me?**

This helps you figure out whether the class is a familiarization class, a sport class, or a self defense class. It also forewarns you if the instructor expects students to come with a bunch of gear you haven't yet purchased.

☑ **Where did you get your training and instructional credentials?**

Excellent answers: I was trained at a nationally known and established firearms school (Gunsite, Thunder Ranch, DTI, Front Sight, Rangemaster, Firearms Academy of Seattle, and many others) or by a nationally-known professional trainer who travels (Massad Ayoob, Ken Hackathorn, Chuck Taylor, Rob Pincus, and many others). Ideally, the instructor will name multiple mentors and multiple schools.

Good answers: I was trained by a locally-known instructor, and have been teaching for more than two years, or, I took instructor classes through the NRA and work with a team.

Bad answer: I've never taken any classes, but I've shot a lot.

A lot of former military and former law enforcement people enjoy teaching firearms classes. These guys often have real-world experience that can be very valuable, however, military and law enforcement training does not address the needs of civilians interested in concealed carry. The missions are very, very different. If your prospective instructor mentions a law enforcement or military background, excellent! But listen closely for civilian-applicable teaching credentials as well.

☑ **Can you give me the names and phone numbers of some former students who are willing to recommend your classes?**

Most reputable instructors will be happy to do that. Be brave and call those people. Ask about their experiences with the instructor, and before you hang up be sure to ask if they have any advice for you when you take the class.

☑ **Where can I find the state laws about concealed carry? What are our state laws about using a gun in self defense?**

This one's sneaky. The instructor's answer will tell you whether or not he really focuses on self defense issues. He doesn't have to know the statute number off the tip of his tongue, but he should be able to tell you in very general terms where you can find the information you're asking about, or how you can look it up for yourself. He may even tell you that these questions will be covered in the class. If the prospective instructor doesn't either answer the questions directly, or point you toward a place you can find the answers you seek, look elsewhere for a school more oriented toward self defense. Crucial: if the prospective instructor blows off your need to understand the laws related to self defense, that's a huge red flag. Beware and steer clear!

The specific answers to these questions don't matter nearly as much as the "feel" you get from the conversation. If the class fits within the category you want, and you hit it off well with the instructor, and you don't spot any major red flags, chances are you will enjoy taking that class.

If it turns out the instructor is not offering the type of class you are looking for, or isn't the type of person you want to work with, conclude your conversation by asking about other instructors you might try. Most trainers have a pretty good idea of who is offering classes within their general area, and will usually be willing to give recommendations to students who aren't a good fit for their own classes.

Women-Only vs. Co-ed Classes

Female students have an additional option not open to men: they can opt to take a firearms class offered for women only. Will such a class be a good fit for you? That depends. Classes for women offer:

- A friendlier, less competitive atmosphere. Women's classes tend to be a lot of fun because the students are more likely to feel comfortable with each other rather than competing with each other.

- More personalized instruction. Women's firearms classes tend to be less crowded than the same classes offered in co-ed format. This often translates to more one-on-one time with the instructor and more time for questions.

- Help with female-specific issues, such as how to find a holster that works with a woman's body shape, or how to most safely carry in a purse.

- A chance to learn how to shoot without a well-meaning loved one pushing you along.

- (Sometimes) Instruction tailored for verbal and visual learners, and fewer assumptions about students' mechanical knowledge.

- (Usually) The same instructional outline and course of fire given to an equivalent level co-ed class.

Co-ed classes offer:

- More choices. At all levels, it is significantly easier to find co-ed classes than it is to find women-only classes.

- More classes at upper levels of training. It isn't too hard to find an entry level class intended for women only. But advanced classes for women are rare and difficult to find.

- More competitive atmosphere. This can be a good thing at intermediate and advanced levels, when increased pressure helps a student focus. At lower levels, it can be a distraction, sometimes a significant one.

Class Costs

Prices for local instruction vary wildly from one part of the country to another. For professional training from an established school with a dedicated range, expect to pay upwards of $200 per day of instruction.[165] Local instruction will cost less than that, sometimes a lot less. If money is an issue for you, discuss this frankly with your prospective instructor. Some schools offer scholarship programs and some instructors, especially for beginning classes at the local level, may be willing to consider a work exchange if you have skills to barter.

In addition to the cost of the class, note the amount of ammunition the course will use. For a two-day weekend class, it isn't unusual to burn through 500 to 1000 rounds of ammunition. When figuring the cost of training, remember to budget ammunition expenses.

The Bottom Line

Although it seems an overwhelming task at first, finding good firearms instruction is really not that hard. Once you get past the initial fear of picking up the phone, you'll find a large network of people out there who are ready to help you get started and eager to help you on your way. Good luck in your search!

---

165 Ballpark figure as of spring 2010.

Having Fun with Firearms

There's one word so taboo, so beyond the pale, that you'll rarely find it in news stories about women and guns.

That word is *FUN.*

It's time to admit the awful truth: shooting is fun. Whether it's just a day spent at the range in informal plinking, or intensely focused competition at the Olympic level, firearms provide untold hours of amusement for millions of people every year.

One of the coolest things about the shooting sports is that, in most firearms games, women are able to compete on an equal footing with men. Nor is age a barrier in many firearms competitions. In fact, the very oldest Olympic contender competed in the shooting sports, and some of the youngest Olympic competitors do, too.[166]

There are a lot of different competitions and other games which involve firearms. These are referred to collectively as "the shooting sports." Although many of the links given in the text below will take you to the sponsoring national organizations for official competitions, you should be aware that most local ranges offer many, many informal matches and shooting events. These unofficial matches are often far more flexible to a beginner's needs, and can be a good way to wet your toes before diving into the more structured official-dom that the national organizations require.

Some shooting games include lots of activity on the part of the shooter: running, crouching, kneeling, even skiing from stage to stage. Others are more sedentary. Many require acute levels of concentration. Some games are *very* particular about the equipment used, and place a premium on wise gear choices and skill at choosing or creating ammunition. Some are all about the

---

166 *Swedish shooter Oscar Swahn won his sixth Olympic medal at the 1920 Antwerp Games at the age of 72 years and 280 days old. Kimberly Rhode was just 17 years old when she won a gold medal in women's double trap shooting at the 1996 Summer Olympics, making her the youngest female gold medalist in shooting. And Hungarian shooter Karoly Takac taught himself to shoot left-handed after a grenade blew off his right arm in 1938. Ten years later, he won two gold medals at the London 1948 Games.*

total package: outfit, gear, shooting skill. Many provide lots of competitive categories so shooters can choose the level of competition which best matches their own experience level.

The following list is by no means all-inclusive. It's just a quick overview. New games are being developed all the time. And no matter what the name of the game may be, you'll find people who are prepared to swear it is the *best game ever!*

Action Games

Biathlon. Call it a race with a difference. Participants shoot highly accurate straight-pull .22LR rifles at small 50-yard targets, making the game similar to most precision target games. The difference is that players must ski cross-country from one shooting station to the next, adding in a high degree of difficulty as they must be able to calm their breathing and slow their heartbeats on demand. Not for the unfit, biathlon is an Olympic sport. (See www. biathlon.teamusa.org).

• Variant: **Summer Biathlon** combines cross-country running with rifle shooting.

Cowboy Action / SASS. Participants in Cowboy Action events sponsored by the Single Action Shooting Society get to dress up fancy in old-time western wear, choose amusingly rustic character names, and shoot historic firearms (and replicas) at reactive targets. The stages often involve some activity, such as climbing atop a barrel designed to simulate a cowboy pony, or swaggering through the doors of a saloon to confront bad guys who look suspiciously like steel plates. Some scenarios are designed to mimic true historic events or even movie scenes. The firearms are single-action revolvers, lever-action rifles, and double-barreled shotguns. The costumes are often hand-crafted by the players. (See www.sassnet.com).

GSSF. The Glock Shooting Sports Federation sponsors matches around the country which are open to anyone who owns a Glock. GSSF matches are somewhat similar to very simple action pistol stages, but GSSF does not require participants to draw from a holster or do any shooting while moving. While everyone competes together, there are separate prize categories for seniors, youngsters, females, law enforcement, teams, and probably others I've forgotten. A special effort is made to be sure that those at the beginning end of the spectrum have a chance to win some good prizes too. For these reasons, GSSF matches are an excellent choice for beginning shooters who would like to get a little taste of what handgun competition is all about. (See www.gssfonline.com).

ICORE (International Confederation of Revolver Enthusiasts). Autoloaders need not apply! Similar in some respects to IPSC, IDPA, and Bianchi Cup, ICORE games revolve around the wheelgun. (See www.icore. org).

IDPA. The International Defensive Pistol Association sponsors action pistol events designed to simulate self defense scenarios and real life encounters. Although superficially similar to IPSC matches, IDPA competition retains more of its martial heritage than IPSC does, including a requirement that participants must shoot from concealment. Intentionally geared toward the new or average shooter, and with very limited gear requirements, IDPA events are very accessible to newcomers. (See www.idpa.com).

IPSC (USPSA). Available in more than 30 countries, shooting events designed around International Practical Shooting Confederation rules provide plenty of excitement for competitors. In the United States, the United States Practical Shooting Association governs these matches, creating an action pistol sport in which the competitor must try to blend accuracy, power, and speed. Most shooting takes place at close range, and stages may involve multiple targets, moving targets, targets that react when hit, penalty carrying targets, partially covered targets, obstacles, movement, competitive tactics, and any other difficulty the course designer can dream up. Some matches even contain surprise stages where no one knows in advance what to expect. (See www.ipsc.org and www.uspsa.org).

Modern Pentathlon. An Olympic sport, Modern Pentathlon requires competitors to master running, swimming, horseback riding, epee fencing, and 10 meter air pistol, competing in all events during a single grueling day. (See www.pentathlon.org).

PPC (Police Pistol Competition). More common years ago before IPSC and IDPA really got going, NRA-sanctioned PPC events are strictly a law-enforcement game, although informal PPC-style matches may be open to the public as well. Participants typically shoot handguns (traditionally revolvers) at human-shaped silhouette targets at distances which range from 4 yards out to 25 yards or more. There are strict time limits. Not a lot of shooter movement is involved, which makes PPC-style competitions a good choice for people who want to practice self defense type shooting without having to work around the run-n-gun style stages common to other action pistol games. Because of PPC's origins, all stages are revolver-friendly. (See www.nrahq.org/law/competitions/ppc).

Sportsman's Team Challenge. To compete in STC, simply get a group of buddies together, practice a bit, and sign up for this team competition. STC uses two or three team members and has six different events for pistol, rifle, and shotgun. The targets are falling steel for the pistol and rifle stages, and moving clays for shotgun. (See www.sportsmansteamchallenge.com).

- Many other games also provide for cooperative team efforts. In many competitions, all you need to do is declare that you and your friend(s) are a "team" and enter the team category as well as your own individual category. If in doubt, ask one of the match coordinators if teams are allowed.

Three gun. This fast-moving sport requires as much strategic planning as the action pistol games. The only real difference is that the competitors use more guns. Participants bring rifles, pistols, and shotguns to the range and compete with all three, including transitioning between the three as often as needed. There is no official parent organization for most three gun matches, although the USPSA has begun to sponsor many three gun competitions and offers a national three gun championship every year.

Precision Games

Benchrest. Benchrest competition involves funky-looking rifles designed to be shot from a rest rather than from field positions. The competition places a premium on good equipment, and the firearms are often heavily modified by participants. Participants usually create their own handloaded ammunition which is custom-matched to the firearms they use.

Bullseye Pistol (sometimes called Conventional Pistol). A precision pistol shooting competition in which the competitor typically fires six strings of five shots in a trio of events at distances of 25 to 50 yards (50 feet for indoor competitions). Bullseye matches require participants to shoot the same courses of fire three times over: once with a .22-caliber pistol, once with anything larger than a .32 caliber centerfire pistol, and once with a .45-caliber pistol. Many shooters opt to use the same .45-caliber gun for both centerfire events. (See www.nrahq.org/compete/conventional.asp and www.bullseyepistol.com).

F-Class Long-Distance Rifle Shooting. Generally shot at distances of 1,000 yards, F-Class Shooting has been called "Belly Benchrest." Competitors shoot scoped bolt-action rifles in the prone position. There are generally two recognized classifications: F-Class Open, which has few restrictions on caliber and configuration, and F-Class Target Rifle which is limited to rifles chambered in .223 and .308. (See www.6mmbr.com/Fclass.html).

High Power. A rifle sport which requires competitors to shoot centerfire rifles accurately over distances of 200, 300 and 600 yards from standing, sitting, and prone positions. The rifles are generally broken down into the categories of Service Rifle and National Match Rifle. Service rifles must conform to certain specifications and must be in an external configuration very similar to those issued in the military. The AR15, M1A, M1 Garand and Springfield rifles are all popular choices for this kind of shooting. National Match rifles do not have nearly as many rules to abide by, and are available in a number of interesting configurations. Scopes are not allowed. The rules are deceptively simple; attaining a competitive score is not. (See www.nrahq.org/compete/highpower.asp).

Olympic Events. Although played during the Olympics, these games are also available to regular people interested in precision shooting competitions.

- **10 Meter Air Pistol.** Participants have a set amount of time to fire 60 (men) or 45 (women) shots offhand with a single-shot air pistol.

- **10 Meter Air Rifle.** Similar to air pistol, competitors fire at targets that are much smaller than those used for air pistol.

- **10 Meter Running Target.** An event with much history and popularity in Europe, running target involves shooting an air rifle at a horizontally moving target that is only visible for a short period of time.

- **25 Meter Centerfire Pistol.** The rules are exactly the same as for 25 Meter Women's Pistol, except that the shooter must use a pistol chambered for a round with a caliber ranging from .30-.38. Most competitors use pistols that are chambered for .32 S&W Long. Many of the .22 LR target pistols on the market also have optional conversion kits for shooting centerfire.

- **25 Meter Rapid Fire Pistol.** From a static standing position, in this Olympic sport the competitor must raise the pistol and fire five shots on five separate targets under time constraints of eight, six, and four seconds. Pistols are chambered in .22 LR and fired from the offhand position.

- **25 Meter Standard Pistol.** The shooter fires a total of four strings consisting of five shots each in a trio of events. Slow Fire allows 2-1/2 minutes for each five shot string. Timed Fire allows 20 seconds for each string, and Rapid Fire allows 10 seconds for each string. Scopes are not allowed.

- **25 Meter Women's Pistol.** In this event, 30 shots are fired in a precision slow-fire segment, and 30 shots are fired in five-shot strings on a turning target. When the target turns to face the competitor, she has three seconds to raise the pistol and fire a single shot. The target then faces away for seven seconds before offering the shooter another three seconds. While this is a women-only sport in the Olympics, many informal club-level competitions allow both male and females to enter.

- **50 Meter Free Pistol**. At a distance of 50 meters using a single-shot, iron-sighted .22 LR pistol, competitors engage a target about the size of those used in 10 Meter Air Pistol. Shooters have a set amount of time to complete a course of fire. The pistols are "free" in the sense that very few rules govern their configuration.

- **50 Meter 3 Position Rifle**. In this competition the shooter fires 40 shots of record in each of three positions: prone, standing, and kneeling using a .22 LR.

- **50 Meter Prone Rifle**. Working from a prone position, the competitor fires 60 shots with a .22 rifle.

Progressive Position Air Pistol. Designed to develop youth interest in the Olympic pistol events it closely resembles, PPP allows children who may not yet possess the dexterity or strength to fire an unsupported air pistol with a single hand to learn the basics of marksmanship and competition by progressing through a number of shooting positions, starting with a benched two-handed position. As skill and strength develop, the shooter is moved towards developing into using the traditional offhand stance. (See www.usashooting. org/youthPistol.php).

Smallbore Rifle. Using .22-caliber rifles, the game is to shoot quarter-sized targets at 25 yards distance, from prone, sitting, kneeling, and standing positions. Accuracy demands are very stringent, and competition targets usually feature 10 separate bullseyes on each target so that scorers have an easier time determining where each shot fell.

- There are lots of variations on this basic accuracy game, with different rules and courses of fire.

- This is still a common sport at the high school level in many rural areas, and some colleges offer scholarships to the best players.

- The NRA Junior Marksmanship program moves youngsters through various levels of smallbore rifle competition.

Shotgun Games

Skeet. Shooters fire a total of 25 rounds from eight different locations arranged around a semi-circle (well, okay—technically there are seven positions around the semi-circle, and an eighth one which is halfway across the semi-circle between stations one and seven). Each location is called a "stand" or a "station." Formal competitions usually divide shooters based upon the shotgun gauge being used. (See www.nssa-nsca.com).

- The targets are called "clays," "clay pigeons," or "birds." They are clay discs, somewhat frisbee-shaped but only a hand's width across.

- When two birds are flown at once, they are called a double. Each round involves a certain number of doubles, and some variations of this game involve *only* doubles.

- One type of skeet game is called Olympic Skeet, because it is an Olympic sport. But there are lots of skeet competitions at the local, regional, and national level which are not in any way connected to the Olympic event.

Sporting Clays—often described as "golf with a shotgun," sporting clays is probably a more challenging game than skeet although it is very similar to that game in a lot of ways. The clays are launched at different velocities from more locations than in skeet, and the course of fire was designed to mimic bird hunting as closely as possible. Participants typically fire from 14 different stations, with varying numbers of birds being thrown for each station. The total number of shots fired by each competitor usually equals 50 or 100 depending upon the exact game variant being played. The shotguns used can be semi-automatics, pumps, over/unders, or side-by-sides, but if you use a semi-automatic your gun should be equipped with a shell catcher. (See www.nssa-nsca.com).

Trap. Another game which uses clay pigeons. In some versions of the game, the end of the trap (out of which the birds fly) may be set to move back and forth, so that it is impossible to know at what angle the birds will be ejected. Other versions require the trap be fixed in place so that the birds appear to be flying straight away from the shooter on some stations. The shotguns used can be semi-automatics, pumps, over/unders, or side-by-sides, but if you use a semi-automatic your gun should be equipped with a shell catcher. Firing distances vary according to the exact version being played, but the usual distances are from 16 to 27 yards. There are five shooting stations. Shooters usually fire once at each of 25 targets in each round of competition.

- There are many different regional and national variations of the basic game.

- Some well-known versions include Single Trap, American Trap, Double Trap, Nordic Trap, and Olympic Trap. Wobble Trap is another version which is even more challenging than most other forms of the game.

Target-Based Games

Bowling Pin. In these informal matches, the game is to knock bowling pins off a table. Sounds simple, right? You'd be surprised how difficult it can be. There are a lot of variations on this game, which can be played with nearly any type of firearm. The fun usually starts when a pin goes over but not off the table—providing lots of hilarity for the watchers and plenty of frustration for the competitors.

Silhouette. In silhouette competitions, the game is to shoot metal plates. The gimmick is that the plates are shaped like various animals: a chicken, a ram, a turkey, a pig. The plates are shot from extreme distances. There are lots of variations on the basic game.

- Handgun Silhouette matches are sponsored by the International Handgun Metallic Silhouette Association (IHMSA), by the NRA, and by many local clubs.

- Smallbore Silhouette matches use .22 caliber rifles. They are sponsored by local clubs and by the NRA. In smallbore silhouette, the metal targets are positioned at 40, 60, 77, and 100 meters. Due to the irregular target shapes, this competition is a lot more difficult than it appears at first glance.

- Highpower Silhouette matches use centerfire rifles and are sponsored by local clubs and by the NRA.

Steel. Most steel targets look somewhat like dinner plates, but they're made out of metal and you knock them over. Sometimes called "falling steel" because when you hit them, they fall down (d'oh!) Steel comes in many shapes other than the familiar round one: stars, triangles, and squares are also common, as well as vaguely humanoid silhouettes. Steel matches are available in pistol, shotgun, and rifle variants. Some steel matches include swinging or rotating targets.

Other Games and Sports

Black Powder. Black powder competitions are a natural for antique buffs, but there are plenty of modern black powder firearms too. Black powder divisions and game variants are also available within many of the other shooting sports.

Hunting. It's not everyone's cup of tea, but there's a lot of joy to be found by spending days in the woods, getting in tune with the natural world and learning its rhythms well enough to play the same game every animal plays.

Paralympic Shooting Sports. The Paralympics are open to athletes with physical disabilities. Many of the Paralympic shooting events are similar to those shot in the Olympic games, but with rules and classifications designed to accommodate the needs of these competitors. (See www.paralympic.org).

Plinking. It's not a competition, but it sure can be fun to just settle in for a pleasant summer afternoon on the range enjoying the sunshine, visiting with a friend while sending rounds downrange. For ultimate plinking satisfaction, pick up some reactive targets and watch the grins begin.

Taking a Friend to the Range

There are few things more satisfying than introducing a newcomer to the shooting world. New shooters are the lifeblood of the firearms rights movement. Beyond that, it is just plain fun to share your hobbies with a friend. If you shoot for very long, you can expect that sooner or later, you will have the urge to invite a friend to visit the range with you.

When your friend agrees to shoot with you, she will very likely have some concerns about safety. Listen to those concerns. Do your best to set her mind at ease by both telling her and showing her how a responsible shooter stays safe at the range. One way you can make your friend more comfortable about the safety of your hobby is to go over range safety long before you set foot on the range. Give her an opportunity to ask questions. This is best done away from the range, so your friend will be able to hear you easily.

Be sure to discuss The Four Rules. If you cannot recite them from memory and explain what they mean, you probably are not yet ready to take a newbie to the range. Learn them!

The Four Rules

1. All guns are always loaded.

2. Never point the gun at anything you are not willing to destroy.

3. Keep your finger off the trigger until your sights are on target (and you have made the decision to shoot).

4. Be sure of your target and what's beyond.

The Safety Briefing

After discussing the Four Rules, make sure your newbie understands and agrees that you will stop her if she is about to do something unsafe. Explain that it's part of the learning process and that you don't mean anything personal by it. If your friend does not seem to be taking this or any other part of the safety briefing seriously, stop right there and don't take her to the range with you.[167]

Tell her that if she is shooting and you say, "Stop," she needs to stop moving and stand still, not turn around to see what's wrong. Tell her you probably won't need to do that but if you do, it doesn't mean anything except that you are taking care of keeping her safe. Warn her that you might tap her on the shoulder to get her attention, but if she is holding a gun she must not turn around.

Talk about the safety gear you'll wear—eye protection, hearing protection, hats, and high-collared shirts. Explain that sometimes people get hit with empty brass cases. Hot brass isn't really dangerous by itself, but sometimes people do very dangerous things when they're hit with brass. Let

> **Priorities**
>
> Your first job is to keep your friend safe. Your second job is to help her have fun. Everything else is a distant third.

her know that she will need to trust her safety gear rather than freak out if a piece of brass hits her. Add that even if a piece of brass goes somewhere it's not supposed to, that she must keep the gun pointed downrange at all times. Tell her to carefully set the gun down on the bench if she needs to get rid of a piece of brass.

Discuss rules specific to your own range, rules such as staying behind the yellow line during cease fires, or not going forward unless the flag is up. Explain that range rules are different from one place to the next, and that the specific range rules are posted so she doesn't have to work too hard remembering that kind of stuff.

Then and only then, you can discuss how to shoot, and the shooting basics of sight alignment, grip, and trigger squeeze. Try not to overwhelm your newbie here. If her eyes glaze over by the time you get to this point, stop talking. The only really important thing she needs to know is how to be safe. Everything else is just gravy.

Equipment Lists

Things to bring with you to the range

- Ear muffs for you and for her. Electronic muffs are best because you will be able to hear questions or comments from your friend, and keep track of what the people around you are doing.

---

167 *This is literally a matter of life and death... possibly yours, because you're the one who'll be standing the closest if she violates the safety rules and something goes wrong. She doesn't have to take it as seriously as you must, but if she blows you off, don't keep pushing. It is absolutely not worth the risk.*

- Ear plugs for her to wear in addition to the muffs, after the safety briefing is over. Remember you'll have to shout to be heard, but it will help her avoid developing a flinch.
- Eye protection for both of you. Basic prescription glasses are not generally good enough. Get a pair of protective glasses that fit over the Rx ones. Make sure they have decent side shields.
- Hat with a brim for both of you. The side shields and the hat brim prevent brass from dropping in behind the glasses, an important issue especially with a newbie who cannot be expected to keep the gun pointed safely downrange when in pain and distress.
- Shirts with high collars. Warn a new female shooter to wear a shirt with a high collar for range outings. The hot-brass dance is dangerous.
- Big targets. And you're going to put them close rather than far away. You want your friend to experience good success. If your range allows it, use reactive targets, things that pop or fall over or make a noise when shot, because reactive targets don't keep a record of misses the way paper targets do.
- Small caliber gun. A .22 is ideal. 9mm is better than .45—at least in this context! A .38 special is a good choice too. Stay away from super-lightweight guns, however. Basically, you want a heavy gun and a small caliber, so recoil is minimized. Your friend may not mind the feel of recoil, but her shooting will definitely be better in the long run if she starts out on something mild.
- Hand wipes for cleanup. You can talk about lead contamination some, but full instruction about that isn't necessary unless and until she becomes a frequent shooter herself.
- Your most patient attitude. A newcomer will do some things "wrong." Don't try to fix everything! Focus on safety issues—those are the only issues that really matter for the first outing.

Things to leave at home

- Your own plans to shoot. The first outing is all about your friend. If things go well, you might have a chance to shoot a little; if they don't, you won't. Understand that going in and you'll be a lot happier if she needs more hand-holding than you expected.
- Arrogance. The attitude you want to convey is that you want to share your world with her, and that safety is important—not that you know

everything there is to know about guns and that you are the source of all shooting wisdom. If she asks a question you don't know the answer to, tell her you don't know.

At the Range

Place the target close. Four to seven yards is ideal. Anything over ten yards will probably frustrate your new shooter, and stymie your attempts to help her have fun.

Set out only one gun. If you've brought more than one, keep the others boxed up until she is ready for the change. Set out only one magazine. Don't put the ammunition out until after dry fire. When you do, set out only one kind of ammunition. Avoid confusing a newcomer with clutter!

Before loading the gun, show your friend how to hold the gun and how to stand. Do not make this complicated. Stick with the basics of keeping her thumbs out of the way of the recoiling slide or her fingers away from the cylinder, so she'll be safe. Tell her she'll need to grasp the gun tightly. Do not talk too much about recoil, but do mention it in passing as a reason to hold the gun firmly.

Show her the gun's controls, and have her practice racking the slide a few times. Watch her trigger finger and remind her to keep it alongside the frame rather than on the trigger while she works the slide.

Show her how to put the magazine in and take it back out again. Show her how to lock the slide back, or how to open the cylinder. Show her how the ammunition feeds into the gun. Show her where the brass comes out and explain again that it isn't anything to worry about.

Talk about what the sights look like and how they are supposed to line up on the target. Draw a quick sketch of that if she seems to need it, otherwise don't.

Have her dry fire. While she dry fires, be especially conscious of her muzzle direction and remind her to watch it if necessary. Watch her trigger finger while she dry fires, and remind her that the instant the gun comes down off target, her finger must also come off the trigger.

> **Important!**
>
> Have your friend load only one round at first.

Going live

Show your friend how to place ammunition into the magazine. Have her watch you while you fire one or two rounds, so she knows what to expect. Fire very, very slowly so she doesn't try to imitate you shooting fast.

Then it is her turn. Start by having her load only one round. You do not know how a new shooter will react to the first shot firing, so it is safer to load only one round at first. You want to familiarize her with running the gun, which she will do as she repetitively loads it. Watch her muzzle direction while she loads the gun. Remind her about muzzle direction if necessary.

Resist the temptation to reach in and fix anything for her unless she asks for help. If she does ask for help, show her again how to do it but then have her do it herself so she can learn. Don't take over.

Everyone likes praise!
If she is doing well, say so.
Say so again.
And then again.

Have her load one, then shoot one, for at least 10 rounds. Stand just barely behind her strong-side elbow, within easy reach, while she is firing. A surprising number of new shooters will turn around with the gun in their hands immediately after the first shot goes. By standing close, you can be ready for this and are able to stop her if needed. Another reason to stand close is that the most common reason a new shooter turns around is to look for her mentor. If you stand close, she won't need to turn around to find you.

Be aware that some new shooters have an emotional reaction to the first shot, and may even get tears in their eyes. Unless the newcomer is working through some personal traumatic event, this is a physical response to the adrenalin dump caused by the unfamiliar sensations of shooting. If it happens to your friend, reassure her that it's a normal reaction and doesn't mean she's weird. Help her settle back down and encourage her to work through it once she has settled down enough to remain safe.

Watch her hands while she fires, not the target. Keep your eye on her trigger finger especially. Remember, the holes in the target will still be there when she is done shooting, but you must see what her hands are doing *right now*. Nag about trigger finger as often as you need to, but do it politely. Don't give up on reminding her if she forgets more than once.

Also watch her weak-hand thumb. Some folks will put it behind the slide sometime during that first trip to the range. For revolvers, watch to be sure her fingers do not get too close to the cylinder. Your new shooter does not need to hurt herself today.

Do not say anything bad about her marksmanship. Marksmanship is not the name of the game today. First priority is to be safe, second priority is to have fun. If she is doing both those things, she is doing very well.

Suggest that she takes her first target home to keep. Write the date on it, and sign it as a witness. Invite her to come shooting with you again. Not "sometime," but for a specific date and time. And follow through.

Appendices

Dear Gunhilda,

When is the best time to tell my friends
I am carrying a gun?

~ Polite in Parkerville

Dear Polite,

At the same point you feel compelled
to inform them what color
underwear you are wearing.

~ Gunhilda

Complete Glossary of Holster Terms

When it comes time to pick out a belt holster, the choices seem overwhelming and the terminology mystifying. A holster maker uses words few other people do, and uses familiar words in unusual ways. A rake is something you use in the garden, right? Not to a holster maker! With all the specialized terminology, it isn't any wonder that the rest of us are often confused. So here's a cheat sheet that might help make your next holster-buying expedition a little less confusing. This glossary includes terms that refer to

- *the angle the muzzle will be held,*
- *where the holster rides in relation to the waistline,*
- *where the holster rides in relation to the hip,*
- *how the holster attaches to the belt,*
- *the overall shape of the holster,*
- *specific features that some holsters might have,*
- *and common holster materials.*

Muzzle Angle

Adjustable rake or **adjustable cant** – The angle at which the holster holds the gun can easily be changed by the user.

Cant – Sometimes called *rake*. The angle at which the holster will hold the gun on the belt. It is measured by degrees. (There's a good explanation of this, with a diagram, on DelFatti Leather's site at http://www.delfatti.com/webdoc20.html.)

Extreme rake or **extreme cant** – The muzzle will be angled more sharply than other designs by the same maker. The exact angle meant by this term varies from one maker to another.

FBI rake or **FBI cant**– A widely used term, but the specific angle it refers to varies greatly from one holster maker to another. Traditionally, it means 12-15 degrees of muzzle-rear cant.

Muzzle forward – The holstered gun will have its muzzle angled toward the front of your body.

Muzzle rear – The holstered gun will have its muzzle angled toward the rear.

Rake – Sometimes called *cant*. The angle at which the holster will hold the gun on the belt. It is measured by degrees. (There's a good explanation of this, with a diagram, on DelFatti Leather's site at http://www.delfatti.com/webdoc20.html.)

Straight drop – The holstered gun will have its muzzle pointed straight toward the floor.

Where the Holster Rides in Relation to the Waistline

Drop or **dropped** – As little of the gun as possible is held above the belt line. This is often more comfortable for people with curvy waistlines, but it is not very concealable. Holsters which combine drop with offset are usually very comfortable and practical for range use.

High ride or **high rise** – As much of the gun as possible is held above the belt line. This is often more comfortable for people with curvy waistlines, and is very concealable even under short cover garments. But it can be difficult for short-waisted people or those with shoulder mobility issues to draw a weapon from a high ride holster.

Offset – The whole top portion of the holstered gun is held away from the shooter's body by the shape of the holster. This is usually more comfortable for people with curves and provides good grip accessibility. But it is bulky, usually isn't very concealable and often makes the wearer look chunky. Holsters which combine offset with drop are usually very comfortable and practical for range use.

Where the Holster Rides in Relation to the Hip

Appendix carry – The holstered gun is placed forward of the hip on the strong side, usually halfway between belly button and hip bone.

Behind the hip – The holster is placed *immediately* behind the hip.

Between pants & belt – The holster is placed outside the pants, but inside the belt.

Cross draw – The holstered gun is placed forward of the hip on the support side, usually halfway between belly button and hip bone. It is usually carried butt-forward in this position.

Combination IWB/OWB – The holster can be worn either inside or outside both pants and belt.

IWB (Inside Waist Band) – The holster is placed inside the pants and inside the belt.

On the hip – The holster is placed on the waistline directly below your armpit.

OWB (Outside Waist Band) – The holster is placed outside the pants and outside the belt.

Small of back – The holster is placed in the center of the back, over the spinal cord. (NOT RECOMMENDED!)

Strong side – The side corresponding to the dominant hand. The holstered gun is usually placed butt-rearward when worn on the strong side.

Weak side or **support side** – The side corresponding to the non-dominant hand.

How the Holster Attaches to the Belt

Clip – A metal or polymer clamp which typically fits over the belt, or over the clothing waistline beneath the belt. Although clips can often also be attached to clothing without a belt, they are less secure when not paired with a belt – and some makers specifically warn against this practice.

C Hook or J hook – A piece which partially encircles the belt, typically placing a hook at the bottom of the belt (J hook) or a hook at both top and bottom of the belt (C hook).

Loop – An attachment which completely encircles the belt.

Paddle – A wide, rounded attachment on the back of the holster which slips inside the waistband while the holster itself is on the outside of the waistband.

Shank – A long, narrow piece typically attached to the outer bottom of the holster, with the belt attachment at the top, allowing a shirt to be tucked in over the top of the holstered gun.

Slot – An opening in the holster body or wing.

Snaps – Typically paired with one or two loops, allowing the holster to be easily removed from the belt without unbuckling.

Tab – A flat piece often covered with Velcro-style hooks to mate with soft loops on the back side of the belt.

Tail – A long piece of material which 'flags' behind the holster body, with a second belt attachment at the end of it. This typically pulls the butt of the gun more firmly into the torso but also creates a wider footprint on the belt.

Tunnel – The belt is completely enclosed within the back side of the holster for some distance.

Overall Shape of the Holster

Paddle – A wide, rounded attachment on the back of the holster which slips inside the waistband while the holster itself is on the outside of the waistband.

Pancake – A wide holster constructed of two flat pieces of leather (the "pancake") sewn together and molded to the shape of the firearm.

Scabbard – Designs which (usually) fully enclose the muzzle end, or which (less usually) cover the entire length of the gun but leave a small molded opening at the muzzle end. These are typically OWB holsters.

Slide – Minimalist OWB holster designs which do not enclose the muzzle end, allowing them to carry otherwise identical guns with different muzzle lengths. Some slide holsters literally look like a single piece of leather covering *only* the trigger area.

Specific Features Some Holsters Might Have

Body guard / sweat guard – A high piece on the back of the holster where it touches your body, designed to prevent contact between your body and the exposed part of the holstered gun.

Collapsible – A holster made of flimsy material which allows the holster mouth to shut as soon as the gun is withdrawn. Comfortable for concealed carry, but a safety issue in range practice as it is impossible to reholster in these designs without muzzling your own non-dominant hand.

Covered trigger guard – The holster completely covers the entire trigger area, and it is impossible to reach a finger in to touch the trigger of the holstered gun. A completely covered trigger guard is absolutely necessary for safety in a carry rig, because of the potential for clothing or gear to get snagged in it and trigger an unintentional discharge.

Grip accessibility – How easy it is to get a complete grasp on the grip while the gun is in the holster.

Liner, lined – Material on the inside of the holster, where the gun rides; occasionally refers to material on the back of the holster, where it touches your body.

One-handed reholstering – The holster will stay open when the gun is drawn, enabling you to reholster without holding the mouth of the holster open with your support hand. Absolutely necessary for safety, because otherwise you will point the gun at your support hand every time you holster.

Open top – Holsters that don't have a retention strap.

Retention holster – A holster which has a retention strap or other device intended to prevent the gun from being drawn by anyone but the person wearing it.

Stability – How much the holster wiggles around on the belt, whether it is prone to flopping or twisting or other movement.

Thumb break / retention strap – A strap that goes over the top of the holstered gun and is (usually) snapped in place for security. Called a thumb break because the thumb must break it open in order to draw the weapon. This feature is frequently desirable on holsters which will be carried openly rather than concealed.

Tension – How tightly the gun is held in the holster.

Tension screws – Screws which allow the user to adjust how tightly the gun is held in the holster.

Tuckable or shirt tuck feature – Enables a shirt to be tucked in over the holstered gun, leaving only the holster's loop(s) or hooks visible on the belt line.

Common Holster Materials

Combination Kydex / leather ("hybrid") – A holster which includes both Kydex and leather in its design. Usually, this means that a leather back (closest to the body) will be paired with a Kydex front (where the gun rides). Sometimes it means that the entire Kydex sheath will be covered with an outer layer of leather.

Custom holster – A holster that is made just for you to your specifications. Often surprisingly affordable, but also often involves a lengthy wait.

Injection-molded – A process used to form Kydex or plastic holsters inside a hollow mold by injecting completely melted polymer into the mold. Non-injection-molded holsters are made by placing sheets of Kydex or plastic over a form and partially melting them until they conform to the proper shape.

Kydex – A very sturdy polymer which has characteristics that make it work well for holsters. Its primary advantages are easy maintenance, and that it holds the gun securely while still allowing a fast draw. Its primary disadvantages are that it is less attractive and (typically) less comfortable to wear than leather. Kydex also creates a distinctive sound when drawn.

Leather – Gunleather is usually made of cowhide or horsehide, but may be trimmed with exotic leathers such as shark or snakeskin. Its primary advantage is comfort against bare skin; its primary disadvantage is that it is not waterproof or sweatproof. Leather can be "squeaky" as the wearer moves.

Nylon – A soft, collapsible holster material which often does not hold the gun securely in place.

Plastic – A polymer which is less expensive and generally less sturdy than Kydex.

Complete Glossary of Firearm and Shooting Terms

A

Accidental Discharge – An unintentional firing of the gun which is caused only by mechanical error. If mechanical error was not the cause, it is a negligent discharge. See also: *negligent discharge.*

ACP – An abbreviation for Automatic Colt Pistol. It is commonly used to designate specific calibers, particularly those which were originally designed by John Moses Browning for the Colt Firearms Company.

Action – A group of moving parts used to load, fire, and unload the firearm. See also: *single action, double action.*

Adjustable Stock – A stock is the wooden, polymer, or metal part of a long gun which is braced against the shooter's shoulder while shooting. An adjustable stock is one which can be easily lengthened or shortened to fit shooters of different sizes.

Adjustable Trigger – A trigger in which one or more parameter may be easily adjusted by the user. The most common adjustment is pull weight, but a fully adjustable trigger may be adjustable for pull distance, individual trigger stage distances, individual trigger stage weights, release point, left/right cant, overtravel, and possibly others. Adjustable triggers are common on specialized target-shooting firearms, but rare on self defense firearms.

Ambidextrous Safety – A manual, external safety which can be easily reached with either hand. It often features dual levers, with one lever on each side of the firearm.

Ammo – See *ammunition.*

Ammunition – Gun food. Typically, the term refers to the complete package of components the firearm needs in order to fire. This often includes a *projectile* (the bullet, slug, or pellets), a *propellant* (the powder), and a *primer* (which produces the spark that ignites the powder). Shotgun ammunition also includes a *wad*, which acts as a buffer between the shot and the powder and seals in the gases which propel the shot out of the barrel. Ammunition components are held together within a *case* (handguns and rifles) or a *shell* (shotguns).

Assault Rifle – A military firearm which fires a reduced power rifle round and is capable of both fully-automatic and semi-automatic modes of fire. See also: *automatic, semi-automatic, assault weapon.*

Assault Weapon – A political term with no fixed definition, being defined differently by different jurisdictions. Because the actual definition is so fluid, laws written to regulate "assault weapons" often define the term by various cosmetic characteristics which do not affect a firearm's power or function in any fundamental way. The term is distinct from the term *assault rifle*, which is a technical term with a specific meaning widely accepted both in law and within the military and firearms communities. Despite public perception, "assault weapons" are not machine guns. They are semi-automatic firearms, not fully automatic firearms.

> **Legal Note:** "Assault weapons" bans do not generally propose to ban fully automatic firearms. Many of the features outlawed by "assault weapons" laws actually function to make these semi-automatic firearms safer for users and bystanders. One specific design feature often mentioned in "assault weapons" bans is an adjustable or collapsible stock. This disproportionately affects female gunowners, who often benefit from being able to adjust a long stock downwards to suit the smaller female frame. Because there is no actual, non-slippery definition for the term *assault weapon*, many proposed and actual assault-weapons bans simply resort to banning specific firearms by brand name, with all the obvious problems of enforcement that entails.

Autoloader – A semi-automatic pistol, shotgun, or rifle. See also: *semi-automatic.*

Automatic – A firearm which rapidly fires multiple shots with a single pull of the trigger. A fully automatic firearm is commonly called a machine gun. See also: *semi-automatic.* In America, fully automatic firearms have been strictly regulated since 1934, and illegal to produce or import since the 1980s. Functioning full-auto guns legal for civilians to own are extremely difficult to find, and very expensive to purchase, often costing $10,000 or more. Existing fully-automatic firearms are generally antiques. They are illegal for civilians to own in many (but not all) states. In states where fully-automatic firearms are legal to collect, federal law requires the purchase of a $200 authorization stamp for each firearm. An extensive background check, which includes approval of local law enforcement and requires full fingerprints and photographs, is conducted before the purchase is approved.

> **Incorrect usage:** Any firearm which uses the energy from the fired shot to eject the empty case and feed the next round into the chamber may sometimes be called "automatic." This is technically incorrect unless referring to a firearm which fires multiple shots with a single trigger pull. If

the trigger must be pulled a second time before a second shot is fired, such a firearm is properly called a semi-automatic.

B

Backstop – Anything that will safely stop a bullet and prevent it from hitting anything else after the target is struck.

Backstrap – A handgun term. The rearmost surface of the grip.

Ball – Often used in casual conversation to mean any ammunition capped with a round-nose FMJ bullet, especially in .45 ACP caliber, but is accurately used to describe standard military ammunition of any standard military caliber. Also, a round, lead bullet used in muzzle-loading firearms. See also: *full metal jacket, hardball.*

Ballistic Fingerprint – A fired case has unique marks upon it from the extractor, ejector, and breechface. A bullet fired through a rifled barrel also has unique rifling marks. A record of these marks, when stored in a central database, is called a "ballistic fingerprint." Some states require this record to be made by law, so that individual guns can be located from bullets or casings found at the scene of a crime.

> *Legal Note:* The primary difficulty with ballistic fingerprint databases is that ejectors, extractors, and barrels all suffer through normal use, and all can (and should) be replaced at regular intervals. Change one part, and the record in the database is no longer accurate. Even absent this normal swapping-out of parts, every time a gun is fired, the "fingerprint" changes a little. New scratches appear; old ones are worn away. As time goes on, the original marks are completely altered and the data in the files becomes useless. Because of this normal process of erosion and parts replacement, a ballistic fingerprint database really isn't like a record of human fingerprints. It's more like trying to keep a permanent record of criminals based solely on their current hairstyle: an expensive and probably useless boondoggle.

Barrel – The metal tube through which the bullet or shot travels.

Battery – Most firearms do not have literal batteries. But a firearm is said to be *in battery* when the breech is fully closed and locked, ready to fire. When the breech is open or unlocked, the gun is *out of battery* and no attempt should be made to fire it. A semi-automatic is *out of battery* when the slide fails to come all the way forward again after the gun has fired, making it dangerous or impossible to fire the next round. This condition can be created by a misfeed, a dirty gun, weak springs, the shooter's thumbs brushing against the slide, riding the slide, or any of several other causes.

Beavertail – On many 1911-style pistols, a large piece of curved metal at the top of the grip which protects the user's hand from getting bitten by the hammer. It is nearly always the top part of the grip safety.

Berm – On an outdoor shooting range, a large pile of dirt that functions as a backstop.

Birdshot – A type of shotgun ammunition which uses very small pellets. It is so named because it is most often used for hunting birds. Birdshot comes in different sizes. Generally speaking, the smaller the pellets, the more of them there are in each round of ammunition.

Black Powder – Black powder is a type of gunpowder invented in the 9th century and was practically the only known propellant until the middle of the 19th century when smokeless powder was invented. It is purchased separately from other ammunition components, and is commonly used in muzzle-loading firearms. It is not used in modern encased ammunition.

Bolt – A bolt is a mechanical part in some firearms which blocks the rear of the chamber while the powder burns. It must be moved out of the way to load and unload the gun; this action may be manually performed by the shooter pulling back on an exterior knob called the bolt handle and then sending it forward again, or the action may be performed by other moving parts within the firearm. When the user must move the bolt manually, the firearm is called a bolt-action firearm. See also: *bolt action.*

Bolt Action – An action type most commonly used in rifles, in which the user ejects the spent round and brings a new round up from the internal magazine by pulling back on an external knob which is called a bolt handle. See also: *bolt.*

Bore – 1) The guy at the range who keeps talking and talking and talking and talking when you just want to shoot. 2) The inside surface of the barrel. A smooth-bore firearm is one that does not have *rifling* on the barrel's internal surface. Except for shotguns, these are generally antiques and collector's items. See also: *rifling.* A big-bore firearm is one which fires a large caliber. A smallbore firearm is one which fires a small caliber. When used to describe a competition, "smallbore" generally means the competition will use rimfire rounds. Not all smallbore calibers are rimfire, however: .223 Remington is one example of a smallbore centerfire round.

Bore Axis – An imaginary line which runs right down the center of the handgun's barrel and out though the back end of the gun. A handgun may have a high bore axis, with the imaginary line running out into space well above the shooter's hand. Or it may have a low bore axis, with the imaginary line running either straight through the shooter's hand or just skimming the surface slightly above her hand. A high bore axis tends to create greater perceived recoil and more muzzle flip when firing the gun than does a low bore axis.

Brass – The most common material used for ammunition cases, so much so that you will often hear people refer to 'picking up the brass' even when the empty cases they are going to pick up are actually made of aluminum or steel.

Brass Magnet – We all want one. But my scientific friends tell me it's impossible.

Break (Trigger Break) – The point at which the trigger allows the hammer to fall, or releases the striker, so that the shot fires. The ideal break is sudden and definite. 'Like a glass rod' is the cliché term shooters use to describe the ideal crisp, clean break.

Breech – The rearmost end of a barrel, closest the shooter (opposite from the muzzle end).

Breech Block – A mechanical piece which seals the rearmost part of the barrel (the breech) while the gun is firing, preventing the rearward escape of gases.

Breech Face – That portion of the breech block which touches the cartridge when the breech is closed.

Breech Opening – The open rear of the barrel through which cartridges are inserted into the chamber.

Brick – A box of ammunition roughly equal in size and weight to a... well, a brick. Most often used to describe a 500-round container of .22 Long Rifle ammunition.

Buckshot – A type of shotgun ammunition which uses medium-sized to large-sized pellets. It is so named because some folks hunt deer with it. Buckshot comes in different sizes. Generally speaking, the larger the pellets, the fewer of them there are in each round of ammunition.

Bullet – The solitary metal projectile which is flung downrange. When shooters refer to the bullet, they mean only the projectile itself, not the complete package which holds the bullet before it is fired. The complete package, which includes the case, primer, powder, and bullet, is usually called a cartridge or a round. See also: *ammunition.*

Bullet Trap – A type of backstop which catches the fired bullet and prevents it from exiting the area.

Bullpup – A rifle configuration in which the action and magazine are located behind the trigger. This is done so the overall length of the firearm is shorter than it otherwise would be, but is controversial because it puts the receiver very close to the shooter's face.

Butt – Handguns – The base of the grip. On semi-automatic handguns, the magazine is inserted into a hollow magazine well located in the butt of the gun.

Butt – Long Guns – The rearmost portion of the stock, the part the user braces against one shoulder.

C

Cable Lock – A short stretch of cable with a padlock at the end. It is threaded through the action of the firearm.

Caliber – Generally speaking, caliber refers to the size of the bullet a gun will fire, and also usually refers specifically to the bullet's diameter or to the bore size of the gun that fires it. But the nominal caliber designation isn't always the actual bullet diameter or chamber measurement. Caliber numbers are usually followed by words or letters to create the complete name of the cartridge. These letters often represent a brand name or an abbreviation for the name of the company that first introduced the round, or otherwise give more information about the cartridge.

Cant – Tilting the gun slightly to the left or right rather than keeping it level, with the front sight vertical in relation to the ground. Canting the firearm can make precision shooting more difficult, but may be necessary in certain circumstances. For example, when shooting a semi-automatic around left-hand cover it may be necessary to cant the gun so that the ejection port is not blocked. A slight cant may also assist a cross-dominant handgun shooter to improve her accuracy when shooting one-handed.

Carbine – (Pronounced "car-bean.") A short, lightweight rifle, usually with a short barrel. Carbines are often designed to shoot a pistol caliber rather than a rifle caliber.

Cartridge – The complete package which makes up a single round of ammunition. It includes the case, primer, powder, and bullet. See also: *ammunition.*

Case – The metal (or, very occasionally, polymer) container which holds the primer, powder, and bullet together. Sometimes it is called the brass, because brass is the traditional and still most common case material.

Centerfire – Ammunition in which the primer is located in a small cup in the bottom center of the case. See also: *rimfire.*

Chamber – 1) The part of the gun which holds the round while the shot is being fired. In semi-automatics, the chamber is located at the base of the barrel. Revolvers have multiple chambers, which are located in the cylinder. 2) A firearm is said to be chambered in whichever caliber it shoots. 'What's that chambered in?' means, 'What size ammunition does it use?'

Chapman Stance – Named for Ray Chapman, this is a modified form of the Weaver stance. It is sometimes called a modified Weaver. The strong side elbow is held straight and locked out, while the weak hand pulls back against the strong hand thus producing the push-pull tension typical of the Weaver stance.

Choke – 1) A constricting tube at the end of a shotgun barrel, which changes the pattern of how the shot spreads out. Chokes come in different configurations to give varying effects. 2) A misfeed or failure to fire. ("My gun just choked.") 3) To mess up under stress, especially the stress of competition. ("Well, I was worried about shooting against Julie Golob, and I just choked.")

Clay Pigeon – A frisbee-shaped chunk of pottery, typically flung into the air to function as a shotgun target.

Clearing – 1) Unloading a gun and double checking that it is unloaded. 2) "Tactical" term meaning to safely enter a room making sure there are no criminals lurking there. 3) Fixing a malfunction so that the gun is ready to fire again.

Clip – A literal clip that holds fresh cartridges together, but does not feed them into the gun. It is not usually encased. Handguns, with a *very* few limited exceptions, do not have clips; they have magazines. Using the word "clip" instead of "magazine" is one of the things that marks a new or uninformed shooter, and often drives experienced shooters right up the wall. See also: *magazine.*

Cock – On hammer-fired guns, to retract the hammer so it is in position to fall forward onto the firing pin, which will in turn strike the primer and fire the shot. If the firearm has an external hammer, the gun may be cocked manually, by pulling the hammer back with the thumb (*thumb cocking*). Some external hammers, and all internal hammers, may be cocked simply by pulling the trigger (*trigger cocking*).

Collapsible Stock – A long gun term which refers to a stock which can be shoved into itself to shorten it, either for storage or to make the gun fit shooters of different sizes.

Concealed – Hidden from view. A handgun is concealed when it is carried in such a manner that an observer cannot tell whether it is there or not. See also: *printing.*

Concealment – Anything that blocks the attacker's view of the intended victim, but which won't necessarily stop a bullet. See also: *cover.*

Controlled Pair – Two shots fired in rapid succession. It is distinguished from a double tap because in a controlled pair, the second shot will be fired after the shooter has obtained a second sight picture, whereas in a double tap both shots are fired based upon the initial sight picture alone.

Cosmoline – An icky, sticky substance in which most of the world's old military firearms were bathed upon retirement, in order to prevent corrosion. Collectors of antique military firearms spend a lot of time swapping recipes for getting the stuff out of the nooks and crannies of their beloved old guns.

Cover – Anything an intended victim hides behind which will probably stop a bullet. Cover is nearly always also concealment, but concealment isn't necessarily cover. See also: *concealment.*

Cover Garment – Any piece of clothing that covers the holstered gun. When the gun is worn on the belt, the most common types of cover garments are vests, sweaters, and jackets.

Creep – 1) A guy at the range or anywhere else who gives you the willies. Always listen to your instincts and avoid being alone with a creep. 2) A trigger is said to creep when it does not have a consistent, clean *break*. Once the trigger reaches the break point, it should not be possible to move it farther to the rear, even slightly or slowly.

Crisp – A trigger is crisp when it breaks in a sudden and definite manner, with no extra movement.

Cross-dominant – Sounds a little hinky, but don't worry. It just means a shooter who is right-handed but left-eyed, or left-handed and right-eyed.

Crosshairs – The cross-shaped object seen in the center of a firearm scope. Its more-proper name is reticle.

Crown – The area inside the bore nearest the muzzle. Damage to the crown can severely and adversely affect the firearm's accuracy.

Cylinder – The part of a revolver which revolves. The cylinder contains 5, 6, or more chambers into which the ammunition is placed.

D

Decocker – On double-action semi-automatic firearms, a lever which mechanically lowers the hammer without firing the gun. Like all mechanical safeties, it can fail. The decocker should never be pressed unless the gun is pointed in an absolutely safe direction.

Deringer or derringer – A small, double-barreled handgun which can fire a single shot from each barrel before it needs to be reloaded. It is loaded by folding the barrels downward and away from the receiver, a process called breaking the action open. The spent cases are then removed, and one fresh round is placed in the base of each barrel before the barrels are snapped shut again. The design was first produced by Henry Deringer, under the brand name Deringer. When used to refer to any other brand of the same design, derringer is spelled with two r's and is not capitalized.

Double Action (DA) – Originally used only for revolvers but now common in semi-autos as well, double action originally meant that the user had two choices for how to cock the hammer. The user could either cock the hammer by pulling it back with his thumb (thumb cocking), or by an extended, heavy trigger pull (trigger cocking). This reason for the use of the term has been widely forgotten. Now it generally means using the single motion of the trigger to both cock the hammer and to fire the shot. Double action firearms tend to have long, heavy trigger pulls.

Double Action / Single Action (DA/SA) – DA/SA firearms are designed to operate in *double action* on the initial shot, and in *single action* on the second and subsequent shots. Consequently, these guns tend to have a long, heavy trigger pull for the first shot, and a relatively short and light trigger pull for subsequent shots. This is because the first trigger pull gets the internal parts into position, while the energy from the first shot is used to prep the mechanism for follow-up shots. See also: *double action, single action.*

Double Action Only (DAO) – Some pistols and revolvers can only be trigger cocked and are impossible to thumb cock. Even though it drives traditionalists nuts (the apparent redundancy irritates some), these are commonly called double-action-only firearms. See also: *double action.*

Double Barrel – A shotgun with two barrels is called a double-barreled shotgun. The barrels may be situated next to each other (side by side), or vertically aligned (over/under). Double-barreled shotguns typically hold only two rounds at a time, and are designed to break open at the base of the barrel (the breech) for reloading.

Doublefeed – A malfunction in which the spent case fails to eject from a semi-automatic firearm, so that when the fresh round is brought forward it cannot fit into the chamber because the other case is still in the way. It is cleared by stripping the magazine from the gun, racking the slide several times to eject the spent case, and then reloading.

Double Tap – Two shots fired in rapid succession. Generally the second shot will be fired more quickly than a new sight picture can be established. If the second shot is fired after a second sight picture is established, a double tap may instead be called a controlled pair.

Drams – A black powder weight measure. Although shotgun ammunition uses smokeless powder, in order to standardize measurements, shotgun ammunition manufacturers use dram equivalents to indicate how much power the load has. The quantity of smokeless powder in the load is compared to the amount of black powder it would require to produce the same velocity with the same projectile(s).

Dremel – A tool used by home handypersons and do-it-yourselfers to damage and destroy firearms. Never let anyone with a Dremel tool anywhere near your firearm. See also *hammer.*

Drop Safety – A mechanical safety which prevents the gun from firing when it is unintentionally dropped. Some state governments require drop-testing of all handgun designs sold within the state, a redundant law because there really aren't any modern firearms which aren't drop safe.

Dry Fire or **Dryfire** – Practicing gun manipulations, including sight alignment and trigger press, with an empty firearm. Dry fire can be very beneficial, but it is also very dangerous.

Dud – A round of ammunition that does not fire when expected.

Dum Dum – A somewhat obsolete term which refers to one of several different shapes of expanding bullets, especially when used by a soldier on the field of war. Most commonly, this term refers to a jacketed bullet illicitly or illegally modified by the user in order to create greater injury. Except in rare cases, the term does not refer to legally-produced hollowpoint ammunition. Legally-produced hollowpoint ammunition is commonly used in self defense and law enforcement applications because its reduced penetration capabilities make it safer for bystanders.

Dummy Round – An inert ammunition-shaped object, used in practice to simulate misfeeds and other malfunctions. Some folks also use them in dry fire practice.

E

Ear plugs – A type of hearing protection which fits inside the ear canal.

Earmuffs – A type of hearing protection which completely covers both ears and is usually attached to a headband (sometimes to a neckband rather than a headband). See also: *muffs, electronic.*

Ears – Casual slang for hearing protection (muffs or plugs). The human ear is very vulnerable to the sharp, loud noise of gunfire. Smart shooters always protect their ears by wearing good ear protection on the range. See also *ear plugs, earmuffs,* and *muffs, electronic.*

Ejection Port – The opening through which the empty, spent ammunition case is cast out of a firearm.

Ejection Rod – A sliding metal dowel located at the muzzle end of a revolver cylinder. The rear end of the ejection rod holds the star, which contacts the case rims when the gun is loaded. After firing, the shooter opens the cylinder and depresses the front end of the ejection rod, causing the star to shove the empty cases out of the cylinder.

Ejector – 1) The part of a semi-auto firearm responsible for tossing the empty case out of the ejection port. 2) In most double action revolvers, empty cases are removed by the user pushing down on the ejector rod (sometimes called the ejection rod). The bottom end of the ejector rod holds the *star*, which shoves the spent cases out of the chambers by pushing against their rims.

Electronic Hearing Protection – See *muffs, electronic.*

Electronic Muffs – See *muffs, electronic.*

External Safety – A safety which is placed on the outer surfaces of the firearm and is accessible to the user. Not all external safeties require user attention. For instance, a grip safety is an external safety, but requires no deliberate act on the part of the shooter in order to do its job. See also: *passive safety, manual safety.*

Extractor – The part of a semi-automatic firearm responsible for grabbing the empty case by its rim and yanking it out of the chamber as the slide travels rearward.

F

Failure to Extract – A semi-automatic firearm malfunction in which the extractor fails to yank the old case out of the way as the slide travels back, so the spent case is still in the chamber as the slide on its return journey tries to stuff the new round into the same space. A failure to extract often causes a doublefeed malfunction. See also: *doublefeed.*

Failure to Feed – A semi-automatic firearm malfunction in which the slide passes entirely over the fresh round, failing to pick it up to insert in the chamber as the slide returns to battery. Failures-to-feed and misfeeds are closely-related malfunctions, and the two problems often share a root cause.

Failure to Fire – Any malfunction which results in nothing happening when the trigger is pulled. Most commonly caused by a failure to feed the ammunition properly into the chamber, a failure to fire can also be caused by bad ammunition or by a broken firing pin.

Firearm – A mechanism which throws metallic projectiles using the energy produced through the rapid, confined burning of a propellant. Pellet guns, BB guns, airsoft guns, paintball markers, and air rifles are not firearms, because their projectiles are propelled by air pressure or a spring rather than by burned propellant.

Firing Pin – Part of the firing mechanism which serves to transfer energy from a spring-loaded hammer to the primer. The firing pin is a lightweight, very hard steel rod with a small, rounded end at its front for striking the primer. Not all firearms are actuated by hammer-struck firing pins. Some firing pins are actually part of the hammer. Others, called *strikers*, consist of a single piece which is directly connected to the spring which powers it. See also: *striker.*

Firing Pin Block – A type of internal safety which prevents the firing pin from moving forward for any reason unless the trigger is pulled.

Flash Hider – See *flash reducer.*

Flash Reducer – A mechanical device which directs the burning gases away from the front sight, making the firearm more pleasant to shoot, especially in low light. Flash reducers lessen glare as seen by the shooter, but do *not* hide the flash from other observers to the front or side of the firearm.

Flash Suppressor – See *flash reducer.*

Flat Point or Flat Nose – A bullet shape with a flat nose rather than a rounded one.

Flinch – Yanking the gun downwards just before the shot fires, causing the shot to go wild. A flinch is commonly caused by learning to shoot with a more powerful gun than the shooter is yet ready to handle. Many shooters have recurring problems with flinching throughout their shooting lives.

FMJ – See *full metal jacket.*

Folding Stock – Long gun term. A stock which features a hinged point so that it may be doubled over for conveniently compact storage.

Follow Through – Holding the trigger to the rear after the shot has fired, until the sights are back on target, at which time the trigger is released.

Fore-end – The fore-end (sometimes spelled *forend*) is the front part of the long gun's *furniture*. It is designed to give the shooter a place to hold the front end of the gun and protects the shooter's hand from getting burned on the hot barrel. Pump-action firearms have movable fore-ends, while other types of firearms have stationary ones. See also: *furniture.*

Fouling – The gritty, grubby, icky stuff that has to swabbed out of the barrel and scrubbed out of every nook and cranny of the firearm in order to clean it.

Four Rules – The four universal rules of firearms safety, which apply every single time a firearm is handled in any way or for any reason.

Frame – The skeleton of the gun, to which all moving parts are attached.

Front Sight – See *sight, front.*

Front Strap – The surface of the forward part of the handgun grip.

Full Metal Jacket (FMJ) – Ammunition in which the front part of the lead bullet is covered with a thin layer of copper or another metal. This reduces fouling and makes the firearm easier to clean at the end of the shooting day, and also reduces the amount of lead dust present in the air on the range. The term is distinct from *total metal jacket* because in ammunition with a total metal jacket, the entire bullet is encased by another metal. See also: *total metal jacket.*

Furniture – A long gun term that basically means the pretty parts of the gun—the stock, the grip if there is one, and the fore-end. It does not include the receiver or the barrel.

G

Gas – The superheated air and other stuff produced by burning powder. Gas pressure is what sends the bullet downrange.

Gas Operated – In this case, gas does not mean gasoline. It means the superheated air and other stuff created by burning powder. A gas-operated firearm is one which uses the energy from these superheated gases to work the action.

The Cornered Cat

Gauge – The shotgun equivalent of caliber. Sort of. Rather than being a direct measurement of bore size, gauge indicates how many lead balls the same diameter as the gun's barrel would equal one pound. For this reason, a 20-gauge barrel is actually *smaller* in diameter than a 12-gauge barrel.

Ghost-Ring Sight – A type of aperture rear sight with a large opening and a thin rim which seems to disappear when the shooter looks through it. Sometimes installed on rifles and shotguns intended for home defense or police use.

Grains – A weight measurement used for bullets. The more grains, the heavier the bullet. Powder is also measured by grains, but this is generally of interest only to reloaders. There are 7000 grains to a pound.

Green Ammunition – Ammunition which contains no lead in any component.

Grip – 1) That part of the handgun which the shooter's hand wraps around. In a semi-automatic pistol, the grip contains the magazine inside the magazine well. The grip's muzzleward surface is called the front strap, while its rearward surface is called the backstrap. Its base is called the butt. See *pistol grip* for long gun usage. 2) The method by which the shooter holds the handgun.

Grip Panels – The interchangeable surfaces which are installed on the part of the gun that you hold. Users change grip panels to improve the look or feel of the firearm, or to personalize it so that the gun is more suited to a different hand size. Some grip panels are chosen for function, while others are chosen for looks. Common grip-panel materials are wood, plastic, and rubber.

Grip Safety – A passive, external safety typically located on the backstrap, which is disengaged by obtaining a firing grip on the handgun. Most 1911-pattern pistols feature a grip safety.

Group – A gathering of holes in the target. Group size is measured center-to-center from the holes which are farthest apart. The smaller the group, the happier the shooter.

Gunpowder – See *powder.*

H

Hair trigger – A trigger that breaks from an extremely light touch. Trigger pull weight is measured by the number of pounds and ounces of pressure required to pull the trigger past the break. A *hair trigger* is a trigger that could be pulled past the break by the weight of a single strand of human hair. Obviously a descriptive term that is never strictly accurate, it is sometimes used in news stories to denote a trigger that can easily be pulled by a normal human being instead of by someone with the hand strength of an upland gorilla.

Hammer – 1) A tool used by a do it yourself home gunsmith to destroy firearms. See *Dremel.* 2) On guns so equipped, the hammer is the part that rotates to provide the percussive impact on the primer, or that strikes the flint to the frizzen. The firing pin may be struck by the hammer, or the firing pin may be a part of the hammer. Not all guns have hammers. Many guns are equipped with strikers: notably Glock pistols and the vast majority of bolt action rifles. Hammers may be exposed or shrouded, spurred or bobbed. See also: *striker*. 3) To hit the target repeatedly.

Handgun – A small firearm designed to be fired while held in one or both hands, rather than while braced against the shoulder.

Hardball – Slang for a full metal jacket bullet with a round nose. In casual conversation, the term is most commonly used in referring to .45 ACP caliber ammunition, but may be used for other calibers as well. "They all fall to hardball." See also *ball, full metal jacket.*

Heavy Trigger – A trigger that requires a lot of pressure to pull it past the break point. It is a subjective term which depends upon the gun type. Speaking very generally, in a defensive handgun anything under around 5 pounds is light, and anything over around 8 pounds is heavy. Rifles usually have considerably lighter triggers than handguns, and even a heavy rifle trigger is often lighter than a light handgun trigger.

High Kneeling – A shooting position in which one or both knees are touching the ground, but the shooter is otherwise erect.

Hollowpoint – A bullet shape. With a deeply dimpled nose, a hollowpoint is designed to expand and spread out on impact. Hollowpoint bullets are most commonly used in law enforcement and self defense applications, because they are most likely to stop an assailant with as few shots as possible, and least likely to overpenetrate the target and harm an innocent bystander. See also: *ammunition.*

Holster – A gun holder which may be strapped to a human body, or affixed to the inside of a pack or bag, or dropped into a pocket. A holster serves to protect the gun's mechanisms and finish, to provide security by covering the trigger so it cannot be pulled inadvertently, and to present the grip of the gun at a constant angle for easy access. Some holsters also serve to obscure the outline of the gun so it may be more easily concealed.

I

Integral Lock – A lock which may prevent the firearm from being fired and which is built into the gun itself. Because of the risk of having a non-functional firearm when you most need it, integral locks are very controversial in the self defense firearms community.

Internal Safety – A safety which is placed within the gun itself and is not accessible to the user. Internal safeties are generally designed to prevent unintentional discharges when the gun is dropped or mishandled.

Iron Sights – The ordinary, mechanical sighting system which usually comes with the firearm. It is so called to distinguish it from laser sights, red dot sights, and scoped sights. Iron sights may be either open sights, most commonly found on pistols, or aperture sights, most commonly found on rifles.

Isosceles Stance – The gun is held thrust straight out from of the body, with both arms straight. The arms and upper body form an isosceles triangle when seen from above. See the Shooting Basics chapter for more information.

> **Isosceles Stance, Classic** – Classic Isosceles positions the feet shoulder width apart, on the same plane, and pointed toward the target. Knees can be locked or slightly flexed. The lower body thus forms a second isosceles triangle.

> **Isosceles Stance, Modern** – Modern Isosceles positions the lower body to fight or run. The feet will be shoulder width apart, knees slightly flexed, with the strong-side foot roughly a half-step behind the weak-side foot. Shoulders will be forward of the hips, and hips forward of the knees.

J

Jam – A malfunction which locks up the gun so badly that tools are required in order to fix it. Sometimes used to denote a simple malfunction, but many people make a distinction between a complete jam and a simple malfunction.

Jam - Revolvers – Contrary to popular misconception, revolvers can jam. They rarely have minor malfunctions. When they do, the problem is often ammunition-related and a second pull of the trigger is the usual cure. If a second pull of the trigger does not clear up the problem, a trip to the gunsmith may be needed. As most people know, such problems are extremely rare, but they can happen.

K

Keyhole – An oddly-shaped hole in the target caused by a bullet which was unstable during its flight and entered the target sideways rather than nose-on. Keyholing sometimes, but not always, indicates a safety issue such as using the incorrect caliber for the gun.

Kick – See *recoil*.

L

Laser – As used around firearms, a laser is an alternative sighting device similar to a laser pointer, which enables the shooter to quickly and accurately see where the firearm is aimed even when lighting or other conditions prevent using the gun's normal sights. Lasers may be located within the grips, hung from accessory rails at the front end of the gun, or placed within the firearm itself as part of the guide rod.

Laser Grip – A type of aftermarket firearms grip which contains a pressure-activated laser pointer which enables the shooter to quickly and accurately see where the firearm is aimed even when lighting or other conditions prevent using the sights.

Lead – [pronounced *leed*] To aim at a spot just in front of a moving target, so that the target moves into the line of fire at the moment the trigger is pulled.

Lead – [pronounced *led*] The metal from which bullets are traditionally made. They may also be made of steel, copper, or other materials.

Lead Fouling – Fouling is the icky stuff that collects in firearm barrels and other parts of the gun, and needs to be swabbed or scrubbed out when cleaning the gun. Lead fouling is fouling that is composed primarily or entirely of lead, and which requires strong solvents to remove. Its presence can be very dangerous in barrels with polygonal rifling, because it can narrow the diameter of the barrel, causing an increase in ammunition pressure to extreme levels which the firearm is not designed to contain.

Length of Pull – 1) The distance between the face of the trigger and the rearmost surface of the gun. On handguns this length is measured from trigger face to backstrap, while on long guns it is measured from trigger face to the butt of the gun. A firearm with a shorter length of pull is generally more apt to fit a small-statured shooter, or one who has small hands. 2) The distance the trigger must travel before it fires the gun.

Less-Lethal Ammunition – Ammunition which, by its design, is less likely to kill someone than traditional ammunition. When used in unaltered firearms, this is almost exclusively a shotgun term. There are a lot of different types of less-lethal ammunition, including beanbag rounds, pepper balls, and rock salt. Although it is entirely possible to kill someone with less-lethal ammunition, such ammunition does not always stop a determined attacker. Because of this, less-lethal ammunition is generally considered a very poor choice for self defense.

> *Incorrect use: Less-than-lethal ammunition* is the old term for the same basic stuff. This term is no longer considered correct because these types of ammunition are fully capable of causing death in many circumstances.

Lever Action – A rifle term. Lever-action rifles have an oversized lever around the area of the trigger guard (often including the trigger guard itself). The user manually brings this lever down and back up again to eject the spent case and bring a new round into the chamber ready to be fired. This motion also typically cocks the hammer of the rifle.

Light Double Action (LDA) – A double-action semi-automatic firearm which is designed to have a much lighter pull than is usual for a double action.

Limp Wristing – Because they function on spring tension, semi-automatic pistols require a solid platform in order for the action to work correctly. Failing to provide this via a solid grip can result in misfeeds or other malfunctions. The problem is called limp-wristing because a floppy, limp wrist is the most common culprit when shooter error is responsible for such failures. However, some gunsmiths claim that any gun which malfunctions when held loosely needs mechanical adjustment.

Loaded Chamber Indicator – A mechanical device which protrudes from the gun when a round is in position ready to be fired, giving a visual and tactile indication of whether the gun is loaded or not. Loaded chamber indicators are required by law in some states. They are a source of some controversy in the shooting community because many shooters believe their presence encourages the ignorant to violate the first, and most important, of the Four Rules.

Loading Gate – 1) Antique, single-action revolvers are loaded by flipping open a tiny little door which allows the user to load or unload one chamber at a time. This tiny little door is called a loading gate. Double-action revolvers do not have loading gates; rather, the entire cylinder swings down so that all the rounds can be loaded at once. 2) Pump and semi-automatic shotguns, and lever-action rifles, often have a spring-loaded cover over the entry to an internal magazine. This cover is called the loading gate. The loading gate moves out of the way when a cartridge is pressed against it, allowing the magazine to be filled.

Long gun – A firearm with an extended barrel, usually designed to be fired while braced against the shoulder. The most common types of long guns are rifles and shotguns.

Long Trigger – A long trigger is one with an exceptional *length of pull*. It is a subjective term which very much depends upon the type of gun being discussed.

Low Kneeling – A shooting position in which one or both knees are touching the ground and the shooter tries to get as low as possible.

M

Machine gun – A fully automatic firearm which rapidly fires multiple rifle-caliber shots with a single pull of the trigger. See also: *submachine gun, automatic.* In America, fully automatic firearms have been strictly regulated since 1934, and illegal to produce or import since the 1980s. Functioning full-auto guns legal for civilians to own are thus difficult to find, and very expensive to purchase, often costing $10,000 or more. Existing fully-automatic firearms are generally antiques. They are heavily regulated, and are illegal in many states. In the few states where fully-automatic firearms are legal to collect, federal law requires the purchase of a $200 authorization stamp for each firearm. An extensive background check, which includes approval of local law enforcement and requires full fingerprints and photographs, is conducted before the purchase is approved.

Made – In casual range conversation, if someone admits they 'got made,' it means someone caught them carrying a concealed handgun. The stories about this can range from pretty funny to downright disastrous.

Mag – See *magazine, Magnum.*

Magazine – An ammunition and storage device located within, or attached to, a firearm. It is sometimes erroneously called a clip. Calling a magazine a clip drives experienced shooters crazy. Handguns, with very few and rare exceptions, don't use clips at all. They use magazines, and a box magazine is the most common type of handgun magazine. Internal magazines are commonly used in rifles and shotguns. Internal magazines may be box-shaped, or they may be tubular. On military rifles, external drum-shaped magazines are common. Magazines can often be found in different types and carrying capacities even for the same make and model of firearm.

> *Legal Note:* From 1994 until 2004, it was illegal for any handgun magazine manufactured for civilian ownership to be capable of holding more than ten rounds. At the time this book was written, the law was no longer in effect at the federal level, but is still on the books in a few restrictive states.

Magazine Disconnect – Sometimes called a *magazine safety.* A mechanism which prevents the gun from being able to fire when the magazine is removed from the gun, even if there is still a round in the chamber. Magazine disconnects are required by law in some states.

Magazine Loader – A mechanical device designed to make it easier to fill magazines using less hand strength, without hurting one's fingertips or thumbs. The author is particularly fond of the UpLula brand universal loader, but many other types are available.

Magazine Pouch – Commonly shortened to *mag pouch,* this is a device to hold extra magazines which fastens to the shooter's belt.

Magazine Safety – See *magazine disconnect.*

Magazine Well – The opening in the bottom of the gun into which a box magazine feeds. On a semi-auto handgun, the magazine well is at the base of the grip; on a rifle, it is usually placed somewhere ahead of the trigger guard.

Magnum – A designation used by ammunition companies to denote a cartridge with more power than one would traditionally expect for the bullet diameter. It generally indicates a round which cannot be interchanged with other loadings of the same caliber (for example, a .22 Magnum shell does not fit within a firearm designed to fire .22 Long Rifle ammunition).

Malfunction – A misfeed or other failure to fire which can be cleared on the spot and without tools.

Manual Safety – A safety which the shooter must deliberately disengage in order to fire the gun. All manual safeties are also external safeties, but not all external safeties are manual safeties as well. See *passive safety*.

Misfeed – In semi-automatic firearms, a failure of the next round to completely enter the chamber. A misfeed can keep the gun from going into battery, which in turn may prevent the gun from firing. Misfeeds and failures to feed are closely related: a failure to feed is a round that never even leaves the top of the magazine, while a misfeed is a round that leaves the magazine but does not enter the chamber.

Moon Clip or **Moonclip** – A flat, circular loading device for revolvers, similar to a speedloader in that it holds the ammunition together and facilitates quick loading. Unlike a speedloader, however, a moon clip is designed specifically for rimless cartridges (such as 9mm Luger or .45 ACP), and it becomes an integral part of the revolver while firing.

Mouse Gun – A gently derogatory name for any palm sized handgun which fires a small caliber.

Muffs – A type of hearing protection which completely covers both ears and is usually attached to a headband (sometimes to a neckband rather than a headband).

Muffs, Electronic – A type of hearing protection which completely covers both ears and is usually attached to a headband (sometimes to a neckband rather than a headband), and which includes internal electronics to amplify human voices while excluding all noises louder than a given decibel rating. Electronic muffs are a godsend to the serious firearms student, because they allow her to safely hear instruction over the sound of gunfire on the range. They also dramatically improve range safety, especially for instructors and range officers who must be able to hear what others are doing around them while they are working.

Mushy – Similar to creep, it denotes a trigger that has a squishy or uncertain feel, especially around the break point.

Musket – A long gun which has a completely smooth bore and is intended to fire a single projectile rather than a collection of shot. Muskets were common before rifles were invented, but now they are mostly collector's items.

Muzzle – The end of the barrel where the bullet comes out.

Muzzle Brake – A system of vents placed near the end of the firearm barrel to reduce recoil and muzzle rise.

Muzzle Control – Being aware of which direction your firearm is pointed at all times, and always keeping it pointed in a safe direction.

Muzzle Loader – A firearm design in which the ammunition and its propellant are loaded into the firearm from the front end. Sometimes called a *black powder* gun, after the type of propellant most commonly used. Some muzzle loaders are antiques, but there are many modern hunting firearms which are loaded in this manner.

Muzzle Rise – How much the muzzle end of the barrel lifts during the recoil process.

N

Negligent Discharge – An inadvertent shot which is not caused by a mechanical failure of the gun. Negligent discharges always involve violating one or all of the Four Rules. See also: *accidental discharge.*

Night Sights – A type of *iron sights* that glow or shine in the dark, intended for use in low light conditions. Some night sights consist of tiny tubes of tritium, while others use painted dabs of phosphorus. Nearly all use a standard three-dot system, with one dot for the front sight and two—spaced on either side—for the rear sight.

O

Off hand – 1) *Shooting off-hand* means to fire while standing, without bracing against a bench, bipod, tree, or any other rest. 2) The non-dominant hand.

Open Sights – The most common type of *iron sights*. Open sights are called open because the rear sight is an open-topped U or a V or a square-notch shape, in contrast to the closed circle commonly found in aperture sights.

Out of Battery – Most firearms do not have literal batteries. But a semi-automatic is said to be *out of battery* when the slide fails to come all the way forward again after the gun has fired. This condition can be created by a misfeed, a dirty gun, weak springs, the shooter's thumbs brushing against the slide, riding the slide, or any of several other causes.

Over / Under – A shotgun with two barrels which are vertically aligned with each other, one on top of the other.

Over-travel – Immediately after the trigger break which fires the shot, the trigger should be unable to move any farther to the rear. If it is able to continue moving to the rear after the shot has fired, the trigger is said to over-travel.

Owner's Manual – A little-read document that contains a surprising amount of necessary information. If you've lost yours, visit the manufacturer's website to download a new one, or pick up the phone and ask the company to send you a fresh copy. At the risk of engaging in a little crazy talk: when all else fails, read the manual.

P

P+ Ammunition (+p and +p+) – Many calibers are available in both standard and +p or +p+ variants. Ammunition marked +p produces more power and higher pressures than the standard ammunition produced in that caliber, while ammunition marked +p+ produces even more power and pressure than the +p loading.

> **Safety issue:** Many older firearms, and some modern ones (especially those made of lightweight alloys), are not designed to cope with the increased pressure produced by +p or +p+ loadings. If in doubt, consult your owner's manual, or call the firearm manufacturer before using any ammunition marked +p.

Passive Safety – Any safety, internal or external, which functions apart from the shooter's conscious control. Grip safeties are one example of a passive external safety; drop safeties are an example of a passive internal safety.

Patridge Sight – A type of sight designed by E.E. Patridge in the late 1800s, often used on handguns. It has a rear sight shaped as a square notch, and a front sight consisting of a thick blade that is flat on top.

Pattern – A shotgun term which refers to the manner in which the pellets spread out as they exit the gun. It is sometimes called the *spread*, although strictly speaking *spread* refers to the actual distance measured between the two most widely-separated points of impact, while *pattern* refers to the overall shape of the entire set. A tight pattern is one in which the pellets are closely grouped when they land on target. A loose pattern is one in which the pellets are widely spread.

Pellet – In target shooting, a chunk of metal fired from a gun. In hunting, a chunk of poop dropped from a deer.

Pistol – Another term for handgun. Some claim it refers only to semi-automatic handguns, but this is an incorrect bit of firearms lore: many early patents refer to revolving pistols.

Pistol Grip – A long gun term with two possible meanings. 1) Some long guns feature a standard stock (one which can be braced against the shoulder) that includes an extra handle behind the trigger for the firing hand to wrap around. The extra handle is called a pistol grip. When used properly by an experienced shooter, a standard stock equipped with such a pistol grip can improve the controllability of the gun, although firing it can be uncomfortable for the wrist. 2) A super-short, pistol-shaped stock which completely replaces a standard stock and makes the long gun impossible to fire from the shoulder. A gun so equipped is most easily fired from the hip without sighting. This looks cool, but is often extremely painful to fire and is no aid to accuracy.

> **Legal Note:** When combined with other features such as an adjustable stock, a flash reducer, and/or the ability to hold over five rounds, a gun equipped with either type of pistol grip becomes an "*assault weapon*" subject to additional regulation or outright prohibition in many states. None of these

devices alter the gun's basic firing mechanism or its power in any way.

Plinking – Recreational shooting, or shooting for fun rather than for scored competition or defense practice: "I just spent an afternoon plinking with the kids." Plinking often involves a brick of .22LR ammunition and some reactive targets.

Point Shooting – Shooting without using the sights. Instead of using sights, point shooters use body position or other cues to provide a rough index of where the shots will land.

Port – An opening. The *ejection port* is the opening in the side of a semi-auto from which spent cases are ejected.

Porting – Openings at the muzzle end of the gun through which some of the spent gases can escape. Porting reduces perceived recoil and lessens muzzle rise, but the trade off is that the gun becomes much louder when fired and produces a brighter flash. Porting is quite safe on the range, but is not generally recommended for defense handguns, because when used for defense, the gun may need to be fired from an odd position while it is still very close to the defender's body or face. When a ported gun is fired from such unusual positions, escaping gases may cause serious burns or even blind the shooter.

Powder – The chemical propellant which is burned to produce the hot gases which send the bullet flying downrange. Sometimes called *gunpowder*, although experienced shooters usually reserve the term gunpowder to mean black powder rather than modern smokeless powder. See also: *black powder, gunpowder, smokeless powder.*

Pre-travel – Some triggers can be pulled slightly backwards before the shooter can feel any tension and before the hammer or striker begins to retract. Thus, pre-travel is any movement of the trigger that begins before the trigger is doing its real work.

Primer – That portion of the ammunition which contains a tiny quantity of explosive compound that detonates when struck with force, igniting the powder. Hot gases from the burning powder then send the bullet downrange. In centerfire ammunition, the priming compound is located inside a tiny metal cup which can be seen by looking at the underside of the case. In rimfire ammunition, the priming compound is distributed evenly around the inside of the bottom rim of the case.

Printing – A condition in which the outline of the concealed handgun may be discerned through the outer clothing. The firearm itself is not visible, but its presence and shape may be apparent to an observer.

Propellant – The chemical whose rapid burning sends the bullet on its way, usually called *powder* or *gunpowder*. Modern gunpowder is sometimes called smokeless powder or simply powder, terms which distinguish it from the original *black powder.*

Pull – 1) The entire process of making the trigger complete its journey past the *trigger break*. 2) What a shotgun shooter yells when she wants a target (typically a clay pigeon) to be thrown into the air for her to shoot.

Pull Distance – The distance the trigger must travel before it reaches the break point and fires the gun.

Pull Weight – See *trigger pull weight*.

Pump Action – A long gun term. Common in shotguns, less common in rifles. Pump-Action guns have a moveable fore-end. After the shot fires, the user pulls sharply back on the fore-end to eject the spent shell or case, and then shoves the fore-end forward again to bring a fresh round into the chamber.

R

Racking the Slide – A semi-automatic handgun term which means pulling the slide back to its rearmost position, and then letting it go forward under its own spring tension. If the magazine is loaded and inserted in the gun, racking the slide loads the chamber and prepares the gun to fire.

Rail – A feature on the underside of the frame below the barrel on many handguns which allows various aftermarket accessories to be attached the firearm. It is most commonly used to attach specially-designed flashlights or laser sights.

Rails – The usually metal surfaces upon which a semi-automatic's slide travels to and fro as each shot is fired. For proper function, they need to be clean and wear a light coating of oil.

Reach – The measurement from the backstrap to the face of the trigger. The shorter the reach, the smaller the hands that will easily be able to fire the gun.

Reactive Targets – Targets that do something when you hit them, such as fall over, burst, send up smoke, or make a noise. Examples of reactive targets include bowling pins, full or empty soda cans, rotten fruit, steel gongs, and balloons. Responsible shooters always clean up any mess left behind by their reactive targets.

Rear Sight – See *sight, rear.*

Receiver – The essential part of the gun, containing the firing mechanism and action. In semi-automatic handguns and revolvers, this part is typically called the *frame*.

Recoil – Sometimes called *kick*, recoil is the rearward force produced by a gun when it is fired. A shooter is said to be recoil sensitive if she does not enjoy the sensation caused by this rearward force. It is possible to scientifically measure the exact amount of recoil produced by a particular gun and ammunition. However, perceived recoil—the amount of force and the type of sensation it produces as felt by the shooter—may differ substantially from actual recoil as measured by the mathematician or scientist. Perceived recoil may be influenced by the gun's internal architecture, by design details, by the spring weight, by the type and size of ammunition chosen, and by how well the firearm fits the shooter. The interplay between these complex variables can be difficult to assess simply by holding or examining the gun without firing it.

Red Dot Sight – A sighting system which replaces the front and rear (iron) sights with a see-through screen upon which a colored dot may be superimposed over the target. It is typically most useful for competition work rather than on guns intended to be used in self defense.

Reload – 1) A form of recycling wherein a shooter reuses empty brass cases and fills them with new primers, powder, and bullets. The old cases must be cleaned, resized, and have the spent primers removed. After the cases are prepared, a new primer is inserted into the primer pocket, a carefully-measured amount of powder is placed in each case, and a new bullet is seated to a precisely-measured depth within each case. Most of these steps are accomplished on a specialized piece of equipment called a *reloading press*. 2) To refill the firearm with ammunition in order to continue shooting.

> *Safety Note:* Although most reloaders are justifiably proud of their handiwork, it can be very dangerous to fire ammunition that someone else has reloaded. It is strongly suggested that shooters purchase new, factory-produced ammunition whenever possible.

Reset – The point of the trigger's return journey at which the gun's internal mechanisms are ready to fire another round. On many guns, after the shot has fired, if you hold the trigger to the rear and then slowly release it, you can feel or sometimes hear an audible click as the trigger reaches the reset point. The reset point varies greatly from one type of gun to another, and some guns do not reset until the trigger has been allowed to complete its entire return journey.

Reticle – The object seen in the center of a firearm scope which assists the rifleman in aligning the shot. The most familiar reticle shape is a simple cross, which is commonly called the crosshairs. Other possible reticle shapes include circles, chevrons, and dots.

Revolver – A type of handgun with one barrel and a rotating cylinder which contains multiple chambers. As the cylinder is rotated, either by cocking the hammer or by pulling the trigger, the chamber containing the spent cartridge is rotated away. This brings a fresh cartridge into alignment with the barrel, ready to fire when the hammer falls. A revolver cylinder typically holds 5 or 6 rounds of ammunition, though it may hold considerably more depending upon the caliber.

Riding the Slide – Racking the slide incorrectly by allowing your hand to rest upon the slide as it moves forward during the loading procedure. Riding the slide is a common cause of misfeeds and other malfunctions.

Rifle – A firearm designed to be fired while braced against the shoulder, and which uses a spiral groove cut along the inside of the barrel to spin the bullet. Spinning improves the projectile's accuracy and range, the same basic principle which makes a football travel in a straight line rather than wobbling when it is thrown correctly.

Rifling – Continuous spiral (helical) grooves cut along the inside surface of a firearm barrel to improve the accuracy and range of the bullet, and stabilize the bullet's flight, by giving it a spin as it leaves the barrel. Rifles, by definition, always have rifling; handguns typically do; and shotguns rarely do. Because shotguns typically do not have rifling in the barrel, some shotgun slugs (very large bullets) feature rifling on their outer surfaces. These are called *rifled slugs*.

Rimfire – Ammunition in which the primer is located in the outer edge, or rim, at the bottom of the case. Typically, rimfire rounds are smaller in diameter than centerfire rounds. Although there are several other rimfire cartridges, the term "rimfire" is often used in casual conversation to refer exclusively to the .22 Long Rifle round. Rimfire ammunition tends to be less reliable than centerfire ammunition. For this reason, it is a poor choice for self defense unless no other alternatives are reasonably available.

Rough Trigger – A trigger which has a gritty or inconsistent feel during the pull.

Round – One complete unit of ammunition, which includes a bullet (or other projectile), powder, and a primer, and is contained in an outer shell or case.

Round Gun – Slang term for a revolver.

Round Nose – The classic bullet shape.

Running the Gun – Performing all necessary manipulations (such as loading, unloading, or clearing jams) to keep the firearm functioning as designed.

S

Safe – 1) A firearm is said to be *on safe* when its safety is engaged and *off safe* when it is ready to fire. Wise shooters place only guarded trust in mechanical safeties, and always follow the Four Rules even when the safety is engaged. 2) A locking container in which firearms should be stored when they are not in use. True safes are rated by the Underwriters' Laboratories as such. Other types of locking storage commonly called safes include "Residential Security Containers" (RSCs) and security lockers.

Safety – 1) A mechanical device which may or may not function as intended. 2) Conscientiously following the Four Rules every single time you handle a firearm... even if you think the gun is unloaded, and even when you think no one's looking.

Scattergun – A casual term for a shotgun, so called because the shot spreads out or

Kathy Jackson

Scope – A magnifying tube through which the shooter may see the target and thus aim the firearm. Scopes contain a reticle, commonly in the shape of a cross, which must be properly centered upon the target for accurate aim.

Sear – The part of the trigger mechanism which holds the hammer or striker back until the correct amount of pressure has been applied to the trigger, at which point the hammer or striker is released to discharge the firearm. The sear may be a separate part, or may be a surface incorporated into the trigger.

Semi-automatic – A firearm which uses the energy from the fired shot to eject the empty case and feed the next round into the chamber. Sometimes called an autoloader, a bottom-feeder, or (inaccurately) an automatic. See also: *automatic*.

Semi-Wadcutter – A modified wadcutter bullet with slightly sloping edges, designed to load smoothly in a semi-automatic pistol.

Shell – An empty ammunition case. Sometimes called the brass, even when it is composed of another material such as aluminum or (rarely) polymer.

Shell, Shotgun – Shotgun ammunition often comes encased in plastic shells rather than in metal cases, so shotgunners often refer to shells in conversations where a rifleman or handgunner would refer to cases, cartridges, or rounds. A shotgun shell usually contains a primer, powder, shot, and a wad. In place of the shot (multiple pellets), the shell might instead hold a single large bullet called a *slug*.

Shooting Sports – There are a lot of different competitions and other games which involve firearms. These are all referred to collectively as the shooting sports.

Short Trigger – A trigger that doesn't have to travel very far before it reaches the break. In a 1911 semi-auto pistol, a short trigger is a different part than a long trigger, and (in addition to providing less motion) it features a shorter reach which may be of benefit to a small-handed shooter.

Short-stroking – On a pump-action firearm, short-stroking means being too gentle with the fore-end and either not pulling it all the way back at the beginning of the stroke, or not shoving it all the way forward at the end of the stroke. If the shooter doesn't pull the fore-end all the way back, the old case or shell fails to eject and the gun often misfeeds. If the shooter doesn't shove the fore-end all the way forward, the gun will not fire when the trigger is pulled. The term is used most often to refer to pump-action shotguns, but it is possible to similarly short-stroke any type of firearm which requires the user to manually cycle the action (lever action rifles, for example).

Shot – In shotgunning, multiple pellets contained in the shell and sent downrange when the shotgun is fired. No matter how many pellets there are, shot in this sense is pluralized without adding an "s" to the end: "a handful of shot."

Shotgun – A firearm typically used to fire a number of small spherical pellets collectively called *shot*. Shotguns usually have a smooth, unrifled bore, but may be fitted with a rifled bore designed for firing a single slug rather than a collection of shot. Sometimes called scatterguns because the shot spreads out in a conical pattern upon leaving the gun.

Shoulder – To bring the butt of a long gun's stock to the shooter's shoulder, preparatory to firing the gun.

Side-by-Side – A shotgun with two barrels which are situated next to each other.

Sight – A mechanical, optical, or electronic device used to aim a firearm. The most common type of sights, generally referred to as *iron sights* or sometimes as *open sights*, consist of specially-shaped pieces of metal placed at each end of the barrel. The sight closest to the muzzle end of the gun is called the *front sight*, while the one farthest from the muzzle (and nearest to the shooter) is called the *rear sight*.

Sight Alignment – The manner in which the sights are lined up properly in front of the shooter's eye, to form a straight path to the target.

Sight Picture – What the shooter sees when looking through the sights at the target.

Sight, Front – The front sight is placed at the muzzle end of the barrel. It is often (but not always) in the form of a dot or a blade. To attain a proper sight picture and shoot with the greatest degree of accuracy, the shooter's eye should be focused sharply upon the front sight while shooting, allowing both the rear sight and the target itself to blur somewhat.

Sight, Rear – The rear sight is placed at the end of the barrel nearest the shooter. It may be in the shape of a square notch, a U, a vee, a ring, or simply two dots designed to be visually placed on either side of the front sight while shooting.

Silencer – See *suppressor, sound*.

Single Action (SA) – A single-action firearm is one in which pulling the trigger does only one thing: fires the shot. The trigger is not used to cock the hammer, rotate the cylinder, or retract the firing pin.

> **Revolvers** – A single-action revolver requires the user to manually pull the hammer back ("cock the hammer") before each and every shot. Pulling back on the hammer causes the cylinder to revolve, and brings a fresh round into alignment with the barrel ready to be fired.

> **Semi-autos** – A single-action semi-automatic firearm has a hammer that is not actuated by the trigger. The hammer may be cocked by hand, or by racking the slide, or by the rearward movement of the slide after each shot is fired. The most widely known single-action semi-auto handgun is the 1911-style pistol designed by John Moses Browning.

Slack – See *pre-travel*. To 'take up the slack' means to pull the trigger through its pre-travel stage.

Slide – On a semi-automatic firearm, the slide is the part of the gun that moves quickly back and forth with every fired shot, ejecting the spent case as it moves to the rear and loading a fresh cartridge into the chamber as it moves forward again. On a handgun, it is often the uppermost portion of the gun and the sights are usually fastened to its top. To *rack the slide* means to pull the slide back to its rearmost position, and then letting it go forward under its own spring tension. To *ride the slide* means to rack the slide incorrectly, allowing your hand to rest upon the slide as it moves forward during the loading sequence. Riding the slide is a common cause of malfunctions.

Slide Lock – When most semi-automatic firearms have been fired until empty, the slide will remain in its rearmost position rather than going forward as if to chamber another round. This condition of the gun is called slide lock. *Shooting to slide lock* means shooting until there is no more ammunition in your semi-automatic gun, because the slide usually locks back with the chamber empty after firing the last round.

Slide Release – The slide release lever, usually located on the left side of the slide, is pushed down to unlock the slide and allow the slide to move forward into its normal position. It is sometimes called the *slide stop* or slide stop lever.

Slide Stop – The slide release lever.

Sling – A long strip of leather, plastic, or nylon which is fastened at the fore and rear of the gun. A sling enables easy carry of long guns. It also allows the shooter to wrap body parts into it and brace solidly against the tension thus produced for a steadier hold.

Slug – A single, very large projectile fired by a shotgun. It may be plain, or it may have spiral grooves, called rifling, cut into its outer surface to help stabilize it during flight.

Slug Gun – Slang for a shotgun which is set up specifically to fire a slug (a large, single projectile) rather than shot (multiple projectiles contained within a single shell). Slug guns are most commonly used for deer hunting in states which prohibit hunting deer with rifles.

Smokeless Powder – Modern gunpowder, so called because it doesn't produce the thick clouds of acrid black smoke that black powder does. See also: *powder, gunpowder*

Snap Cap – An inert ammunition-shaped object, used in practice to simulate misfeeds and other malfunctions. Some folks also use them during dry fire practice to cushion the firing pin as it strikes.

Snubby – Casual slang for a short-barreled revolver.

Snubnose – Casual slang for a short-barreled revolver.

Speed Strip – A flat piece of rubber which holds revolver cartridges preparatory to loading them into the revolver's cylinder. It is designed to lie flat in the pocket, so it is a boon to concealed carry folks who want to carry extra ammunition discreetly. Using a speed strip to load a revolver is slightly faster than rummaging around in your pockets for loose ammunition before stuffing rounds into the cylinder one by one. But only slightly.

Speedloader – A circular gadget which holds revolver cartridges preparatory to loading them into the revolver's cylinder. It holds the rounds in the correct configuration to plunk all of them at once straight into the chambers.

Spread – See *pattern*.

Springs – Most guns have springs. Big springs, little springs, tiny springs that bounce across the room and hide under the couch while you hunt for them in vain. Not that we're bitter about that.

> *Mainspring* – The mainspring provides the initial source of energy needed to fire the gun. Cocking the hammer compresses the mainspring, capturing potential energy. That energy is released when the hammer falls, striking the firing pin which in turn strikes the primer, igniting the powder. Not all firearms have mainsprings and hammers. Some are striker-fired instead. See also: *striker, hammer, firing pin.*

> *Recoil Spring* – The recoil spring is the powerful spring that cushions the slide in its rearward travel and then sends the slide forward again with enough force to drive the fresh round firmly into the chamber. The strength of the recoil spring is calibrated to run the slide without any outside assistance. See also *riding the slide.*

Squib – A round of ammunition which has far less power than it is supposed to, often having no powder at all. Squib loads can result in a bullet getting lodged in the barrel, which can be dangerous if the gun is fired again before clearing the obstruction out of the way. Squib loads are very uncommon when shooting commercial ammunition.

Stacking – A noticeable increase in pull weight as the trigger travels. Ideally, the trigger pull should feel as if it remains the same weight throughout its entire journey.

Stance – How the shooter positions her body while shooting. The three most widely-known handgun stances are *Weaver, Chapman,* and *Isosceles.*

Stock – 1) The back part of a rifle or shotgun, excluding the receiver. It is commonly made of wood, wood laminate, metal, or synthetic materials. 2) In competition, an unaltered firearm, used in the same configuration in which it came from the factory. 3) Some people and companies refer to handgun grips as stocks.

Stovepipe – Failure of a spent case to completely eject from a semi-automatic firearm. This malfunction is called a stovepipe because the case usually stands on end while lodged in the ejection port, thus resembling a stovepipe sticking up out of a roof.

Striker – On guns so equipped, the striker is the device that moves linearly to provide the percussive impact on the primer. Not all firearms have strikers; many have firing pins which are struck by a hammer instead. See also: *firing pin*.

Striker Fired – A striker is a form of firing pin that replaces the hammer and firing pin with a single unit. So a striker-fired handgun is a semi-automatic which uses a striker, rather than a hammer or a firing pin, to hit the primer and fire the round.

Stripper Clip – See *clip*.

Submachine Gun – A fully automatic firearm which fires a pistol caliber. See also: *automatic, machine gun*.

Suppressor, Flash – See *flash reducer*.

Suppressor, Sound – A device that fits on the muzzle end of a firearm to reduce (but not eliminate) the loud noise created when the gun is fired. Suppressors cannot reduce the loud *crack* caused by the bullet as it exceeds the speed of sound, but can reduce the noise caused by the escape of gases from the end of the barrel. Like fully-automatic firearms, sound suppressors have been strictly regulated in the United States since 1934. Purchase requires a $200 federal authorization stamp, a background check, the approval of local law enforcement, and nearly the same paperwork required to purchase a fully automatic weapon. Although strictly regulated in the US, many European laws require shooters to use sound suppressors, because the sound of gunfire can cause permanent hearing damage and is sometimes considered a nuisance by neighbors who live within earshot of a range.

T

Tang – The recurved top part of a semi-automatic handgun's grip at the point where it meets the slide. On long guns, the tang is the top strap used to screw the receiver to the stock.

Tap, Rack, Bang – The slang term for the procedure to clear a misfeed. To clear a misfeed, *tap* the base of the magazine firmly to be sure it is properly seated, *rack* the slide to eject an empty case or feed a new round, and assess to be sure your target still needs shooting. If it does, pull the trigger to create the *bang*, the final step in the complete sequence which gives this procedure its name.

Thumb Safety – An external, manual safety which is typically disengaged with the firing-hand thumb.

Total Metal Jacket – A type of ammunition in which the lead bullet is entirely encased inside another metal, usually copper. This reduces fouling and makes the firearm easier to clean at the end of the shooting day, and also reduces the amount of lead dust present in the air on the range. Ammunition with a total metal jacket is distinct from ammunition with a full metal jacket because *full* metal jacket simply means the nose of the lead bullet is covered with another metal, while *total* metal jacket means the entire lead bullet is encased in another metal. See also: *full metal jacket*.

Trigger – The bang switch. Pulling the trigger sets in motion the whole chain of mechanical events which results in a bullet coming out of the muzzle end of the gun. Typically, pulling the trigger releases the striker or allows the hammer to fall, causing the firing pin to strike the primer. The primer then ignites the powder within the round. Burning gases from the powder force the bullet out of its case and through the barrel, causing the bullet to exit the muzzle end of the gun and strike the target. In addition to releasing the hammer or striker, some triggers may cock the hammer or striker (see *double action*), rotate a revolver's cylinder, deactivate passive safeties, or perform other functions.

Trigger Control – Never putting your finger on the trigger until your sights are on target, then pulling the trigger smoothly, without jerking or yanking, and following through by realigning the sights before allowing your finger to come off the trigger. Every time. Even when you're in a hurry.

Trigger Group – The entire collection of moving parts which work together to fire the gun when the trigger is pulled. It may include trigger springs, return springs, the trigger itself, the sear, disconnectors, and other parts.

Trigger Guard – The hoop encircling the area around the trigger. The shooter's finger should never be within the trigger guard unless the sights are on target and the shooter has made the decision to fire.

Trigger Jerk – No, not the guy in the lane next to you—well, probably not, anyway. Jerking the trigger means yanking it back abruptly, thus pulling the muzzle of the gun downward at the moment the shot fires. This does not help accuracy.

Trigger Lock – A walnut-sized lock which fits into the trigger guard area and is designed to prevent the trigger from moving. Its chief disadvantage is that, ignoring or defying the cautionary warning labels, too many users install these on loaded firearms. Most experienced shooters believe that unnecessarily fiddling around in the trigger guard area creates many mishaps.

Trigger Pull – The entire process of moving the trigger from its forwardmost position to its rearwardmost position, causing the hammer to fall and the shot to fire.

Trigger Pull Weight – How much pressure the trigger finger must put on the trigger before the gun will fire. Trigger pull weight is measured in pounds and ounces.

Trigger Safety – An external, passive safety which can be found on the face of some trigger designs (most notably found on Glock firearms). It is intended to prevent the trigger from being pulled by objects which find their way into the trigger guard area.

Trigger Scale – A specialized type of hanging scale designed to test trigger pull weight.

Trigger Slap – 1) Flapping your finger onto the trigger and yanking it to the rear, usually accompanied by flopping your finger immediately back off the trigger at the moment the shot fires. Trigger slap is generally a bad thing, because unless the firearm has an incredibly short, light trigger (such as is used in high end competition), it almost inevitably misaligns the sights and sends the shot wild. 2) An uncomfortable sensation caused by the trigger springing back into the shooter's trigger finger while firing.

Trigger Stop – A mechanism for adjusting overtravel.

Trigger Weight – See *trigger pull weight*.

W

Wad – 1) In shotgunning, a clump of something, commonly cardboard or plastic, which acts as a buffer between the shot and the powder in shotgun ammunition. It seals in the gases which propel the shot out of the barrel. Without a wad, the gases would go whistling past the shot instead of propelling it out the barrel. 2) In muzzle loading, a piece of cloth used to seal the bullet in the barrel. Its purpose and function is the same as a shotgun wad.

Wadcutter – A cylinder-shaped bullet with sharp front edges. When used on a paper target, it creates a very tidy hole with crisp, easily-measured edges, and is thus often used in target competitions.

Weapon – A tool designed for a human being to enable her to defend herself and her community, or to commit aggression against other people, or (sometimes) to take game animals. By definition, firearms used for concealed carry are weapons both by design and intent. And *all* firearms are defined as weapons under the law.

Weaver Stance – A shooting position named after Jack Weaver, who was a Deputy Sheriff in the 1950s when he first began using this stance in competition. In the Weaver stance, the body is bladed slightly in relation to the target rather than squarely facing it. The elbows are flexed and pointed downward. The strong-side arm pushes out, while the weak hand pulls back. This produces a push-pull tension which is the chief defining characteristic of the Weaver stance. See the Shooting Basics chapter for more information.

Wheel Gun – Casual slang for a revolver.

Y

Youth Rifle – A short, lightweight rifle. Some are small enough for a young child to easily handle, while others are large enough to perfectly suit teenagers, average-sized adult women, and small-statured adult males.

Youth Stock – A short stock, often ideally sized for teenagers, average-sized adult women, and small-statured adult males.

Z

Zero – A firearm is said to be "zeroed in" when its sights have been adjusted so that the bullet will hit the center of the target when the sights are properly aligned upon the center of the target. Because of the effects of gravity and inertia on the bullet as it travels, there is no such thing as a gun with sights that are accurate at all distances. Sights need to be "re-zeroed" to compensate for different distances, or the shooter must adjust her point of aim (aligning the sights a bit higher on the target, for instance). If the gun's sights are adjusted for shooting at 200 yards, the gun is said to have a 200-yard zero.

Index

A

Also by Kathy Jackson

Whether you are new to the concept of armed defense or have long since made it a part of a prudent lifestyle, you'll find much that is useful in this book. Read it the way Kathy and Mark wrote it, that is, don't just look at it, but study it for its lessons! -Massad Ayoob Founder, Lethal Force Institute Author of "In the Gravest Extreme- These are serious words from Massad, the Master of self defense!

Don't rely on others to protect yourself and your loved ones. "Lessons from Armed America" is the essential primer for self defense. Kathy and Mark are the experts that answer all your questions on stalking, real-life firefights, prevention and awareness, as well as carjacking and use of nonlethal force. They tell it like it is with candor and compassion, speaking through both experience and well-thought-out-research. If you're serious about protecting your family, this is the one book you MUST read!

Made in the USA
Las Vegas, NV
10 February 2023

67297722R00223